ISBN 978-0-282-15772-2
PIBN 10272350

1 MONTH OF
FREE
READING

at
www.ForgottenBooks.com

By purchasing this book you are eligible for one month membership to ForgottenBooks.com, giving you unlimited access to our entire collection of over 1,000,000 titles via our web site and mobile apps.

To claim your free month visit:
www.forgottenbooks.com/free272350

STAGS

Vol. II. p. 283

FALLOW DEER

Vol. II. p. 298

REMARKS

ON

FOREST SCENERY,

AND OTHER

WOODLAND VIEWS.

BY THE LATE

WILLIAM GILPIN, A.M.

EDITED BY

SIR THOMAS DICK LAUDER, BART.

IN TWO VOLUMES.

VOL. II.

EDINBURGH:
FRASER & CO. NORTH BRIDGE;
SMITH, ELDER & CO. CORNHILL, LONDON;
W. CURRY, JUN. & CO. DUBLIN.
MDCCCXXXIV.

EDINBURGH:
Printed by Andrew Shortrede, Thistle Lane.

FOREST SCENERY.

BOOK II.

SECTION XIII.

BRITAIN, like other countries, abounded once in wood. When Cassibalan, Caractacus, and Boadicea, defended their country's rights, the country itself was a fortress. An extensive plain was then as uncommon as a forest is now. Fitz-Stephen, a monk of Canterbury, in the time of Henry II, tells us, that a large forest lay round London, " in which were woody groves, in the coverts whereof lurked bucks and does, wild boars, and bulls." To shelter beasts of the latter kind, we know a forest must be of some magnificence. These woods, contiguous even to the capital, continued close and thick, many ages afterwards. Even so late as Henry VII's time, we are informed by Polidore Virgil, that " Tertia propemodum Angliæ pars pecori, aut cervis, damis, capreolis (nam et ii quoque in ea parte sunt, quæ ad septentrionem est) cuniculisve nutriendis relicta est inculta : quippe passim sunt ejusmodi ferarum vivaria, seu roboraria, quæ lignis roboreis sunt clausa : unde multa venatio, qua se nobiles cum primis exercent." *

* Almost the third part of England is uncultivated, and possessed only by stags, deer, or wild goats, which last are found chiefly in the northern parts. Rabbits, too, abound everywhere. You everywhere meet with vast forests, where these wild beasts range at large, or with parks secured by pales. Hunting is the principal amusement of all the people of distinction.

VOL. II.   A

In this passage the forest seems to be distinguished from the park, which latter was fenced, in those days, with oak pales, as it is now.

As Britain became more cultivated, its woods, of course, receded. They gave way, as in other places, to the plough, to pasturage, to ship building, to architecture, and all other objects of human industry in which timber is the principal material ; obtaining, for that reason, among the Romans, the pointed appellation of *materies*.

That our woods were often cut down, merely for the sake of tillage and pasturage, without any respect to the uses of timber, seems to be evident, from the great quantities of subterraneous trees dug up in various parts of England. They are chiefly found in marshy grounds, which abounded, indeed, every where, before the arts of draining were in use. Nothing was necessary, in such places, to produce the future phenomenon of subterraneous timber, but to carry the trees upon the surface of the bog, which might easily be done in dry summers. Their own weight, the oozing of the springs, and the swelling of the mossy ground, would soon sink them, as they were generally stripped of their branches, which were probably burned. Dr Plot, who had examined subterraneous timber with great exactness, gives good reasons for supposing it might have been buried in this way, merely to make way for the plough, and imagines that the English might begin to clear their woodlands, for tillage, as early as the times of Alfred the Great.* Others account for the phenomenon of subterraneous timber, from the havoc made in woods by the violence of storms. In marshy grounds, especially, where trees take but feeble hold, they would be most liable to this destruction. Both this hypothesis and Dr Plot's may be equally true.

We have perhaps had occasion to examine as many of these subterranean trees as Dr Plot, though we did so in a different country, and should therefore hesitate to venture to question the particulars of his theory, so far as Oxford-

* See Plot's *History of Oxfordshire*, chap. vi. sec. 56.

shire may be concerned. But we are quite clear, that the operations of the axe are not visible on the roots and trunks which fill the mosses of Scotland. The trees which are found in the Scottish mosses, and particularly the pines which are found in those of the northern parts of Scotland, all invariably exhibit marks of fire, as, indeed, do the stocks from which they have been severed, and near to which they are always discovered. It is quite evident, that these aboriginal forests, of Scotland at least, have been destroyed by great conflagrations, kindled either purposely or accidentally, and, perhaps, in each of these ways, at different times. Some of the pine logs are excavated longitudinally by the fire, so as to form spouts, such as are often applied to the eves of the roofs of houses, for catching and carrying off the rain. These appear to have been so hollowed out by the fire, which had continued to burn and smoulder on the upper side, after the tree had fallen into some wettish place, the damp of which prevented its being consumed below. We have legendary accounts enough in Scotland of the burning of great tracts of forest, to bear out the explanation of the appearances which these ligneous remains exhibit.

The Rev. J. Farquharson, F.R.S.E. in his paper on the Native Forests of Aberdeenshire, in the second volume of the *Edinburgh Journal of Geographical and Natural Science*, tells us of one stretch of forest, in the parish of Coldstone, which seems to have been overturned by some hurricane. But this is only an exception to the great general rule. He says that the trees are buried from four to ten or twelve feet deep in the moss, the extent of which is about one hundred acres. They are found in such numbers, as to prove that a close growing forest must have been overturned. Some of them have been overthrown with the root, and others broken off, leaving the roots in the position in which they originally grew. They lie generally towards the east, so that they must have been prostrated by a strong blast from the west.

But, notwithstanding this general extermination of timber, for the purposes of human industry, still many forests were left, in the time of our ancestors, in every part of the island, under the denomination of Royal Chases, which our ancient kings preserved sacred, for their amusement. Forests, indeed, have ever been in use in all parts and ages of the world, as the

The woods that rear themselves over the steeps of the Alps and Apennines, often form appearances of this kind, but of a more cheerful cast. The following description is a beautiful contrast to the gloomy aspect of a Scotch forest; though I fancy the poet has drawn a more woody species of scenery than is at this time commonly to be found in Italy:

> Far to the right, where Apennine ascends,
> Bright as the summer, Italy extends.
> Woods over woods, in gay theatric pride,
> Well mass'd, yet varied, deck the mountain's side;
> While towering oft, amidst the tufted green,
> Some venerable ruin marks the scene.

As we have already had occasion to mention the magnificent forests which clothe many parts 'of the Apennines, we need hardly say, that Mr Gilpin is mistaken in believing that the poet is describing what does not exist in Italy. We remember to have heard quoted, as applied to Valombrosa, those beautiful lines of Milton, in which he describes the woody walls of Paradise:

> Where delicious Paradise,
> Now nearer crowns with her enclosure green,
> As with a rural mound, the champain head
> Of a steep wilderness, whose hairy sides,
> With thicket overgrown, grotesque and wild,
> Access denied; and, overhead, upgrew
> Insuperable height of loftiest shade,
> Cedar, and pine, and fir, and branching palm,
> A sylvan scene; and, as the ranks ascend,
> Shade above shade, a woody theatre
> Of stateliest view.

We have often felt the aptitude of this quotation as applied to Valombrosa; from which place, indeed, some people suppose that Milton borrowed the description. Certain it was, that the poet was peculiarly attached to the spot. He describes Satan's legions lying

> Entranced,
> Thick as autumnal leaves that strew the brook,
> In Valombrosa, where the Etrurian shades
> High overarch'd embower.

But well as the first quotation may describe the Valombrosan scene, we have no hesitation in saying, that if the palm be exchanged for the birch, and the cedar classed, as it ought to be, under the pine race, we have seen Scottish glens which presented the very beau ideal of Milton's lines.

The animals which inhabit the Scotch forest, are the roebuck, the eagle, and the falcon. Heretofore it was frequented by the cock of the wood, a noble bird, dressed in splendid plumage, of nearly the size of a turkey. He was often seen, amidst the dark foliage of the pine, rearing his glossy crest, and crowing at intervals; but he is now seldom found. The stag also sometimes shelters himself among the thickets of the forest; but it is the heat only of a meridian sun that drives him thither. The storm he values not, but continues browsing in defiance of it, on the side of the bleakest mountain on which it happens to overtake him.

When engaged in investigating the ravages of the great floods of August, 1829, we had occasion to see three of these magnificent birds at Marr Lodge,—a young cock and hen, kept in one place, and an old cock, who resided in a separate apartment. The hen had laid eggs, which she had uniformly destroyed. But, since that period, we have been informed by that distinguished naturalist, Mr James Wilson, that, in his visit to Braemar, about the first week of August, 1831, he saw five young ones alive, which, though only a few weeks old, were larger than the largest moor game. Two of these, both females, lived for a considerable time; but they have since died. They fed upon ants, larvæ, and crysalids; and, as they grew stronger, they began to eat oats and pot barley. The old birds were chiefly fed on grain and heather tops, and also with the young shoots, and other tender parts, of the Scottish fir. However unpromising this first attempt may have proved, it is to be hoped that farther endeavours will be made to restore to the Scottish forests this bird, which was for centuries their noblest winged inhabitant.

The English forest (except in the northern counties which border on Scotland) exhibits a very different species of landscape. It is commonly composed of woodland views, interspersed, as we have described them,* with extensive heaths and lawns. Its trees are oak and beech, whose lively green corresponds better than the gloomy pine with the nature of the scene, which seldom assumes the dignity of a mountain one, but

* See Vol. I. p. 312.

generally exhibits a cheerful landscape. It aspires, indeed, to grandeur; but its grandeur does not depend, like that of the Scottish forest, on the sublimity of the objects, but on the vastness of the whole,— the extent of its woods, and wideness of its plains. In its inhabitants, also, the English forest differs from the Scotch. Instead of the stag and the roebuck, it is frequented by cattle and fallow deer, and exchanges the screams of the eagle and the falcon for the crowing of pheasants and the melody of nightingales. The Scotch forest, no doubt, is the sublimer scene, and speaks to the imagination in a loftier language than the English forest can reach. This latter, indeed, often rouses the imagination, but seldom in so great a degree, being generally content with captivating the eye.

The scenery, too, of the Scotch forest is better calculated to last through ages than that of the English. The woods of both are almost destroyed. But while the English forest hath lost all its beauty with its oaks, and becomes only a desolate waste, the rocks and the mountains, the lakes and the torrents of the Scotch forest, make it still an interesting scene.

In Sutherland, which is the most northern county in Scotland, are found the forests of Derrymore, and Derry-monach.

We believe that these forests no longer exist in Sutherland, at least as timber forests. A deer forest is a very different thing from a forest of trees. The term implies no more than a very large tract of wild country, set apart for red deer, and where the princely sport of hunting, or rather of stalking, that noble animal may be enjoyed in perfection. Many parts of Sutherland exhibit traces of ancient wood. On the banks of Loch Brora, in particular, we remember to have seen a very large oak, growing behind the house of Carrail, which, though exhibiting symptoms of decay, was yet by no means far gone in the wane, and still carried a very grand head. The glen which runs up from Strathfleet, some miles above the place where the celebrated mound of Fleet has been formed, shews all the symptoms of ancient forest, and is even now very beautifully wooded with natural birches and other trees. There is a good wood on the banks of Loch

Shin, and great appearances of timber of other years in several parts of the parish of Creech, where there are still considerable quantities of natural wood. Several oak woods, indeed, have been cut down in this parish within these fifty years, some of them about the beginning of this century; and a number of these have vigorous successors springing from their roots. But the grown woods and young plantations about Dunrobin Castle, and the old and large trees about the ancient place of Tongue, on the very north coast of Sutherland, sufficiently prove that nothing is wanting but to select the proper districts for planting, and then to plant on a sufficiently great scale. The trees, especially the hard wooded trees, on a bank overhanging the sea at Dunrobin, are growing as vigorously as trees can grow. It is true that Caithness gives little promise of rewarding its patriotic proprietors for the indefatigable attempts which many of them are making to rear timber in that county; but this is by no means owing to the climate or latitude, or else we should not find those really magnificent trees of all kinds growing around the old mansion-house at Tongue. The cause of wood not thriving in Caithness is, the great and general flatness of the surface of that county, which permits the wind from the ocean to sweep over it from one end to the other with so great fury, that nothing can withstand it; and the same cause operates, in a great measure, to produce very nearly the same effect throughout the greater part of Buchan. The sea, we think, acts in these cases very much in the same manner as any plane of the same extensive and level surface would do; for the moment a spot is found sheltered from the fury of its blast, there trees will certainly be found to succeed; as in the land-locked portions of the sea in the New Forest, on the west coast of England, and in many parts of the west of Scotland. At Roseneath, for example, we have seen magnificent beeches, dipping the tips of their spray in the rising tide. But to plant trees in places where they are exposed to such a blast as that which sweeps over Caithness, is to create bushes, or walking-sticks, and not trees.

In Ross-shire, in the district of Assynt, lies the forest of Coygach; and, along the confines of Lochmari, which is one of the most extensive lakes in Scotland, runs another forest, which bears the name of the lake.

So far as we can discover, from our own imperfect knowledge, and from the as yet very imperfect statistics of

Ross-shire, the natural forests which once abounded in this county, and which were, many of them, very extensive, have disappeared almost entirely. We speak of forests, in the wide Highland acceptation of that word, when applied to miles of naturally wooded country. As to woods, both natural and planted, and, above all, as to well timbered gentlemen's seats, Ross-shire can boast of many; and, so far as scenery depends upon trees, much of that of Ross-shire is exquisitely wooded. The remains of the ancient fir forests, and of oaks of immense size, are to be found all over this extensive and highly varied county.

In the county of Moray are the forests of Abernethy and Rothimurcha, winding along the banks of the Spey. They both belong to the family of the Grants, and make a part of the extensive demesnes of Castle Grant, which stands in their neighbourhood.

Mr Gilpin has fallen into an error here, very allowable to a stranger, such as he was, to the country he writes about. The forests of Abernethey and Rothiemurchus (not Rothiemurcha) are not in the county of Moray, but in that of Inverness; and although both forests belong to the Clan Grant, yet the former belongs to Grant, now Earl of Seafield, and the other to Sir John Peter Grant of Rothiemurchus. Of these forests we have already spoken pretty fully, in a former part of our notes. We cannot, however, now pass them by, without a smile at the idea of considering a forest such as that of Abernethey, which consists of many miles of country, as being capable of forming part of the *demesne*, or pleasure ground, of Castle Grant! Of the *domain*, or territory, it certainly does form a part, and a very important part; but under the head of Morayshire, we must tell the reader, that the whole of its hills and heaths exhibit the relics of one continued forest, chiefly of pines, thickly set, even on the flat summits of some of the highest hills; and great part of the country, from the Spey to Cawdor Castle, near Nairn, was covered with forest, within little more (if any more) than a century back; of which the very picturesque, and, in many respects, noble woods of Dulnan and Dulsie are the only fragments remaining. The forest of Tarnawa, surrounding the castle of that name, once the favoured seat of Randolph, Earl of Moray, Regent of Scotland, had fallen into sad decay; but the late Earl of Moray conceived and executed the highly laudable undertaking of its restoration, by planting between four and five thousand acres, along the left bank of the Findhorn. This noble example was immediately followed by the neighbouring proprietors; and we think we state matters within the limits of safety, when we say, that there is now along the course of that river and its tributaries, in one continued tract of forest, not less than from sixteen to eighteen thousand acres of wood, young and old, great part of which is composed of oak, larch, and other valuable trees. Besides this modern forest, which in some measure makes up for the extinction of the ancient forest of Drummyne, by which name this great woodland part of the country was known in the olden time, we have also large plantations, amounting almost to a forest, in the vicinity of Gordon Castle, a creation by the late Duke of Gordon. We should have mentioned, that many of the ancient oaks of the Tarnawa forest still remain. Some of them rise ten or twelve enormous and perfectly vigorous trees, together, from one stool; and in Nairn, the adjacent county, the remains of the ancient forest that surrounded the venerable Castle of Cawdor, yet exhibits some magnificent and luxuriant trees, as specimens of those which have disappeared.

In the shire of Inverness are the remains of several forests,—those of Loch Loyn, Glenmoriston, Strathglass, Loch Garrie, Loch Artrig, and Kinlochleven.

We have already hinted that the large county of Inverness not only possesses very extensive forests at this day, such as those of Loch Arkeg, Glengarry, Glenmorriston, Strathglass, Glen Strathfarrar, that at the head of Loch Sheil, and others, some of which we have already noticed, but it everywhere exhibits remains indicating the existence of one continued forest in ancient times. The fir was no doubt the most abundant tree, but the birch, the hazel, the oak, the ash, the Scotch elm, the mountain ash, the alder, the holly, and the yew, (of which last we have the living remains,) all certainly occupied such places in these ancient forests as were best adapted to encourage their natural growth. In a canal, cut by Mr Macpherson Grant, at Invereshie, in Badenoch, three ranges of fir roots were found standing, one above the other, in the growing position; and at Abernethey, six or eight different strata of them were discovered similarly placed, one

over the other, in the course of digging a ditch in a deep
moss. This we have noticed in the *Account of the Moray
Floods.*

In the county of Banff lies the forest of Glenmore,
which belongs to the Duke of Gordon, whose castle rises
among the woods on the confines of it.

The boundaries of the counties of Moray, Inverness, and
Banff, are rather ill defined in the vicinity of the Cairngorum
mountains ; but, with our present knowledge, we cannot
hesitate a moment in saying that Glenmore is in Inverness-
shire. Of one thing we are decided, that although it belongs
to the Duke of Gordon, his Grace's residence is so far from
rising among the woods on the confines of Glenmore, that it
stands above thirty miles distant from that secluded mountain
valley. All these, however, are excusable mistakes in a
stranger to the country, such as Mr Gilpin was, where we,
who are familiar with the country, find it so difficult to go
right. Banffshire is not remarkable as a wooded country.;
on the contrary, the general flatness of great part of its
surface makes it rather a dfficult matter to get trees to
grow on it. But there are some grand exceptions to] this
rather general remark, as exemplified in the noble and extensive wood and park scenery around the mansions of Cullen
House and Duff House, which sufficiently shew that where
glens and sheltered districts are chosen, timber may be brought
to the greatest possible perfection in a country otherwise
unfavourable to its production.

On the banks of the Dee, in the southern part of the
county of Aberdeen, lies the forest of Glentanner, which
belongs to Lord Aboyne ; and, more to the west, the
forests of Braemar and Invercauld.

The former is a very romantic scene, especially in the
eastern parts. Here we find, in great perfection, every
species of the wildest and most awful country. The
beetling rock assumes nowhere a more tremendous
form ; nor the pine, bursting from its fissures, a more
majestic station ; nor does the river, in any place, throw
itself into more furious contortions. This wild and
extensive forest is much frequented by game of every
kind ; which used formerly, in the summer season, to
draw together a great resort of nobility and gentry, from
all parts of Scotland. Their meeting had the appearance

of a military expedition. They wore a uniform, and encamped together in temporary huts. Their days were spent in the chase, and their evenings in jollity. Such meetings were common in Scotland, and of great antiquity. A hunting party of this kind gave occasion to the celebrated ballad of Chevy Chase.

The forest of Invercauld is likewise a very romantic scene. The pines which at this day grow in some parts of it, are thought to be superior to any in Europe, both in size and quality. Many of them attain the height of eighty or ninety feet, and measure four feet and a half in diameter. They are sold, even in that country, for five or six guineas a tree. The timber which they yield is resinous, heavy, and of a dark red colour. Considerable quantities of it are still carried into the lower parts of Scotland in floats down the Dee, when that river happens to be swollen with rains. The forests of Braemar and Invercauld are supposed to be the remains of the ancient Caledonian wood.

On the banks of the Dee, in truth, as we have already said, the most magnificent, as well as the most extensive, forests now existing in Scotland, are to be found. Those of Invercauld and Braemar are so united, that they may be almost considered as one remnant—and a very grand remnant they are—of the ancient Caledonian forest, of which, indeed, all the forests upon the Spey are also fragments. Here the endless fir woods run up all the ramifications and subdivisions of the tributary valleys, cover the lower elevations, climb the sides of the higher hills, and even, in many cases, approach the very roots of the giant mountains which tower over them; yet, with all this, the reader is mistaken if he supposes that any tiresome uniformity exists among these wilds. Every movement we make exposes to our view fresh objects of excitement, and discloses new scenes produced by the infinite variety of the surface. At one time we find ourselves wandering along some natural level under the deep and sublime shade of the heavy pine foliage, upheld, high over head, by the tall and massive columnar stems, which appear to form an endless colonnade; the ground dry as a floor beneath our footsteps, the very sound of which is muffled by the thick deposition of decayed spines with which the seasons of more than one century have strewed it; hardly conscious that the

sun is up, save from the fragrant resinous odour which its
influence is exhaling, and the continued hum of the clouds of
insects that are dancing in its beams over the tops of the trees.
Anon the ground begins to swell into hillocks, and here and
there the continuity of shade is broken by a broad rush of
light streaming down through some vacant space, and brightly
illuminating a single tree of huge dimensions and of grand
form, which, rising from a little knoll, stands out in bold
relief from the darker masses behind it, where the shadows
again sink deep and fathomless among the red and gray stems,
whilst Nature, luxuriating in the light that gladdens the little
glade, pours forth her richest Highland treasures of purple
heath bells, and bright green bilberries, and trailing whortle-
berries, with tufts of ferns and tall junipers irregularly intermingled. And then, amidst the silence that prevails, the red
deer stag comes carelessly across the view, leading his whole
herd behind him ; and, as his full eye catches a glimpse of
man, he halts, throws up his royal head, snuffs up the
gale, indignantly beats the ground with his hoof, and then
proudly moves off with his troop amid the glistening boles.—
Again the repose of the forest is interrupted by the music of
distant waters stealing upon the ear ; curiosity becomes alive,
and we hurry forward, with the sound growing upon us, till
all at once the roar and the white sheet of a cataract bursts
upon our astonished senses, as we find ourselves suddenly
and unexpectedly standing on the fearful brink of some deep
and rocky ravine, where the river, pouring from above, pre-
cipitates itself into a profound abyss, where it has to fight its
way through countless obstructions, in one continued turmoil
of foam, mist, and thunder. The cliffs themselves are shaken,
and the pines quiver where they wildly shoot, with strange and
fantastic wreathings, from the crevices in their sides, or where,
having gained some small portion of nutriment on their summits,
they rear themselves up like giants aspiring to scale the gates of
heaven. And here, perhaps, a distant mountain top may appear
blue over the deep green fir tops.— By and by, after pursuing
the windings of the wizard stream for a considerable way
upwards, we are conducted by it into some wide plain, through
which it comes broadly flowing and sparkling among the
opposing stones, where the trees of all ages and growths stand
singly, or in groups, or in groves, as Nature may have planted
them, or the deer may have allowed them to rise—where
distant herds are seen maintaining their free right of pasture
—where, on all sides, the steeps are clothed thick with the

portly denizens of the forest, and where the view is bounded by a wider range of those mountains of the Cairngorum group which are now ascertained to be the highest in Great Britain. — And finally, being perhaps led by our wayward fancy to quit this scene, we climb the rough sides of some isolated hill, vainly expecting that the exertion of but a few minutes will carry us to its summit, that we see rising above all its woods. And we do reach it — but not until we are toilworn and breathless, after scrambling for an hour up the slippery and deceitful ascent. Then what a prospect opens to us, as we seat ourselves on some bare rock! The forest is seen stretching away in all directions from our feet, mellowing as it recedes into the farthest valleys amid the distant hills, climbing their bold sides, and scattering off in detachments along their steeps, like the light troops of some army skirmishing in the van — and, above all, the bold and determined outlines of Benmachdhuie, that king of British mountains, and his attendant group of native Alps, sharply, yet softly, delineated against the sky, look down with silent majesty on all below.

The Rev. J. Farquharson, F. R. S. E., in his paper on the Native Forests of Aberdeenshire, formerly referred to, tells us, that the highest grown fir trees there are at an elevation of about one thousand six hundred feet above the level of the sea; but these are large serviceable trees. Those of Glentanner, belonging to Lord Aboyne, farther down the country, are six or seven hundred feet only above the sea, and are very valuable native trees. The finest native trees are in a part of the Invercauld forest, called Glenbeg. Some trees have been cut there having three hundred rings.

It was indeed in these forests of the Dee that some most interesting hunting meetings were held, in times past, — hunting meetings remarkable for their political interest, as well as for the pomp and pageantry under which their deeper purposes were veiled. But perhaps there were none of these so important in its consequences as that which preceded the rising of 1715. We shall make no apology for laying this before the reader, in the words of Sir Walter Scott : —

" Upon leaving Fifeshire, having communicated with such gentlemen as were most likely to serve his purpose, Mar proceeded instantly to his own estates of Braemar, lying along the side of the river Dee, and took up his residence with Farquharson of Invercauld. This gentleman was chief of the clan Farquharson, and could command a very considerable body of men. But he was vassal to Lord Mar for a

small part of his estate, which gave the earl considerable
influence with him; not, however, sufficient to induce him to
place himself and followers in such hazard as would have been
occasioned by an instant rising. He went to Aberdeen, to
avoid importunity on the subject, having previously declared
to Mar, that he would not take arms until the Chevalier St
George had actually landed. At a later period he joined the
insurgents.

" Disappointed in this instance, Mar conceived that as
desperate resolutions are usually most readily adopted in large
assemblies, where men are hurried forward by example, and
prevented from retreating or dissenting by shame, he should
best attain his purpose in a large convocation of the chiefs and
men of rank who professed attachment to the exiled family.
The assembly was made under pretext of a grand hunting
match, which, as maintained in the Highlands, was an occasion of general rendezvous of a peculiar nature. The lords
attended at the head of their vassals, all, even Lowland guests,
attired in the Highland garb, and the sport was carried on
upon a scale of rude magnificence. A circuit of many miles
was formed (by men) around the wild desolate forests and
wildernesses which are inhabited by the red deer, and is called
the tinchel. Upon a signal given, the hunters who composed
the tinchel began to move inwards, closing the circle, and
driving the terrified deer before them, with whatever else the
forest contains of wild animals, who cannot elude the surrounding sportsmen. Being in this manner concentrated and
crowded together, they are driven down a defile, where the
principal hunters lie in wait for them, and shew their dexterity by marking out and shooting those bucks which are in
season. As it required many men to form the tinchel, the
attendance of vassals on these occasions was strictly insisted
upon. Indeed, it was one of the feudal services required by
the law, attendance on the superior at hunting being as regularly required as at hosting, that is, joining his banner in war,
or watching and warding,—garrisoning, namely, his castle in
times of danger.

" An occasion such as this was highly favourable; and the
general love of sport, and the well known fame of the forest
of Braemar for game of every kind, assembled many of the
men of rank and influence who resided within reach of the
rendezvous, and a great number of persons besides, who,
though of less consequence, served to give the meeting the
appearance of numbers. This great council was held about
the 26th of August, and, it may be supposed, they did not

amuse themselves much with hunting, though it was the pretence and watchword of their meeting.

" Among the noblemen of distinction, there appeared in person, or by representation, the Marquis of Huntly, eldest son of the Duke of Gordon; the Marquis of Tulliebardine, eldest son of the Duke of Athol; the Earls of Nithsdale, Marischal, Traquair, Errol, Southesk, Carnwath, and Linlithgow; the Viscounts of Kilsythe, Kenmuir, Kingston, and Stormount; the Lords Rollo, Duffus, Drummond, Strathallan, Ogilvy, and Nairne. Of the chiefs of clans, there attended Glengarry, Campbell of Glendarule, on the part of the powerful Earl of Breadalbane, with others of various degrees of importance in the Highlands.

" When this council was assembled, the Earl of Mar addressed them in a species of eloquence which was his principal accomplishment, and which was particularly qualified to succeed with the high-spirited and zealous men by whom he was surrounded. He confessed, with tears in his eyes, that he had himself been but too instrumental in forwarding the union between England and Scotland, which had given the English the power, as they had the disposition, to enslave the latter kingdom. He urged that the Prince of Hanover was an usurping intruder, governing by means of an encroaching and innovating faction; and that the only mode to escape his tyranny, was to rise boldly in defence of their lives and property, and to establish on the throne the lawful heir of these realms. He declared that he himself was determined to set up the standard of James III, and summon around it all those over whom he had influence, and to hazard his fortune and life in the cause. He invited all who heard him, to unite in the same generous resolution. He was large in his promises of assistance from France, in troops and money, and persisted in the story that two descents were to take place, one in England, under the command of Ormond, the other in Scotland, under the Duke of Berwick. He also strongly assured his hearers of the certainty of a general insurrection in England; but alleged the absolute necessity of shewing them an example in the north, for which the present time was most appropriate, as there were few regular troops in Scotland to restrain their operations, and as they might look for assistance to Sweden as well as to France.

" It has been said, that Mar, on this memorable occasion, shewed letters from the Chevalier de St George, with a commission nominating the Earl his Lieutenant-general, and Commander-in-chief of his armies in Scotland. Other

accounts say, more probably, that Mar did not produce any
other credentials than a picture of the Chevalier, which he
repeatedly kissed, in testimony of zeal for the cause of the
original, and that he did not, at the time, pretend to the
supreme command of the enterprise. This is also the account
drawn up by Mar himself, or under his eye, where it is plainly
said, that it was nearly a month after the standard was set up
ere the Earl of Mar could procure a commission.

" The number of persons of rank who were assembled, the
eloquence with which topics were publicly urged, which had
been long the secret inmates of every bosom, had their effect
on the assembled guests ; and every one felt, that to oppose
the current of the Earl's discourse by remonstrance or objection, would be to expose himself to the charge of cowardice,
or of disaffection to the common cause. It was agreed that
all of them should return home, and raise, under various
pretexts, whatever forces they could individually command,
against a day, fixed for the 3d of September, on which they
were to hold a second meeting at Aboyne in Aberdeenshire,
in order to settle how they were to take the field. The
Marquis of Huntly alone declined to be bound to any limited
time ; and in consequence of his high rank and importance,
he was allowed to regulate his own motions at his own
pleasure.

" Thus ended that celebrated hunting in Braemar, which, as
the old bard says of that of Chevy Chase, might, from its consequences, be wept by a generation which was yet unborn. There
was a circumstance mentioned at the time, which tended to shew
that all men had not forgotten that the Earl of Mar, on whose
warrant this rash enterprise was undertaken, was considered
by some as being rather too versatile to be fully trusted. As
the Castle of Braemar was overflowing with guests, it chanced
that—as was not unusual on such occasions—many of the
gentlemen of the secondary class could not obtain beds, but
were obliged to spend the night around the kitchen fire,
which was then accounted no great grievance. An English
footman, a domestic of the Earl, was of a very different
opinion. Accustomed to the accommodations of the south,
he came bustling in among the gentlemen, and complained
bitterly of being obliged to sit up all night, notwithstanding
he shared the hardship with his betters, saying, that rather
than expose himself to such a strait, he would return to his
own country and turn Whig. However, he soon after com-
forted himself by resolving to trust to his master's dexterity

for escaping every great danger. " Let my Lord alone," he said; " if he finds it necessary, he can turn cat-in-pan with any man in England."

In the county of Athol is the forest of Lochrannoc; and, in that of Argyl, the forest of Lochtulla, where Mr Pennant tells us he saw the last pines, which he supposed to be of spontaneous growth in Scotland.

The " county of Athol," is a strange mistake for Mr Gilpin to have fallen into. We need not tell the domestic geographer, that there is no such county. Our author means the county of Perth, in which the Loch Rannoch Forest is a very important feature ; that of Loch Tulla, or Loch Tollie, in Argyleshire, is also well known to us as possessing pines of truly ancient growth. The extensive moor of Rannoch, which now presents one of the largest and most dreary wastes in Scotland, was once, like all the other wastes both of Argyleshire and of Perthshire, covered with a forest, of which these are the fragments. In both counties, natural oak woods are found, the most extensive tracts of which occur at Dun-keld, and in various other places along the banks of the Tay and the Tunnel, as well as on the skirts of different lochs throughout these counties. Most of these are copsed, and this fate attends the classic wood of Birnam, which is still to be found near Dunkeld. Natural birch woods, too, are as numerous and beautiful as in the more northern counties: as examples of these, we need only instance those of the well known Pass of Killikrankie, and the hills of Loch Cateran. But much has been done by the proprietors of both the great counties we are now considering, and among these, the patriotic exertions of the late Duke of Athol have been the most prominent. We have already said,* that the plantations executed by his Grace, amounted to above fifteen thousand five hundred and seventy-three acres, of which the most important lie in the neighbourhood of Dunkeld and Blair. By far the larger part of these consist of larch, but there is also a considerable mixture of trees of other sorts, and within later years many Norway spruces have been planted. The highest plantations are those near Loch Ordie, at an elevation of about one thousand, or twelve hundred feet, and at this height the larches promise to grow.

* Vol. I. p. 152.

In the county of Stirling lies the forest of that name, or Torwood, as it is often called. Here the country, though still abrupt and rough, begins to assume a milder form. Here, too, the oak begins to mix its cheerful verdure with the dark green tint of the pine. As we approach nearer the English border, it is probable the oak became still more frequent, and occupied large tracts in those vast woods, which, on better evidence than that of ballad history, we believe existed formerly in the wilds of Teviot and Cheviot.

In former times, the greater part of the county of Stirling was covered with forests, vestiges of which are everywhere to be found, and even now the natural woods are calculated to cover about thirteen thousand acres, whilst the plantations extend to about ten thousand acres. As to the forests of the Scottish Border, we know, from early history, that they were almost unbroken in their extent. The whole hills and rising grounds which discharge water to the eastern sea, through the channel of the Tweed, and those of its tributaries, were covered with forests. The Forest of Ettrick still retains its name, and some of its oak woods still exist, the children and the representatives of noble and ancient ancestors. Then there were the Forests of Lauderdale and of Wedale, which covered the hills of Gala Water, and the Forest of Romannoch. Wedale, which comprehended the whole parish of Stowe, belonged to the monks of St Andrews, and many of their charters are dated from thence. The lower part of that valley belonged to the monks of Melrose, and frequent disputes about territory took place between these two bodies of holy men. The ancient forest of Jedwood, so famous both in border history and border ballad, formed a very important integral part of the vast woodland country of the south of Scotland. It is melancholy to have to record, that the two remarkable oaks—the King of the Wood and the Capon Tree—which we have particularly described in page 252 of our first volume, are now the only remaining fragments of Jed Forest. We think it necessary to particularize these forests only, but they may be considered as samples merely of the ancient state of the western as well as the eastern border of Scotland.

As we enter England, the large county of North-umberland affords the remains only of two forests,—

KING OF THE WOOD, OAK

Rothbury in the middle of it, and Lowes on the western side, a little to the north of the Roman wall.

Little living remains of these forests do now comparatively appear. In 1201, the inhabitants of Rothbury held their town of the crown. It has the privilege of three annual fairs, and King John bestowed on them free forest here, with certain other franchises. As to the Forest of Lowes, the ancient family of that name, and of that neighbourhood, are so called from their being possessors of the Forest of Loughs, or Lakes.

In Cumberland we find five, — Nicol, Knaredale, Westwood, Inglewood, and Copeland; all now desolate and naked scenes, except where some of the lands have been cultivated.

Notwithstanding the inexpressible beauty of its lake and hill scenery, the general face of the county of Cumberland is bleak and naked in appearance, from the extensive moors which stretch themselves over its surface ; but these were, no doubt, anciently covered with these great forests, which have now hardly left a vestige behind them.

The wild county of Westmoreland consisted formerly of little besides forests, with the appendages of lakes and mountains. Six are still traced in it. On the north lies the forest of Milburn, in which rises one of the loftiest mountains in England, that of Crossfell. On the west lie the forests of Whinfield, Martindale, and Thornthwait. Martindale is bounded by the beautiful lake of Ullswater, and Thornthwait by that of Broadwater. On the eastern side of this rough county, lie the forests of Stainmore and Mellerstang. Stainmore is a wild scene, noted only for being one of the great western passes into Scotland. At the northern extremity of it is presented a gran piece of distant mountain scenery. On the borders of Mellerstang stand the ruins of Pendragon Castle, the walls of which are full four yards in thickness. Pendragon Castle gives Westmoreland perhaps a better title to that celebrated hero, Uter Pendragon, than any the Welsh can boast. It stands upon the river Eden ; and the tradition of the country is, that the noble founder proposed to draw that great stream around it, like a trench. His enterprise miscarrying gave rise to the following adage, applied to the attempting of an impossibility :

> Let Pendragon do what he can,
> Eden runs, where Eden ran.

This forest was likewise celebrated for being formerly the haunt of wild boars; and a part of it, to this day, retains the name of Wild-boar-fell. Here also stands the mountain of Mowil, from whence three of the largest rivers in the north of England take their source,—the Eden, the Ewer, and the Swale.

Westmoreland exhibits the unequivocal proofs of its having been at one period a great forest country, for the remains of trees are found in the mosses on the highest hills; and statutes made long after the Conquest, are full of notices of its forests, chases, parks, mastage, pannage, vert, venison, green hue, regarders, foresters, verderers, and numerous other names and titles respecting the preservation of woods and game. The valuable woods of the Earl of Lonsdale, in the neighbourhood of Lowther, shew how well the soil and climate of this county are adapted for the growth of timber, as are also the detached groves which surround the dwelling houses in the dales situated high up in the mountains. In some parts of the county, considerable portions of land are covered with coppices of oak, ash, alder, birch, and hazel, many of which may be considered as living remains of the ancient forests which covered the country. Besides the forests mentioned by Mr Gilpin, those of Musgrave Fell, of Sleddale, and of Fawcet, still exist, at least by name, and numerous local appellations also attest the existence of former sylvan scenes. King John granted the Forest of Milbourne to William de Stuteville. Rowgill Castle, the capital of the extensive manor of Milbourne, stands on elevated ground, under Dunfell, overlooking all the champain parts of Westmoreland. Some of the walls still remaining, are ten feet thick, and underneath it were large arched vaults for ensuring the safety of the cattle by night, from the depredations of the Border moss-troopers. It is now occupied as a farm house. Martindale has its name from the Martern, or Martin, an animal inhabiting woods, and well known for its valuable fur. This creature is noticed by Manwood, in his *Treatise on the Forest Laws*, first published in the reign of Queen Elizabeth, and he particularly mentions that it was scarce in all other parts of England, but in this dale. This manor anciently belonged to the Multons and Dacres; and now by purchase to the Hasells of Dalemain. There is still a kind of chase or forest here of great extent, and even yet plentifully stocked with red deer. The tenants are called Strones, and are bound to assist their lord in hunting and turning the deer on the tops of the mountains. Each time they are called out, every four of them have an allowance of eightpence in ale or other liquor; and if they disobey their summons, they are finable at the Court Baron. Thornthwaite, means " the tower in the wood-girt plain." The Folds-in-the-wood, on Knype Scar, denote the site of a British village.

In the bishoprick of Durham we find only the forest of Langden, or Teesdale, which latter name it assumes from running along the banks of the Tees. When the woods of this forest were in perfection, they must have afforded a great variety of very picturesque scenery. For the Tees is one of the most romantic rivers in England, and forms many a furious eddy, and many a foaming cascade, in its passage through the forest, particularly that celebrated cataract which, by way of eminence, is called the Fall of the Tees.

There is also the Weardale Forest. But the general aspect of this county is hilly and mountainous, and the sides, as well as the summits of the hills, are moorish wastes. The whole western angle, indeed, is a bleak, naked, and barren region, crossed by the ridge of hills termed the English Apennines, though they do not here rise to any great elevation.

In Lancashire we find three forests, — Lancaster Forest, which, I suppose, is the same as Wiresdale; Bowland, a little to the south; and Simon's Wood, extending almost to Liverpool.

The chief part of the king's property, as Duke of Lancaster, consists of what are generally styled the Forests of Myerscough, Fullwood, Bleasdale, Wyersdale, and Quernmore, all of which are situated in the most northern parts of the county. In these his majesty is entitled to the estrays, and the game, the right of holding the courts, &c. and is lord of the manor for all the forests. The township of Quernmore is situated in the Hundred of Lonsdale and parish of Lancaster, and contains a considerable quantity of enclosed and waste land, which last amounts to three thousand acres. There is a separate court for this forest, held half-yearly by the master forester of Amounderness, whose duty it is, in right of his office, to hold the several courts for the said forests. Wyersdale is similarly situated to Quernmore. The river Wyer rises in this forest, and flows through a valley about the middle of it. The open and enclosed parts together are computed to contain more than twenty thousand statute acres. The greater part consists of mountainous land not worth enclosing; but it produces abundance of game. The court is held exactly like that of Quernmore. Bleasdale is situated in the Hundred of Amounderness, and parish of Lancaster, and lies coextensive with the township of Bleas-dale. According to the receiver-general's report in 1777, it contained from three thousand five hundred to four thousand five hundred acres of unenclosed, and about the same quantity of enclosed, land. The court of this forest is held jointly with those of Myerscough and Fulwood. Myerscough township is understood to be of equal extent with the ancient forest, and consists of nearly two thousand two hundred statute acres; about three hundred of which are private property. The remainder, belonging to the king, is called Mayerscough Park, and is held under a lease by Mr Heatley, with the exception of a small portion of woodland. The whole of this forest is enclosed. Fulwood is situated near Preston. The ancient forest comprised a great quantity of land, which is now enclosed; the whole, or a considerable part, of the town of Preston, is said to have been originally within its boundaries. Preston race ground forms a part of it. Previous to the Norman dynasty, and under the early part of it, this county was distinguished as an Honour, and was of the superior class of Seigniories, on which inferior lordships and manors depended, by the performance of certain customs and services to the lords who held them. Landed Honours belonged exclusively to kings originally, but were afterward granted in fee to noblemen. " These keep their honour courts," as Hopkinson's MSS tell us, " every year at least, or oftener, if need be; at which court all the freeholders of all the manors that stand united to the said honour, shall make their appearance; which suitors shall not sit, but stand bare-headed; and over that court shall be hanged a cloth of state, with a chair of state, upon which chair shall be laid a cushion, either of cloth of gold or velvet, seemly and decent for such a place of honour, upon which there ought to be embroidered the arms of the honour." That the honour of Lancaster existed before the Conquest, is demonstrated by an agreement (still preserved) made between King Stephen and Henry Duke of Normandy. Soon after the Conquest, three noblemen held the honour of *Luncaster*, as it was then termed; but Roger of Poictou is the first person whose name has been recorded as the possessor; and that nobleman forfeited it for high treason. Stephen then gave it to his son William. After this the honour was held by several great personages, till Henry III conferred it on his second son, Edmund Plantagenet, surnamed Crouchback, when it became an earldom in consequence of the possessor being an earl by birthright, in addition to which Parliament passed an act, in which Edmund was styled Earl of Lancaster. The title of Duke of Lancaster was created by Edward III in favour of Henry Plantagenet, whose daughter and heiress, Blanche, married John of Gaunt, fourth son of Edward III, from whom it descended to his son, Henry IV, who decreed, that the title and revenues should remain to him, and to his heirs, for ever, as a distinct and separate inheritance from the crown.

The site of Browsholme is on a commanding elevation in a tract of land, formerly part of the forest of Bowland, which, though now enclosed and mostly cultivated, was, not many years ago, rànged by several herds of wild deer, the last of which was destroyed so late as the year 1805. Browsholme has long been the seat or lodge of the bow-bearer, or master forester, of the district, a title and office retained by the possessor. " Here have been two lawnds," says the *History of Whalley*, " or enclosures for deer,—Radholme Lawnd, and Lathgram Park. The beautiful river Hodder, famous for its umber or grayling, intersects the forest, and forms the only ornamental scenery of a tract otherwise bleak and barren, by its deep and wooded banks. On one of these is the little chapel of Whitewell, together with an inn, the court house of Bowland, and undoubtedly a very ancient resting-place for travellers journeying from Lancaster to Clithero or Whalley. The landscape here is charming. The Hodder, brawling at a great depth below the chapel, washes the foot of a tall conical knoll, covered with oaks to its top, and is soon lost in overshadowing woods beneath. On the opposite hill, and near the keeper's house, are the remains of a small encampment, supposed to be Roman. On an adjoining height, a quarry and manufactory of querns, or ancient hand-mills, was discovered, the use of which was probably introduced into Britain by the Roman soldiers. In the hall of Brows-holme is preserved an interesting vestige of the forest laws. This is a stirrup through which every dog, excepting those belonging to the lords, must pass. There is a portrait here of Edward Parker, Esq. who was bow-bearer of Bowland, about 1690; he is in the costume of his office, with a staff tipped with a buck's horn, and a buglehorn tucked under his girdle.

In the northern parts of Yorkshire lie a cluster of small forests,—Lime, Applegarth, Swaledale, and Wenseleydale. Whether each of these had a separate jurisdiction, or whether their rights were intermingled, would be difficult at this day to ascertain. They must formerly, however, in their rude state, have been delightful scenes. Even now they contain some of the most picturesque country we have in England; rivers, valleys, rocks, and woods in great profusion, though intermingled and deformed with patches of human industry.

On the eastern side of Yorkshire lies the forest of Pickering, extending itself almost to Scarborough. This forest, with that of Wiresdale, were royalties belonging to the Duchy of Lancaster; and, in the time of John of Ghent, the jurisdiction of forest law was maintained in both of them with so much exactness, that the determinations of the courts of Lancaster and Pickering were always esteemed sufficient precedents for all the other forest courts in England.*

In the middle of Yorkshire lies the wide forest of Knaresborough, once a very romantic scene; a little to the south lies Harewood; and, on the east, lies Galtries, still a woody district, extending almost to the walls of York.

Around Halifax lies Hardwicke Forest, within the precincts of which Halifax Law, as it was called, took place. It was a very severe jurisdiction, vested in the

---

* See Manwood *On Forest Law*, in various parts.

magistrates of the town, to punish cloth stealing. The offender, within the space of two or three market days, was tried, condemned,. and executed. The instrument of his execution was called a maiden. It was a machine in which an axe was drawn up a considerable height between two posts, and, under the pressure of a heavy weight, fell rapidly on the criminal's neck. The axe is still shewn at Halifax.

There were probably many other forests in Yorkshire, but we can only trace, with any degree of certainty, the site of one more, which is Hatfield Chase : and this might likewise have been forgotten, had it not been for a piece of history belonging to it,—the death of Edwin, king of Northumberland, which happened in this forest, together with the destruction of his army, by Penda, the pagan king of Mercia.

Knaresborough Forest extends, from east to west, above twenty miles ; and it is in some places eight miles broad. At the time of Doomsday Book, there were only four townships in it, but in 1368, there were three towns and sixteen hamlets. At present, it consists of eleven constabularies. Till the year 1775, those comprised a large extent of old enclosed land, and also a tract of about thirty thousand acres of common, on which Knaresborough, and several other townships not within the constabularies, claimed and exercised a right of common and turbary, equally with the owners of property within their limits. This waste, in its open state, was of little benefit to any one except to some of the more opulent yeomanry, who derived a considerable profit from it. But an act was obtained in 1770 for its division and enclosure, and this no sooner began to be carried into effect, than the proprietors, and especially the smaller ones, commenced a spirited system of improvement. The poor cottager and his family exchanged their indolence for active industry, and obtained extravagant wages. Labourers and workmen of every description poured in from different quarters, and met with high wages and constant employment, and a great part of the forest was speedily brought into cultivation ; and a turnpike road was opened through the centre of it ; in consequence of all which the rent has trebled, and the population increased in an extraordinary degree, for the old enclosed lands, as well as the common, being free from tithes, a full

3

scope was given to spirited cultivation. The village of Harrowgate, remarkable for its mineral waters, is situated in this forest.

From Bentley's account of Halifax and its gibbet law, we learn, that " the inhabitants within the forest of Hardwick had a custom, from time immemorial, that if a felon were taken within their liberty, with goods stolen out of, or within the liberty of the said forest, either hand-habend, back-berand, or confessand, any commodity of the value of thirteen pence halfpenny, he should, after three markets, or meeting days, within the town of Halifax, next after such his apprehension, and being condemned, be taken to the gibbet, and have his head cut off from his body." But the felon was to be publicly and deliberately tried by the frith burghers, within the said liberty, which comprised about twenty townships and hamlets, from the names of some of which it would appear that the forest of Hardwick was the same as the forest of Lowerby. The history of the gibbet law is so extremely curious, that we conceive an abridgment of it, extracted from the *Beauties of England and Wales*, will not be unacceptable to the reader.

" The process of the gibbet law was this :— Out of the most wealthy persons, and those of the greatest repute for integrity and understanding in the liberty, a certain number were selected for the trial of the offenders ; for, when a felon was apprehended, he was immediately brought before the Lord's Bailiff at Halifax, who, by virtue of the authority granted him from the Lord of the Manor of Wakefield, under the seal of the manor, kept a common jail in the town, had the custody of the axe, and was the legal executioner. On receipt of the prisoner, the bailiff issued out his summons to the constables of four several towns within the precincts of the liberty, to require four frith burghers within each town to appear before him on a certain day, to examine into the truth of the charge. At the time of appearance, the accuser and the accused were confronted before them, the thing stolen was produced, and the prisoner acquitted and condemned according to the evidence, without any oath being adminis- tered. If the party accused was acquitted, he was instantly liberated on paying his fees ; if condemned, he was either immediately executed, if it was the principal market day, or kept till then, if it was not ; and in the meanwhile, set in the stocks on the less meeting days, with the stolen goods on his back, if portable, or, if not, they were placed before him. But the executions always took place on the great market day, in order to strike greater terror into the neighbourhood. And so strict was this customary law, that whoever within the liberty, had any thing stolen, and not only discovered the thief, but secured the goods, could not receive them back without prosecuting the delinquent, but was obliged to bring him with the stolen property to the chief bailiff at Halifax, and to carry on the prosecution. Without this procedure, he both forfeited the goods to the Lord of the Manor, and was liable to be accused of theft-bote, for his private connivance and agreement with the felon. After every execution also, it appears, that the coroners for the county, or some of them, were obliged to repair to the town of Halifax, and there summon a jury of twelve men, sometimes the same persons who condemned the felon, and administer an oath to them to give in a true and precise verdict relating to the fact for which he was executed, in order that a record might be made of it in the crown office.

" This custom, which has been noticed by every historian and antiquary who has treated of this town and parish, has obtained the distinguishing appellation of the Halifax law. It attracted the attention of Camden and his commentators, and is amply explained by Bentley, Wright, and Watson. It is first to be noted that the felon was liable to suffer, if he was taken within the liberty or precincts of Hardwick. This refers us directly to the privileges of infangthefe, and outfangthefe, the origin of which is of great antiquity. These privileges are mentioned in the laws of Edward the Confessor, which William the Norman afterwards confirmed, in the twenty-first chapter, ' De baronibus, qui suas habent curias et consuetudines,' concerning the barons, who have their courts of law and customs. In this article there is an express mention of infangthefe and outfangthefe, which is thus explained, ' Justitia cognoscentis latronis sua est, de homine suo, si captus fuerit super terram suam;' he has the right of taking cognizance of felony, in respect of his own vassals, if the felon be taken within his own manor. But here is nothing said, *de homine extraneo*, or such as did not belong to the manor, whom the lord had power to execute by the privilege of outfangthefe, if taken as a thief within his manor, let the robbery have been committed wherever it might. This power was undoubtedly exercised at Halifax, as appears in the following entries in the register : ' Quidam extraneus capitalem subiit sententiam 1° Jan. 1542 ;' a certain stranger suffered capital punishment, and Richard Sharp and John Learoyd, beheaded the 5th day of March, 1568, for a robbery done in Lancashire.

" But there is such a variety of opinions brought forward by different writers concerning the power of infangthefe and outfangthefe, that the recital of them would be tedious ; and Spelman very justly observes, that the true signification must be sought in the customs of particular places.   At Halifax, it appears, that the felon was to be taken within the liberty, and that if he escaped out of the liberty, even after condemna- tion, he could not be brought back to be executed ; but if ever he returned into it again, and were taken, he was liable to suffer, as was the case of a person named Lacy, who, after escaping, remained seven years out of the liberty, but, venturing to come back, was beheaded on the former verdict, in the year 1623. In the next place, the fact was to be proved in the clearest manner : the offender was to be taken either hand-habend, or back-berand, that is, having the stolen goods either in his hand, or bearing them on his back, or, lastly, confessand, confessing that he took them.   This is what the writers on ancient laws denominate ' Furtum manifestum ;' and perhaps the abhorrence which our ancestors had of that crime, might give rise to the ample power that was so long left to the barons of punishing offenders of this description ; for nothing surely could more effectually deter from the prac- tice of theft, than capital punishment, inflicted in this summary way, without much trouble or expense to the prosecutors. But it must, however, be remarked, that there was a great defect in this law ; for, unless the felon was taken with the stolen goods in his actual possession, which would seldom be the case, he could, by pleading not guilty, avoid conviction ; and the person injured had no farther redress.   The value of the goods was to amount to thirteen pence half-penny or more ; and Dr Gray seems to think, that thirteen pence half- penny may have been called hangman's wages, in allusion to the Halifax law.   Mr Watson also supposes, that this sum of money might ·be given at this place as a gratuity to the executioner.

" When the condemned felon was brought to the gibbet, which stood a little way out of the town, at the west end, the bailiff, the person who had found the verdict, and the attending clergyman, placed themselves on the scaffold with the prisoner. The fourth psalm was then played round the scaffold on the bagpipes, after which the minister prayed with the prisoner till he received the fatal stroke.   The execution was performed by an engine similar to the guillotine. It consisted of two upright posts, fifteen feet high, joined at the top by a transverse beam ; within these was a square block of wood, four feet and a half long, which moved up and down between the uprights by means of grooves. To the lower end of this sliding block was fastened an axe of the weight of seven pounds twelve ounces. The axe, thus fixed, was drawn up to the top by a cord, or pully. At the end of the cord was a pin, which, being fixed to the block, kept it suspended till the moment of execution, when, by pulling out the pin, or cutting the cord, it was suffered to fall, and the criminal's head was instantly severed from his body. The mode of this proceeding has been differently described. Harrison says, that every person present took hold of the rope, or at least stretched forth his arm as near to it as he could, in token of his approbation, and that the pin was pulled out in this manner ; but if the offender was condemned for stealing an ox, sheep, or horse, the end of the rope was fastened to the beast, which, being driven, pulled out the pin. Camden informs us that if this was not performed by a beast, the bailiff or his servant cut the rope ; with which Bentley's representation agrees. From these descriptions of the Halifax gibbet, it evidently appears that the French guillotine is not a recent invention.

"Mr Watson, with great probability, supposes that the gibbet law had its beginning about the manor of Wakefield, which included the present parish of Halifax, and was bestowed on the Earl of Warren. In the reign of Edward I, at the pleas of assizes and jurats, John Earl of Warren and Surrey, answering to a writ of *quo warranto*, said that he claimed gallows at Coningsburgh and Wakefield, and the power of doing what belonged to a gallows in all his lands and fees, and that he and his ancestors had used the same from time immemorial ; to which it was answered, on the part of the King, that the aforesaid liberties belonged merely to the crown, and that no long seisin or prescription of time ought to prejudice the King, and that the Earl had no special warrant for the said liberties : therefore judgment was desired, if the seisin could be to the said Earl a sufficient warrant. But the prescriptive right of the Earl was deemed good.

"It seems to be universally agreed, that theft was the only thing cognizable in this court ; but, as Mr Watson informs us, that in a MS in the Harleian Collection in the British Museum, No. 797, under the title of Halifax, is the following entry : — ' The Court of the Countess, held 30th January,

33, Edward III, it is found by inquisition, that if any tenant of this lordship of Halifax be beheaded for theft, *or other cause,* that the heirs of the same tenant ought not to lose their inheritance,' &c.   But Mr Watson says, it is difficult to understand how the power of beheading for other offences than theft could have existed in early times, and not afterwards in later times, except upon the supposition that the whole power being about to be done away by Edward IV, that part of it which referred to theft was left as an encouragement to the manufactures, which were then in their infancy.

" This power of capital punishment was kept up at Halifax a considerable time after it had ceased in every other part of the kingdom.   The privilege was in no place taken away by act of Parliament, but fell, by degrees, from the liberties becoming extinct.   But as Halifax was a place of so much manufacture and trade, the old laws were kept up there as long as the people dared to exercise them.

" It seems that theft was exceedingly common in this neighbourhood, and also that the law was rigidly executed whilst it endured ; for the register books exhibit a list of forty-nine persons beheaded at Halifax gibbet, between the 20th day of March, 1541, and the 30th April, 1650.   Of these, five were executed in the six last years of Henry VIII ; twenty-five in the reign of Elizabeth ; seven in the reign of James I ; ten in that of Charles I ; and two during the interregnum.   And it cannot be supposed that, in any part of this period, the number of inhabitants in the whole district could equal one third of the present population.   The list of executions, indeed, is so formidable, that there is no reason to wonder at the proverbial petition of the thieves and vagabonds,—' From Hell, Hull, and Halifax, good Lord deliver us !'   Hull was formerly noted for the strictness of its police, and the walls and fortifications were great impediments to escape.

" The extensive level of Hatfield Chase contains about one hundred and eighty thousand acres, which was one great morass, till Charles I sold it to Cornelius Verminden, a Dutchman, who drained and improved it at an expense of £400,000, but who was unfortunately ruined by the lawsuits his operations led him into.   In almost every part of these extensive levels, numerous trees are dug out of the boggy earth.   These unquestionably grew on the spot, and the notion is, that they were cut or burned down by the Romans, to dislodge the conquered Britons, who had retired within their fortresses.   Many of the trees bear evident marks of fire, and some are said to be found with the marks of the tools on them by which they had been cut down, whilst a great proportion are found attached to the root.

In Cheshire, we have the forests of Delamere and Macclesfield. The former is an extensive district of ground, rising, as it approaches Chester, and presenting, at the extremity, a grand view of the flat country below, bounded by the mountains of Wales. The Castle of Beeston, seated on a hill in the second distance, appears to great advantage in the view. In this forest Edelfleda, a Mercian princess, founded a little town for her retirement, which obtained the title of the Happy City. The site is still known by the name of the Chamber in the Forest.

Besides these two forests in Cheshire, there was formerly another of larger dimensions than either of them. It occupied, under the name of Wireall Forest, that whole peninsula which lies between the estuaries of the Mersey and the Dee.

There are few large woods of any kind in Cheshire. That which was the forest of Delamere is a very extensive tract, comprising great part of the Hundred of Eddisburg. In the time of Leland it abounded with red and fallow deer; but it is now a bleak and dreary waste, composed of deep sand and steril heath, and chiefly inhabited by rabbits, with a few black terns which skim over the pools and stagnant waters that occupy some parts of it. Some stunted trees still remain near the Chamber of the Forest, which was once in the centre of the woodland. This Hundred contains no town of consequence, though tradition reports that a large town was formerly situated in it. Macclesfield Forest has long been a dreary and bleak district, with little or no wood.

In the county of Nottingham is the celebrated forest of Sherwood, which was formerly the frequent scene of royal amusement. Mansfield, a town in that forest, was the seat of the king's residence on those occasions; and it was here that he made an acquaintance with the miller of famous memory. This forest was also the retreat of another personage, equally celebrated in the chronicle of ballad, the illustrious Robin Hood, who, with Little John and the rest of his associates, making the woody scenes of it his asylum, laid the whole country under contribution. Sherwood forest is, at present, a scene of great desolation, though its woods, in various parts, are reviving, under the auspices of several eminent patrons,* whose estates either lie within it, or on its confines.

Sherwood, or Shirewood Forest occupied a large part of the county of Nottingham. " The famous forest," says Camden, " anciently thick set with trees, whose entangled branches were so twisted together, that they hardly left room for a single person to pass. At present," he adds, writing in the time of Elizabeth, " it is much thinner, but still breeds an infinite number of deer and stags with lofty antlers."

Leland seems not to have paid much attention to this woodland district during his journey. ' " Coming out of the town of Mansfield," says he, " withyn a little way, passed over the brooke that renneth in the vale hard by it. This brooke a three miles by west above the town of Mansfield, and a three miles lower goeth by Clypstone, as I harde. Soone after I entered, withyn the space of a mile or lesse, into the very thick of the woddy forest of Sherwood, where is greate game of deere, and so I rode a V miles in the very woddy grounds of the forest, and so to a little pore streete, a thoroughfare at the end of the wood," (this was Papplewick.) " A little or I came to the end of this wodde, I left, about a quarter of a mile on the right hand, the ruins of Newstead, a priory of chanons."

Thoroton tells us, a century after this, that the pleasant and glorious condition of this noble forest is now wonderfully declined; and, he adds, " there is at present, (1675,) and long hath been, a justice-seat held under my Lord's Grace the Duke of Newcastle, justice in Eyre of all his Majesty's forests north of Trent, wherein it seems his deputies or lieutenants have allowed such and so many claims, that there will not shortly be woode enough left to cover the bilberries, which every summer wont to be an extraordinary great profit and pleasure to poor people who gathered them, and carried them all about the country to sell." But, notwithstanding this alarming description, there is still much woodland scenery left, enough at least to suggest ideas of the forest life that once existed there.

* The Dukes of Norfolk, Kingston, Newcastle, and Portland; Sir George Saville, Sir Charles Sedley, and others, have made large plantations in several parts.

The author of the Account of Sherwood Forest in the *Beauties of England and Wales*, says, that " if this forest does not possess all that the landscape gardener would call beautiful, it has in itself every variety of sylvan scenery, consisting of pasture, tracts of woody country intermixed with pasturage, and in many places with cultivated enclosures. These intermingled scenes are again divided from other intermixtures of the same kind by wild heaths, which are sometimes bounded by a naked line of horizon, at others skirted with wood; and this intermixture of wood and pasturage, with large separations of heath, gives a variety to many tracts of Sherwood Forest, which could not be expected in a boundless continuance of woody scenery alone. The forest heath, too, becomes a most interesting scene to the admirer of Nature, when bounded, as it generally is in this forest, by woods in various directions, and interspersed here and there with lately planted clumps, which almost imperceptibly unite its woody boundaries with the wide foreground of heath and gravel. A very pleasing contrast, too, may be discovered in the broad masses of colour in the wild extent of heath, and the various portions of gravelly surface, broken as they often are by the rude forest tracks, or dotted in deeper shades with patches of furze, fern, or other wild plants, which stain it, as it were, with every shade of green, or enliven it with the yellow furze blossoms. In some places, too, the most pleasing ideas of animated Nature break in upon the desert scene, from the woodman's cottage, or groups of cattle, or the starting deer; and when these circumstances come in unexpectedly, and happily unite with the time of day, or with the general expression given to the scene by the state of the atmosphere, it does not require much taste to perceive, that, to a picturesque eye, the wild heath may become one of the most interesting scenes of the forest. To this must be added the incidental appearance of smoke, either from the low-roofed cottage, or from the frequent practice of burning the gorse, or fern, for agricultural purposes, which is always attended with peculiar beauty in woodland scenery. In the latter case, its effect is always striking; for then we see it in large masses spreading in the forest glades, and forming a soft background to the trees which intercept it; and as this process generally takes place in autumn, it contrasts more happily with their russet foliage, or withered ramifications. The open heath, with its accompaniments, may be traced through these broad tracts that lie between

Beskwood and Mansfield, skirting Newstead Abbey, and extending to the right towards Oxton and Farnsfield. The wild expanse, overgrown with gorse and fern, and skirted with woodland scenery, may be traversed between Mansfield and Ollerton, round Edwinstow and Rufford, and including the scenery of Clipstone Park ; whilst the more varied scenery of ancient forest, of thickening foliage, intermixed with open lawns and breaks of cultivation, may be found round Warsop and Carburton, including much of the park landscape of Welbeck, Worksop, Clumber, and Thoresby, and extending to the northern limits of the forest land to the right of the road from Worksop to Retford. The whole of which is finely contrasted, on the eastern bounds, by the rich scenes of cultivation and enclosure extending from Haughton Park to Southwell, and where, in general, the ground is sufficiently broken to add the picturesque to the beautiful. Such are the scenes that, even in its denuded condition, may be traced through Sherwood Forest ; we shall now slightly touch upon its ancient history and present state.

" The forest was anciently divided, or rather known by the names of Thorny Wood and High Forest ; the first of which, although by much the smallest, contained, within its limits, no less than nineteen towns and villages, among which Nottingham was included ; and the High Forest is described as abounding with fine stately oaks, and as being entirely free from underwood. The first time we find it particularly mentioned was in the reign of Henry II, it being then a place of royal resort. It appears, by an inquisition held at Nottingham in that reign, that the archbishop of York had a right, or a custom, of hunting in the forest nine days in every year, — three at Christmas, three at Easter, and three at Whitsuntide ; and also, that the archbishop, and his canons, and his men, had here their proper foresters, and aeryes of hawks, and pannage. It is evident, indeed, that, although not mentioned by any writers before this reign, it must have been for some time previous of considerable consequence ; for the first session of justices in Eyre, held by order of Henry, was under the superintendence of the bishops of Durham and Lincoln, and the Earl of Leicester. The last of these sessions upon record in the Tally Office of the Exchequer, is in a book in which is entered the claims and commencement of a justice-seat held here before the then Lord Cromwell, who was Chief Justice in Eyre, north of Trent, and which must have taken place sometime after the

twenty-sixth year of Henry VIII, (1534.) In the same
reign there was also a perambulation, which is preserved by
Thoroton, much more minute than any preceding ones, but
not essentially differing in the extent of its limits.

ₜ " The old forest books contain a copy of a charter made by
King John, before his coming to the crown, and whilst Earl
of Moreteyn, to Matilda de Caux, and Ralph Fitzstephen, her
husband, and to their heirs, of all the liberties and free
customs, which any of the ancestors of the said Maud
(Lords of Laxton) held at any time in Nottinghamshire
and Derbyshire, as their ancestors ever held the same. It
then descended to John Birking, her heir, and then to the
family of Everington, who having lost their rights by
forfeiture, it came to the crown in the reign of Edward I,
since which time it has come generally under the jurisdiction
of the sheriffs of the county, and its forest jurisdiction has
been granted to various individuals among the nobility and
gentry as special marks of royal favour.

" Its manners and customs are curious, and very illustrative
of the olden times. By an inquisition taken before Geoffry
de Langley, the king's justice in Eyre, north of Trent, it
appears, that the chief keeper ought to have three deputy
keepers over three districts, in order to attach all trespassers,
and to present them at the attachment before the verdurers.
In the first keeping, which lay between the rivers Lene and
Doverbeck, he was to have one forester riding, with a page
and two foresters on foot, two verdurers, and two agisters.
This keeping contained the three Hays of Beskwood, Lindeby,
and Willay. The High Forest formed the second keeping;
and here were two foresters riding, with two pages and two
foresters on foot; here also were two verdurers and two
agisters. This keeping also included the two Hays of Birkland and Billahay, with the park of Clipstone, which were to
be under the care of two verdurers and two agisters. The
third keeping, Rumwoode, was to have one forester on foot;
and two wood wards, one at Carburton, and the other at
Badby; also two verdurers and two agisters. It was farther
found, that the chief keeper ought also to have a page, bearing
his bow, through all the forest, to gather chiminage, which
seems to have been a fee for the making and mending of
roads.

" The whole extent of the forest, from north to south, is
about twenty-five miles, and its breadth from seven to nine;
which seems to agree with its ancient boundaries; for the

perambulation in the sixteenth of Henry III (1231) began at Coningswith Ford, by the highway towards Nottingham, on to Blackstonehaugh, and thence forward, by the course of the Doverbeck, into the Trent. Westerly it went from Coningswith by Mayden Water, to the town of Worksop, following the course of the river to Pleasby, so to Otterbrigs, and by the great highway to the Millford, Mayneshead, Hardwick, and Kirkby, to Nuncarre and Annesley, and thence by the highroad through the town of Linbye, to Lene Water and Linton, and thence by the said water, as it was wont of old time to run into the Trent, to the fall of Doverbeck."

The present forest officers consist of a lord warden, a bow-bearer, and ranger, which situation was held by Lord Byron, four verdurers, a steward, and nine keepers, having so many different walks. There are also two sworn wood wards for Sutton and Carleton. Thorny Wood Chase, being a branch of the forest, was granted by Queen Elizabeth, in 1559, to John Stanhope, Esq. as hereditary keeper, and is now held by the Earl of Chesterfield. The surveyor-general of the woods has also a jurisdiction over the forest, so far as regards the timber of the crown, and he has a deputy in the forest.

The soil of the forest has been granted by the crown to different lords of manors, reserving only, in forest language, the vert and venison, or trees and deer. The deer were very numerous in former times, and were all of the red kind, except in Thorny Wood Chase, where they were of the fallow kind. Within the memory of many persons now living, herds of an hundred or more might be seen together in different parts of this woodland district; but cultivation has gradually driven them from their accustomed haunts, and, except in preserved parks, there are none now to be found. The forest is now so decayed, that Robin Hood and his merry men could scarcely find shelter in it. The principal remains of it are now only to be found in the Hays of Berkland and Bilhagh, which form an open wood of large ancient oaks, free from underwood, except in one place, where some natural birch is growing; but most of these old trees are in a state of decay. The extent of this tract is about three miles, by one and a half, or about fifteen hundred acres. In a survey made about thirty years ago, they only contained ten thousand one hundred and seventeen trees, valued at little more than £17,000. Clumber Park contains the remains of two venerable woods called Clumber and Hardwick woods; and there are some ancient districts of small extent, called Harlow Wood, Thieves Wood, and Mansfield Wood, containing little timber of value. Welbeck Park contains extensive groves of very ancient and majestic oaks, with some beautiful birches. Some of the oaks, as we have already had occasion to notice, are of extraordinary size, and are perhaps one thousand years old, being upwards of thirty-four feet in girth. Among other trees worth mentioning, there is an oak called the Parliament Oak, from Edward I having held a parliament under its shade; and there is another called the Broad Oak, measuring twenty-seven feet and a half in circumference. Near Blidworth, also, there is a very large and ancient elm called Langton Arbour, which, even some centuries ago, was sufficiently remarkable to give a name to one of the forest walks, and to have a keeper appointed to it.

Major Rooke tells us, that a curious discovery was made in cutting some of the trees in Birkland and Bilhagh: letters were found cut or stamped in the body of them, denoting the king's reign in which they were thus marked. The bark seems to have been taken off, and the letters cut in, after which year after year's growth was added to the tree, without any ligneous matter adhering when the bark had been removed, so that, when that which was restored came to be again cut away, the letters were distinctly discovered. The cyphers were of James I, of William and Mary, and one of King John. One of these, with James's cypher, was one foot within the tree, and one foot from the centre. It was cut down in 1786. This tree, therefore, must have been two feet in diameter, or two yards in girth, at the time the mark was cut. Now, estimating a tree of that size at one hundred and twenty years' growth, and subtracting that number from the middle year of James's reign, would make the year 1494 as the date of the planting of the tree. One of William and Mary had the mark about nine inches within the tree, and three feet three inches from the centre. It was also cut down in 1786.

The mark of John was eighteen inches within the tree, and something more than a foot from the centre. It was cut down in 1791; but the middle year of John's reign was 1207, from which if we subtract one hundred and twenty, the number of years requisite for a tree of two feet diameter to arrive at that growth, it will make the date of its planting 1085, or about twenty years after the Conquest. The tree, therefore, when cut down, in 1791, must have been seven hundred and six years old, a fact scarcely credible ; for it appears, from the trees whose marks are better authenticated, that those exactly of the same size, where marked, had increased twelve inches in diameter in one hundred and seventy-two years ; whilst this one had increased no more than eighteen inches in five hundred and eighty-four years. But the surplus six inches contained a greater cubic quantity than the six inches immediately within them, and would therefore require a longer time for their increase, and that in the proportion of our increasing progression. Major Rooke accounts for these phenomena, by supposing that, as the increasing wood never adheres where the bark has been taken off, the sap, which rises from the roots through the capillary tubes of the wood to the branches, returns in its circulation, between the blea and the bark. " I have often," says he, " examined many of the ancient hollow trees in Birkland and in Bilhagh, and always found that where the bark remained, even in their mutilated trunks, there they frequently put out small branches with leaves ; but where the necessary covering of the returning sap was wanting, there was no appearance of vegetation."

It is some satisfaction to know that the proprietors interested in the Forest of Sherwood, are doing much to restore its sylvan honours ; but ages must pass away before the trees now planted can well harmonize with our ancient associations connected with this great scene of England's ballad story. It never can be forgotten that these woodland retreats have been haunted by the daring muse of Byron. The poet's residence of Newstead Abbey was formed out of the ancient Priory of Black Canons of that name, which was founded by Henry II, about the year 1170. It stands in a vale in the midst of an extensive park, finely planted, with a large artificial lake flowing almost up to the building. But even Byron's memory and Byron's fame will fail to excite that interest in Sherwood with which the name of Robin Hood has long inspired the inhabitants of Britain of all ages and conditions, — an interest which has been recently extended from the narrow sphere of these islands to the boundless theatre of the civilized world, by the magic wand of the enchanting author of Ivanhoe ! For our own parts, we must candidly confess that we hardly believe that we should have troubled the reader with so much regarding this classic ground of Sherwood, had it not been for our own ardent affection for our nursery recollections of Robin Hood and Little John, refreshed, and brightened, and polished as they have been by the powerful descriptions and poetical imaginings of the Scottish Shakespeare. Trusting, therefore, that we are certain of finding responsive feelings everywhere, we hope to be forgiven for going as fully into the history of the bold outlaw as our materials and space will admit.

Mr Thorsby, in his addition to Thoroton, observes, that the songs in *Robin Hood's Garland*, are simply and historically poetized, and have been the favourites of the lower classes ever since his time ; but the author of the article Nottinghamshire, in the *Beauties of England*, seems very much to doubt that these ballads had any particular claim to antiquity, at least in their present dress. Their internal evidence is certainly not in favour of their antiquity, — the style and turn of expression are not those of the twelfth century, nor of many centuries afterwards. One fact in particular is well worthy of attention, — that they are free from indelicacy, which is not the case with the popular ballads, even so late as the reign of Elizabeth ; and this simple fact alone must place the date of their composition, or rather of their present dress, at a period by no means very remote. But still these ballads bear every semblance of having originated from older and ruder traditions ; and the circumstances recorded in these traditions have, in all probability, had corresponding circumstances and actions from which they have sprung ; and it is even possible that the ballads of *Robin Hood's Garland*, though comparatively modern, may have been altered to suit the taste of the period that produced them, from the yet ruder and less delicate rhymes which had been in the mouths of the people, even from the olden times, but which these more chastened lays have now for so many years superseded. Whilst Mr Thorsby believes that their antiquity cannot be doubted, he also supposes that they have been altered in their phraseology to suit the different periods through which they have descended to the present.

But be this question settled as it may, there can be no doubt that Robin Hood is no fabulous hero. Camden calls him " The gentlest thief that ever was ;" and Major says of him,—

From wealthy abbots' chests, and churl's abundant store,
What oftentimes he took, he shared amongst the poor :
No lordly bishop came in Robin's way,
To him before he went but for his pass must pay.
The widow in distress he graciously relieved,
And remedied the wrongs of many a virgin grieved.

As early as 1594, his story seems to have become a favourite subject for the drama ; for we find, that " The pastoral comedy of Robin Hood and Little John," was printed in that year. Again, we meet with " Robin Hood's Pastoral May Games," printed in 1624; and in 1730 Robin Hood was performed as an opera, at Bartholomew Fair.   Soon after this, " Robin Hood and his crew of Soldiers " appeared ; and in 1751, a musical entertainment, under the name of " Robin Hood," came out at Drury Lane ; besides which we have had " Robin Hood, or Sherwood Forest," of a recent date; all founded on the original *Garland.* Now, the *Garland* itself might have been lost, and if it had, we might have as well reasoned against the probability of its ever having existed with an argument drawn from the more modern style of these later productions, as reason now that older traditional rhymes did not beget those of the *Garland.* This collection of ballads is well known, but the real historical biography of Robin Hood differs considerably in its particulars from those recorded by them.   In a romantic point of view however, his legendary biography is of as much importance to us as the historical ; nay, we may even be excused for considering it as more so.   It is, notwithstanding, made up in a great degree of exaggeration and improbability, and, in some instances, of improbability mixed up with what may be considered as truth.   It tells us, that his father was a forester, who could send an arrow to a distance of *two north country miles,* a fact which we leave to the judgment of those who have had the happiness to encounter that species of land measure, on some long Highland hill, towards the conclusion of a hard day's pedestrian exertion. Then, by a glaring anachronism, it describes his mother as having been niece to Guy, the Saxon Earl of Warwick. This lady is stated to have had a brother, ' a notable squire," who lived at Gamewell Hall, in Nottinghamshire, a name probably corrupted from Gamelston, or Gamston.   This gentleman was desirous that Robin should spend the years of his youth with him ; but his unconquerable passion for field sports, and his attachment to a rambling life, induced him to go to Tutbury, in Staffordshire, not far from Loxley, the place of his birth, where he married a shepherdess, under the poetical name of Clarinda, having been smitten by her charms, and still more by the dexterous manner in which she slew a buck in the forest.   Drayton, in the twenty-sixth song of his *Poly Olbion,* gives some particulars of Robin Hood, and his maid Marion, called Clarinda in the *Garland.*

Even at this early period of his life, his exploits against the foresters must have been frequent; for we are told, that he killed no less than fifteen of them, all of whom were buried in one row, in one of the churchyards at Nottingham. A singular discovery took place a few years ago, which was immediately supposed to be connected with these slaughters, by those who heard of it. Some men digging in a garden at Fox Lane, near Nottingham, found six entire human skeletons deposited in regular order, side by side, and these were immediately conjectured to be the remains of those fifteen foresters slain by Robin Hood. And this idea is in some degree borne out by the fact, that close to the spot where they were found stood a church dedicated to St Michael, which was utterly destroyed at the Reformation. Robin's fame now became so great, that nearly one hundred followers joined him; and in a short time, his robberies and frolics, his kindness and charity to the poor, became the general theme in all men's mouths, and produced a kind of friendly feeling towards the outlaw. The *Garland* exhibits him as a merry thief, making his business his amusement, for he not only takes the purses of the bishop and the sheriff of the county, but he takes his sport out of them by making them food for his wit. He was not always victorious, however, in bodily conflicts; for, on more occasions than one, he was roughly handled by the tinker, the shepherd, the friar, and several other characters.

He is next described as going to London, and being received at court, where he appeared in a scarlet dress, followed by his men, clad in Lincoln green, all of them wearing black hats and white feathers; a species of costume which was unknown in the thirteenth century, in which age he lived, the head covering of those days being a sort of cowl of cloth, folded or tied under the chin, and bonnets for ceremonial occasions. Soon after this he is stated to have fought a desperate battle with Little John, or John Little, who, *lucus non lucendo*, was seven feet high. In this combat he was worsted; but the result was, that Little John joined the troop, and became the hero's attached and faithful friend. There is a loose paper, in the handwriting of Ashmole, and of the date of 1612, which says, " The famous Little John, Robin Hood's companion, lies buried in Heathersedge churchyard, in the Peak of Derbyshire; one stone at his head, another at his feet, and part of his bow hangs up in the church." The *Garland* concludes the eventful history of the bold outlaw with his death, which it states to have been produced by a monk who was called to bleed him, when all his brave bow-men fled to different countries to escape that justice which they could not otherwise avoid, now that they had lost that head by which all their plans and movements were organized and directed.

The author of the *Anecdotes of Archery*, who seems to have bestowed considerable research to discover the real events of the outlaw's life, gives us some particulars, which have every semblance of authenticity. He describes him as at the head of two hundred strong, resolute men, who were all expert archers, who were generally occupied in ranging the Forest of Sherwood, but who often went into other quarters also.

Fuller says, that his principal residence was in Sherwood Forest, though he had another haunt near the sea, in the North Riding of Yorkshire, where Robin Hood's Bay still bears his name; and Charleton, in his *History of Whitby*, tells us, that when Robin Hood was closely pursued by the civil or military power, he frequently found it necessary to abandon his usual haunts, and that on such occasions he crossed the moors to Whitby, in Yorkshire, where he had always some small fishing vessels lying ready for his occasions, in which he put to sea, and so provided for his security on an element which, in those days, was much less the high road of British shipping than it now is; and Robin Hood's Bay was the place where these small craft were kept always ready for his service. He was thus not only strong in his land forces, but well equipped also as a naval power. There is a tradition, that Robin and his friend Little John, being in this neighbourhood, were hospitably received by Richard, the Abbot of Whitby; and the abbot, having heard much of their skill in archery, requested of his guests to give him a speci-men of their powers in that art. To oblige their courteous entertainer, the two bold bowmen accompanied the abbot to the top of the abbey tower, whence each of them discharged an arrow, which fell close to Whitby Laths, a distance of more than a measured mile. The abbot was so delighted with this marvellous exhibition, that he ordered two pillars to be erected to mark the spots where the arrows fell, and certain it is, that two such pillars were standing at Whitby some few years ago, and it is also true, that they were called after the two friends, but as to the accuracy of the tradition in regard to the shots, we are not prepared to speak.

The *Anecdotes of Archery* then proceed to state, that he was outlawed, and a price set upon his head; and they detail several stratagems which were vainly practised to ensnare him, he always repelling force by force, and stratagem by stratagem. At length, overwhelming numbers were sent against him, and many of his followers being slain, and the remainder having fled, he sought shelter and protection in the Priory of Kirklees, in Yorkshire, the prioress of which was his near relative. Here, it is said, that age, mortification at his defeat, and the fatigue he had undergone, brought on a disease which required bleeding, and that a monk performed the operation, so as, either ignorantly or wickedly, to wound an artery, and so to cause his death. As his end approached, he called for his bow, and, summoning up his departing strength, he let fly two arrows. The first dropped into the river Calder, but the second falling into the park, he pointed to that spot as the place where his remains should repose. This event is said to have taken place on the eve of Christmas day, 1274; and on his tomb the following epitaph is said to have been inscribed by the prioress:—

> Hear, undernead dis latil stean,
> Lais Robert Earl of Huntington;
> Nea arcir ver az hie sa geud,
> And pipl kauld im Robin Heud:
> Sick utlaz as hi an iz men,
> Vil England nivr see agen.

A drawing of this tomb is preserved by Gough in his sepulchral monuments. Mr Ritson, on the authority of one of the Sloanian MSS, says, that it was the prioress who bled him to death.

It is certain that, so far as history speaks, no Earl of Huntingdon existed in England at that time. John Le Scot, of the Scottish royal family, was Earl of Huntingdon in 1219. He died shortly after, and the title was extinct, until 1337, when it was conferred on William de Clinton, which completely fills up the period of Robin Hood's life. It has been said by some, that his name was Head, or Hood, and that he was the son of a nobleman. Others, again, think that he was one of those youths of good family, who, in the unsettled reign of Richard the First, resented the act of the enclosure of the forest; and being prosecuted by the officers of the crown for some infringement on it, was tempted, by revenge and for his own security, to raise a band of archers, with whose assistance he infested all the towns within the forest and its vicinity, robbing all rich travellers, but never proceeding to acts of bloodshed, except in self defence. It is said, too, that he was a great favourite in many parts of the country, in consequence of his hoarding up the different articles which he obtained in the course of his robberies, until they amounted to a considerable stock, when he exposed them to sale at a well known place on the borders of the forest, where his regular fairs were held, and where bargains so very tempting were always got, that they gave origin to the well known proverb of " selling Robin Hood's penny worths." There is another proverb regarding him recorded by Fuller, in his *Worthies of England :* " Many talk of Robin Hood who never shot out of his bow;" that is, " Many prate of matters wherein they have no experience." This proverb has extended all over England, though originally of Nottingham-shire birth. Fuller says, " that he was an arch robber, and withal an excellent archer ; though surely the poet gave a twang to the loose of his arrow, making him shoot one a cloth yard long, at full forty score mark, for compass never higher than the breast, and within less than a foot of the mark." But herein our author hath verified the proverb, " talking of Robin Hood, in whose bow he never shot."

So far as historical fact goes regarding Robin Hood, he is certainly mentioned in the writings of most of our annalists. In the Harleian collection of MSS in the British Museum, in No. 1233, p. 199, there is the following article, though the author of Nottinghamshire, who quotes it, says, that he knows nothing as to the name of the writer. " Robin Hood, accompanied with one Little John, molested passengers on the highway, temp. Rich. I. Of whom it was said, that he was of noble blood, no less than an earle. Having wasted his estate in riotous courses, very penury forced him to steale. The king, at last, set forth a proclamation to have him apprehended ; at which time it happened he fell ill at a nunnery in Yorkshire, called Birkleys," (Kirklees ;) " and desiring there to be let blood, he was betrayed, and made bleed to death."

But Stukeley, in his *Polæographia Britannia,* vol. ii. page 115, seems to have nearly settled the question with regard to the identity of Robin Hood. He says that his true name was Fitz Oeth, and that he was descended from a Norman chief of that name, who was Lord of Kyme in Lincolnshire imme-diately after the Conquest ; and farther, that his mother was daughter of Payne Beauchamp and Roisia de Vere. And this lineage will somewhat explain the supposed difficulty as to his having been called Earl of Huntingdon. In 1068 Waltheof was Earl of Huntingdon in right of his wife, Judith, niece of William the Conqueror. Their daughter Alice married Richard Fitz Gilbert, or De Clare, Earl of Brian in Normandy. These had a son, Robert Fitz Gilbert, whose daughter, Roisia, married Gilbert de Gaunt. These had a daughter, Maud, who married Ralph Fitz Ooth, or Oeth, a Norman, the Lord of Kyme in Lincolnshire. These had William Fitz Ooth, who was brought up by Robert de Vere, Earl of Oxford, and who afterwards married his patron's relative, the daughter of Paganel Beauchamp and Roisia de Vere, of the Oxford family, of which marriage was born Robert Fitz Ooth, or Robin Hood, and so he could certainly prove his descent from the first Earl of Huntingdon, and might thus have been induced to claim that title; and when it is remembered that Waltheof, the first Earl, left no son, and that the title of Huntingdon, after his death, was carried by another of Maud's daughters to her husband, Simon St Luz, who was the second Earl, but who likewise left no issue; that Maud married, as her second husband, David, Prince, and afterwards King, of Scotland, who thus, in right of his marriage, became third Earl of Huntingdon; that this line also failed in John Le Scot, who was the tenth Earl of Huntingdon, but who died without issue in 1237, from which time it was as it were dormant, until the year 1337, when the title was conferred as a new grant on William de Clinton,—it will be seen, that not only had Robin Hood a line to lay hold of as a claim, much better than many a claim which in those days was admitted as good, but he actually had what may be called the succession to the peerage opened to him by the failure of all other claimants.

We are therefore disposed to agree most perfectly with Thorsby, who believes that the title may have been absolutely claimed by Robin Hood; and, in this view of the matter, it is by no means improbable that he may have been driven to his predatory life from dissatisfaction arising from his claims on the title of Huntingdon having been refused by Henry II, whose troubled reign might have rendered justice inaccessible to the claimant, and so exasperated him. Another probability is worthy consideration, we mean the likelihood that his father, William Fitz Ooth, may have been implicated in the rebellion of Prince Henry, the king's eldest son, and so have been in bad odour with the reigning monarch; for in that rebellion the Earl of Ferrers took the Prince's side, and he was Lord of Loxley, which was said to have been the birthplace of Robin Hood. It is also well urged by the author of Notting-hamshire, that the fact of his being something more than a mere robber, is evident from the considerable force which he was able to raise and to keep together, which must have been even much greater than is mentioned in the legendary ballads, as he was so long able to bid a bold and open defiance to all the attempts of the sheriff, with the royal army at his back; and, in our opinion, he must have been an individual of no ordinary character, and of no ordinary fame, during his own time, who could make England ring with his name from one end of it to the other for so many ages after his death—who, during his life, could command the use of a little fleet when it pleased him to use it—and, above all, who has actually bequeathed his *nom de guerre* to a portion of the maritime geography of our island, with which no one who has sailed between the Scottish and English capitals can be ignorant. We feel that we have dwelt very much at large on Robin Hood; but, in doing so, we do not conceive that we have been talking irrelevantly to the subject of our present con-sideration; for it appears to us to be impossible even to think of a forest, without the ideal picture of Robin Hood and his merry men being immediately associated with it, as the natural figures for its animation, and we should consider that mind devoid of all proper share of feeling for the romance or poetry of life which could not sympathize with us in these our sentiments.

In Shropshire are the vestiges of at least four forests, —Huckstow, King's Wood, Bridgenorth, and Clune. Clune Forest deserves ever to be remembered in British Annals, as the scene where Caractacus is supposed * to have made his last noble stand against the Romans. Having resisted them nine years with various success, and being now pushed to extremity, he fortified himself on a hill in this forest. Tacitus tells the story at length.† Ostorius led his legions against him. The British camp was forced, and through treachery the gallant chief was delivered to his conqueror. At Rome, says the historian, the senate considered the triumph over Caractacus as splendid as those over Syphax and Perses.

---

* See Camden *On Shropshire.*
† See Tacitus' *Annals,* lib. xii. chap. 33.

The Clune Forest in Shropshire has now little more than the name. The spot fixed upon by Gough, the editor of Camden, for the scene of the treacherous capture of Caractacus, is a hill about two miles south of Clun, called Caer Caradoc, or the Gaer, near the junction of the rivers Clun and Teme, among several dangerous fords. There is a very large camp on the point of this hill, which is accessible by one way only, for it is fortified on the east and south by ramparts of stone. Mr Gough says that the description given by Tacitus is so perfectly applicable to this spot, that it places it before our eyes.

Some consider the name of Bridgenorth to have been originally Burg Morfe, that is, the town of the Morfe, a forest once existing in this neighbourhood. Leland tells us, that Morfe was, in his time, " a hilly district, well wooded; a forest or chase having deer." Not a single tree is now remaining in it. From the time of Edward I, to Elizabeth, it had its forester and steward. King Althelstan's brother was said to have led a hermit's life in a rock here, where there is a cave still called the Hermitage. There are five tumuli in a quincunx position on the Morfe; in some of these, human bones were found, and an iron shell of the size of a small egg, supposed to have been the boss of a sword.

In the map of Shropshire, we find various forests laid down which have now no substantial existence; the forests of Coirdegar, Longmot, Mogg, Tiefton, and Wire, may be said to have nothing left to them but their names. There are, however, the remains of a fine oak forest in Oakley Park, about two miles north-west of Ludlow, where the grounds, naturally romantic, are laid out with great taste and judgment, and where the meanderings of the river Teme contribute greatly to the beauty of the scenery. The prospects here are everywhere delightful; and there is one in particular, which looks towards the south-east, and embraces the town and castle of Ludlow, which is much and deservedly celebrated.

In the county of Stafford, the forest of Needwood still affords a variety of pleasing country. It is bounded by the Trent and the Dove, and is in the neighbourhood of those romantic scenes in which the latter of these rivers makes so pleasing an appendage.

On the confines of this forest stand the ruins of Tutbury Castle; where the princes of the house of Lancaster formerly held their residence. Their hospitality, diversions, and jovial housekeeping, are not yet forgotten in the traditions of the country. One instance, called the bull running, remains, I b ieve, to this day. On the 16th of August, a bull is turned loose, 'nd is .ι. ɼ roperty of those who seize him. This amusement, which was formerly given to the Duke of Lancaster's servants, is now become the subject of great contention between the youth of Staffordshire and Derbyshire, who exercise their prowess on the occasion, for the honour of their respective counties.

The middle parts of Staffordshire are occupied by a very extensive forest, known by the name of Cank Wood.

Needwood Forest is interesting and beautiful. It extends from the confines of Hanbury to Yoxal, which lies about a mile to the north of the river Trent. According to a survey made in 1765, it consists of nine thousand nine hundred and twenty acres of soil, as fine as any in the kingdom, which was left, till of late years, very much in a state of Nature, and of little use, except as a harbour for deer and other game. In ancient times, Needwood Forest belonged to the Dukes of Lancaster, by whose right it came to the English monarch, and so it has been the property of the crown for several centuries, subject, however, to certain privileges of common, enjoyed by the owners and inhabitants of some of the adjacent villages. It is ¬vided into the four wards of Marchington, Yoxall, Barton, and Tutbury, each ward containing about five miles in compass, exclusive of the Uttoxeter Wood, Boughay, &c. The officers of the forest are a lieutenant and chief ranger, assisted by a deputy, four lieutenants, four keepers, and an axe-bearer. A court is still held every year by the king's steward of the honour of Tutbury, when a jury of twenty-four persons, resident within the jurisdiction, present and amerce all persons guilty of " encroaching on the forest, or committing offences in vert or venison." There were formerly eight parks impaled within the ring of the forest, called the Parks of Agardesley, Stockley, Barton, Heylyns, Sherrold, Castle Hay, Hanbury, and Rolleston. That of Castle Hay was three miles and a half in compass, and that of Hanbury two miles and a half.

The natural disposition of Needwood Forest is beautiful

and varied in its aspect. It consists of gently swelling eminences, and vales watered by murmuring rills, whilst here and there the ground swells more boldly and abruptly. The eminences are much more numerous and lofty in the northern parts, and especially in Marchington woodlands, than in the middle or southern divisions of the forest. In the northern parts, the scenery exhibits a series of deep glens, enclosed by steep and rugged precipices, incapable of agricultural improvement, and covered with a variety of trees, among which the native oak shoots up in great abundance. Mr Shaw estimates the oak timber in the forest at fully one thousand acres. The venerable Swilcar Oak, already particularly noticed by us, in pages 208 and 253 of our first volume, stands in an open lawn, surrounded by extensive woods. It is thus addressed by the author of the poem of *Needwood Forest:*

> Hail! stately oak, whose wrinkled trunk hath stood,
> Age after age, the sovereign of the wood :
> You, who have seen a thousand springs unfold
> Their ravell'd buds, and dip their flowers in gold—
> Ten thousand times yon moon relight her horn,
> And that bright eye of evening gild the morn,—
> * * * * * *
> Yes, stately oak, thy leaf-wrapp'd head sublime
> Ere long must perish in the wrecks of time ;
> Should, o'er thy brow, the thunders harmless break,
> And thy firm roots in vain the whirlwinds shake,
> Yet must thou fall. Thy withering glories sunk,
> Arm after arm shall leave thy mouldering trunk.

The village of Yoxal is beautifully watered by the stream of Swarbourne, which is one of the tributaries of the Trent. At a short distance from the village, a number of vessels, probably Roman, were discovered a few years ago, but most of them were unfortunately destroyed in raising them. One of the few that were got up entire, was deposited in Mr Green's museum at Litchfield, and is engraved, and described in the *Gentleman's Magazine,* vol. xliv. p. 358. A little way east from Yoxal lies the village of Wichnor, or Whichmore, famous for the flitch of bacon which the lord of the manor is bound to provide for any married couple who may claim it after the union of a year and a day without having had a quarrel. Since the institution of this extraordinary practice, few have dared to claim the prize, and only three couples have obtained it. But, alas! one of these pairs having quarrelled about the mode of preparing the bacon for the table, the parties were compelled to return it; and another couple are said, by the *Spectator*, No. 608, to have been a sea officer and his wife, who had never seen one another from the day of their marriage till they met at the hall—a simple pair,—the husband a good-natured, sensible man, and the wife luckily dumb.

The Cannock Chase is now 'an extensive waste of about forty square miles. Some derive the name from the Cango, and others from Canute, the first Danish King of England. This was entirely a forest during the period of the Mercians; for it was the favourite hunting district of their kings, in which time it was filled with majestic oaks. The change which took place in it, when these were gradually extirpated, is well described in Mr Williams' poetical version of the *Iter Boreale* of Mr Masters:

> A vast, a naked plain confines the view,
> Where trees unnumber'd in past ages grew,—
> The green retreat of wood nymphs — once the boast,
> The pride, the guardians of their native coast.
> Alas, how changed! each venerable oak
> Long since has yielded to the woodman's stroke.
> Where'er the cheerless prospect meets the eye,
> No shrub, no plant, except the heath, is nigh;
> The solitary heath alone is there,
> And wafts its sweetness in the desert air;
> So sweet its scent, so sweet its purple hue,
> We half forget that here a forest grew.

In the southern parts of Leicestershire lies the wide forest of Charnwood, in which the park of Beaumanòur, twenty miles in circumference, was walled round by the lords of Beaumont, and was thought to be one of the largest works of the kind in England. In this county also lies the forest of Leicester, on the borders of which is the celebrated field of Bosworth, where, after so much bloodshed in the contest between the two houses of York and Lancaster, their quarrel was finally decided.

Although the district called Charnwood Forest is almost without a tree, yet it is a very striking feature in the county of Leicester. It contains about sixteen thousand acres, "three-fourths of which," observes Mr Monk, "might be made very useful good land. The chief proprietors are the Earl of Stamford, Earl of Moira, William Herrick of Beaumanor, and a few others." Mr Marshall gives us the following description of this tract: " The Charnwood Hills are too striking a feature of this district to be passed over without especial notice. When seen obscurely, they appear like an extensive range of mountains, much larger, and of course much more distant, than they really are. When approached, the mountain style is still preserved, the prominences are distinct, sharp, and most of them pointed with ragged rocks. One of these prominences, Bardon Hill, rises above the rest; and though far from an elevated situation, comparatively with the northern mountains, it probably commands a greater extent of surface than any other point of view in the island. It is entirely insulated, standing, in every way, at a considerable distance from lands equally high. The horizon appears to rise almost equally on every side : it is quite an ocean view, from a ship out of sight of land—at least, more so than any other land view I have seen. The midland district is, almost every acre of it, seen lying at its feet. Lincoln cathedral, at the distance of near sixty miles, makes a prominent object from it. With a good glass, the Dunstaple Hills, at little less than eighty miles, may, it is said, be distinctly seen. The Malvern Hills, May Hill, and the Sugar Loaf in South Wales, are distinctly in view. Enville, the Wrekin, and other mountains in Shropshire and North Wales, are equally distinguishable; and the Derbyshire hills, to the highest peak, appear at hand. An outline described from the extremity of the views, would include nearly one fourth of England and Wales. It may be deemed one of the most extraordinary points of view in Nature."

In Rutlandshire is the forest of Lyfield, still in some parts in its original state, and stocked with deer: and in Hertfordshire are the remains of the forests of Bringwood, Deerfield, Hawood, and Acornbury.

The woods in Rutlandshire were once very extensive. Oakham has its name from the oak woods which grew where it now stands ; and the whole Vale of Cotmore is supposed to have been once an extensive tract of woodland. The Forest of Leafield, or Lyfield, once occupied the greatest part of Oakham Hundred; and Beaumont Chase, a part of it, once extended over great part of Martinsley Hundred, having several towns within its purlieus, though they are now destroyed. The author of the article Rutlandshire, in the

Beauties of England, tells us that "It is supposed that this forest took its name from the Manor of Leigh, or Lee, which is nearly in its centre; it must be, however, rather of recent erection, for there is no mention of it in Doomsday Book, nor in any of the subsequent reigns, as the editors of *Magna Britannia* assert, until that of Edward II, when Theobald de Menyle, (or rather, as some think, Neville,) was lord of the Manor of Leigh.   But this is incorrect; for though its origin is uncertain, yet several grounds, parcels of it, were afforested in the reign of King John, which is fully proved by a perambulation made in the twenty-eighth year of Edward I. Several of the towns in its vicinity, as well as these within its limits, still claim certain forest rights. It may not be irrelevant, therefore, to trace its bounds from a manuscript, whose date is uncertain, but which came into the possession of the Noel family on their purchase of its rights in the reign of James I. This perambulation is stated as commencing at Flitteris Corner, in the field of Oakham; from whence it goes westward, including all Braunston High Meadow, with the Wisp and Withcot Sail; thence it proceeds towards the south-west, taking in Brittlewell Sail, and Corkleg Sail, and so to Steerwood, where it takes in Tinford Bridge, Belton and Wardly towns, and thence to Beaumont Sail, and Preston Underwoods; thence by Caldecot to Longbridge, including Caldecot and Snelston Fields, and thence to Lyddington, taking in all Uppingham Brand and the East Field; after which, taking in all Ayston Commonfield, it proceeds by Riddlington to Brooke, thence up to Brooke Mill, and so on to Flitteris, where it commenced.

From Theobald de Menyle, already mentioned, the office of chief forester passed by inheritance to the family of Cheseldine; but there is no evidence remaining of the length of their tenure, only it is known that the property was in the crown in the reign of Edward IV, as that monarch bestowed the grant of the Manor of Leigh, or Lyfield, and of the office of chief forester in Rutland, upon his great favourite and faithful adherent William Lord Hastings. This nobleman having been murdered by the usurper Richard, and his lands confiscated, they were again restored by Henry VII to his son, Edward Lord Hastings, whose son and heir, George, was created Earl of Huntingdon, as we have noticed above in our account of Robin Hood. But his son, Henry, sold it, with the manor, to Sir James Harrington, Knight, who was obliged, in the twenty-fourth year of Queen Elizabeth, to apply for a pardon for having purchased it without a licence of alienation, it being held of the crown *in capite.* The last Lord Harrington in whom it became vested, settled the Manor of Leigh, and all the forest rights, &c. in the hands of trustees, for payment of debts, after which it was purchased by Sir Edward Noel, Baronet.

Leland, when speaking of this forest, in the reign of Henry VII, says, " From Wiscombe, partely through woddy ground of the Forest of Leafield, and so to Ruthlandshire, by woddy first, and then all champain ground, but exceeding rich of corn and pasture." This description may be considered as strictly applicable at the present day, as there is not a tract of the same extent in England which presents a richer prospect of wood and cultivation than this, when viewed from the rising grounds on the road between Uppingham and Wardley. The forest and parish of Leafield consist of a good rich red clay soil, and the mere fact that a great part of the cheese that goes by the name of Stilton, is made in this district and in the vale of Cotmore, is of itself a sufficient proof of fertility.

Hertfordshire was once almost entirely covered with forest. Leofstan, the twelfth Abbot of St Albans, who was confessor to Edward, and Edith his queen, occupied himself in rendering the roads safe. At that time the Watling Street, and many parts of the Chiltren Hills, were covered with thick woods, which were the haunts of wolves, wild boars, stags, and wild bulls, as well as of numerous robbers and outlaws; but, comparatively speaking, there is little forest wood now in this county.

Wire Forest, once famous for its stately timber, lies on the north-west of Worcestershire, along the banks of the Severn. In this county also, we have the forest of Malvern and Feckingham : the former winds among the hills whose name it bears, and the latter is famous for its salt springs, in the boiling of which its woods have been almost exterminated.

Wyre Forest, has long been in a great measure denuded; even as early as the days of Drayton, who sings of it,—

> When soone the goodlie Wyre, that wonted was so hie
> Her statelie top to reare, ashamed to behold
> Her straight and goodlie woods unto the furnace sold,
> And, looking on herself, by her decay doth see
> The miserie wherein her sister forests bee.

Leland says of it, that " summe part is sett in Wicester-shire, but the most part in Shropshire, and stretchythe up Fronthalt upon Severn, on to Brugenorth.   Bewdley is set in the marches of this forest."   It seems, however, that more of it is now considered as belonging to Worcestershire than at that period.   It is now a great nursery for oak poles and underwood, which are cut at the proper seasons, reserving the timber trees to remain at proper distances as standards.

Worcestershire, like many of the other counties, was com-pletely covered with forests.   Even in the time of the Conquest it was held to have five distinct forests.   Of these Wyre Forest occupied the north-western part of the county, and extended into Shropshire and Staffordshire.   Feckenham Forest was very extensive, as appears by an old perambula-tion in the reign of Edward I.   It commenced at the Foregate Worcester, and passed to Beverburn by Stour to Bordesley, round by Evesham to Spetchley, and so to Sidbury.   It was disafforested in 1629, in the reign of Charles I, and has now decreased, and almost ceased to exist, from the continual demands for the salt-works at Droitwich, until within these few years that the supply of coals has been found sufficient for all the purposes of manufacture.   Ombersley Forest began at the north gate of Worcester, and extended along the banks of the Severn.   Horewell Forest was in the southern district, beginning at the south gate, and extending along the eastern road to Spetchley, thence to Thurgarton, and across the Avon, and including all the country between the two principal rivers. These last two forests have ceased to exist since the reign of Henry III.   Malvern Forest, or Chase, as it was latterly designated, extended, in length, from the river Teme in the north, towards Gloucestershire in the south, and from the Severn to the top of the Malvern Hills, where may still be traced the trench dug along the ridge to mark its limits, and to divide it from the possessions of the see of Hereford.   This trench is also the divisional line of the two counties, and was dug in consequence of a long contest between the Bishop and the Earl of Gloucester, to whom the forest had been granted by Edward I, after his marriage with Joan of Acres, that king's daughter.   At the same time this Gilbert, Earl of Gloucester, received a grant of the small Forest of Cors ; but in consequence of these royal demesnes becoming the pro-perty of a subject, Malvern was called a Chase, and Cors received the name of a Lawn, losing also considerable privi-leges by this change.   Nash tells us, in his *Survey,* that a chase is a place for the reception of deer and wild beasts, and holds a middle place between a forest and a park. The distinction of a forest depends on its having a Justice in Eyre, which none can constitute but the crown; therefore a forest, when coming into the hands of a subject, must lose this privilege, and thereby change its name. A chase, also, is defined to differ from a park in not being enclosed, being of a larger extent, and having a greater variety of game, under the superintendence of a greater number of keepers, verdurers, &c.

More than half the county of Warwick was formerly a continued forest scene, and was known by the name of Arden, an old British word, which signifies a wood. Whether this vast district of woodland was divided into different jurisdictions, would be difficult to ascertain. There seems at least to have been one separate chase in it, which belonged to the Castle of Kenelworth; and it is probable there might have been others.

The early writers describe Warwickshire as naturally divisible into two parts,—the Feldon, or Champaign, and the Arden, or Woodland, a name given by the Celtæ to forests, however situated. The Avon formed the line that separated these tracts. Drayton asserts, with great probability of truth, that the Arden of Warwickshire was the most important of the forests of southern Britain. It extended from the banks of the Avon to the Trent on the north, and to the Severn on the west, being bounded on the east by an imaginary line drawn from Highcross to Barton. At the time the shire divisions of England were established, certain portions of this wild fell to the share of Worcestershire and Staffordshire, which counties bestowed on them those names which they still hold. The Warwickshire part has been long generally cleared of its thick and tangled woods, but in some spots an occasional air of wildness is found, as if a colouring of its ancient character remained, to afford some notion of what the complexion of the county was when occupied by the Cangi of the Cornavii, and their numerous herds. In Shakespeare's time, doubtless the forest fragments were more entire and continuous, to have induced him to have selected it as the spot where some of his most interesting and beautiful scenes are acted.

In the county of Northampton is the large forest of Rockingham, which stretches along the river Welland, almost to Stamford. In this forest stands the Castle of Rockingham, formerly a pile of vast importance, built by William the Conqueror. In Northamptonshire, also, there are three other forests,—Sacy, Yardly, and Whittlebury. I have been assured, that in the first and last of these forests, Rockingham and Whittlebury, there remains, at this day, sufficient timber to build the navy of England twice over; and as canals are now forming in those parts, it may soon be no difficult matter to convey it from 'its deep recesses to any of the king's yards. These forests also, particularly Whittlebury, are infested by the wild cat, which the naturalists call the British tiger.

" Though numerous in many of the wild woods, and mountainous and thinly inhabited parts of this island," says a writer in the *Sporting Magazine*, vol. iii. p. 281, " the wild cat is almost, if not entirely, extirpated in most of the southern counties. ' The fur is soft and fine, of a yellowish dun colour, mixed with gray; a dusky list runs along the middle of the back, the sides are streaked with dark gray, pointing from the back downwards; the tail is thicker and shorter than that of the domestic cat, and marked with alternate bars of black and whitish dun. The animal is much larger and stronger than the common one, and its fur thicker and longer.' It resides and breeds principally in holes in almost inaccessible rocks, the levels of old mines, &c. and haunts and preys in the adjacent woods; it destroys every species of game; it will even kill lambs, kids, and fawns, and is the most fierce, destructive, and dangerous beast of prey in these islands.

" In proof of this, a fellow well known in the vicinity of Richmond, in Yorkshire, who kept a most hardy and excellent breed of terriers, and almost made a livelihood by bagging foxes and badgers among the woods and precipices up the Swale, being for this purpose one night in Wycliffe Wood, hearing his dogs baying something among the brushwood at the bottom of the Scaur, made all speed to their assistance, and though armed with a good hatchet, had great difficulty in destroying an old wild cat, which he did not effect till she had left marks which lasted very long on him, and two or three couple of his best dogs. A wild cat was killed in

Cumberland, measuring from the nose to the end of the tail upwards of five feet."

The extensive forests in Northamptonshire go under the different names of Forests, Chases, or Purlieu Woods. Rockingham is the most important of the forests; it lies in the northern part of the county, and extends for nearly twenty miles in one direction. The large forests of Whittlewood and Salcey lie towards the southern border of the county. There are two chases, Geddington and Yardley: the former was once a part of Rockingham Forest, but permission was many years ago granted by the crown to the Montague family to disforest it, and to convert it into a chase. Yardley Chase was once a part of Salcey Forest, but has also been disforested. Purlieu woods are those which are situated in the vicinity of the forests, and which at one time formed a part of them; but the respective owners having at some former periods obtained grants from the crown to disforest them, and to consider them as their own private property, they are not now subject to forest regulations. The purlieu woods are numerous and extensive in this county, particularly towards the southern side, and upon the borders of Rockingham Forest; and besides these, there are other tracts of woodland in the county.

The Forest of Salcey is situated near the south-eastern border of the county, where it joins Buckinghamshire. From a perambulation made in the time of King Edward I, its limits appeared to have been extended by King John, but the woods and lawns afforested by that king, were disafforested by Edward, according to the tenure of the *charta de foresta*, and in consequence of a grant of a fifteenth part of the moveables of all his subjects. But though the forest was, by this proceeding, brought back to its ancient bounds, and though the limits thus established were followed and confirmed by usage for more than three hundred years, Charles I made an attempt again to enlarge the forest, and with that view, in the year 1639, a new perambulation was made, by which a considerable extent of country was added to it, and subjected to the burden of the forest laws; but this oppressive measure, which was also extended to several other forests, was rendered ineffectual by an act of parliament in 1641, which confined all the royal forests to their reputed limits in the twentieth year of the preceding reign. The lands now considered as forests, and in which the crown is possessed of the timber and other valuable rights, extend in length about two miles and a half, and in breadth nearly one mile and a half, containing one thousand eight hundred and forty-seven acres. The whole is divided into four walks,—Hanslop, Piddington, Hodwell, and the Deputy Ranger's Walk.

In the seventeenth year of Charles II, this forest, together with that of Whittlewood, was settled on Queen Catharine, for her life, as part of her jointure, reserving all the timber trees and saplings for the use of the crown. And in the twenty-fifth year of that king, the woods, coppices, and woodlands in these forests, were granted to Henry, Earl of Arlington, for his life, after the decease of the queen ; and after his death to the king's three sons, Henry, afterwards Duke of Grafton, Charles, Earl of Southampton, and George, Lord Fitzroy, otherwise Lord George Palmer, and their heirs male for ever. On the death of the Queen Dowager, 31st December, 1705, the Grafton family thus became proprietors of the underwood, which seems to be the only property they have in Salcey Forest. We learn from the *Beauties of England*, that the officers of this forest are a warden, or master forester, lieutenant, or deputy warden, two verdurers, a woodward, three yeomen keepers, one page keeper, and the surveyor general of the woods and forests. The warden possesses a well built house called the Great Lodge, with gardens and pleasure grounds attached to it. There are about one thousand deer of all sorts kept in this forest ; and the number killed annually is about twenty-eight brace of bucks, and twenty-four of does, of which four bucks and four does are supplied for the use of the king's household, by warrants from the board of green cloth ; and six bucks and six does are killed under warrants from the cofferer's office, or clerk of the venison warrants, for the use of the public offices, and for persons accustomed to have venison from the royal forests. Besides these, the other officers of the forest have each their share of venison, and the rest are disposed of by the warden.

The verdurers in this, as in all forests, are chosen by the freeholders of the county. Their office is to preside at the forest courts, and to take cognizance of all trespasses relative to vert and venison ; but no courts are now held for this forest.

By a survey of the timber, taken in 1608, it appears that there were then growing in this forest fifteen thousand two hundred and seventy-four oak timber trees, then valued at £11,951, besides four hundred and forty decaying trees, valued at £140. On a survey taken in 1783, there were reported to be then in this forest only two thousand nine hundred and eighteen oak trees fit for the navy, including all trees down to thirty feet of timber; so that the timber fit for the navy, according to this survey, was even then reduced nearly to one-tenth of what it was in 1608. The soil of this forest is peculiarly well adapted to the growth of large timber, of which the celebrated Salcey Forest Oak, already particularly noticed by us in the first volume, page 255, affords a most magnificent sample. The trees in general are larger and longer than those of Whittlewood Forest.

The forest of Whittlewood, though chiefly belonging to the county of Northampton, extends into the adjoining counties of Oxford and Buckingham. A perambulation made in the reign of Edward I, distinctly describes the parts lying within the three counties above named. Charles I extended its bounds as he did those of Salcey, but they were also again restricted by act of Parliament. The part now considered as forest, contains five thousand four hundred and twenty-four acres, and is almost entirely surrounded by a ring mound, which has been its boundary beyond the memory of the oldest man. The rest of the land within the ancient perambulation, consists of estates belonging to several proprietors, some wholly, some partially exempted from forest laws. The whole is divided into five walks,—Hazleborough, Sholbrook, Wakefield, Hanger, and Shrobb. This forest is under the care of a lord warden, or master forester; lieutenant, or deputy warden; two verdurers; woodward; purlieu ranger; five keepers, and six page keepers; and the surveyor general of the woods and forests. The Duke of Grafton, as lord warden, holds Wakefield Lodge, with the gardens, pleasure grounds, one hundred and seventeen acres of enclosed land, and various other advantages, and, with the exception of a few deer to be provided by venison warrants for the royal household, the whole are left at the Duke's disposal. The author of Northamptonshire reckons about one thousand eight hundred deer of different kinds, and about one hundred and thirty-eight bucks, and he says that about one hundred does were killed annually.

The survey of 1608, makes Whittlewood Forest to have contained about fifty thousand and forty-six oak timber trees, then valued at £25,755, and three hundred and sixty decaying trees, valued at £123. The produce of the timber felled in this forest, from the death of the Queen Dowager in 1705, to the end of the year 1786, including four hundred and eighty loads taken for the works at Blenheim, and the value of £7648 felled for the navy, appears, after deducting all expenses, to be about £145 a-year only. By the survey of 1783, there were five thousand two hundred and eleven timber trees fit for the navy then growing in it, besides scrubbed, dotard, and decayed trees; besides which, there were six thousand three hundred and thirty-five oak trees, and twelve thousand two hundred and eighty-two ash trees, constantly lopped for browse for deer.

The forest of Rockingham, in the northern part of the county, was anciently one of the largest forests in the kingdom. The perambulation of it, during the 14th of Edward I, describes it as extending, from Northampton to Stamford, about thirty miles; and from the river Nen on the south, to the Welland and Maidwell in the northwest, being about eight miles of a medium breadth. The bounds of it were particularly specified and settled in the 17th of Charles I. It contains three separate districts, called the Bailiwicks of Rockingham, Brigstock, and Clive, or Cliff. Rockingham is divided into the Lawn of Benefield, the West Bailiwick, or West Walk, Gretton Woods and Little Weldon Woods, Weedhow, Thornhow, and Corby Woods. Brigstock consists of Geddington Woods and Farming Woods; and Cliff into Westhay, Moorhay, and Sulehay Farms, and Shortwood. The whole was anciently under the superintendence of one warden, with his subordinate officers; but Charles I abolished the office, and constituted three master foresters of separate districts; since which period, and since the discontinuance of the forest courts, the forest has been principally under the care of the hereditary keepers.

The bailiwick of Rockingham contains many extensive woods, amounting to about three thousand five hundred acres; also a large open plain, called Rockinghamshire, and several smaller plains, amounting, in all, to about five hundred and sixty acres, and an enclosed lawn, called Benefield Lawn, of about three hundred and eighty-four acres. These belong to the Earls of Harcourt and Cardigan, Lord Sondes, and other proprietors; and are subject to the feed of deer, and are commonable at certain seasons, and under certain conditions, to the adjacent towns and parishes. The Lawn of Benefield is a tract of pasture land of the nature of a park, enclosed and set apart for the feeding of deer, and not subject to any right of common. Four brace and a half of bucks, and the same number of does, for the use of the crown, and eleven brace of each for the use of the forest officers, are supplied from this bailiwick.

The bailiwick of Brigstock comprehends that part of the town and fields of Geddington, lying to the north of the river Ise,—Geddington Woods, containing about seven hundred acres; the town and part of the fields of Brigstock; Farming Woods, also containing about seven hundred acres; and Farming Woods Lodge, with an enclosed lawn of about two hundred acres. Thirty-four bucks, and as many does, are supplied from this bailiwick.

Cliffe is the largest bailiwick of the forest. It comprehends four extensive tracts of woodland,—Westhay Woods, belonging to the Earl of Exeter; Moorhay Woods, belonging to the Earl of Westmoreland; Earl's Woods, in Moorhay Walk, the property of Mr Blackhorne and others; and Sulehay Woods, belonging also to Lord Westmoreland. These woods, with the open plains and wastes adjoining, and two enclosed lawns, called Moorhay Lawn and Sulehay Lawn, held by Lord Westmoreland, in right of the keepership of those walks, contain together about four thousand five hundred and eighty-two acres. The town and fields of King's Cliffe, except Cliffe Park, and parts of the towns and fields of Duddington, Apethorpe, Newton, Nafsington, and Yarwell, are also comprised within the limits of this bailiwick; but the woods and lands above mentioned are the parts which are chiefly subject to the haunt and feed of the deer.

Huntingdon takes its name (as etymologists suppose) from being a country adapted to hunting.* We may imagine, therefore, that in elder times, when such beasts were hunted as required large covers, a great part of the county was forest. At present, though we have the vestiges of several woods, we meet with no forest directly named, but that of Wabridge.

Huntingdonshire, as Leland tells us, " was in old time much more woody than it is now, and the dere resorted to the fennes; it is full long sins it was deforestid." Camden corroborates this, and states, that " the inhabitants say it was once covered with woods; and it appears to have been a forest till Henry II, in the beginning of his reign, disforested the whole, except Weybridge, Sapple, and Herthei, which were the lord's woods and remain forest." Sir Robert Cotton

* See Camden's *Huntingdonshire.*

says, this country was not completely disafforested till Edward I.'s time, when that sovereign, in his twenty-ninth year, confirmed the great charter granted by Henry III, and left no more forest than his own demesne. Dugdale records, that "the tenants of the abbots of Ramsay, in the town of Ramsay, and the tenants of the abbots of Thorney, in Whittlesea, had wasted all the feu of King's Delf, of the alders, hassocks, and rushes, estimated at one thousand acres, so that the King's deer could not have harbour there." There are about forty-four thousand acres of fens in this county, exclusive of about five thousand acres of what are called skirty lands.

In Gloucestershire, the Forest of Dean has ever been esteemed one of the most celebrated forests in England. It is of large extent, not less than twenty miles in length, and half as many in breadth; stretching on the south-east along the Severn, and on the north-west along the Wye; the picturesque scenes of which latter river it greatly improves, by often presenting its woody distances. The timber in this forest was formerly more in request than any other timber for the service of the navy. But it is, at this time, much diminished, owing chiefly to the neighbourhood of several iron forges, which it has long supplied with fuel. There is, however, still more the appearance of a forest preserved here, both in the scenery and in the jurisdiction, than in almost any other part of England. The courts are held in a large house, which was built for this purpose in the middle of the forest. In the county of Gloucester, also, is the forest of Micklewood, on the confines of which stands Berkly Castle, of celebrated antiquity. Kingswood, too, is another forest in this county, which being bounded by the Avon, spreads itself almost to the walls of Bristol.

The forest district of Gloucestershire is separated from the rest of the county by the river Severn, and is principally occupied by the Forest of Dean, which in former times was considered as peculiarly valuable for the goodness and strength of its timber. Evelyn tells us, that he heard, " that in the great expedition of eighty-eight, it was expressly enjoyned the Spanish commanders of that signal armada, that if, when landed, they should not be able to subdue our nation, and make good their conquest, they should yet be sure not to leave a tree standing in the Forest of Dean. It was like the policy of the Philistines, when the poor Israelites went down to their enemies' smiths to sharpen every man his tools; for, as they said, lest the Hebrews make them swords or spears; —so these, lest the English build them ships and men of war." If the Spaniards were destined to fail in overcoming the English, it appears to be a curious question, how were they to effect the Herculean labour of cutting down the Forest of Dean, with the English looking on? The Forest of Dean has probably received its name from the British *Danys Coed*, which signifies the Wood of Fallow Deer; for which animal it was for centuries famous. It abounds with beech trees, as well as with oaks; but its iron ore has operated severely in causing the destruction of its timber. The iron seems to have been wrought here even in the Roman times, and so early as the reign of Edward I there were seventy-two furnaces built here for smelting iron. Evelyn frequently and grievously deplores the exterminating effects of iron furnaces. A survey in the reign of Charles I makes the Forest of Dean contain upwards of forty-three thousand acres, of which about fourteen thousand were woodland; but several thousand acres have been since disafforested, and granted away by different sovereigns. The quantity of ground now belonging to the crown, is about twenty-three thousand acres. Some notion of the manner in which our national forests are destroyed, may be formed from the account, given in the *Beauties of England and Wales*, of the mischief done by Sir John Wyntour, to whom Charles I, made a grant of all the King's coppices and waste soil of the forest of Dean, except the Lea Bailley with all mines and quarries, in consideration of £10,600, and a fee farm rent of £1950 for ever. At that time, there were one hundred and five thousand five hundred and fifty-seven trees, containing sixty-one thousand nine hundred and twenty-eight tons of timber, besides one hundred and fifty-three thousand two hundred and nine cords of wood. The Civil War put an end to the patent; and the enclosures which had been made were thrown down, and the whole reafforested. At the Restoration, the grant was revived; but on a representation of the injury done to the neighbouring inhabitants and to the public, being made to Parliament, a commission was issued to inquire into the state of the forest; and upon an accurate survey, there were found twenty-five thousand nine hundred and twenty-nine oaks, and four thousand two hundred and four beeches, containing one hundred and twenty-one thousand five hundred and seventy-two cords of wood, and eleven thousand three hundred and thirty-five tons of ship timber. On the return of the commissioners, a new grant was made to the nominees of Sir John Wyntour, of all the above trees, excepting the timber fit for the navy. Five hundred fellers of wood were immediately employed; and so rapid was the devastation, that an order of Parliament was made to prevent any farther felling of timber, or cutting of wood. Before a bill could be passed, however, the Parliament was prorogued, and Sir John left to pursue his pleasure, which he did so effectually, that on a new survey, in 1667, only two hundred of the oak and beech trees were standing, and a deficiency of seven or eight thousand tons was found in the quantity that should have been reserved for the navy. To repair these mischiefs, eleven thousand acres were immediately enclosed, planted, and carefully guarded, and it is from these that the supply of the dockyards is now principally obtained. Other enclosures have been made within the last sixty-five years, of upwards of two thousand eight hundred acres; but the fences of the chief part having been demolished, not more than three hundred and twenty-three acres are expected to produce useful timber. About one thousand loads are annually supplied for the use of the navy.

In its present state, the forest is divided into six walks, under the government of a lord warden, who is constable of the Castle of St Briavels, six deputy wardens, four verdurers, chosen by the freeholders, a conservator, seven woodwards, and a chief forester in fee, who has no salary, but claims to be entitled to the left shoulder of all bucks and does killed within the forest, also to ten fee bucks, and ten fee does, annually to be thence taken and killed, according to his own will; with unlimited right of hunting, hawking, and fishing, within the forest. As bow-bearer, he is to attend the king with a bow and arrows, and six stout bowmen clothed in green, whenever his majesty hunts within the forest. There are also eight foresters in fee, a gaveller, and a steward of the swanimote. These officers are empowered to hold a court of attachment every forty days; a court of swanimote thrice every year, and another court called the Justice Seat, once in three years. These courts are held at the King's Lodge, or Speech House, situated nearly in the centre of the forest. The whole forest is extraparochial, and its inhabitants are exempted from rates and taxes. They have free liberty of pasturage, access to the woods and timber, and the privilege of sinking mines. These advantages have induced many to form residences here; and according to the returns previous to 1803, the population amounted to three thousand three hundred and twenty-five, and the number of houses to seven hundred and twenty, nearly all built within the last hundred years; the six lodges erected for the keepers being the only houses in the forest in the time of Sir Robert Atkyns. The crown has the right of keeping eight hundred deer here, at all times; but these animals are so scarce, that the annual warrant issued from the crown for four bucks and four does, is frequently sent back unexecuted.

Henry II gave a right to the Cistercian Abbey of Flaxley, in this neighbourhood, to erect an iron forge, together with liberty to cut two oak trees weekly, to supply it with fuel. But Henry III revoked this latter grant, as being prejudicial to the forest; and a wood, called the Abbot's Wood, was gifted to the abbey in lieu of it.

This abbey was founded in the reign of Stephen; and, in contradiction of the notion that the chestnut is an introduction, and a comparatively recent introduction, into Britain, we may mention, that the early records of Flaxley notice it as a native timber tree, and it is found in the composition of many of the old roofs.

The free miners and colliers claim a right, not only to dig for coal and ore in the forest, with the consent of the gaveller, but also to be supplied with wood and timber for their works; and on an average of seven years, nearly one thousand five hundred trees are annually delivered to them.

The scenery of Dean Forest is extremely beautiful, the surface being finely varied with rising grounds, interspersed with deep valleys, and the majestic oaks and wide expanding beeches are delightfully intermixed with pensile birch trees, hawthorns, and different kinds of underwood. In many parts of it very copious chalybeate springs are seen to give a rich ochre tint to the ground and plants. The forest abounds with orchards, and the cider made from the styre apple, its almost peculiar produce, is remarkaly fine, and bears a high price.

In Oxfordshire we have only the single forest of Whichwood.

Camden describes the woods of this county as forming

one of its chief boasts; and Plott admits, that anciently such might have been the fact, but says, that, " owing to the late unhappy wars," (those of Charles I,) " wood has become so scarce, that it was a common thing to sell it by weight; and not only at Oxford, but in many other places in the northern part of the shire, where, if brought to mercat, it is ordinarily sold for about one shilling the hundred; but, if remote from a great town, it may be had for seven-pence." This fact can only be accounted for by the want at that period of inland coals, which are now so plentiful in the county. Except in the very northern districts, and omitting the article of oak, Oxfordshire may be termed a well wooded county. The whole of the Chiltern division abounds in beeches, and has been supposed by some, with much appear-ance of truth, to have formed a part of that great forest described by Leland as stretching one hundred and twenty miles westward from the border of Kent. " The beech woods of Oxfordshire," says Mr Dávis in his *Original Report*, " consist of trees growing on their own stems, pro-duced by the falling of the beech mast, as very little is permitted to grow on the old stools, which are generally grubbed up. It requires much judgment to thin these woods, so that the present stock may not hang too much over the seedlings, at the same time that, in a south aspect, injury may take place by exposing the soil too much to the sun; for it is to be observed, that the north side of a hill will produce a better growth of beech than the south side. There are some oak and ash trees dispersed among the beech, which have sprung up in places where the seeds have dropped, or been carried by birds.

In the forest of Whichwood, the oak, the ash, the beech, and the elm, are intermixed; but the oak is the prevailing tree, though there are not many of them likely to be ready for naval use for at least half a century. The ash is every where remarkably flourishing. The coppices are the most profitable production of Whichwood Forest. There are thirty-four of these; eighteen of which belong to the king, twelve to the Duke of Marlborough, and four to other indi-viduals. The whole extent of the forest is about five thousand five hundred and ninety-three acres, to which fall to be added the Chase Woods, four hundred and eighty-seven acres, and about six hundred and thirty-nine acres which form the con-tents of Blandford Park.

' In the vicinity of Stanton St John, are considerable tracts of woodland, called the Quarters, in which the oak is frequent, and there are many similar stretches in various parts of the county. The great price of timber, and the high rent offered for land during the war, induced many landlords to grub up considerable ranges of wood; but many plantations were made throughout the country. The great Belt at Blenheim extends of itself not less than thirteen miles.

In Buckinghamshire, we have the forests of Bernwood and Clitern. Bernwood runs along the hilly country from Aylesbury, almost to Oxford. Clitern was formerly a very thick impervious wood, and noted for being the haunt of banditti, who long infested the country, till a public spirited abbot of St Alban's broke their confederacy, by bringing many of them to justice, and destroying their retreats.

Bernwood Forest was a favourite hunting ground of Edward the Confessor, who had a palace at Brill, to which he frequently retired to enjoy the pleasures of the chase. The forest was at that time infested by a wild boar, which was at last slain by a huntsman named Nigel, whom the king rewarded for this service with a grant of some lands to be held by a horn,—a mode of livery which was common in that age. Nigel built a large manor house on the land thus given him, and called it Bore Stall, or Borstal, in memory of the event which gave it to him. The estate has descended in uninterrupted succession by several heirs female from the family of Nigel to that of Aubrey, who now possess the original horn, as well as a folio volume, composed about the time of the reign of Henry III, containing transcripts of papers relating to the manor, with a rude delineation of the site of Borstal House and lands; beneath which is the figure of a man on one knee, presenting a boar's head, on the point of a sword, to the king, who is returning him a coat of arms. The horn is of a dark brown colour, variegated and veined like tortoiseshell: the ends are tipped with silver, and fitted with wreaths of leather to hang round the neck. Borstal Tower was frequently the scene of contest during the Civil Wars.

In Essex are the two forests of Epping and Hainhault; the latter of which, it is probable, was once an appendage to the former. For Epping Forest was anciently a very extensive district; and, under the name of the Forest of Essex, included a great part of that county. It afterwards took the name of Waltham Forest; but Epping being a place better known, it now commonly takes that denomination.

Epping Forest is an extensive tract of good woodland, which was formerly called Waltham Forest, and, in yet more remote ages, the Forest of Essex, but which is now called by the name of the neighbouring town. In receiving its modern appellation, it has been greatly curtailed, many thousand acres having been grubbed up, and the land culti- vated. It is under the control of a lord warden and four verdurers; the latter, who are elected by the freeholders of the county, retain their offices during life. The forest rights are as various as the tenures of the different manors that surround it. Wild stags are still found in this forest, though within twelve miles of London, and a stag is annually turned out on Easter Monday, under an establishment patronized by the merchants of the city, and attended by hundreds of sports- men from within reach of the sound of Bow Bells. And then, indeed, may be seen, (to use the language of Froissart when speaking of tilting,) " good emptying of saddles : " so much so, indeed, that we have been told a thoroughly sportsman looking person was once seen standing, booted and spurred, and with a whip in his hand, by the side of the first fence that lay in the way of the riders, and being asked by an inquisitive traveller what he did there? " I am waiting for a horse," replied he, " there will be horses to spare very soon ;" and, to be sure, in a very few moments after the deer had dashed off, the pedestrian sportsman was seen leading the way over furrow, ditch, hedge, and gate, mounted on one of the best horses in the field.

Hainault Forest is about one mile from Barking Side. In page 217 of our fist volume, we have already noticed the celebrated Fairlop Oak, which grows in it. The fair, which is held round this tree on the first Friday of July, originated above a century ago from a man of singular character called Day, who was a block and pump maker at Wapping. He had a small estate near the Fairlop Oak, and used to invite a large party of friends on the first Friday of July annually to dine, on beans and bacon, under the shade of the tree. In the course of a few years other parties were formed on Mr Day's anniversary, and suttling booths were erected for their accommodation ; these progressively increased, and booths began also to be set up for the sale of various articles, and so early as 1725, the place began to exhibit the appearance of a regular fair. Mr Day continued to resort annually to his favourite spot as long as he lived ; and, to keep up the memory of its origin, he never failed to provide several sacks of beans, with a proper proportion of bacon, which he distributed from the trunk of the tree to the persons assembled at the fair. For several years before his death, the pump and block makers of Wapping went regularly to the fair in a boat made of one piece of entire fir, covered with an awning, mounted on a coach carriage, and drawn by six horses, attended by people carrying flags and streamers, a band of music, and a great number of persons both on foot and on horseback. A few years before Mr Day died, his favourite tree lost a large limb, out of which he had a coffin made, to remain with him for his use, as he said himself, " when Day should be turned into Night." His death happened on the 19th of October, 1767, at the age of eighty-four. His remains were conveyed to Barking by water, according to his own directions, accompanied by six journeymen pump and block makers, to each of whom he bequeathed a new leathern apron and a guinea. There is a tombstone to his memory in Barking churchyard.

Wiltshire, also, was formerly a very woody county, and once probably almost the whole of it was a forest. Even at this day we find in it the vestiges of four forests,— Peevisham, Blakemore, Bradon, and Savernack. Bradon was a scene of dreadful bloodshed in the year 905, when the Danes under Ethelred invaded it, and slaughtered all the inhabitants of its environs, among whom were a number of women and children, who had fled for refuge to its recesses. Savernack forest is still a woody scene, and adorns a part of the road between Bath and London. It belongs to the Earl of Aylesbury, and is almost the only privileged forest in England in the hands of a subject, by whom, in strict language, a chase only is tenable. This forest is about twelve miles in circuit, and is still well stocked with deer and timber.

The ancient forest of Peevisham, extended from Chippenham nearly to Devizes, and from Lacock to Calne,

3

being bounded on the north and west by the river Avon. King James I took especial delight in hunting in this forest. After his death, it seems to have been disafforested, and one half of it granted to the ancestors of Lord Dudley, and the other to the family of Carey, in Devonshire. The magnificent place of Bowood, now belonging to the Marquis of Lansdowne, was included in the former half; and its extent and grandeur may be imagined when we state, that no less than nine various valleys, each characterized by its own peculiar style of scenery, are to be found within the boundary of its demesnes. Bowood was also comprised among those estates seized by the Parliament as forfeited, after the establishment of the Commonwealth. It was then laid open, and it is said that the Parliamentary Commissioners, having wished to convey the deer over Lockshill Heath to Spye Park, were enabled to do so by the clothiers in the neighbourhood, who skirted the way between the two places with broad-cloth.

Bradon Forest is a large tract of country, which is now almost denuded of trees, and a great part of it enclosed for cultivation. It was anciently called Bredon Wood, and, by some of the old writers, it is called Brithendune. It is mentioned as a forest as early as the reign of Henry IV. It then extended many miles beyond its present nominal limits, at which time one of its keepers was Edmond de Langley, Earl of Cambridge and Duke of York. On Charlton Common, which is comprehended within the limits of the forest, is Bradon Pond, three quarters of a mile long, and half a mile in breadth.

Selwood Forest, which was chiefly situated in Somersetshire, also comprehended a portion of the south-western side of Wiltshire. It was a forest in the Anglo Saxon era; and it was the retreat of Alfred, at the time his forces were too weak to oppose the Danes in the open field.

Melksham Forest, which covered a large tract of country, extended from the vicinity of the town whence it had its name northward towards Chippenham. Matthew Fitz-John, governor of the Castle of Devizes, had the keeping of it in the reign of Edward I.

Chippenham Forest was also committed to Fitz-John's custody by the same monarch. It seems to have been attached to the palace of the West Saxon kings when they resided at Chippenham.

Clarendon Forest seems to have been a branch of the New

Forest, in Hampshire, which also occupied a part of Wiltshire; and it is even said by some writers to have extended as far as Devizes. Clarendon Forest was a favourite resort of the English monarchs. It was on his return from hunting in this forest that Edward the Martyr was murdered by order of his mother-in-law, with the view of securing the throne to her son Ethelred. Henry II and Edward III also frequently enjoyed the pleasures of the chase during their visits to the palace whence the forest had its name.

Chute Forest, situated on the eastern confines of the county adjoining Hampshire, was probably a branch of New Forest.

Savernake Forest is the only one in Wiltshire which remains in a well wooded condition; and it is also the only forest in England in the possession of a subject. It belongs to the Earl of Aylesbury, into whose family it came by the marriage of Thomas Lord Bruce with Lady Anne Seymour, daughter of Henry Lord Beauchamp, sister and heiress of William Seymour, Duke of Somerset, the sixth in descent from the Protector. Whilst annexed to the crown, it was usually assigned by the reigning monarch as part of the jointure of the Queen Consort, and was, in particular, long held by Eleanore, wife of Edward III. Several warrants to the keepers, signed by her, and of most beautiful manuscript, are still extant. Many of the oaks here are very large and majestic. In page 257 of our first volume, we have already noticed one of them, the King's Oak, as being very remarkable. This forest, with the adjoining park of Tottenham, the residence of the Bruce family, comprehends an extent of country nearly sixteen miles in circumference. The whole is intersected by numerous walks and avenues, eight of which diverge from a common centre. It is well stocked with deer, and exhibits some highly interesting scenery, being beautifully diversified with hills, valleys, and lawns.

Windsor Forest includes that portion of Wiltshire which is situated near Oakinghame in Berkshire, though thirty miles from the eastern border of the county.

The chases within Wiltshire are believed to have been anciently very numerous; but Cranbourne Chase, Vernditch Chase, and Albourn Chase, are now the only woodland districts retaining that appellation. The first two are immediately adjoining to each other, and occupy a long narrow tract of country in the southern confines of Wiltshire, where it unites with Dorsetshire. The last is situated almost in the very centre of Marlborough Downs, and forms a remarkable contrast to the naked appearance of the country immediately around it. Besides these, there are many patches of woodlands throughout the county.

In Berkshire is the celebrated Forest of Windsor. It was formerly the property of Queen Emma, and was afterwards distinguished by William the Conqueror, who built lodges in it, and established forest law. He himself used commonly, after the chase, to sleep at an abbey in the neighbourhood. There is now little scenery left in any part of it. Some of the finest of the old forest trees still remaining, stand on the left of the road leading from the great park to Cranburn Lodge. The scenery here, chiefly from the ornament of the trees, is beautiful. The most pleasing part of Windsor Forest is the Great Park, which, though in many places artificially and formally planted, contains great variety of ground. The improvements of Duke William of Cumberland were magnificent, rather than in a style suitable to a forest. All formalities should have been, as much as possible, avoided, and the whole formed into noble lawns and woods, with views introduced, where they could be, into the country. The great avenue to Windsor Castle, though in a style of great formality, is, however, in its kind, so noble a piece of scenery, that we should not wish to see it destroyed. Besides great numbers of red and fallow deer, this park was, in the duke's time, much frequented by wild turkeys, the breed of which he encouraged. It could hardly have had a more beautiful decoration. Birds are among the most picturesque objects : their forms and plumage are both picturesque; yet they are generally so diminutive, that, beautiful as they are, they have little effect. But the turkey is both a large bird, and, being gregarious, forms groups, which become objects of consequence. Its shape, also, is picturesque, and all its actions. Its colour, also, especially if it be of the bright copper, varying in the sunbeam, is more beautiful than the plumage of any other bird. The peacock, neither in form nor in colour, is equal to the turkey. As this bird was reclaimed from

the unbounded woods of America, where it is still indigenous, its habits continue wilder than those of any
domestic fowl. It strays widely for its food; it flies
well, considering its apparent inactivity, and it perches
and roosts on trees. On all these accounts it is a proper
inhabitant of parks. Windsor Forest is about thirty
miles round, the Great Park fourteen, and the Little
Park three.

Windsor Forest was the delight of many of our monarchs,
and of none more than our worthy King George III,
who took very great pleasure in it. The park is rich in
forest scenery, and some of its prospects command a vast
extent of country. Here it was that the king carried on
his agricultural experiments and improvements. When his
majesty succeeded to it, the contents were about three
thousand eight hundred acres, abounding with moss, fern,
rushes, and ant-hills; and it was even dangerous in some
places, from its bogs and swamps. In this state it hardly
afforded nutriment for three thousand deer. But although the
park was afterwards reduced to two thousand four hundred
acres, the king's improvements, in draining, &c. were such,
that it still supported the same number of deer, and in
excellent condition. The remaining one thousand four hundred
acres were laid out in what were called the Norfolk Farm,
and the Flemish Farm, so denominated from the different
kinds of husbandry practised experimentally upon each.
Windsor Forest, which extended over seventeen parishes,
was disafforested in 1814. The people then ignorantly took it
into their heads to imagine, that the deer would become
common property the moment the enclosure bill should pass;
and they immediately began an immense slaughter, which
the forest officers found it impossible to arrest. Government,
thinking it the wisest plan to endeavour to drive the deer into
the park, a regiment of horse guards was ordered out, in
addition to which, hundreds of horsemen assembled from all
parts of the neighbourhood, and for several days the thickets
and coverts of that richly wooded country echoed with the
trumpet calls of cavalry giving the order to charge; and in
this way some hundreds of deer were saved and enclosed.
The Little Park contained Hearne's Oak, immortalized by
Shakespeare, in his *Merry Wives of Windsor*. Hearne was
a keeper in the forest in the time of Elizabeth, who hanged

himself upon this oak, from fear of being disgraced for
some offence he had committed; and his ghost was believed
to have haunted the spot, which was probably the cause of
the poet selecting this place as the scene for exposing the
cowardice of his fat knight.

In Middlesex is the forest of ·Enfield. After the
death of Charles I, it is said that Cromwell divided it
into farms among his veterans; but, if they ever took
possession, they were dispossessed at the Restoration, and
deer, its ancient inhabitants, were again settled in their
room.

Middlesex was certainly at one time covered with a forest.
The curious tract, written in 1174, by Fitz-Stephen, a monk
of Canterbury, entitled *Descriptio nobilissimæ civitatis Lon-
doniæ*, states, " that there were open meadows of pasture
lands on the north side of the city, and that beyond these
there was a great forest, in whose woody coverts lurked the
stag, the hind, the wild boar, and the bull."

Enfield Chase seems to be a fragment of this ancient
forest of Essex. It first appears under this name in a record
of the reign of Edward II, having been previously called the
Great, or Outer Park. After the decapitation of Charles I,
it was seized as crown lands, and was surveyed by order of
the House of Commons, in 1750, when the deer were valued
at £150; the oak timber, exclusive of two thousand five
hundred trees, marked for the use of the navy, at £2100;
and the hornbeam and other wood, at £12,100.   The chase
was soon afterwards divided into parcels, and sold to different
individuals; and the enclosures which followed this measure
created great disturbances among those who claimed a right
of common, and of fuel, on it.   It was afterwards entirely
divided in 1777, its contents then being eight thousand three
hundred and forty-nine acres, of which three thousand two
hundred and eighteen went to the king. At this time a large
portion of the chase remained in wild and beautiful woodland,
browsed by deer; but the enclosure destroyed much of its
picturesque character. For several centuries, it had its due
proportion of forest officers, and three lodges,— South Lodge,
occasionally used as a retirement by the great Earl of
Chatham, but since allowed to become dilapidated, East Lodge,
and West Lodge.

Surrey and Kent were formerly very woody counties, of which we need no evidence besides that of Cæsar, when he invaded Britain. There are no traces, however, of any nominal forest in either of them, except the forest of Tunbridge. Woods, indeed, there are in various parts; and much more the appearance of a woody country is still left than in most of those countries in which forests are known to have existed.

A great portion of the county of Surrey was reserved as crown demesnes, under the Norman race of kings. Henry II extended the limits of Windsor Forest by the enclosure of his manors in Surrey, till at length he had afforested the whole county. The general discontent which arose from this proceeding compelled his son Richard to undo in part what his father had been so desirous to accomplish. In the first year of his reign he consented to disafforest the county from the river Wey, eastward, and from Guildford Down, southward, which amounted to about three-fourths of it, and his charter to this effect was confirmed by King John. What remained forest, upon the footing of this charter, was called the Bailiwick of Surrey, as being exempted from the jurisdiction of the sheriff, and subject to that of its own bailiff alone. It contained the parishes and townships of Chobham, Bisley, Horshill, Byfleet, Purford, Wanborough, Pirbright, Ash, Windlesham, Tongham, Warplesdon, Woking, and Stoke. Within the same jurisdiction also lay Chertsey, Egham, and Thorpe; but these being the estates of the Abbey of Chertsey, were not subject to the bailiff's authority. Manwood tells us, that King John "followed the example of his brother and father in afforesting the lands of his subjects, so that the forests were everywhere so much enlarged, that the greatest part of the kingdom was turned into forests, the boundaries of which were so large, and the laws so very severe, that it was impossible for any man who lived within these boundaries to escape the danger: and thus it continued till the 17th year of his reign, A.D. 1215." By this time afforestation had become so general a grievance, that several of the nobility and gentry petitioned the king against it, and especially, that all the new afforestations made by him and his predecessors might be disafforested. The king was unwillingly obliged to comply; and in this way originated the great charter, and the charter of forests stipulated for by the barons, and granted

6

by John at Runnymede in 1215. In obedience to this, John
was bound to have disafforested all that part of the county of
Surrey which his brother had afforested, but he died in the
following year, and his son, Henry III, having granted a
charter in the ninth year of his reign, the whole of Surrey, with
the exception of the park of Guildford, was thus disafforested;
and notwithstanding the after attempts of Edward I and II
to set it aside, the commons of the county maintained their
rights with so much perseverance, that in the first year of
Edward III, they obtained a full confirmation of the above
charter. Charles I, in the seventh year of his reign, had the
weakness to revive the royal pretensions, which attempt,
added to his after aggressions, cost him his crown and
his life. From this period, the Bailiwick of Surrey is only
reckoned *purlieu* of the royal forest, in which the king still
has a right of property over any of his deer escaping into
it, against every one except the owner of the woods or lands
in which they are found, but which is exempted from the
general laws of the forest, and the ordinary jurisdiction; and
so far free and open to all owners of land within the same,
that, under certain limitations, they may chase and kill any of
the deer actually found therein. The king has rangers
appointed by letters patent, for the preservation of all deer
escaping into the purlieus, whose office it is to drive them
back towards the forest. Langrove Lodge, near Chertsey, is
the residence of the ranger of this purlieu.

Norwood, in Surrey, is described by the survey of 1646, as
containing " eight hundred and thirty acres, in which the
inhabitants of Croyden have herbage for all manner of cattle,
and mastage for swine without stint." The whole of this
waste was covered with wood at no very remote period; and
Aubrey mentions a remarkable tree called Vicar's Oak. The
Magna Britannia says, that Norwood consisted entirely of
oak, "and among them was one that bare misselto, which
some persons were so hardy as to cut, for the gain of selling it
to the apothecaries of London, leaving a bunch of it to sprout
out. But they proved unfortunate after it; for one of them
fell lame, and the others lost an eye. At length, in the year
1678, a certain man, notwithstanding he was warned against
it upon the account of what the others had suffered, adven-
tured to cut the tree down, and he soon after broke his leg.
To fell oaks, hath long been counted fatal, and such as believe
it, produce the instance of the Earl of Winchelsea, who, having
felled a curious grove of oaks, soon after found his countess

dead in her bed suddenly, and his eldest son, the Lord Maidstone, was killed at sea with a cannon bullet."

The Weald of Kent anciently extended to Winchelsea, in Sussex, and was one hundred and twenty miles long by thirty broad. It now stretches from Romney Marsh to Surrey—is bounded on the north by the range of hills entering Kent near Well Street, and extending, in a due west direction, to Sutton and Egerton, and thence south-eastward to Hythe; and, on the south, it goes to the confines of Sussex, and includes the Isle of Oxney. In ancient times, all this was one immense forest, destitute of inhabitants, and stored with hogs and deer only. By degrees, however, it became peopled, and it is now everywhere interspersed with towns and villages, though it still contains some extensive and flourishing woodlands, among which, as our experience enables us to say, many very interesting scenes are to be found. Its present name is Saxon, and signifies a woody country; but the Britons called it Coit Andred, the Great Chase, or Forest. The whole was ancient demesne of the Saxon kings; and there are still certain provisions attached to the possession of the lands, which induce the proprietors to wish to be considered as within its limits. The views over the Weald, enjoyed from some of the adjoining hills, are very delightful, the landscape being varied by small eminences with rich cultivation, interspersed with farm houses, seats, and villages, promiscuously scattered among groves and groups of towering oaks, happily mingled with other trees.

The Forest of Tunbridge is noticed in the foundation charter granted to the canons regular of the priory of Tunbridge, founded by Richard de Clare, first Earl of Hertford, who gives them yearly the privilege of " one hundred and twenty hogs in his forest of Tunbridge, free from parsonage; and that the canons should have two horses every day, freely and quietly to carry home the dead wood out of those his woods which were nearest and most convenient for them; together with one stag yearly, on the feast of St Mary Magdalene, for ever, to be taken by the Earl's men."

Sussex, which has ever been remarkable as one of the finest timber counties in England, abounds, at the same time, with nominal forests. It contains no fewer than seven,—St Leonard's, Word, Ashdown,

Waterdown, Dallington, Arundel, and Charlton, which last forest was settled on the Dukes of Richmond. Ridings through it have lately been cut, and many plantations made; but I never saw them.

Sussex has been celebrated for its timber, and especially for its oak, from the remotest antiquity. Before the Norman Conquest it was one continued forest, and even now it contains not less than one hundred and eighty thousand acres of woodland. The Weald here is every where overspread with wood, which is so natural to the soil, that if a field were sown with furze only, the ground would be covered with young oaks in the course of a few years. The quality of the wood is so well known to be superior, that the navy contractors have generally stipulated for Sussex oak in preference to every other kind.

Ashdown Forest, or Lancaster Great Park, occupies a considerable part of the lower division of the Rape of Pevensey. According to the parliamentary survey in the seventeenth century, the impaled ground was estimated at thirteen thousand nine hundred and ninety one acres, worth £2256 per annum, exclusive of various parcels of land without the pale. James I appointed the Earl of Dorset master of the forest, governor and master of the game, and keeper and surveyor-general of all the woods; but this grant was voided by the Parliamentary commissioners. It was afterwards granted to the Earl of Bristol for ninety-nine years, for £200 per annum; but he surrendered his lease because he could make no profit from it. It is now vested in the Duke of Dorset.

In Cornwall, it does not appear that there has ever been any thing like a forest.

In Devonshire there are two,—the Forest of Dartmore, which runs along the mountainous and barren country on both sides of the river Dart, before it enters the South Hams; and the Forest of Exmore, which accompanies the river Ex till it enter the more fertile country about Dulverton.

Dartmoor, and the waste called the Forest of Dartmoor, occupy the greatest portion of the western district of Devonshire, which, extending from the vale of Exeter, nearly reaches to the banks of the Tamar. These uncultivated lands amount to more than two hundred and fifty thousand acres, of which Dartmoor alone occupies above eighty thousand. The forest is a part of the duchy of Cornwall. This was originally made a forest by King John, and its bounds were set by perambulation in the reign of Henry III. Although it is now destitute of trees, it presents many interesting objects. Its surface is diversified by vast masses of granite, called *Tors*, which may be seen at the distance of many miles. The principal of these are High Tor, Bellever Tor, Hessary Tor, Stepherton Tor, Ham Tor, Mist Tor, Row Tor, and Crockern Tor. This last has been long celebrated as the place where the Stannary Parliaments of this country held their meetings; and Mr Polwhele imagines it to have been a seat of British judicature, even prior to the invasion of the Romans. "Distant as it has always been," says he, "within the memory of man, from every human habitation, we might well be surprised that it should have been chosen for the spot in which our laws were to have been framed, unless some peculiar sanctity had been attached to it in consequence of its appropriation to legal or judicial purposes, from the highest antiquity. On this Tor, not long since, was the warden's, or president's chair, seats for the jurors, a high corner stone for the crier of the court, and a table, all rudely hewn out of the rough moor stone of the Tor; together with a cavern, which was used in latter ages as a depository for wine. Notwithstanding this provision, Crockern Tor was too wild and dreary a place for our legislators of the last generation, who, after opening their commission, and swearing the jurors on this spot, merely to keep up the old formalities, usually adjourned the court to one of the Stannary towns. From the nature of this spot, open, wild, and remote,—from the rocks that were the benches, and from the modes of proceeding,—all so like the ancient courts, and all so unlike the modern,—I judge Crockern to have been the court of a Cantred, (a district of a number of townships,) or its place of convention for the purposes of legislature."

In Somersetshire there are two forests,—Nerohe Forest, which lies a little to the south of Taunton; and Selwood Forest, a little to the south of Froom. These scenes will ever be famous in British history while the remembrance continues of Alfred the Great. Frequent inundations of Danes, and repeated losses, had driven him from the management of affairs; but he retired before the enemies of his country only to attack them with more advantage. Seeing the time ripe for action, he emerged from his retreat, sent his emissaries around, and called his friends together in the forest of Selwood, which sheltered and concealed his numbers. Here, arranging his followers, he burst from the forest like a torrent upon the Danes. They gave way at once, and suffered so terrible a defeat, that they never again molested his repose.

In Somersetshire, the ancient forests were Selwood, near Frome; Mendip, between Frome and the Bristol Channel; Exmoor, between the port of Watchet and the north-west part of Devon; Neroche, near Ilminster; and North Petherton, near Bridgewater. The forest of Selwood, which, as we have already noticed, p. 72, also ran into Wiltshire, gave the name of Selwoodshire, or Sealwardscire, to the adjoining country.

On the north of Dorsetshire lies Gillingham Forest, remarkable also for a great defeat which Edmund Ironside gave the Danes on the confines of it. A little to the east, lies Cranburn Chase; and on the west, Blackmore Forest, commonly called the Forest of White Hart, from a celebrated stag which afforded great diversion to Henry III. The whole of the island of Purbeck was once a forest. In the midst of it stands Corf Castle, where Elfrida, to open the throne for her son Ethelred, murdered her son-in-law Edward, when he called for refreshment at her castle after a toilsome chase.

Between the years 930 and 980, the manor of Cranbourne Chase belonged to a noble soldier called Haylward de Mean, from his pale, or fair complexion. His grandson, Brictricus, was sent ambassador into Norway, where the Princess Matilda became enamoured of him; but he refused to marry her, and the lady was so irritated against him for his frigidity, and so provoked by the affront she had received by his refusal, that when she came into England as the queen of William the Conqueror, she procured an order to seize Brictricus at his castle of Hanley, in Worcéstershire. After the Conquest, this manor was given to Queen Matilda, on whose death it reverted to the crown, and was bestowed by William Rufus on Robert Fitz-Hamon, nephew to the Conqueror ; and, on his decease, it became the property of Robert, first Earl of Gloucester, illegitimate son of Henry I, who had married one of Robert Fitz-Hamon's four heiresses. It then passed through a female to the Earls of March, and só it has since descended through various families.

The forest of Gillingham was, in Leland's time, " foure miles in length, and a mile, or thereboute, in bredth." In the reign of Charles I, by whom it was disforested, the lessee was obliged to keep four hundred deer for the king's recreation. Great disaffection was created among the peasantry by its enclosure, and several persons were fined, and otherwise punished, in consequence of the riots that ensued. It was near this, at a place called Peonne, or Penn, in Somersetshire, that the battle between Canute and Edmond Ironside was fought ; and the pursuit is supposed to have extended to the spot called Slaughter Gate, in this parish.

The Forest of Blackmore, otherwise called Whitehart Forest, comprehends a large tract in the northern and western parts of the county of Dorset. Its first name seems to have been derived from the black clay soil, and the name of Whitehart was given to it from the following event recorded by Camden :— " Henry III, hunting in this forest, among several deer he had run down, spared the life of a beautiful white hart, which afterwards Thomas de la Lind, a neighbouring gentleman of ancient descent and special note, with his companions, hunted, and killed, at a bridge, since from thence called Kingstag Bridge, in the parish of Pulham. The king, highly offended at it, not only punished them with imprisonment and grievous fine, but severely taxed all their lands which they then held. The owners of which yearly, ever since to this day, pay a sum of money by way of fine, or amercement into the Exchequer, called Whitehart Silver, in memory of which this county needeth no better remembrance than this annual payment." Leland says, " this forest reached from Joelle into the quarters of Shaftesbyri."

In Hampshire are the vestiges of five forests. On the north near Sylchester lies Chute Forest, through which passes the great southern Roman road still visible

in many parts. On the west lies the Forest of Harewood, which is still a woody scene, though its larger
trees are in general gone. This place was formerly
celebrated for the unfortunate loves of Athelwold and
Elfrida. Here Edgar slew his rival; and the supposed
place is traditionally marked by the name of Dead Man's
Plot. The abbey of Whorwell, which Elfrida founded
on this occasion, is not now to be traced, except by a
monumental stone which marks its situation. On the
east of Hampshire, lies Holt Forest; more to the south,
the Forest of Waltham, which belongs to the Bishop of
Winchester; and near Tichfield, the Forest of Bere.
Some parts of these forests still afford remains of woody
scenery.

At the south-west extremity of Hampshire lies New
Forest; which, as it hath given occasion to these remarks,
and is besides the noblest scene of the kind in England,
I shall in the following book consider more at large, and
endeavour to illustrate, by its scenes, some of the observations which have already been made.*

Besides the New Forest, of which enough will be said
anon, important parts of Hampshire were occupied by the
forest of Alice Holt and Woolmer, and the forest of Bere. The
first of these is separated into two portions by the intervention of private property. Its limits comprehended about fifteen
thousand four hundred and ninety-three acres, eight thousand
six hundred and ninety-four of which belong to the crown.
In the survey of 1608, there were one thousand three hundred
and one oaks returned as fit for the use of the navy, and
twenty-three thousand nine hundred and thirty-four loads as
defective. This quantity has since greatly decreased; and

---

* To this account of the forests of England I shall only subjoin, that
Mr St John (see his *Observations on the Land Revenues of the Crown*,
p. 118) enumerates seventy-seven, of which, Windsor, Waltham, Dean,
Rockingham, Whittlewood, Salcey, Sherwood, Whichwood, New
Forest, Bere, and Walmer, are the only forests, he says, which are
reputed to have preserved their rights. Of the rest indeed he gives the
names, many of which I meet with nowhere but in his catalogue. He
says, however, that several of them were disforested, and changed into
private property, by an act of Charles I, which was wrested from him,
in consequence of his having revived the vexations of forest law at the
beginning of his difficulties.

in 1783, the sound and defective wood together amounted only to fifteen thousand one hundred and forty-two loads; and those were of trees mostly of one age, — that is, from one hundred to one hundred and twenty years,—without any having been planted to succeed them. In the division called Alice Holt, which contains about two thousand seven hundred and forty-four acres of crown lands, the growing timber has been estimated at £ 60,000. This forest is situated on the borders of Surrey and Sussex. The Forest of Bere extends northward from the Portsdown Hills, and according to the perambulation made in 1688, and now considered as the boundary, it includes about sixteen thousand acres, of which one third is enclosed. This forest is divided into the east walk and the west walk, to each of which are annexed several smaller divisions called purlieus, though all of them are subject to the forest laws. From the survey of 1783, the wood then growing was only a twenty-eighth part of what was standing in the year 1608, and its boundaries were continually decreasing by encroachments. It contains about two hundred head of deer, from which about seven brace of bucks are annually killed. The officers are a warden, four verdurers, two master keepers, two under keepers, a ranger, a steward of the Swainmote Court, twelve regarders, and two agisters.

In addition to these English forests, we may notice, that Radnorshire in South Wales was anciently distinguished for its forests, of which the Great Forest of Radnor was the most important. But from carelessness and neglect, it was found to have been much curtailed and deteriorated, even in the time of Elizabeth, when an inquisition was held in it, the names of the members of which, together with their judgments, are still extant. " Which individuals, upon their oath, do say and present, that the said Forest of Radnor doth extend to the number of three thousand acres of all sorts and kinds of land, or thereabouts ; unto two thousand of waste heath, wild fogge, moorish ground ; eight hundred acres of land, roots, and bushes of small hazzles and thorns, utterly destroyed, by reason the same have been hewn and cut by inhabitants dwelling thereabouts, always out of season, and at the spring time eaten and consumed by wild beasts and goats ; two hundred acres thereof, lying in sandy places of the said forest, is somewhat more bateful than the rest are, whereon sheep and cattle most commonly depasture : And do say and present, that the yearly rent of the said forest is now £19, paid and answered by the tenant's commoners thereunto, to one Stephen Vaughan, yet under forester to Gibes, who hath the said forest in farm, or ortherwise, in bargain from William Abbott, Esq. * * * * * * And finally, the said jury doth say and present that the said forest is worth yearly to be let out to farm £19, and not above."

OBSERVATIONS

ON

FOREST SCENERY.

BOOK III.

SECTION I.

WE concluded the last book with a catalogue (for it was little more) of the princi al forests which formerly overspread the island of Britain. None of them at this day possesses its original grandeur. A few have preserved some little appearance of scenery, but the greater part are wastes. New Forest, in Hampshire, is among the few which have retained any ideas of their ancient consequence ; at least it is superior to the rest, on account of the extent of its boundaries, the variety of its contents, and the grandeur of its scenes.

With these scenes I propose, in the following book, to illustrate the observations which have been made in the two preceding books ; and shall, in several excursions through the different parts of this woody country, endeavour to point out its peculiar beauties. But though I shall chiefly consider it in a picturesque light, I shall vary my subject by giving a general idea of the ancient history and present state of this celebrated forest.

This tract of woodland was originally made a forest by William I, in the year 1079, about thirteen years after the battle of Hastings, and is indeed the only forest in England whose origin can be traced. It took the denomination of New Forest, from its being an addition to the many forests which the crown already possessed, and which had formerly been appropriated in feudal times. The original name of this tract of country was Ytene.

As several forests were more commodiously situated for royal diversion than New Forest, the historian hath been sometimes led to conceive, that William must have had other ends than amusement in making this addition to them ; and observing, farther, its vicinity to the coast of Normandy, he hath, from this circumstance, drawn a surmise that, under the idea of a forest, William meant to preserve an unobserved communication with the continent, which would enable him to embark his troops on either side without giving alarm.

But this surmise depends on no historical evidence, neither indeed is it probable. The coasts of Kent and Sussex were more commodious for the embarkation of troops than any part of New Forest; and it is absurd to suppose an army could be embarked any where without observation. Southampton, indeed, was commodious enough; but this port neither lies in New Forest, nor does the forest in any degree skreen its avenues. Besides, the affairs of William were never in so perplexed a situation as to require privacy, especially at the time when he made this forest, which was after he had defeated all his enemies, and was of course in the height of his power. Nor, indeed, was it agreeable to the general character of this prince to do things secretly. He rather chose, on all occasions, to sway the sceptre with a lofty hand. The judicious Rapin seems to close the whole debate very justly, by observing, that this surmise seems to have arisen merely from an opinion, that so politic a prince as William could do nothing without a political end ; whereas the most politic princes, no doubt, are swayed, where their pleasures are concerned, by passions and caprice, like other men.*

The means which William used in afforesting these extensive woodlands, create another question among historians. The general opinion is, that he destroyed a number of villages and churches, drove out the inhabitants, laid their lands waste, and formed New Forest in their room.

* Rapin, vol. i. fol. page 178.

This opinion has appeared to some ill-founded; and Voltaire, in particular, has stood up in defence of the humanity, or rather the policy, of William. It is absurd, he thinks, to suppose that a prince, so noted for prudent and interested conduct, should lay waste so much cultivated ground; plant it with forest trees, which would be many years in coming to perfection; and for the sake of a few deer, turn adrift so large a body of his industrious subjects, who might have contributed so much to the increase of his revenues.*

Voltaire's conclusion may be just, but his reasoning is certainly ill-founded. It proceeds on the improbability of so wide a desolation; whereas it might have proceeded better on the impossibility of it. For how could William have spread such depopulation in a country, which, from the nature of it, must have been from the first very thinly inhabited? The ancient Ytene was undoubtedly a woody tract long before the times of William. Voltaire's idea, therefore, of planting a forest, is absurd, and is founded on a total ignorance of the country. He took his ideas merely from a French forest, which is artificially planted, and laid out in vistas and alleys. It is probable that William rather opened his chases by cutting down wood, than that he had occasion to plant more. Besides, the internal strata of the soil of New Forest are admirably adapted to produce timber; yet the surface of it is, in general, poor, and could never have admitted, even if the times had allowed, any high degree of cultivation. Upon the whole, therefore, it does not seem possible that William could have spread so wide a depopulation through this country as he is represented to have done.

On the other hand, there is no contending against the stream of history; and though we may allow that William could not make any great depopulation, we are not to suppose he made none at all. Many writers who lived about his time, unite in lamentable complaints of his devastations. According to them, at least thirty miles of cultivated lands were laid waste; above fifty

* See his *Abridgment of Universal History.*

parish churches and many villages destroyed, and all
the inhabitants extirpated.* But it is to be considered,
that these writers were monks, who had taken high
offence at William for his exactions on their monasteries,
and were neither, as it appears, informed themselves,
nor disposed, through their prejudices, to inform others.
Many things they say are palpably false.

In this dearth, therefore, of historical evidence, we
are still at a loss. To suppose that William made no
devastation, and to suppose that he made all which these
prejudiced monks lay to his charge, seem to be sup-
positions equally unsupported. On the whole, therefore,
the truth of the matter, as of most others, lies probably
between the two opinions.

* In sylva, quæ vocatur Nova Foresta, ecclesias, et villas eradicari ;
gentem extirpari, et a feris fecit inhabitari. — *Hen. de Huntingdon.*
In that wood, which is called New Forest, he ordered the churches
and villages to be destroyed, the people to be driven out, and the whole
to be inhabited by wild beasts.
Nova Regia Foresta, anglice Ytene, quam Gulielmus Bastardus, homi-
nibus fugatis, desertis villis, et subreptis ecclesiis per 30, et eo amplius
milliaria, in saltus, et lustra ferarum redigit. — *Brompton.*
That tract of country, a space of more than thirty miles in extent,
now called New Forest, but formerly called Ytene, William the Bastard
ordered to be despoiled of all its churches, villages, and inhabitants, and
to be turned into a habitation for beasts.
Per 30, et amplius milliaria, ubi erat hominum mansio, terra fructi-
fera, necnon frugifera, extirpatis domibus, cum pomariis, et hortis, et
etiam ecclesiis, cum cæmetariis, in forestam, vel potius in deserta, et
ferarum lustra, rege jubente, redacta erant. — *Hist. Winton.*
Through the space of thirty miles, the whole county, which was fruit-
ful in a high degree, was laid waste. The churches, gardens, and
houses were all destroyed, and the whole reduced by the king's order
into a chase for beasts.
Hic Gulielmus (Rufus) fecit forestas in multis locis, per medium
regni ; et inter Southampton, et prioratum Twynam, qui nunc vocatur
Christ-church, prostravit, et exterminavit 22 ecclesias matrices, cum
villis, capellis, maneriis, atque mansionibus ; secundum vero quosdam,
52 ecclesias parochiales ; et fecit forestam novam, quam vocavit suum
novum herbarium ; et replevit eam cervis, damis, et aliis feris ; parcens
illis per septem annos primos. — *Knighton.*
This prince (Rufus) made forests in various parts ; but his capital
forest occcupied that tract of country which lies between Southampton
and Christ-church. Here, to make room for his beasts of chase, he
destroyed twenty-two churches, — some say fifty-two, — together with
villages, chapels, and private houses, and formed New Forest, which he
called his garden, filling it with game, which he spared for seven years.

We are disposed to agree perfectly in the judgment which Mr Gilpin has here pronounced, as to the degree of oppression with which William the Conqueror is chargeable. He was certainly not a monarch likely to be guilty of wanton or gratuitous cruelty; and to whatever extent he may have carried afforestation, and however little scrupulous he may have been in providing for the gratification of his well known passion for the chase, it is not to be imagined that he would authorize the execution of any acts of tyranny which were not absolutely necessary to ensure him a full enjoyment of its pleasures.

On reference to Walter, Mapes, Hemingford, Knyghton, and other writers, we find that their accounts of the devastation produced by William are very widely different from each other. In one circumstance alone, that of the number of churches destroyed, their evidences vary from twenty-two to sixty, a circumstance which sufficiently shews the vagueness of their accusations. " With respect to the monkish writers who first raised the cry against the Conqueror," says the author of the article Hampshire in the *Beauties of England,* we should cautiously admit their evidence in matters wherein themselves were interested. Indeed, our caution should be doubled in the present instance, since these ecclesiastics, the only biographers of William, were his bitterest and most rancorous foes. Exasperated by injuries and contumely, which his power prevented them from revenging, they seized the means of retaliation to which impotent and little minds too frequently have recourse, and took every method to traduce his name and blast his memory, magnifying each small deviation from propriety into enormous wickedness, each exertion of prerogative into unbounded tyranny ; and, when real sources of abuse failed, inventing excesses which never occurred, and evils that never had a being.

"It is peculiarly remarkable that the author of the latter part of the *Saxon Chronicle,* who was indisputably contemporary with William, and who seems to have viewed his vices with a severe eye, should not take the least notice of the afforestation of the New Forest, nor of the cruelties said to have been inflicted on its inhabitants in consequence of it. Every other memorble event of this reign he particularly relates,— the total devastation of Northumberland—the compilation of the Doomsday Book—the universal and formal introduction of the feudal system into the kingdom—and the fearful famine

and pestilence, which other monkish writers have converted
into an infliction from Heaven as the punishment of William's
supposed acts of tyranny, — these are all circumstantially mentioned ; but not a hint occurs relative to the formation of the
New Forest.   What is still more singular, he paints the
Conqueror's passion for the chase in the warmest colours, and
condemns it with the greatest severity, lamenting the excesses
which the indulgence of it led him to commit; in the enu-
meration of which, he would most assuredly have included
the remarkable one of the devastation in Hampshire, if the
circumstance had reached his knowledge. May we not, then,
fairly infer, from the silence of this accurate and impartial
writer, that the afforestation, which, from the authority of the
Doomsday Book, was incontrovertibly made by William, was
effected with so little injury to the subject, and so little dis-
turbance of social intercourse, that it was scarcely known, or
perhaps entirely unnoticed, beyond the immediate scene of
its occurrence ?

" It is farther observable, that no particular era is marked by
these annalists at which this afforestation was made, a very
extraordinary instance of omission in writers whose chief
merit is accuracy in arranging events under the years when
they respectively happened. Surely so obnoxious an exaction
of power, attended with so many instances of tyrannical
oppression, involving so large a tract of country in desolation,
and such numbers of people in utter distress, and giving so
violent a shock to the opinions of the age, by throwing down,
without ceremony, the walls of so great a number of churches,
must have been generally known, and as universally execrated.
Can we suppose, then, that writers who were on the watch
for opportunities of loading William with blame, would not
immediately have seized on so striking an instance of his
unfeeling tyranny, and minuted down with the nicest accuracy
every circumstance of time, place, and manner attending it,
since they must have been sensible that these minutiæ are
what stamp every recorded fact with the appearance of
authenticity ? The destruction of so many churches would
have been a noble theme for monkish declamation; and we
may rest assured that these ecclesiastics would have detailed
every sacrilegious circumstance with malignant particularity.
Instead of these distinct notices, we have nothing but general,
confused, and discordant accounts, neither specifying the
period of the afforestation, nor agreeing in the number of

churches destroyed. It would be a waste of time to enter into a more detailed refutation of the extravagant falsehoods of these monkish writers. Even the most modest of them has .egregiously overstepped the line of probability in his account. In tracts of country which (from their nature) must have been but thinly peopled in ancient times, places of public worship were but thinly scattered, and one church frequently served a very extensive district. Such, probably, was the case in the New Forest; for if these edifices ever existed in such numbers as are said to have been destroyed, some remains of them would surely have been discovered in subsequent periods, and would even now be discoverable.

" In thus vindicating the Conqueror from the extreme injustice that has been done to his memory as to the tyranny exercised in forming the New Forest, it is by no means our intention to absolve him from all reproach respecting devastations. With the evidence in Doomsday Book before us, such an attempt would be inexcusable ; and sufficient proof of his oppression and cruelties may be found in other records. In regard even to the New Forest, it is evident that many persons must have been dispossessed of their lands, ere such an extensive tract could have been wholly at his disposal; but yet this was no more than had been previously done in every part of the kingdom, and would therefore appear to be undeserving of particular reproach. On the whole, it may be fairly surmised, that William ' being passionately fond of hunting, and wishing to extend the scenes of his favourite amusement, fixed on this corner of Hampshire as a spot proper for his purpose, and accordingly converted a large proportion of it into forest ; but that the ¨afforestation was made without much injury to the subject, or offence to religion, from the scantiness of its population, and the barrenness of its surface.' That the afforestation of this district took place between the end of Edward the Confessor's reign, and the time of the compilation of the Doomsday Book, is evident from that invaluable record itself, in which will be found, in many instances, the contents of each field or estate laid into the forest in hides, carucates, or virgates, (terms then used in the admeasurement of land,) the names of the hundreds and villages, and of the former proprietors, (for the most part Saxon,) the rent, or yearly value, of each possession, and the tax paid for each to the crown during the reign of Edward the Confessor."

With regard to the situation and boundaries of this extensive forest, it occupies the south-west extremity of Hampshire; and in its earlier form was a kind of peninsula, bounded by the bay of Southampton on the east, by the river Avon on the west, and on the south; by the channel of the Isle of Wight as far as the Needles, and to the west of those rocks by the ocean. Thus the boundaries of New Forest were determined by the natural lines of the country.

It does not, however, appear that William I extended the bounds of New Forest thus far. They are supposed rather to have been enlarged by succeeding princes, particularly by Henry I, who was probably tempted by the natural limits of the country. By this prince, or at least by some of the early successors of William, the whole peninsula was taken in, and the bounds of the forest were fairly extended, as I have described them, to the bay of Southampton, the river Avon, and the sea.

In those days it was a matter of little ceremony either to make or to enlarge a forest. Thus saith the law:— " It is allowed to our sovereign lord the king, in respect of his continual care and labour for the preservation of the whole realm, among other privileges, this prerogative,— to have his places of recreation and pastime wheresoever he will appoint. For as it is at the liberty and pleasure of his grace to reserve the wild beasts and the game to himself for his only delight and pleasure, so he may also, at his will and pleasure, make a forest for them to abide in."*

Agreeable to this spirit of despotism the royal forests were regulated. Each had its laws and government; and as these differed from each other in very few particulars, all were equally grievous to the subject. Forest law, indeed, was one of the greatest encroachments that ever was made upon the natural rights of mankind; and, considering the disparity of the object, one of the greatest insults of tyranny.

The Romans had no idea of appropriating game. Under their government, the forests of England, like

* See Manwood *On Forest Law*, chap. ii.

those of America, were common hunting grounds. The northern barbarians first pretended to the right of making private property of what, being naturally wild, belonged equally to all.

The idea of forest law and forest rights obtained early, indeed, in Saxon times. But the Saxon Princes were in general a mild race, and there were some traces of liberal sentiment in their institutions. Under them, untenanted wastes only were afforested—the penalties of forest laws were gentle, and the execution of them never rigid. So that, in those equitable times, forest law was hardly esteemed a burden upon the people.

The Norman princes were a different race: they were fierce, haughty, violent, and despotic. Under them the language of English law, in general, assumed a new tone, and of forest law in particular; for, as the Norman princes were all mighty hunters, this part of jurisprudence engaged their peculiar attention. It was conceived in the highest spirit of despotism, and executed with the utmost rigour of vindictive tyranny:*

* If the reader wish to see the mischiefs of forest law, heightened by poetic images, the following lines of Mr Pope set them in a strong light:

> Thus all the land appear'd, in ages past,
> A dreary desert and a gloomy waste,
> To savage beasts and savage laws a prey,
> And kings more furious and severe than they;
> Who claim'd the skies, dispeopled air and floods,
> The lonely lords of empty wilds and woods.
> Cities laid waste, they storm'd the dens and caves,
> For wiser brutes were backward to be slaves.
> What could be free when lawless beasts obey'd,
> And even the elements a tyrant sway'd?
> In vain kind seasons swell'd the teeming grain,
> Soft showers distill'd, and suns grew warm in vain;
> The swain, with tears, his frustrate labours yields,
> And, famish'd, dies amidst his ripening fields.
> What wonder, then, a beast or subject slain,
> Were equal crimes in a despotic reign!
> Both doom'd alike, for sportive tyrants bled;
> But, while the subject starved, the beast was fed.
>   Proud Nimrod first the bloody chase began,
> A mighty hunter,—and his prey was man.
> Our haughty Norman boasts that barbarous name,
> And makes his trembling slaves the royal game.
> The fields are ravish'd from industrious swains,
> From men their cities, and from gods their fanes:

It is true, indeed, the principal object of forest law was the preservation of game, which the offender killed at his own peril.   But, when we recollect how extensive the royal forests were, including little less than an eighth part of the kingdom—when we consider the mischievous nature of every species of game, and particularly of forest deer, in cultivated lands—when we observe, farther, that many of the royal forests were blended with private property—that the limits of others were very undefined—and, lastly, when we reflect how easy a matter it was, by a stretch of royal authority, to fix the locality of a trespass in a forest, though it was never committed there,—we may easily conclude, from the whole, how fertile a source of vexation forest law might be made, though it merely respected game.

But other grievances accrued.   Many encroachments were made on private property : extravagant claims were pretended by forest officers ; and heavy tolls were levied on such merchandise as passed through the king's forests, though, in fact, it could pass in no other direction.* Sometimes also needy princes, (and most of them were needy,) with a view to raise money, would send commissioners purposely to examine into forest trespasses ; and on these occasions, we may be sure, there was always exaggeration enough.

> The levell'd towns with weeds lie cover'd o'er ;
> The hollow winds through naked temples roar ;
> Round broken columns clasping ivy twined ;
> O'er heaps of ruin stalk'd the stately hind ;
> The fox obscene to gaping tombs retires,
> And savage howlings fill the sacred quires.
>   Awed by his nobles, by his commons curst,
> The oppressor ruled tyrannic where he durst ;
> Stretch'd o'er the poor and church his iron rod,
> And served alike his vassals and his God.
> Whom even the Saxon spared, and bloody Dane,
> The wanton victims of his sport remain.
>   But see the man, whose spacious regions gave
> A waste for beasts, denied himself a grave !
> Stretch'd on the land, his second hope survey,
> At once the chaser, and at once the prey :
> Lo ! Rufus, tugging at the deadly dart,
> Bleeds in the forest, like a wounded hart.
>   *Windsor Forest.*

* See King John's Charter of Forests.

This accumulation of hardship was at all times deeply felt and resented, and whenever the reins of government slackened in the hands of a weak prince, the spirit of the nation arose, and endeavoured to resume its native rights. Success at last attended these repeated struggles. Forest law was abolished, at least its mischievous effects were repressed.

But if the people imagined this victory would reinstate them in their native rights over the forest, they were mistaken. A new species of law, under the denomination of game law, arose upon the ruins of forest law. This law had from its institution an aristocratic cast. For the barons and great men, who had wrested the rigour of forest law from the prince, did not mean to free the people from the imposition; but only to administer it themselves, and thus a thousand tyrants started up instead of one. Some of the severer penalties indeed were abolished. A man preserved his eyes or his hands, though he killed a pheasant or a partridge: but he was fined, he was imprisoned, his dog was shot, his arms were taken from him, and he was continually teased with vexatious suits. Besides, as game law was more extensive than forest law, it involved greater numbers within its influence.

At the time when forest law was abolished, all the encroachments which the crown had made on the confines of forests were given back. Then it was that New Forest was reduced within its ancient bounds; and all those lands, which bordered on the bay of Southampton, the river Avon, and the sea, were restored to their old possessors. These lands were then distinguished by the name of the Purlieus of the Forest, and their owners, at least some of them, by way of indemnification for injuries received, enjoyed several privileges, particularly the right of commoning in the forest, and of killing trespassing deer, provided they were killed before they entered the forest, which was always esteemed their sanctuary.*

The shape of New Forest is a kind of irregular triangle, wide at the south, and drawing to a point

* See Manwood *On Forest Law.*

towards the north, contained within a circumference of about fifty miles. · Its limits on every side are very accurately known and described; but, in a work of this kind, it will answer no end, either of amusement or of utility, to walk its bounds. So far indeed am I from intending to be accurate in this matter, that I propose, in the following descriptive view of New Forest, to take very great liberties with its boundaries, and to consider the forest in its ancient and most extended state, limited by the bay of Southampton on the east, by the river Avon on the west, and by the sea on the south. Without taking this liberty, I should lose the description of some of the most beautiful scenery that formerly belonged to it.

The oldest perambulation extant was made in the eighth year of Edward I. Its boundaries include all the country from Southampton river on the east to the Avon on the west; its southern limit being the sea shore between these two rivers. It extended northwards as far as North Charde-ford, or Charford, in the west; and to Wade and Orebrugge, or Owerbridge, on the east. In another peram-bulation, in the twenty-ninth of the same king, the forest is confined to the limits followed in the twenty-second of Charles II, when it was again perambulated. It was then made to extend about twenty miles, from Godshill on the north-west, to the sea on the south-east, and about fifteen miles, from Hardley on the east to Ringwood on the west; its limits containing about ninety-two thousand three hun-dred and sixty-five statute acres. The whole of that quantity, however, is not forest-land, or now the property of the crown. There are several manors and other freehold estates within the perambulation, belonging to individuals, to the amount of about twenty-four thousand seven hundred and ninety-seven acres. About six hundred and twenty-five of these are copyhold, or customary lands, belonging to his majesty's manor of Lyndhurst; about three hundred and eighty-seven leasehold, under the crown, granted for certain terms of years, and forming part of the demised land revenue under the management of the surveyor general of the crown lands. About nine hundred and one acres are *purprestures*, or encroachments on the forest. About eleven hundred and ninety three acres are enclosed lands, held by the master keepers and groom keepers, with their respective lodges. The remainder, being about sixty-three thousand eight hundred and forty-five acres, are the woods and waste lands of the forest. The interests or rights of the crown are very various, in the different kinds of property we have noticed. In the freeholds, the rights preserved by the crown are those of deer and game, now of little value to the superior; but if exercised according to the ancient forest laws, they might be very prejudicial to the owners of the lands. The copyholds are subject to small fines and quit rents; and the timber and trees are the property of the crown. The estates granted by lease are the entire property of the crown. These are Cox Leaze and Pondhead farm, which, with the woods adjoining, contain about five hundred and eighty-seven acres; for New Park, which was once similarly situated, is now in possession of the crown, and is used as a farm for furnishing hay for the deer. In these leases the timber is reserved to the crown. The encroachments, or *purprestures*, consist chiefly of cottages built by poor people, and small parcels of land adjoining. Some encroachments have, however, been made by the proprietors of the neighbouring estates. The lands held with the lodges, or the greatest part of them, which have been enclosed from time immemorial, are the entire property of the crown, not subject to right of common, or any other claim.

The forest lands, containing sixty-three thousand eight hundred and forty-five acres, are the property of the crown, subject to certain rights of common, of pasture, pannage, and fuel, belonging to the proprietors of estates within or adjacent to the forest, and defined and ascertained by the act ninth and tenth of William III, for the increase and preservation of timber in this forest. By this act the crown was empowered to enclose six thousand acres, " to remain in severalty in the actual possession of the crown for ever, freed and discharged from all manner of right, title, and pretence whatever, and to be called, made, and kept, a nursery for wood and timber only." The crown was likewise empowered, so soon as the trees in all or any part of such enclosures should be past all danger of being hurt by cattle or deer, to throw open the same, and enclose an equal quantity in any other part of the forest; thus keeping six thousand acres constantly enclosed as a nursery for timber. The crown has also a right to keep deer on the unenclosed part of the forest at all times, without limitation. By this act, also, the rights of all parties were distinctly ascertained, and no hardship or injustice was done to the neighbouring inhabitants or proprietors of estates ; for, while the bill was depending, a most attentive inquiry was made, not only into the condition of the forest generally, but into the rights as well of individuals as into those of the crown, the abuses which prevailed, and the means of remedying them ; with which view, different commissions of inquiry were issued to men of knowledge and consideration, to which full and distinct answers were returned ; and it was not until after the fullest investigation, on behalf of those who had claims on the forest, that the act was passed.

For local purposes, the New Forest is divided into nine bailiwicks, viz. Burley, Fritham, Godshill, Lynwood, Battramsley, South End, the Nodes Inn, and North.   These are subdivided into fifteen walks, viz. Burley, Holmsley, Bolderwood, Eyeworth, Ashley, Broomy, Rhinefield, Wilverley, Whitley Ridge, Lady Cross, Denny and the Nodes, Ashurst, Ironshill, Castle Malwood, and Bramble Hill.

Before I enter on the picturesque part of my work, it remains, as I have already given a short account of the ancient state of New Forest, to add a short account also of its present state, — its government, demesnes, and inhabitants.

SECTION II.

THE government of New Forest is, at this time, nearly what it originally was, excepting only that the abolition of forest law hath restrained the power of its officers.*

The chief officer belonging to it, is the lord warden, who is generally some person of great distinction.   The present lord warden is the Duke of Gloucester.   Under him are two distinct appointments of officers, the one

* I had many particulars with regard to the present state of New Forest from Mr Samber of Castle Malwood Lodge, who was intimately acquainted with it.   After his death, his son, Captain Samber of the navy, obligingly put into my hands other useful papers, on the same subject, which had belonged to his father.

to preserve the venison of the forest, and the other to preserve its vert. The former term, in the language of forest law, includes all species of game; the latter respects the woods and lawns which harbour and feed them.

The lord warden is appointed, during the king's pleasure, by letters patent under the great seal. By this patent he holds the Manor of Lyndhurst and Hundred of Redbridge, or New Forest Hundred, and the office of keeper of the decoy ponds, with the herbage, and pannage, and rents of free tenants. He has also possession of the king's house at Lyndhurst, with an allowance of £70 per annum for repairs, which has, for many years, been diverted from its object, towards a person appointed by the lord warden as housekeeper of the king's house, and called the lord warden's steward; and the repairs are done at the charge of the crown. Besides this sum of £70, the steward receives £48, and the lord warden's emoluments amount to about £214. There are also the lieutenant, the riding forester, and the bow-bearer. The first of these officers is appointed, during pleasure, by the king's letters patent. His duty is to ride before the king when he goes into the forest. His salary is £500 per annum, with a fee buck and doe yearly. The bow-bearer is appointed by the lord warden during his pleasure. His office is to attend the king with a bow and arrows whilst in the forest. His salary is forty shillings per annum, with a fee buck and doe yearly. The services of this officer, however, are rarely called for.

Of those officers who superintend the game are first the two rangers.

The rangers are appointed by the lord warden during pleasure. Their office is to drive the deer found straying in the purlieus back into the forest. The salary is £2, 13s. 4d. per annum, and £4 per annum in lieu of wood formerly allowed, and one fee buck and doe yearly to each ranger.

But the office of ranger, as well as that of bow-bearer, and a few others, have been long in disuse; at least they seem to be delegated to the keepers: of these there are fifteen, who preside over as many walks, into which the forest is divided. In each walk is erected a lodge: a few of these lodges are elegant mansions, and are the habitations of the keepers, who are generally men of

fashion or fortune.   Prince William of Gloucester has
one, the Duke of Bolton another, and Lord Delawar a
third; but in general the lodges are but moderate buildings, and are inhabited by the under keepers, or groom
keepers, as they are called; on whom the executive part
of the keeper's office devolves.

The under keeper feeds the deer in winter, browses
them in summer, knows where to find a fat buck,
executes the king's warrants for venison, presents
offences in the forest courts, and prevents the destruction of game.   In this last article his virtue is chiefly
shewn, and to this purpose the memory of every sound
keeper should be furnished with this cabalistic verse,—

> Stable stand,
> Dog draw,
> Back bear, and
> Bloody hand.*

It implies the several circumstances in which offenders
may be taken with the manner, as it is phrased.   If a
man be found armed, and stationed in some suspicious
part of the forest— or if he be found with a dog pursuing
a stricken deer— or if he be found carrying a dead deer
on his back—or lastly, if he be found bloody in the
forest, — he is, in all these cases, seizable, though the fact
of killing a deer cannot be proved upon him.   The
under keeper also drives the forest; that is, he annually
impounds all the cattle that pasture in his walk, and
sees them examined and properly marked.

The duty of the master keeper and groom keeper is to
preserve the vert and venison in their respective walks, to
prevent the destruction of either, as well as all encroachments
on the forest.   The master keepers have no salary nor perquisites, except a fee buck and doe each annually.   Those of
the under keepers, which once arose chiefly from deer, browse-
wood, rabbits, and swine, amounted to from £100 to £170
a-year; but after the Parliamentary investigation in 1789,
they were materially diminished, by the browsing having been
abolished by law; and the incomes of some of them are farther
most essentially affected by the destruction of rabbits.   The

* See Manwood *On Forest Law*, ch. xviii. 9.

master keepers seem to have considered their appointments rather as marks of distinction than as offices of responsibility or business. The protection of the enclosures, and the preservation of the young timber, therefore, depended chiefly, if not altogether, on the conduct of the groom keepers. The greatest care should have been taken to allow no perquisite to these men, that could make it for their interest to do any thing that might be prejudicial to the forest, or to lead them to counteract the great public object of increasing and preserving the wood and timber; but if a keeper had performed his duty in every particular necessary for promoting that object, he would have lost thereby a great part of his emoluments, which arose chiefly from fees for deer, profits by sales of browse-wood, and by breeding rabbits and swine.

With regard to the woods of the forest, which were originally considered only as they respected game, the first officer under the lord warden is the woodward. It is his business, as his title denotes, to inspect the woods. He prevents waste, he sees that young trees are properly fenced, and he assigns timber for the payment of forest officers. This timber is sold by auction at the court at Lyndhurst, and annually amounts to about seven hundred pounds, which is the sum required.

The woodward is an officer appointed by his majesty by letters patent during pleasure. He has £200 per annum for himself, besides the salary of the deputy; and he also receives perquisites arising from the bark of timber assigned for repairs to the tenants of Lyndhurst Manor, amounting to about £10 per annum. The office of woodward is at present wholly executed by the deputy, whose only duty has been to attend on the assigning of wood for fuel, to direct the digging of the moor-wood, or roots of trees, and to dispose of it, and to take care of windfall trees, or trees casually thrown down in the forest. Such of those trees as are fit for the navy are delivered to the purveyor to be sent to the dockyard, and navy bills for the value are issued to the high woodward. The rest are valued by the regarders, and sold by the deputy woodward, who accounts to the high woodward, who is accountable for the whole to the crown. The deputy woodward has a salary of £50, and perquisites to the amount of about £13, 12s. and an assignment of four loads of fuel-wood.

Under the woodward are twelve regarders, and to these, indeed, chiefly is delegated the executive part of his office. The regarders seize the hedge-bills and axes of trespassers, present offences in the forest courts, and assign such timber as is claimed by the inhabitants and borderers of the forest, for fuel and repairs. Of this inferior wood, there are great quantities assigned on every side of the forest. I can only speak of my own assignment as vicar of Boldre, which is annually twelve load.

The regarders are chosen by the freeholders of the county. Their business, as now executed, is to attend the marking of all trees to be felled, to value the timber for sale, and to attend the sales. They have a fee of two shillings and sixpence per day when on actual duty.

Besides these officers, who are in effect the officers of the crown, as they are appointed by the lord warden, there are four others called verdurers, who are commonly gentlemen of property and interest in the neighbourhood, and are elected, like the knights of the shire, by the freeholders of the county. These officers, since the justiciary in eyre has been a sinecure, are the only judges of the forest courts. The verdurer is an ancient forest officer. His name occurs in the earliest account of forest law. But though his appointment has at present a democratical cast, it is probable that he was formerly a royal officer, and that his election by the freeholders of the county was extorted from the crown in some period favourable to liberty. As New Forest was always considered as the great magazine of navy timber, the verdurers were empowered, by an act of Parliament in King William's time, to fine delinquents to the amount of five pounds in their attachment courts; whereas, in all the other forests of England, the fine does not amount to more than a few pence, which was the original amercement. The verdurer is an officer without salary; but by ancient custom he was entitled to course, and take what deer he pleased in his way to the forest court; but this privilege is now compounded by an annual fee of a buck and a doe.

The verdurers, who are the judges of the swanimote and attachment courts, are chosen by the freeholders of the county, by virtue of the king's writ. They have no salary, nor any consideration, nor perquisite, except a fee buck and doe yearly. The high steward is appointed by the lord warden during pleasure. He has no perquisite but an old annual fee of five guineas paid him by the warden. But his office may be considered as a sinecure. The under steward is also appointed by the lord warden. His duty is to attend at, and to enroll the proceedings of, the courts of attachment and swanimote. He also holds the court leet for Redbridge, or New Forest Hundred, and the baron courts for the manor of Lyndhurst. He has no salary; his emoluments arise from fees paid by individuals having business in the courts.

Besides these ancient officers of the forest, there is one of later institution, since timber became valuable as a material. He is called the purveyor, and is appointed by the commissioner of the dock at Portsmouth. His business is to assign timber for the use of the navy. The origin of the purveyor is not earlier than the reign of Charles II, in whose time five hundred oaks and fifty beeches were annually assigned for the king's yards, and this officer was appointed to assign them. But it being found that the forest could ill supply so large a quantity of oak, instead of five hundred, the number was afterwards reduced to sixty, which, together with fifty beeches, are still annually assigned.* The purveyor has a salary of fifty pounds a-year, and six and eightpence a-day when on duty.

The duty of the purveyor being to assign timber for the use of the navy, and to prevent any fit for naval purposes from being cut for other uses, he is paid as an officer of the dock-yard, and has no salary or emolument from the forest, except about eight loads of fuel-wood yearly, worth about £4. Besides these officers, the surveyor general of the woods appoints a deputy, whose office is to execute all warrants for felling timber, or for any other works in the forest. He has a salary of £50 per annum, and takes as perquisites the old posts, pales, and rails, left in repairing the fences; five shillings a-year from each of the regarders, and one shilling

* Mr Samber's MS.

per lot for every lot of timber wood and bark sold in the forest, which is paid by purchasers.

I shall conclude this account of the officers of the forest, with the singular character of one of them, who lived in the times of James and Charles I. It is preserved in Hutchin's *History of Dorsetshire.**

The name of this memorable sportsman — for in that character alone he was conspicuous, — was Henry Hastings. He was second son to the Earl of Huntingdon, and inherited a good estate in Dorsetshire from his mother. He was one of the keepers of New Forest, and resided in his lodge there during a part of every hunting season. But his principal residence was at Woodlands, in Dorsetshire, where he had a capital mansion. One of his nearest neighbours was the Lord Chancellor Cooper, first Earl of Shaftsbury. Two men could not be more opposite in their dispositions and pursuits. They had little communication therefore; and their occasional meetings were rendered more disagreeable to both, from their opposite sentiments in politics. Lord Shaftsbury, who was the younger man, was the survivor; and the following account of Mr Hastings, which I have some-what abridged, is said to have been the production of his pen.

Mr Hastings was low of stature, but very strong and very active, of a ruddy complexion, with flaxen hair. His clothes were always of green cloth. His house was of the old fashion, in the midst of a large park, well stocked with deer, rabbits, and fish ponds. He had a long narrow bowling green in it, and used to play with round sand-bowls. Here, too, he had a banqueting room built, like a stand, in a large tree. He kept all sorts of hounds, that ran buck, fox, hair, otter, and badger; and had hawks of all kinds, both long and short winged. His great hall was commonly strewed with marrow-bones, and full of hawk-perches, hounds, spaniels, and terriers. The upper end of it was hung with fox-skins of this and the last year's killing. Here and there a pole-cat was intermixed, and hunter's poles in great

* See vol. ii. p. 63.

abundance. The parlour was a large room, completely furnished in the same style. On a broad hearth, paved with brick, lay some of the choicest terriers, hounds, and spaniels. One or two of the great chairs had litters of cats in them, which were not to be disturbed. Of these three or four always attended him at dinner; and a little white wand lay by his trencher, to defend it, if they were too troublesome. In the windows, which were very large, lay his arrows, cross-bows, and other accoutrements. The corners of the room were filled with his best hunting and hawking poles. His oyster-table stood at the lower end of the room, which was in constant use twice a-day, all the year round; for he never failed to eat oysters both at dinner and supper, with which the neighbouring town of Pool supplied him. At the upper end of the room stood a small table with a double desk; one side of which held a Church Bible, the other, the Book of Martyrs. On different tables in the room lay hawk's hoods, bells, old hats with their crowns thrust in, full of pheasant eggs, tables, dice, cards, and store of tobacco pipes. At one end of this room was a door, which opened into a closet, where stood bottles of strong beer and wine, which never came out but in single glasses, which was the rule of the house, for he never exceeded himself, nor permitted others to exceed. Answering to this closet, was a door into an old chapel, which had been long disused for devotion; but in the pulpit, as the safest place, was always to be found a cold chine of beef, a venison pasty, a gammon of bacon, or a great apple pie, with thick crust, well baked. His table cost him not much, though it was good to eat at. His sports supplied all, but beef and mutton; except on Fridays, when he had the best of fish. He never wanted a London pudding; and he always sang it in with, " My part lies therein-a." He drank a glass or two of wine at meals, put syrup of gilly-flowers into his sack, and had always a tun-glass of small beer standing by him, which he often stirred about with rosemary. He lived to be an hundred, and never lost his eye-sight, nor used spectacles. He got on horseback without help, and rode to the death of the stag till he was past fourscore.

HAVING given an account of the government and officers of New Forest in the last section, I shall now examine the state of its demesnes* and inhabitants.

The soil of New Forest, which is in general a sandy loam, is well adapted to the production of oak timber. This tract of woody country therefore hath long been considered as one of the great magazines for the navy. It was formerly thought to be inexhaustible; but by degrees it was observed that it began to fail. So early as in Queen Elizabeth's reign, Manwood tells us, that " the slender and negligent execution of the forest law hath been the decay and destruction (in almost all places within this realm) of great wood and timber; the want whereof, as well in this present time, as in time to come, shall appear in the navy of this realm."+

In Queen Elizabeth's reign, Manwood's remark was speculation; but in the reign of Charles II, it took the air of prediction. The decay of timber, which had long been gradually coming on, began then to be felt. Its

---

* In the year 1788, a survey of New Forest was taken, by order of the commissioners of the land-revenue of the Crown; in which survey the following account was given in of its contents.

	Acres.
Forest lands	63845
Lands held with lodges	1192
Encroachments	900
Leaseholds under the Crown	1003
Freeholds, and other intermediate property	25422
Total within the perambulation	92362

A few fractions, which make about two or three acres more, I have omitted. From this survey a splendid map of New Forest has been engraved, (by order of the commissioners,) by William Faden, geographer to the King, in which the curious may see the boundaries and contents of New Forest, with all the lands granted by the crown, the leaseholds, and encroachments, very accurately ascertained.

+ See Manwood *On Forest Law*, chap. ii. 6.

sources failed as the demand increased. In most commodities the demands of a market immediately produce a supply; but timber requires ages to make it marketable. It may be added, that the navy magazines had not then those resources which they have since found. Timber was with difficulty brought from the inland parts of the country, on account of the badness of the roads — little foreign timber was imported — and what rendered the evil more conspicuous in Charles's time, the nation was on the eve of a naval war. Such pressing necessity urged strongly the propriety of making provision for a future supply. Charles, who had a sort of turn for ship building, and had on that account, a kind of affection for the navy, was easily induced to issue an order, under his sign manual, to Sir John Norton, woodward of New Forest, to enclose three hundred acres of waste, as a nursery for young oak,* the expense of which was to be defrayed by the sale of decayed wood. This order bears date, December 13, 1669.

But though the enclosure here specified was trifling in itself, yet it had the merit of a new project, and led to farther improvements. A few years afterwards the same idea was taken up, on a more enlarged scale. In the 10th of King William, an act passed, empowering certain commisioners to enclose two thousand acres in New Forest for the growth of timber, and two hundred more every year, for the space of twenty years afterwards.

This provident act was as well executed as it had been projected. A very considerable part of the quantity prescribed, at least four thousand acres, were enclosed and planted,† and the timber of these enclosures is now secure from all danger, and is thrown out again into the forest. None of it hath yet been felled, as it is not yet in a state of perfection; but it is in a very flourishing condition, and is at this day the glory of the forest.

---

* Mr Samber's MS.

† In Burley walk, above six hundred acres were enclosed—in Rhinefield walk, the same number—in Boldre Wood walk, above four hundred —in Egworth walk, one thousand—in Bramble Hill walk, above seven hundred—in Dinney walk, above five hundred—in Castle Malwood walk, a quantity not ascertained. Mr Samber's MS.

In the reigns of Queen Anne and George I, I believe no new plantations were made, which is the more to be wondered at, as the severe hurricane in the November of the year 1703 did great injury in New Forest. Not fewer than four thousand of its best oaks were destroyed,* together with great quantities of growing timber.

In the reign of George II, three enclosures were made; but they were injudiciously, or dishonestly managed; and Mr Coleman, who undertook the business, was fined in the forest court at Lyndhurst, by the verdurers, for his neglect.† Some attempts have been made in the present reign; but for want of being properly planned, or honestly managed, very little advantage hath accrued.‡

The great defect indeed here, as in other national matters, is the want of honesty. Public affairs become private jobs. Large enclosures have been made merely to enrich the undertakers, by the profits of enclosing, or the plunder of the underwood. It is said, that although the flourishing plantations made by King William are at this time receiving injury from growing too close, they are rather suffered to grow as they are, than to run the hazard of being dishonestly thinned. For it has sometimes been found, that in thinning trees, the best, instead of the worst, have been removed; nor can any thing prevent such mischief, but the care and honesty of forest officers, and the persons they employ.

What a general rapacity reigns in forests, may be conceived from the devastation which even inferior officers have been able to commit. Not many years ago, two men of the name of Batten, father and son, succeeded each other in the office of under-keeper, in one of the forest walks. The under-keeper is supposed to cut holm, and other underwood of little value, to browse his deer; and when the rind and spray are eaten off, he

* See Evelyn's *Sylva.*
† Mr Samber's MS.
‡ In the year 1782, an inquiry was instituted, by an order from the treasury, into the quantities of navy timber in New Forest,—that is, such timber as would measure thirty-five cubic feet. The quantity given in, after a very nice survey, was fifty-two thousand load. Forty cubic feet make a load. At the same time, the timber in Dean Forest was surveyed; which, though of much smaller dimensions than New Forest, contained sixty-two thousand load.

faggots the dry sticks for his own use. But these fellows cut down the young timber of the forest, without distinction, and without measure, which they made up into faggots and sold; and for this paltry gain, I have been informed, they committed waste in the forest, estimated at fifty thousand pounds damage. The calculation seems large; but we may well imagine, that in the unremitted course of sixty or seventy years, great mischief might be done. For though a young sapling may not intrinsically be worth more than half-a-crown; yet the great difficulty of getting another thriving plant to occupy its room in the forest, raises its consequence to the public much beyond its mere specific value.

The commissioners, in their reports in 1789, observe, that the mode adopted for paying by perquisites, &c. those who have the care of this valuable forest, was such as no one would follow in the management of his own property; and they state the effects of it upon the forest to have been as follows:—1. That it was so much overstocked with deer, that many died yearly of want in the winter; and that not less that three hundred died in one walk in the winter of 1787. 2. That great waste and destruction was made of the hollies and thorns which afforded the best nursery and protection for young trees; and much more wood, and of a larger size than was necessary or proper for browsing, was cut by the keepers under that pretence to increase their own profits. 3. That the breed of rabbits was encouraged by several of the keepers, but particularly in the two walks of Wilverley and Rhinefield, where three enclosures, made for the growth of timber, had been converted into warrens by the under-keepers, insomuch that in two of them, containing about six hundred and eleven acres, there was not one young tree; and in the third, containing two hundred and twenty-four acres, only a very small number. 4. That some of the keepers dealt largely in swine, which were suffered to remain in the forest at all seasons. 5. That the fences of the enclosures made for nurseries of timber, were neglected; and for want of repairing slight defects when they happened, often required large and expensive repairs; but were in general in such bad condition as to keep out neither deer, horses, cattle, nor swine. 6. That the lodges were repaired often, and at a great charge, but never substantially, or in a workman-like manner. 7. That the salutary provisions of the act of the ninth and tenth of William III were almost wholly disregarded in many other respects.

The more early surveys, viz. those of 1608, 1707, 1764, not only shew the quantity of timber in the forest at the times they were taken, but furnish us with the strongest proofs how very opposite were the effects produced by that attention which was formerly bestowed on the management of the royal forests, as contrasted with the neglect which took place in after periods, and which arose from a variety of causes. At the period of the first of these surveys, the landed property of the crown was the chief fund at the disposal of government; great attention was therefore given to it; and though the forest laws were sufficiently bad in themselves, yet they served at least to protect the forests from plunder and destruction. During the contest between Charles I and his Parliament, the trees in almost every one of the royal forests were much destroyed by the different parties, so that, after the Restoration, the New Forest was found greatly denuded of trees, the fences of its coppices broken down, and the young shoots destroyed by the deer and cattle, which were everywhere admitted. To remedy these evils, the act of 9th and 10th William III was obtained, and if the powers which it vested in the crown had been duly exercised, thirty thousand acres of land, formerly bare, might now have been covered with noble trees, in addition to the former woodlands of the forest. But the act was speedily allowed to go into disuse, and it was not till the act passed in the 1800, that any real benefit was done to the forest. This act entirely put a stop to the pernicious practice of browsing, or feeding the deer with young branches, under colour of which great abuses were committed, and it also settled all disputed boundaries, and accurately ascertained the limits of the forest. The forest courts are now regularly held by the verdurers who preside in them, and who are vested with new and extended authorities, under the act for preventing waste, as well as encroachments, and the destruction of the rabbits which overran the forest was provided for. Fixed salaries have been adopted instead of perquisites, and the surveyor general has a fixed office established for him, for the preservation of all books and papers, and proceedings. Other measures have also been taken from time to time, for the renovation of the woodlands, so that it is to be hoped that the New Forest bids fair, through improving management, to become a great and important resource for national defence, by furnishing abundant supplies of timber for the British dockyards.

But the decay of forests is not owing solely either to the legal consumer or the rapacious trespasser. The oak of the forest will sometimes naturally fail. Mr Evelyn remarks,* that every forest in which oak and beech grow pomiscuously, will in a course of ages become entirely beechen. If this be a just remark, the oak, we are to suppose, has not so strong a vegetative power as the beech, which, in time, prevails over the whole. Whatever truth there may be in the observation, certain it is, that this appearance of decay is found in many of the woodlands of New Forest, which consist chiefly of beech and unthriving oak.

Besides these sources of mischief, the woods of the forest are subject to another,— that of fire. In sultry weather, its furzy heaths are very combustible, and the neighbouring cottagers are supposed sometimes to set them purposely on fire to make pasturage more plentiful. The danger arises from the difficulty of stopping these fires, which will sometimes continue burning more or less, at the mercy of the wind, during several days. In the early part of the summer, 1785, which was remarkably dry, many of these fires were lighted, particularly one near Fritham, which did great damage.

From these, and other causes, many parts of this extensive forest are now in a state of extreme decay; being overspread merely with holms, underwood, and stunted trees, which, in the memory of man, were full of excellent oak.†

In planting oak, it hath been a doubt, whether it is more judicious to sow the acorn, after enclosing and grubbing the ground — or to sow it, without either operation, in the wild parts of the forest, in the midst of thorn bushes and hollies, which will defend the sapling from cattle, till it be able to stand alone, and will draw it in its early state to much quicker maturity, than it can arrive at without such shelter. The latter way of sowing acorns, in the wild parts of the forest, is not so sure, but much larger quantities may be sown at a much less expense ; and if one tenth part of the acorns succeed, the

* See his *Sylva*.　　　　　　　† Mr Samber's MS.

saving is great on an equal quantity of timber. I cannot, however, help doubting the efficacy of this mode of raising timber, though I have often heard sensible people, who have lived in the neighbourhood of the forest, speak favourably of it, and it is certain that timber is often raised fortuitously in this manner. We see, in the wild parts of the forest, trees which have attained the growth of ten, twenty, or thirty years, as far as we can judge, without any aid; and we are at a loss to know, how Nature manages a work of this kind, and rears this exposed part of her offspring amidst deer and cattle. And yet we see the same kind Providence in a higher part of the creation. We see the children of the cottage exposed to mischief on every side, and continually running risks, which delicate mothers would tremble at: yet, befriended by a Gracious Protector, they get forward in life, and attain maturity, like the wildings of the forest, in a manner which they who speculate only on human means cannot easily conceive.

In planting the forest, some again have been advocates for uniting the two modes I have specified. The ground is enclosed but not grubbed, and the acorns sown at random. The late Duke of Bedford, when he was lord warden, was very intent on raising timber in this fortuitous manner. He merely enclosed, and left it to chance to fill his enclosures; but I do not find that any of them have succeeded. If the ground were enclosed, and a spot here and there grubbed, in which two or three acorns were sown, and some little care taken afterwards of the infant wood, it might be of all others, perhaps, the most certain and the least expensive way of raising timber.

Mr Sang recommends a method of sowing acorns, in cases where the ground cannot be prepared by regularly ploughing, harrowing, manuring, and cropping. This is by digging pits at the distance of six feet from each other, from centre to centre, or more, according to the fancy of the planter. The pits must be eight or ten inches deep, if the soil will admit of their being made so, and they must be fifteen inches diameter at the least. Each should be filled successively with the earth dug from the next one, the sward having been first thinly pared off, chopped in pieces, and put into the bottom.

All this should, if possible, be done during the month of May of the preceding year, or rather, as we conceive, a whole year of seasons should intervene between the time the pits are made, and the sowing of the acorns, and if a spadeful of short well rotted manure can be mixed up with the soil of each pit, we conceive it would be of very great advantage. The best time, we think, for planting the acorns in the pits, is the season when they naturally drop from the trees. But this will only apply in cases where mice are not numerous, for where these animals abound, we would recommend that the acorns should be put into the ground in the spring, so as to be left exposed to their attacks for as short a time as possible. Mr Sang advises planting seedling larches, or Scottish firs, exactly in the centre, between each four pits, by way of sheltering the seedling oaks. And in very bleak situations, he recommends that this should be done, one, two, three, or even more years before the acorns are planted. After the young oaks have appeared, great attention will be requisite to prevent their being choked by weeds or grass at first, or afterwards by the more rapid growth of those trees intended as nurses.

But the woods of the forest have not alone been the objects of devastation,—its lands also have suffered. After the forest had lost its great legal support, and reasons of state obliged the monarch to seek his amusements nearer home, the extent of these royal demesnes began insensibly to diminish. New Forest, among others, was greatly curtailed. Large portions of it were given away in grants by the crown. Many gentlemen have houses in its interior parts, and their tenants are in possession of well cultivated farms ; for though the soil of New Forest is in general poor, yet there are some parts of it which very happily admit culture. Thus the forest has suffered in many places, what its ancient laws considered as the greatest of all mischiefs, under the name of an assart; * a word which signifies grubbing up its coverts and copses, and turning the harbours of deer into arable land. A stop, however, is now put to all grants from the crown. The crown lands became public property, under the care of the treasury, when the civil list was settled. The king can only grant leases

* See Manwood, chap. ix. sec. 1.

for thirty years; and the parliament seldom interferes in a longer extension, except on particular occasions.

Besides these defalcations arising from the bounty of the crown, the forest is continually preyed on by the encroachments of inferior people. There are multitudes of trespassers on every side of it, who build their little huts, and enclose their little gardens and patches of ground, without leave or ceremony of any kind. The under keepers, who have constant orders to destroy all these enclosures, now and then assert the rights of the forest by throwing down a fence; but it requires a legal process to throw down a house, of which possession has been taken. The trespasser therefore here, as on other wastes, is careful to rear his cottage, and get into it as quickly as possible. I have known all the materials of one of these habitations brought together—the house built—covered in—the goods removed—a fire kindled —and the family in possession, during the course of a moonlight night. Sometimes indeed, where the trespass is inconsiderable, the possessor has been allowed to pay a fine for his land in the court of Lyndhurst. But these trespasses are generally in the outskirts of the forest, or in the neighbourhood of some little hamlet. They are never suffered in the interior parts, where no lands are alienated from the crown, except in regular grants.

We have been informed that instances have occurred of small wooden houses having been secretly constructed in Southampton, and then actually transported upon wheels during the night to some spot in the New Forest, where they were set down, occupied, and afterwards added to by degrees, the ground around them being taken in from time to time as opportunity offered; nay, we have even been assured that some of the most splendid residences in the forest have had no other origin.

The many advantages which the borderers on forests enjoy, such as rearing cattle and hogs, obtaining fuel at an easy rate, and procuring little patches of land for the trouble of enclosing it, would add much, one should imagine, to the comfort of their lives. But in fact it is otherwise. These advantages procure them not half the enjoyments of common day labourers. In general, they are an indolent race, poor and wretched in the extreme. Instead of having the regular returns of a week's labour to subsist on, too many of them depend on the precarious supply of forest pilfer. Their ostensible business is commonly to cut furze, and carry it to the neighbouring brick kilns; for which purpose they keep a team of two or three forest horses; while their collateral support is deer stealing, poaching, or purloining timber. In this last occupation they are said to have been so expert, that in a night's time, they would have cut down, carried off, and lodged safely in the hands of some receiver, one of the largest oaks of the forest. But the depredations which have been made in timber, along all the skirts of the forest, have rendered this species of theft, at present, but an unprofitable employment. In poaching and deer stealing, they often find their best account; in all the arts of which many of them are well practised. From their earliest youth they learn to set the trap and the gin for hares and pheasants; to ensnare deer by hanging hooks, baited with apples, from the boughs of trees; and (as they become bolder proficients) to watch the herd with fire-arms, and single out a fat buck, as he passes the place of their concealment.

In wild rugged countries, the mountaineer forms a very different character from the forester: he leads a life of labour—he procures nothing without it—he has neither time for idleness and dishonest arts, nor meets with any thing to allure him into them. But the forester, who has the temptation of plunder on every side, finds it easier to trespass than to work. Hence the one becomes often a rough, manly, ingenuous peasant; the other a supple, crafty, pilfering knave. Even the very practice of following a night occupation leads to mischief. The nightly wanderer, unless his mind be engaged in some necessary business, will find many temptations to take the advantage of the incautious security of those who are asleep. From these considerations Mr St John draws an argument for the sale of forest lands. " Poverty," says he, " will be changed into affluence—the cottager will become a farmer—the wilderness will be converted into rich pastures and fertile fields, furnishing provisions for the country and employment for the poor. The borders and confines of forests will cease to be nurseries for county jails, the trespasser will no longer prey upon the vert, nor the vagabond and outlaw on the venison. Nay, the very soil itself will not then be gradually lost and stolen by purprestures and assarts. Thus forests, which were formerly the haunts of robbers, and the scenes of violence and rapine, may be converted into the receptacles of honest industry." *

I had once some occasional intercourse with a forest borderer, who had formerly been a noted deer stealer. He had often, like the deer stealer in the play,

—— struck a doe,
And borne her cleanly by the keeper's nose.

Indeed, he had been at the head of his profession, and during a reign of five years, assured me he had killed, on an average, not fewer than an hundred bucks a-year. At length he was obliged to abscond; but composing his affairs, he abjured his trade, and would speak of his former arts without reserve. He has oftener than once confessed the sins of his youth to me; from which an idea may be formed of the mystery of deer stealing, in its highest mode of perfection. In his excursions in the forest he carried with him a gun, which screwed into three parts, and which he could easily conceal in the lining of his coat. Thus armed, he would drink with the under keepers without suspicion; and when he knew them engaged, would securely take his stand in some distant part, and mark his buck. When he had killed him, he would draw him aside into the bushes, and spend the remaining part of the day in a neighbouring tree, that he might be sure no spies were in the way. At night he secreted his plunder. He had boarded off a part of his cottage, (forming a rough door into it, like the rest of the partition, struck full of false nail heads,) with such artifice, that the keepers, on an information, have searched his house again and again, and have gone off satisfied of his innocence; though his secret larder perhaps at that very time contained a brace

* See *Observations on the Land Revenue of the Crown*, page 168.

of bucks. He had always, he said, a quick market for his venison; for the country is as ready to purchase it, as these fellows are to procure it. It is a forest adage of ancient date, " Non est inquirendum unde venit venison.—No inquiry must be made how venison is procured."

Nothing can be more appropriate to the present subject, or more powerfully illustrate the evil effects produced by those temptations to idleness and poaching, with which the life of a New Forest settler is beset, than the following, which, though inconsiderable in length, does yet exhibit, in a very remarkable degree, all that strength and truth of drawing for which the genius of its great author, Sir Walter Scott, was so remarkable. The scene is in the New Forest. It was originally published as an anonymous imitation of Crabbe, and in this respect, too, it is eminently successful:—

THE POACHER.

Welcome, grave stranger, to our green retreats,
Where health with exercise and freedom meets !
Thrice welcome, Sage, whose philosophic plan,
By Nature's limits, metes the rights of man ;
Generous as he who now for freedom bawls,
Now gives full value for true Indian shawls ;
O'er court, o'er customhouse, his shoe who flings,
Now bilks excisemen, and now bullies kings ;
Like his, I ween, thy comprehensive mind
Holds laws as mouse-traps baited for mankind ;
Thine eye, applausive, each sly vermin sees,
That baulks the snare, yet battens on the cheese ;
Thine ear has heard, with scorn instead of awe,
Our buckskinn'd justices expound the law,
Wire-draw the acts that fix for wires the pain,
And for the netted partridge noose the swain ;
And thy vindictive arm would fain have broke
The last light fetter of the feudal yoke,
To give the denizens of wood and wild,
Nature's free race, to each her free-born child.
Hence hast thou mark'd, with grief, fair London's race
Mock'd with the boon of one poor Easter chase,
And long'd to send them forth as free as when
Pour'd o'er Chantilly the Parisian train,
When musket, pistol, blunderbuss, combined,
And scarce the field-pieces were left behind !
A squadron's charge each leveret's heart dismay'd,
On every covey fired a bold brigade :
La Douce Humanité approved the sport,
For great the alarm indeed, yet small the hurt ;

Shouts patriotic solemnized the day,
And Seine re-echoed *Vive la Liberté!*
But mad *Citoyen*, meek *Monsieur* again,
With some few added links resumes his chain;
Then since such scenes to France no more are known,
Come, view with me a hero of thine own!
One, whose free actions vindicate the cause
Of sylvan liberty o'er feudal laws.

    Seek we yon glades, where the proud oak o'ertops
Wide-waving seas of birch and hazel copse,
Leaving between deserted isles of land,
Where stunted heath is patch'd with ruddy sand;
And lonely on the waste the yew is seen,
Or straggling hollies spread a brighter green.
Here, little worn, and winding dark and steep,
Our scarce mark'd path descends yon dingle deep:
Follow — but heedful, cautious of a trip, —
In earthly mire philosophy may slip.
Step slow and wary o'er that swampy stream,
Till, guided by the charcoal's smothering steam,
We reach the frail, yet barricadoed door
Of hovel, form'd for poorest of the poor:
No hearth the fire, no vent the smoke receives,
The walls are wattles, and the covering leaves;
For, if such hut, our forest statutes say,
Rise in the progress of one night and day,
(Though placed where still the Conqueror's hests o'erawe,
And his son's stirrup shines the badge of law,)
The builder claims the unenviable boon,
To tenant dwelling, framed as slight and soon
As wigwam wild, that shrouds the native frore
On the bleak coast of frost-barr'd Labrador.

    Approach, and through th' unlatticed window peep —
Nay, shrink not back, the inmate is asleep;
Sunk 'mid yon sordid blankets, till the sun
Stoop to the west, the plunderer's toils are done.
Loaded, and primed, and prompt for desperate hand,
Rifle and fowling-piece beside him stand,
While round the hut are in disorder laid
The tools and booty of his lawless trade;
For force or fraud, resistance or escape,
The crow, the saw, the bludgeon, and the crape.
His pilfer'd powder in yon nook he hoards,
And the filch'd lead the church's roof affords —
(Hence shall the rector's congregation fret,
That while his sermon's dry, his walls are wet.)
The fish-spear barb'd, the sweeping net, are there,
Doe-hides, and pheasant plumes, and skins of hare,
Cordage for toils, and wiring for the snare.
Barter'd for game from chase or warren won,
Yon cask holds *moonlight*,* run when moon was none;
And late-snatch'd spoils lie stored in hutch apart.
To wait the associate higgler's evening cart.

* A cant term for smuggled spirits.

Look on his pallet foul, and mark his rest :
What scenes perturb'd are acting in his breast !
His sable brow is wet and wrung with pain,
And his dilated nostril toils in vain ;
For short and scant the breath each effort draws,
And 'twixt each effort Nature claims a pause.
Beyond the loose and sable neckcloth stretch'd,
His sinewy throat seems by convulsion twitch'd,
While the tongue falters, as to utterance loath,
Sounds of dire import, — watchword, threat, and oath.
Though, stupified by toil and drugg'd with gin,
The body sleeps, the restless guest within
Now plies on wood and wold his lawless trade,
Now in the fangs of justice wakes dismay'd.
  " Was that wild start of terror and despair,
Those bursting eyeballs, and that wilder'd air,
Signs of compunction for a murder'd hare ?
Do the locks bristle and the eyebrows arch,
For grouse or partridge massacred in March ?"
  No, scoffer, no ! Attend, and mark with awe,
There is no wicket in the gate of law !
He that would e'er so lightly set ajar
That awful portal, must undo each bar ;
Tempting occasion, habit, passion, pride,
Will join to storm the breach, and force the barrier wide.
  That ruffian, whom true men avoid and dread,
Whom bruisers, poachers, smugglers, call Black Ned,
Was Edward Mansel once — the lightest heart
That ever play'd on holiday his part !
The leader he in every Christmas game,
The harvest feast grew blither when he came,
And liveliest on the chords the bow did glance,
When Edward named the tune and led the dance.
Kind was his heart, his passions quick and strong,
Hearty his laugh, and jovial was his song ;
And if he loved a gun, his father swore,
" 'Twas but a trick of youth would soon be o'er ;
Himself had done the same some thirty years before."
  But he whose humours spurn law's awful yoke,
Must herd with those by whom law's bonds are broke.
The common dread of justice soon allies
The clown, who robs the warren or excise,
With sterner felons train'd to act more dread,
Even with the wretch by whom his fellow bled.
Then, as in plagues the foul contagions pass,
Leavening and festering the corrupted mass,
Guilt leagues with guilt, while mutual motives draw,
Their hope impunity, their fear the law ;
Their foes, their friends, their rendezvous the same,
Till the revenue baulk'd, or pilfer'd game,
Flesh the young culprit, and example leads
To darker villainy and direr deeds.
  Wild howl'd the wind the forest glades along,
And oft the owl renew'd her dismal song ;
5

Around the spot where erst he felt the wound,
Red William's spectre walk'd his midnight round.
When o'er the swamp he cast his blighting look,
From the green marshes of the stagnant brook
The bittern's sullen shout the sedges shook!
The wading moon with storm-presaging gleam,
Now gave, and now withheld her doubtful beam;
The old oak stoop'd his arms, then flung them high,
Bellowing and groaning to the troubled sky:—
'Twas then that, couch'd amid the brushwood sere,
In Malwood Walk young Mansel watch'd the deer;
The fattest buck received his deadly shot—
The watchful keeper heard, and sought the spot.
Stout were their hearts, and stubborn was their strife,
O'erpower'd at length the outlaw drew his knife:
Next morn a corpse was found upon the fell—
The rest his waking agony may tell!

The encroachments of trespassers, and the houses and fences thus raised on the borders of the forest, though, at this time, in a degree connived at, were heretofore considered as great nuisances by the old forest law, and were severely punished under the name of purprestures,* as tending "ad terrorem ferarum — ad nocumentum forestæ"— and, as might be added, at this time, by the neighbouring parishes, " ad incrementum pauperum."† When a stranger, therefore, rears one of these sudden fabrics, the parish officers make him provide a certificate from his own parish, or they remove him. But the mischief commonly arises from a parishioner's raising his cottage, and afterwards selling it to a stranger, which may give him parish rights. These encroachments, however, are evils of so long standing, that at this day they hardly admit a remedy. Many of these little tenements have been so long occupied, and have passed through so many hands, that the occupiers are now in secure possession.

Where the manor of Beaulieu Abbey is railed from the forest, a large settlement of this kind runs, in scattered cottages, at least a mile along the rails. This nest of encroachers the late Duke of Bedford, when lord warden of the forest, resolved to root out. But he met with such sturdy and determined opposition from the foresters of

* See Manwood, chap. x. sec. 1.
† As tending to destroy the harbour of beasts — to injure the forest — and to increase the poor.

the hamlet, who amounted to more than two hundred men, that he was obliged to desist* — whether he took improper measures, as he was a man of violent temper — or whether no measures which he could have taken, would have been effectual in repressing so inveterate an evil. And yet in some circumstances, these little tenements (encroachments as they are, and often the nurseries of idleness) give pleasure to a benevolent breast. When we see them, as we sometimes do, the habitations of innocence and industry; and the means of providing for a large family with ease and comfort, we are pleased at the idea of so much utility and happiness arising from a petty trespass on a waste, which cannot in itself be considered as an injury.

I once found, in a tenement of this kind, an ancient widow, whose little story pleased me. Her solitary dwelling stood sweetly in a dell, on the edge of the forest. Her husband had himself reared it, and led her to it as the habitation of her life. He had made a garden in the front, planted an orchard at one end, and a few trees at the other, which in forty years had now shielded the cottage, and almost concealed it. In her early youth she had been left a widow, with two sons and a daughter, whose slender education (only what she herself could give them) was almost her whole employment, and the time of their youth, she said, was the pleasantest time of her life. As they grew up, and the cares of the world subsided, a settled piety took possession of her mind, Her age was oppressed with infirmity, sickness, and various afflictions in her family. In these distresses, her Bible was her great comfort. I visited her frequently in her last illness, and found her very intelligent in Scripture, and well versed in all the Gospel topics of consolation. For many years she every day read a portion of her Bible, seldom any other book:

> Just knew, and knew no more, her Bible true ;
> And in that charter read, with sparkling eyes,
> Her title to a treasure in the skies.

When she met with passages she did not understand, at one time or other, she said, she often heard them

---

* Mr Samber's MS

explained at church. The story seems to evince how very sufficient plain Scripture is, unassisted with other helps, except such as are publicly provided, to administer both the knowledge and the comforts of religion even to the lowest classes of people.

The dialect of Hampshire has a particular tendency to the corruption of pronouns, by confounding their cases. This corruption prevails through the country; but it seems to increase as we approach the sea. About the neighbourhood of New Forest, this Doric hath attained its perfection. I have oftener than once met with the following tender elegiac in churchyards:

> Him shall never come again to we:
> But us shall surely, one day, go to he.

Having thus given a short account of the present state of New Forest, and its inhabitants, I hasten to the more agreeable part of my work,—the description of its scenery. I have already apprised the reader,* that I propose to consider its boundaries in their widest extent, as advancing to the bay of Southampton on the east, to the river Avon on the west, and to the sea on the south. Within equal limits perhaps few parts of England afford a greater variety of beautiful landscape. Its woody scenes, its extended lawns, and vast sweeps of wild country, unlimited by artificial boundaries, together with its river views and distant coasts, are all in a great degree magnificent. It must still, however, be remembered, that its chief characteristic, and what it rests on for distinction, is not sublimity, but sylvan beauty.

But before I enter on a particular description of the scenery of New Forest, in a picturesque light, it may not be improper to give the reader a kind of table of contents of what he is to expect.

SECTION IV.

On looking into a map of New Forest, and drawing an imaginary line from Ringwood on the Avon, to Dibden on the bay of Southampton, the whole forest

* See ante, p. 98.

NEW
FOREST

Romsey

Redbridge
Millbrooke

Fritham
Cadnam
Fling

Poulto

Bramble Hill Lodge
Wounds-down
Tibden
Deer trap

Hythe

tton Abbey

Castle Malwood
Rufus's Monument
Minstead
Mount-royal

Lyndhurst

Hill top
Cuddland

Beaulieu
am Abbey

Boldrewood Lodge
Cuffnells
Foxlees

Denny lodge
Cadnerly

Newpark

Bucklers

Pinkneyspout

Witley ridge lodge
Lodghouse Lodge
Hundsby Pilton

Fighting Cocks

hlemore Point

Ringwood

Burley lodge

Abre Church

St

Burley

Rymfield Lodge

Ober Green
Brokenhurst
Setley Wood
Begdon

Brokenley Lodge
Hincheley Lodge
Longslade bottom

Wilverley Lodge
Hungwood House
Buttramsley
Pennington
Common
R.
Ls

ington R.

Eldern

Sopley

Christchurch
Chewton
Lt Pages
Milton
Priestlands

ur

Shingles

Yarmouth
water

easily divides itself into four parts. That district which lies north of this imaginary line, we may call one part; the river Avon and Lymington river make the boundaries of a second; Lymington river and Beaulieu river of a third; and the country between this last river and the bay of Southampton may be considered as a fourth.

When I spoke of forests in general, as consisting of large tracts of heathy land and carpet lawns, interspersed with woods,* I had a particular view to the scenery of New Forest, which is precisely of this kind. Its lawns and woods are everywhere divided by large districts of heath. Many of these woods have formerly been, as many of the heaths at present are, of vast extent, running several miles without interruption. Different parts, too, both of the open and of the woody country, are so high as to command extensive distances, though no part can, in any degree, assume the title of mountainous.

Along the banks of the Avon, from Ringwood to the sea, the whole surface is flat, enclosed, and cultivated. There is little beauty in this part. Eastward from Christ Church, along the coast, as far as to the estuary of Lymington river, we have also a continued flat. Much heathy ground is interspersed, but no woody scenery, except in some narrow glen, through which a rivulet happens to find its way to the sea. In two or three of these there is some beauty. Here the coast, which is exposed to the ocean, and formed by the violence of storms, is edged by a broken cliff, from which are presented grand sea views, sometimes embellished with winding shores. As we leave the coast, and ascend more into the midland parts of this division, the scenery improves: the ground is more varied, woods and lawns are interspersed, and many of them are among the most beautiful exhibitions of this kind which the forest presents.

In the next division, which is contained between the rivers of Lymington and Beaulieu, we have also great variety of beautiful country. The coast, indeed, is flat, and unedged with cliff, as it lies opposite to the Isle of

* See Vol. I. p. 312.

Wight, which defends it from the violence of the ocean; but the views it presents are sometimes interesting. It is wooded, in many parts, almost to the water's edge; and the island appearing like a distant range of mountains, gives the channel the form of a grand lake. As we leave the sea, the ground rises, and the woods take more possession of it, especially along the banks of the two rivers I have just mentioned, which afford on each side, for a considerable space, many beautiful scenes. There are heathy grounds in this district also; but they occupy chiefly the middle parts between these two tracts of woodland.

In that division of New Forest which is confined by Beaulieu river and the bay of Southampton, the midland parts are heathy, as in the last; but the banks and vicinity, both of the river and the bay, are woody, and full of beautiful scenery. This division is, perhaps, on the whole, the most interesting of the forest. For besides its woods, there is greater variety of ground than in any other part. Here also are grander water views than are exhibited any where else. The views along the banks of Beaulieu river, it has in common with the last division; but those over the bay of Southampton are wholly its own. One disagreeable circumstance attends all the sea views which are opposite to the Isle of Wight, and that is, the ooziness of the beach when the sea retires. A pebbly or a sandy shore has as good an effect often when the sea ebbs as when it is full,— sometimes, perhaps, a better; but an oozy one has an unpleasant hue. However, this shore is one of the best of the kind, for the ooze here is generally covered with green sea-weed, which, as the tide retires, gives it the appearance of level land, deserted by the sea, and turned into meadow. But these lands are meadows only in surface, for they have no pastoral accompaniments.

Nothing, truly, can be more exquisite than the scenery of this division of the New Forest. It is now many years since we first visited it; but we have still a fresh recollection of the delights of that day, when, having left Yarmouth in the Isle of Wight early in the morning, we were landed somewhere near the mouth of the Lymington river, whence, without a guide or companion of any kind, we set out to find our way instinctively, as it were, through the labyrinths of the forest towards Beaulieu and the Southampton river. Limbs which had been trained upon the Scottish mountains gave but little consideration to the fatigue occasioned by those continued deviations from the direct line which fancy prompted, or ignorance of the localities betrayed us into; our route, therefore, was of the most careless description, and we gave ourselves entirely up to the luxurious enjoyment of these solitudes amongst which we wandered. Sometimes we seated ourselves under the shade of a wide spreading oak to listen in vain for sounds indicating life, and pondering on the huge stems which everywhere upreared themselves around us, and on the many and the mighty events which had followed one another in succession since they had first developed themselves from the tiny acorns whence they had sprung; and whilst thus indolently disposed, some of the leather-coated citizens of these wilds, full of the pasture, would sweep past us, scarcely deigning to throw a look of inquiry towards us. Again we would arise to wander whither fancy led us, striving to penetrate amid the mysteries of the forest, and becoming more and more perplexed at every step by the depth of its shades; and anon, an increase of light before us would gradually disclose an embayed portion of the sea, surrounded by magnificent oaks in all their splendour of head, and animated by the cheering operations of shipbuilding. In short, the variety and beauty of these forest scenes were so fascinating, that we forgot time, space, and position, and were nearly paying the forfeit of our pleasure by spending the night beneath the shelter of some of the tangled thickets of these sylvan wildernesses.

The northern division of New Forest contains all those parts which lie north of Ringwood and Dibden. As this district is at a distance from the sea, and not intersected by any river which deserves more than the name of a brook, it is adorned by no water views, except near Dibden, where the forest is bounded by the extremity of the bay of Southampton. The want of water, however, is recompensed by grand woody scenes, in which this part of the forest equals, if not exceeds, any other part. In noble distances, also, it excels; for here the ground swells higher than in the more maritime parts; and the distances which these heights command, consist often of vast extensive forest scenes.

Besides the heaths, lawns, and woods, of which the forest is composed, there is another kind of surface found in many parts, which comes under none of these denominations, and that is the bog. Many parts of the forest abound in springs; and as these lands have ever been in a state of Nature, and, of course, undrained, the moisture drains itself into the low grounds, where, as usual in other rude countries, it becomes soft and spongy, and generates bogs. These, in some places, are very extensive. In the road between Brokenhurst and Ringwood, at a place called Longslade Bottom, one of these bogs extends three miles without interruption, and is the common drain of all those parts of the forest. In landscape, indeed, the bog is of little prejudice. It has, in general, the appearance of common verdure. But the traveller must be on his guard. These tracts of deceitful ground are often dangerous to such as leave the beaten roads, and traverse the paths of the forest. A horse track is not always the clue of security; it is, perhaps, only beaten by the little forest horse, which will venture into a bog in quest of better herbage; and his lightness secures him in a place where a larger horse, under the weight of a rider, would flounder. If the traveller, therefore, meet with a horse path pointing into a swamp, even though he should observe it to emerge on the other side, he had better relinquish it. The only track he can prudently follow, is that of wheels.

Having thus presented the reader with a general view of New Forest, I shall now endeavour to give him a more intimate acquaintance with it, and shall lead him into some of its most beautiful scenes. Nor was the beauty of the forest a matter of no concern, even at a time when we might have supposed the pleasures of the chase engrossed men's whole attention. " There are three special causes," says Manwood, " why the forest laws have so carefully provided for the preservation of the vert of the forest. The first is for the sake of cover for the deer; the second for the sake of the acorns, mast, &c. which feed them; the third is, *propter decorem,* for the comeliness and beauty of the same in a forest. For the very sight and beholding of the goodly green and pleasant woods in a forest, is no less pleasant and delightful in the eye of a prince, than the view of the wild beasts of chase ; and, therefore, the grace of a forest is, to be decked and trimmed up with store of pleasant green coverts."* One should scarce have expected such a passage as this in a law book. On such authority, however, I hope I may consider the scenery of the forest as essential to the very existence of it, and shall proceed with more confidence in the description of those goodly green and pleasant woods, the sight and beholding whereof is so comely and delightful.

In this detail, I shall rarely go in quest of views into the intricacies and recesses of the forest. These sweet retreats would often furnish a great variety of pleasing scenes ; but it would be difficult to ascertain and point them out to the observation of others. I shall satisfy myself, therefore, with following the great roads, or, at least, such as are commonly known, where views may easily be ascertained ; reserving only the liberty of stepping a little aside when any thing of peculiar excellence deserves attention. I should in this detail also pursue my route through the forest, with a careful eye to the arbitrary division I have made of it into four parts ;† but as the roads will not always admit such exactness, I must be content to follow the route prescribed by the surveyors of the highways, keeping within the division I have prescribed as nearly as I can.

The whole of the roads through the New Forest are delightful, and the rides and drives they yield are all sufficiently charming in themselves. But if one would

> Find tongues in trees, books in the running brooks,
> Sermons in stones, and good in every thing,

one must abjure the common every day path, and dive into the depths of the forest. We well remember having visited a very hospitable and kind friend of ours, who had a sweet cottage in the neighbourhood of Lyndhurst. He was a keen sportsman ; and common civility compelled us to restrain the

* Manwood, chap. vi.   † See ante, page 124.

ardent wishes we felt to rush into the woods, in search of
Nature, till we had first gratified him by a minute survey
of his hunters, and by listening to the panegyric he pronounced upon each of them in succession ; and, truth to
tell, this our forbearance required no little effort on our
part, for we had read Gilpin, our imagination had been
excited, we had eagerly panted for an opportunity of indulging
ourselves in gazing upon those sylvan scenes in which our
fancy had long delighted to revel ; and now we were, for
the first time, on the eve of being gratified.   Our impa-
tience was great ; and we had no sooner gone through
the stud, than we delicately hinted our wishes to our friend.
" The forest ! " said he, with an air of some surprise, mingled,
as we thought, with a spice of pity, " why, you 'll see
nothing in the forest but trees.   But, never mind, I 'll
soon shew you the forest.   Here, Bill ; get out the *tandem !* "
In a very few minutes the *tandem* was at the door, and
a very nice carriage it was, though, like the cattle which
drew it, the whole equipage, harness and all, was of New
Forest origin.   The body was very neatly made of basket
work, and the harness was chiefly constructed of hempen
girths, and the New Forest ponies were beautiful, spirited,
blood-looking animals ; and, what was not the least merit
of all, the whole was set a-going for little more than
£30.   We took our seats ; and our friend, who was a first-
rate whip, started, in what would be called *good style ;* and
the ponies kept up a pace of twelve or fourteen miles an
hour, with great ease to themselves, and no inconsiderable
rapture to us ; for if we are so far disposed to agree with
Dr Johnson, that there are few pleasures equal to that of
being rapidly whirled along in a post chaise, how much
more delightful was the motion of such a winged vehicle as
that which we rode in ? and so rapidly did these rich
woodland scenes fly past us, that our senses became bewil-
dered, and we felt as if buoyed up by intoxicating draughts
of the well known nitrous oxide, or *Paradisaical gas.*   But
when we were fairly landed at home, and had begun to
compose our limbs and our thoughts on a sofa, we discovered
that our minds were left in the same state of void, and
confusion, and inanity, that is so apt to follow all sudden
and unnatural excitations.   But it is in such states of the
mind that good resolutions are most likely to be formed ;
and accordingly we determined that nothing should prevent us from next day following out our own inclinations.

Accordingly, we had no sooner risen from the breakfast table than, afraid that our friend might catch and detain us, we stole forth unseen, and with all the eagerness of a bird escaping from a cage, or a boy from school, we flew into the woods, and halted not till we had buried ourselves in their innermost recesses ; and there, forgetful of all but Nature, we wandered about, hand in hand with her, from one wild and silent retreat to another, till our minds were filled with the exquisite woodland pictures on which it had luxuriated. It was well for us that our footsteps accidentally led us to one of those picturesque cottages which are to be found in the forest. The sight of it brought man and his affairs back to our recollection ; and " drawing our dial from our poke," we discovered that we had already spent nearly an entire summer's day ; and reflecting for a moment on the scurvy retreat we had made from our kind host, we quickly obtained a guide from the cottage, and hastened to join him under his own roof. But the gleanings of that day's ramble formed an enduring treasure in our minds, from which we have drawn materials for the happy and rational enjoyment of many a contemplative hour.

SECTION V.

REMARKS ON THE WESTERN PARTS OF NEW FOREST, FROM VICAR'S HILL TO RINGWOOD ; AND FROM THENCE, THROUGH CHRIST CHURCH, TO LYMINGTON.

FROM Vicar's Hill, we passed Boldrebridge.

Boldre is an ancient village, being recorded in Doomsday Book (as we are told by the *Beauties of England and Wales*) by the name of Booreford. It stands two or three miles to the north of Lymington, and on the eastern bank of the river. The church was in existence in the beginning of the twelfth century, and it still displays some interesting specimens of its original architecture, though parts of it have been altered at subsequent periods. The north side appears to have been added about the time of King John ; on one of the windows are the arms of Lewis, the Dauphin of France, who had been invited ˙from England during that troublesome reign ; of William de Vernun, grandson to Richard de Redvers the elder; and of some of the other barons that favoured the cause of Lewis, who so ingloriously quitted the kingdom for which he had contended, that history is silent as to the place of his embarkation. The church is finely situated on an eminence to the north of the village, and, as noticed in different parts of this work, commands a variety of pleasing views. Here our author, the Reverend William Gilpin, the celebrated and very exemplary vicar of this parish, was buried. In the year 1791, he founded two schools here for the instruction of twenty boys, and an equal number of girls. These schools are judiciously regulated. The parsonage house at Vicar's Hill overlooks a wide extent of beautiful scenery.

Ascending the opposite bank, called Rope Hill, to Battramsly, we had a beautiful view of the estuary of Lymington river, which, when filled with the tide, forms a grand sweep in the sea. It is seen to most advantage from the top of the hill, a few yards out of the road on the right. The valley through which the river flows, is broad; its screens are not lofty, but well varied and woody. The curves of the river are marked by long projections of low land, and on one or two of them some little saltern, or other building, is erected, which breaks the lines. The distance is formed by the sea and the Isle of Wight. Altogether the view is picturesque. It is what the painter properly calls a whole : there is a foreground, a middle ground, and distance, all harmoniously united. We have the same view, only varied by position, from many high grounds in the neighbourhood; but I know not that it appears at such advantage any where as from this hill. At Battramsly we join the London road.

From hence to Brokenhurst, the forest exhibits little more than a wild heath, skirted here and there with distant wood.

Brokenhurst is a pleasant forest village, lying in a bottom, adorned with lawns, groves, and rivulets, and surrounded on the higher grounds by vast woods. From the churchyard an expanded view opens over the whole. On the left rise the woods of Hinchelsea, and adjoining to these, the woods of Rhinville. The centre is occupied by the high grounds of Boldre Wood. The little speck just seen among them, is a summer house, built by Lord Delawar to command a forest view. The house among the woods on the right is Cuffnel's, the seat of Mr Rose ; and still more to the right, are the woods of Lyndhurst.

Brokenhurst is a village of Saxon origin, and is recorded in the Doomsday Book by the name of Broceste ; notice is also taken of its church, which is still standing, though somewhat disguised by subsequent alterations. The arch over the southern doorway is ornamented with the zigzag moulding. The descent into the church is by several steps, and it is surrounded by an artificial mound of earth four or five feet high. The font is a very antique and curious piece of workmanship, evidently formed when the custom of total immersion was prevalent. In the *Beauties of England*, notice is taken of a very fine yew tree in the churchyard here, which is more than sixty feet high, and measures fifteen feet in girth ; also an old and venerable oak, " measuring upwards of eight yards in diameter ;" but this must surely be a mistake, and it is probable that, for *diameter*, we ought to read *circumference ;* for Mr Gilpin could not have passed by unnoticed, a tree which would have rivalled the great Cowthorpe Oak. We are informed, that in the twelfth century a carucate of land in Brokenhurst was held by an ancestor of Sir Henry Spelman, by the service " of finding an esquire, with a hambergell, or coat of mail, to give attendance for forty days in England ; and of finding litter for the king's bed, and hay for the king's palfrey, when the king should be at Brokenhurst."

At the entrance of Brokenhurst, a little to the right, Mr Morant's house commands a very grand and picturesque forest view. Both the foreground and the distance are complete.

The former is an elevated park scene, consisting of great variety of ground, well planted, and descending gently into the plain below. Among the trees which adorn it, are a few of the oldest and most venerable oaks of the forest. I doubt not but they chronicle on their furrowed trunks ages before the Conquest.

From this grand foreground is presented an extensive

forest view. It consists of a wide range of flat pasturage, (one of the spreading lawns of the forest, *) garnished with tufted clumps and woody promontories shooting into it; and contrasted by immense woods, which occupy all the rising grounds above it, and circle the horizon. The contrast between the open and woody parts of the distance, and the grandeur of each part, are in the highest style of picturesque beauty.

This grand view is displayed to most advantage from the front of the house; but it is seen also very advantageously through other openings among the trees of the foreground.

Watcombe House, in Brokenhurst Park, was for three years the residence of the philanthropic Howard, whose memory is still cherished by the poor inhabitants of the neighbourhood. To the south-west of Brokenhurst, there is a heath called Sway Common, over which various tumuli, or barrows, are scattered. Mr Warner supposes them to have been constructed about the time when the Britons, Natonleod, or Ambrosius, and the Saxons under Cerdic, were contending for empire. This conjecture is strengthened by the appearance of a rude earthen work on the Lymington river, which is still called Ambrose Hole, as well as by the historical evidence of several battles having been fought by Ambrosius in this country. Several of the barrows are situated within the area of an intrenchment on the brow of a hill, a few hundred yards to the south-east of a wood called Setley Wood. Mr Warner informs us, that " two of these probably cover the remains of chieftains, since considerable labour and care have evidently been exerted in their formation. They have each a regular fosse and vallum ; the mound, or tumulus, is composed of a part of the earth taken from the fosse ; another portion of it forms the surrounding vallum. It is evident that these barrows were raised at the same time, since [they are connected together, and have only a single vallum at the point of their junction. I paced the fosse of each, and found the larger to measure one hundred and ten yards ; the smaller, ninety-five yards. A short distance to the south of these there is another barrow, of a similar construction, and standing entirely alone. This, and one of the two connected with each other, I opened in company with the Rev. W. Jackson, vicar of Christ

* See Vol. I. p. 312.

Church. Large quantities of burnt earth, and parcels of wood, reduced by fire to charcoal, were found in each ; but, after searching with great attention, removing all the factitious earth, and digging to a considerable depth below the surface of the natural land, we were convinced, that simply burning the body, and covering its ashes with mould, had been the mode observed in these instances of inhumation. These tumuli, then, I refer to the Saxons; and I think it will be allowed I have authority for so doing, when it is considered that the German tribes seldom, if ever, used urn burial." Mr Warner ascribes the other barrows, lying half a mile to the southward, to the Britons. He opened two of them about four feet high, and fifteen feet in diameter ; and he found similar appearances. They were both formed of a white gravel, mixed with loose sand ; underneath four feet of this, a quantity of black earth was found, which had evidently undergone the action of fire, and among it were large parcels of wood ashes. After digging into the natural surface below these, a cell, or excavation, was perceived, about two feet square, formed for the reception of an urn. In one of the barrows the urn was in a perfect state ; but it was broken by the carelessness of a workman before it could be taken out. It was composed of unbaked clay ; its form was very clumsy, and its workmanship rude. Within it were ashes, and fragments of human bones, in a calcined state, mixed with an earth of the texture and consistence of peat. The urn in the second barrow, which was situated in a more moist spot, had been resolved into its original clay.

As you leave the village of Brokenhurst, the woods receive you in a noble rising vista, in which form the road is cut through the forest. This vista is exceedingly grand. A winding road through a wood has undoubtedly more beauty than a vista, and in a smaller scene we always wish to find it, and even reprobate the vista wherever it occurs. But through a vast forest the vista is in better taste ; though I do not in the least apprehend we are under obligations on this score to the surveyor of the highways. He took the direct road, which happened on this occasion to be the line of beauty. On other occasions under the same principle, he has missed it ; but here it suits the greatness of the scene, and shews the depth of the forest and the vastness of the woods to more advantage. Regular forms are certainly unpicturesque, but from their simplicity they are often allied to greatness. So essential is simplicity to greatness, that we often see instances in which the stillness of symmetry hath added to grandeur, if not produced it; while, on the other hand, we as often see a sublime effect injured by the meretricious charms of picturesque forms and arrangements.

We are not, however, to conceive of the forest vista, as we do of the tame vistas formed by the hand of art. As it is cut through a tract of woody country, there is first, of course, no formality in the disposition of the trees. In the artificial vista, the trees are all of one age, and planted in regular growth. The whole plan is the offspring of formality; and the more formal it is, the nearer it approaches that idea of perfection at which it aims. But in the forest vista the trees are casually large or small, growing in clumps, or standing single, crowding upon the foreground, or receding from it, as the wild hand of Nature hath scattered them. And it is curious to see with what richness of invention, if I may so speak, Nature mixes and intermixes her trees, and shapes them into such a wonderful variety of groups and beautiful forms. Art may admire, and attempt to plant and form combinations and clumps like hers; but who-ever examines the wild combinations of a forest, (which is a delightful study to a picturesque eye,) and compares them with the attempts of art, has little taste if he do not acknowledge, with astonishment, the superiority of Nature's workmanship.

The artificial vista again is rarely composed of more than one species, — it is the fir, the lime, or the elm. But in the forest vista, you have not only different kinds of trees intermixed, but bushes also, and underwood, and wild plants of all kinds, which are continually producing new varieties in every part.

Open groves, too, make another variety in the forest vista. In the woods between Brokenhurst and Lynd-hurst, an open grove is continued on the right, with little interruption, between the seventh and eighth stones. The woods on the left are chiefly close.

Besides, these grand vistas are not only varied with such smaller openings and recesses as are formed by the irregular growth of trees ; they are broken also by lawns and tracts of pasturage, which often shoot athwart them. One of this kind, and a very beautiful one, occurs at the sixth stone ; and another, though of inferior size and beauty, at the seventh.

Added to this intermixture of lawn and wood, the rising and falling of the ground, in various parts of this vista, produce another species of variety. The elevation is nowhere considerable, but it is sufficient to occasion breaks in the convergency of the great perspective lines. It creates also new beauties in the scenery, particularly in some parts on the left, where you look down from the road, among trees retiring and sinking from the eye, till the stems of the most distant are lost in the deep shadows of the descending recesses.

All these circumstances, though the last is more general, give the forest vista a very different air from the artificial one, diversifying the parts of which it is composed so much, that the eye is never fatigued with surveying them ; while the whole together presents one vast sublime object. Like a grand gallery of exquisite pictures, it fills the eye with all its greatness, while the objects on each side, continually changing, afford at every step a new entertainment.

A late traveller through Russia, does not see these beauties in a forest vista. " The country," says he, " through which we passed, was ill calculated to alleviate our sufferings by transferring our attention from ourselves to the objects around us. The road ran as straight as an arrow, through a perpetual forest : through the dreary extent of a hundred and ten miles, the gloomy uniformity was only broken by a few solitary villages."* No doubt the continuation of a hundred and ten miles in any one mode of scenery, may be rather fatiguing ; but I should have thought that few modes of scenery were better calculated to transfer the attention fron a disagreeable

---

* I beg the reader's pardon for not quoting my author. I certainly met with the passage, but not noting the reference at the time, and not opening my MS. for some time afterwards, it has now escaped me.

subject. I know not indeed what the nature of a vista through a Russian forest may be ; but if it partake of the circumstances that I have just been describing in this vista through New Forest, it must consist of varieties which could not easily be exhausted.

We suspect that the Russian vista consisted of a road cut through a thick pine forest, where the tall, upright, branchless stems of the firs could afford neither diversity in the parts, nor in the whole. Nothing could be more dull and monotonous than this! 'It must be even worse than the " continual dropping," mentioned in Scripture.

The account I have here given of the forest vista is the sober result of frequent examination. A transcript of the first feelings would have been rhapsody, which no description should indulge. The describer imagines that his own feelings of a natural scene can be' conveyed by warm expressions. Whereas nothing but the scene itself can convey his feelings. Loose ideas (not truth, but verisimilitude) is all that verbal description pretends to convey ; and this is not to be done by high colouring ; but to be aimed at by plain, appropriate, intelligible terms.

I should add, before I leave this pleasing vista, that to see it in perfection, a strong sunshine is necessary. Even a meridian sun, which has a better effect on the woods of the forest than on any other species of land-scape,* is not, perhaps, too strong for such a scene as this. It will rarely happen, but that one side or the other of the vista will be in shadow, and this circumstance alone will produce contrasts, which will be highly agreeable. I may add, also, that this vista appears to much greater advantage, as we rise through it to Lyndhurst, than as we descend to Brokenhurst.

As we passed this vista, we saw, in many parts through the trees, on the left, the pales of New Park, just removed from the road. This park, which is the only one in the whole district of New Forest, is about four miles in circumference. It was first used to secure stray cattle forfeited to the lord warden : but in the year 1670,

* See Vol. I. page 329.

it was strongly fenced by Charles II, for the reception of a particular breed of red deer which he procured from France.*   It is now converted into a farm, having been granted in the last reign to the Duke of Bedford, for the term of thirty years.

In all the grand scenery of the forest, which we have just examined, we see little appearance of fine timber. Most of the best trees have been felled.   The landscape, however, is not much injured.   On a foreground, indeed, when we have a single tree, we wish it to be of the noblest kind; and it must be confessed, that, in our passage through this vista, which in every part as we pass along becomes a foreground, there is a great deficiency of noble trees.   Many of the oaks are scathed and ragged, and though in composition trees of this kind have frequently their effect,† yet in a rich forest scene, if they present themselves too often, offend.   For all the other purposes of scenery, inferior trees, if they be full grown, answer tolerably well; and when intermixed with stunted trees and brushwood, as they are in all the wild parts of the forest, they are more beautiful than if the whole scene was composed of trees of the stateliest order.   Interstices are better filled, and a more uniform whole is produced.   Considered in this light, a forest is a picture of the world.   We find trees of all ages, kinds, and degrees,—the old and the young—the rich and the poor — the stately and the depressed — the healthy and the infirm.   The order of Nature is thus preserved in the world, and the beauty of Nature is thus preserved in the forest.

A gentleman once consulted his friend, who pretended to a degree of taste, about the propriety of cutting down some trees, which shaded a winding avenue to his back-front, where his offices were placed.   His friend advised

---

* The expense of this work stands thus in the treasury books:

Fencing New Park and Holm Coppice . . .		£ 100
Winter provision for red deer		50
Pens to feed them		20
Paddocks to catch them, and turn them out . .		20
		£ 190

† See Vol. I. page 49.

him by all means to leave them untouched. "They are beautiful," said he, "in themselves; and, you see, they skreen that part of your house which you would wish to have skreened." The gentleman seemed convinced, and the next time he met his friend, "I have taken your advice," said he, "and have left the trees standing." And so, indeed, he had; but all the stunted wood and under growth, which he considered as offensive rubbish, he had rooted up, overlooking their use in composition. The consequence was, he laid all the offensive part of his house open, let in the light, and entirely destroyed the scene.

In the first book, I mentioned the different effects of soil and climate on trees.* In New Forest these observations are well illustrated. The oaks there seem to have a character peculiar to themselves. They are the most picturesque trees of the kind we meet with. They seldom rise into lofty stems, as oaks usually do in richer soils : but their branches, which are more adapted to what the ship-builders call knees and elbows,† are commonly twisted into the most picturesque forms. In general, I believe, the poorer the soil, the more picturesque the tree — that is, it forms a more beautiful ramification.

Besides, the New Forest oak is not so much loaded with foliage as the trees of richer soils. An overloaded foliage destroys all form. On the other hand, when the leaf is too thinly scattered, the tree looks blighted, shrivelled, and meagre. The point of picturesque perfection is, when the tree has foliage enough to form a mass, and yet not so much as to hide the branches. One of the great ornaments of a tree, is its ramification, which ought to appear here and there, under the foliage, even when it is in full leaf. It is the want of this species of ramification which gives a heaviness to the beech.‡

The great avenue from Brokenhurst leads through the space of five or six miles. After we have mounted the summit of the hill, the close views in the descent on the other side are very beautiful, consisting of little

* See Vol. I. page 64.   † See *ibid*.
‡ See Vol. I. page 98.

woody recesses, open groves, or open glades, varied as they were before in different forms.

As we approach Lyndhurst, we pass Foxlees on the left. The situation here is just the reverse of Mr Morant's: the one stands high, and commands the forest at a distance; the other, in a bottom, is surrounded by it. Both modes of situation have their beauty; but an extensive forest view before the house, with a few noble trees on the foreground, is not only, at all times, a better picture, but it is also more agreeably varied by the occasional incidents of light and weather, of which the other is not capable.

In a part of the skreen which divides these grounds from the road, we have an opportunity of remarking the disagreeable effect of trees planted alternately. The eye is disgusted with looking first on a fir, secondly on an elm; thirdly on a fir; fourthly on an elm again; and so on. And yet this tiresome monotony, under the name of variety, is one of the commonest modes of planting. In planting, we should certainly endeavour at least to plant like Nature, which gives us the best criterion of beauty. This alternacy is a direct and studied opposition to all her pleasing forms of composition. It not only shews the hand of art, but of the most tasteless art. How much more beautiful would such a skreen appear, made up of different kinds of trees in masses of each, or in an indiscriminate mixture of all together!

The town of Lyndhurst makes a picturesque appearance as we approach it; but instead of entering it, we left it on the right, and turned abruptly into the road to Minsted. The ground here is much varied. It is hilly, broken, and wooded in clumps, with cottages here and there interspersed. Nothing in the pastoral style can be more picturesque. We have also extensive views through the woods, particularly a grand retrospect towards Southampton. But as we approach Minsted, the woods fail: all becomes cultivation, and the idea of a forest is in a great degree lost. Soon after, we enter the western road to Ringwood, over a spacious heath.

At the eighty-second stone, about a quarter of a mile down the hill on the right from the road, we are shewn the scene of the celebrated event of Rufus's death. When I mentioned the tree on which the arrow of Tyrrel glanced,* I offered some reasons for supposing it might be admitted as evidence in identifying the place. The scene also in some degree bears the same testimony. For history informs us, the diversion of the day was now over, the sun was declining, and William, dismounting his horse, was enjoying a moment's rest after the fatigue of the chase,† when a stag darted suddenly across the heath. The king, turning towards it, and lifting his hand to skreen his eyes from the sun,‡ at that moment received the arrow. The scene is a sweet sequestered bottom, open to the west, where the corner of a heath sinks gently into it; but sheltered on the east by a beechen grove, and on every other side by clumps of trees forming an irregular skreen around it, among which are several winding avenues of greensward. It is the very place where a person, heated with toil, might be allured to stop for a moment's repose. But the chief circumstance of evidence is, that as the place is open only to the west, where the heath was never probably covered with wood, the king could there only have been incommoded by an evening sun.

"It must be observed," says the author of the article Hampshire, "that the real circumstances attending the death of Rufus are involved in some obscurity, as several of our early historians say not a word of any tree being accessory to his fall. Eadmer says only that he was shot through the heart. Symeon Dunelmensis and Hoveden say, by an arrow incautiously directed, *Sagitta incaute directa.* Matthew Paris, whose account is followed by Speed, is the first who affirms that the king's heart was pierced by an arrow obliquely glancing from a tree: *Exiit ergo telum, et obstante arbore in obliquum reflexum faciens medium cordis regem sauciavit.* Alanus de Insulis is quoted by Baxter, to prove that Tyrrel was engaged by Anselm, the Pope's legate, to shoot Rufus, and the deed itself is extolled as *pulcherrimum facinus* by Alanus, who, in the reign of Henry I, was promoted to the divinity chair of Paris."

---

* See Vol. I. p. 244.
† See William of Malmsbury, and Henry of Huntingdon.
‡ See an account which Rapin gives in a note, from Sir John Haywood.

Having taken a view of this scene, which in itself, unconnected with the history it records, is a pleasing one, we ascended again into the great road, and pursued the heath over which it led. It is a wild expanse, unadorned with wood, but bounded on every side by very extensive distances. In front you discover the high grounds of the Isle of Purbeck. On the left, you have a large range over the Isle of Wight. In the retrospect you overlook the bay and town of Southampton; and on the right is spread before you a vast stretch of distant country, bounded by the hills of Wiltshire and Dorsetshire. This last is the only part of these distances which hath any picturesque value. About the eighty-sixth stone, the parts of it are best disposed; but it is the richest about the eighty-ninth, where it is seen over a woody bottom, which makes a middle ground.

In this part of the forest, the paling of one of the new enclosures to secure timber, which ran a considerable way in a straight line, deformed our views. Sometimes indeed the paling of parks and forests is picturesque, where it runs winding round a hill, and appears again perhaps in some opposite direction; but in general, it is an unpleasing object, and what in adorned scenery we should wish to hide. Indeed all divisions of property are great nuisances to the picturesque eye, which loves to range at large, and it adds peculiar beauty to the forest, that in general the grand lines of Nature, and various swelling of the ground, are unbroken by these intrusions, and have their full play and undulation. In remote distances, hedge rows, pales, and other objects, offensive on the spot, became one rich blended surface. And yet, even on the spot, winding lanes, with full grown hedges on each side, are often beautiful. It is clipping, and making, as they phrase it, which ruin the picturesque idea. Utility is always counteracting beauty. No sooner is the hedge in perfection than it is destroyed.*

* If the reader wish to know an ancient mode of making hedges, he will find it as follows, in the fifth book of Q. Curtius. "Having planted twigs very close in the situation they wished, they bent their branches, as they made shoots, and inserted their extremities into the earth. Here they took root, and from these roots shot into new branches.

The approach to Ringwood, as we leave the wild heath, which gave occasion to this digression, is woody and pleasant. Ringwood was formerly the boundary of the forest in this part, and in times of still more remote antiquity, was a place of great note. I know not whether in Saxon times it did not claim the honours of regal residence. At present, it is a cheerful village, seated in a flat country, on the banks of the Avon, which spreads near the town into a large piece of water, full of little islands, and frequented by swans.

The Doomsday Book speaks of Ringwood as a place of more importance and greater value than Thuinam or Christ Church. It now contains about seven hundred houses, and about three thousand three hundred inhabitants, who are chiefly employed in the manufacture of woollen cloths and stockings, and in brewing ale and strong beer, for which the town has acquired a considerable name.

Somewhere near this part of the river the Duke of Monmouth is said to have been taken, on the 8th of July, 1685, after his defeat at Sedgmore, near Bridgwater. Thus far he had travelled in disguise, and generally by night, feeding on pulse and green corn, which he found growing in the fields. But I think the account more probable, that he was taken near Woodlands, in Dorsetshire.* It was thought, however, that he intended to have secured himself in the woods of New Forest, with which he was well acquainted from having frequently hunted in them. I have heard a tradition, that his body, after his execution, was sent down into the forest, and buried privately in Boldre churchyard; but I cannot find any ground for the surmise. The register of the year is yet extant, in which no notice is taken of any such burial; unless he were buried, as might possibly have been the case, under a fictitious name.

Fox is silent as to the precise spot where Monmouth was taken. He says, that he first directed his course towards the

---

These again were bent into the earth, and so on, till a fence was obtained of the dimensions wanted." I have seen this mode, I believe, practised in some parts of England.

* See Hutching's *History of Dorset*, p. 60, and 499.

Bristol Channel, and, at the suggestion of his faithful and honest adviser, Dr Oliver, he had thoughts of embarking for the coast of Wales, to conceal himself for some time in that principality. "Lord Grey, who appears to have been in all instances his evil genius, dissuaded him from this plan, and the small party having separated, took each several ways. Monmouth, Grey, and a gentleman of Brandenburg, went southward, with a view to gain the New Forest in Hampshire, where, by means of Grey's connections in that district, and thorough knowledge of the country, it was hoped they might be in safety till a vessel should be procured to transport them to the continent. They left their horses, and disguised themselves as peasants; but the pursuit, stimulated as well by party zeal, as by the great pecuniary rewards offered for the capture of Monmouth and Grey, was too vigilant to be eluded. Grey was taken on the 7th of July, 1685, in the evening; and the German, who shared the same fate early in the next morning, confessed that he had parted from Monmouth but a few hours since. The neighbouring country was immediately and thoroughly searched, and James had, ere night, the satisfaction of learning that his nephew was in his power. The unfortunate Duke was discovered in a ditch, half concealed by fern and nettles." Such is the sum of the account given by Fox.

From Ringwood to Christ Church, the country is flat, and the lanes close and woody. Scarce any distant view is admitted, except here and there among the meadows on the right. On the left, Mr Compton's park at Bistern affords some variety, running a considerable way along the road, and grazed with herds of large speckled cattle without horns.

As we leave the village of Sopley, the meadows on the right form a better landscape than we had yet had. The parts are large, though flat, and the whole is bounded with wood, in which the town of Christ Church appears as a principal object. The church to which it belongs was formerly monastic. It is a grand pile, partly Saxon and partly Gothic. Some of its Gothic members are beautiful, particularly a small chapel, near the altar, dedicated to the Virgin Mary, which for proportion and beauty of workmanship, is a very elegant piece of Gothic architecture.   The church is now parochial.

The town of Christ Church, which takes its name from the church, is a place of great antiquity.   Here we find the ruins of a castle, which was intended formerly to secure the mouth of the Avon.   This river is joined by the Stour below the town, where, uniting in a full stream, they wind together through a bleak coast, forming it first into large flat meadows, and then opening into a bay before they enter the sea.   The view, which is not very interesting, is bounded by a ridge of high lands called Christ Church Head, on the right; and, on the left, by the western end of the Isle of Wight, which in this part makes a remarkable appearance.   It is seen nearly in front; and its broken cliffs, when the noontide sun in winter shines strongly upon it, appear like the ends of two fractured walls, with a dark cavity between them.

Christ Church Bay is spacious, but so shallow and dangerous as not to be frequented by vessels drawing more than five feet and a half water.   There is a curious circumstance peculiar to this harbour, and the neighbouring port of Poole in Dorsetshire, — that of the tide producing two high waters, a phenomenon quite inexplicable from the general laws of tides, and only to be accounted for by the situation of this coast as regards the Isle of Wight, and from the contraction of the channel by the jutting out of the point of land on which Hurst Castle stands.   The tide flows into this channel from the west; and though it sets in with uncommon violence at Hurst Castle, it does not meet the tide that sets round the island till it has reached Spithead; and the passage being too narrow for all the water to pass through, the time of high water at Christ Church Head, or, as it is otherwise called, Hengistbury Head, is of course much earlier than either at Portsmouth or Chichester; at the full and change of the moon, the difference is three hours and a half.   When the water begins to ebb, by flowing off from the west, the contraction in the channel operates in a contrary direction; and by confining the water which has been spread over the Southampton estuary, and of the channel within the Isle of Wight, it gives the water in Christ Church Bay an opportunity of flowing off much quicker, by which means it becomes so low, that the water that now pours through with great velocity at Hurst Castle, is sufficient to produce a second rise at Christ Church and Poole harbours, of nearly three feet. Hengistbury Head is generally called Christ Church Head by seamen, from the church of that place appearing in connection with it when seen from the sea. It is a bold headland, forming the western termination of Christ Church Bay. About a mile from the extremity of the point, the cliff dips for a considerable distance, and the estuary of the Stour and the Avon is there only separated from the sea by a thin neck of land, and at the place where it is narrowest, an ancient fosse and double rampart, about six hundred and thirty yards in length, are drawn across it. The outer rampart has been formed by the earth thrown up from the ditch, and the innermost, which is the most considerable, is about eight yards in perpendicular height from the bottom of the fosse. It has three entrances, the most northern of which is flanked by two irregular mounds; between this and the middle entrance the works are the most perfect, the southern extremity having been partly obliterated by the drifting sand hills which are heaped up on this coast. Near the southern termination, there is a large barrow, in which an urn and human bones were found. It seems most probable that these works were of Saxon origin, seeing that the name of the promontory is derived from Saxon appellations. Gough describes another ancient fortification on the ridge, called St Catherine's Hill, about one mile and a half north of Christ Church, and a mile west from the Avon. This seems to have been an exploratory camp, fifty-five yards square, double trenched on every side, except the south, with three entrances. At about twenty yards from the east end of the north side, a small rampart runs south, and at length unites with the south front ; the east side seems to have continued sixty yards north, till it is crossed by another line. Six small mounts are scattered round this camp, and not far from the foot of the hill are two large barrows, one of which was found to contain some human bones. About three hundred yards north of the last mentioned line, there is an eliptical earth work, measuring thirty-five yards by twenty-five. Other remains of intrenchments may be traced in this vicinity.

The origin of Christ Church, Twyneham, or Twynam-bourne, or, as it was called in Saxon times, Tweon-ea, or "the place between the two rivers," is very ancient, and, if not of British origin, it was probably first established by the Romans.

A singular discovery was made by the late Gustavus Brander, of a cavity existing within the foundations of the priory. It was about two feet square, and was covered with a stone carefully cemented with lead into the adjoining pavement, and it contained about half a bushel of the bones of herons, bitterns, cocks, and hens. Mr Warner says, that there is no difficulty in accounting for this phenomenon, " if we advert to the superstition of the ancient Romans, and to the practices of the early Christians. Among the former, many species of birds were held in high veneration, and carefully preserved for the purposes of sacrifice and augural divination. Adopting the numerous absurdities of Egyptian and Grecian worship, those tolerating conquerors had affixed a sacredness to the cock, the hawk, the heron, the chicken, and other birds, the bones of which, after their decease, were not unfrequently deposited within the walls of the temple of the deity to whom they were considered as peculiarly appropriated. It seems, then, probable, that the spot on which the priory of Christ Church was erected, had originally been occupied by some heathen temple." This, we know, was a common practice. Many, if not the greater proportion, of the churches in Rome thus originated, and we find that, in numerous instances, even the heathen names were retained; a singular proof of which we ourselves possess, in a bull granted by Pope Alexander III to the abbey of Kinloss, dated in 1174, attached to which, among other signatures, we have that of " Hugo, Cardinal, *Sancti Sergii et Bacchi!* " But, indeed, it was natural for those who undertook the conversion of the heathens, to fix on such spots for their new places of worship as had been hallowed, in the opinion of the converts, by ancient consecration; and therefore we find that they did so all over Europe.

The priory of Christ Church was founded, early in the Saxon era, for a fraternity of secular canons of the order of Saint Augustine, consisting of a dean and twenty-four canons. William Rufus bestowed the church and convent upon Ralph Hombard, Bishop of Durham, who curtailed the canons of their revenue, and rebuilt the church on a more superb scale with it; but Henry I. being offended at his after attempts to remove the secular canons altogether, and to replace them by regular canons, he was deprived of his wealth and honours, and imprisoned in the Tower, whence he escaped to Normandy by stratagem. He was afterwards restored to his bishopric. The last abbot of Christ Church was John Draper, whom Henry VIII.'s commissioners reported to be " a very honest conformable person." " We found," say they, in their letter, " the house welle furnyshede with juellys and plate, whereof some be meete for the king's majestie's use." The author of *Hampshire* tells us, that " some remains of the wall that enclosed the conventual buildings are yet standing ; and without it, to the south-east, is a meadow still called the convent garden ; in a field adjoining to which are the vestiges of several fish-ponds and stews. Another trace of this religious foundation may be found in a walk, or ambulatory, called Paradise, now used as a place of recreation for the scholars of Christ Church school. What seems to have been the lodge of the priory, is now occupied by a miller, and, from the initials J. D. which appear in various parts of the building, it is thought to have been erected by John Draper, the last prior. The site, and part of the walls of the refectory, which measured thirty-six feet by twenty, and of some other buildings, were laid open by the late Mr Brander, when he attempted to ascertain the ground plan of the whole pile." The church is a very interesting specimen of the Norman style, though more modern additions have been here and there made since the first erection of Bishop Flambard. The chancel contains some interesting specimens of ancient carvings on the oak wainscot. The under sides of the benches of the canons' stalls which still remain, exhibit a curious series of grotesque subjects, which, Mr Warner says, are supposed to refer to the arts of the mendicant friars, who began to establish themselves in England in the thirteenth century. In one of those pieces of carved work, a friar is represented under the emblem of a fox, with a cock for his clerk, preaching to a set of geese, who are greedily listening to his deceitful words. In another, a zany, intended to represent the people at large, turns his back on a dish of porridge, which is greedily licked up by a friar in the form of a rat. Under another of the seats is a baboon, with a cowl on his head, reposing on a pillow, and exhibiting an enormous swollen paunch. The altarpiece is also curiously carved in wood, and Mr Warner supposes it to be of the time of Bishop Flambard. It represents the genealogy of Christ, by a tree springing from the loins of Jesse, who appears in a recumbent posture, supporting his head on his left hand. On each side of him is a niche, in one of which is David playing on his harp, and in the other, Solomon in a musing attitude. Above these, the Virgin is seated with the child Jesus in her lap, and near her Joseph with the Magi, and the projecting heads of an ox and an ass, in allusion to the circumstances of our Lord's birth. These are, again, surmounted by shepherds and sheep in high relief, the former looking upward to a group of angels, immediately over whom God the Father, decorated with wings, extends his arms. Besides all these figures, there are those of a great number of saints. Under the altar there is a subterraneous chapel, or crypt; and, north from the altar, there is a beautiful, but, unfortunately, much mutilated, chapel, erected, in the reign of Henry VII, by the venerable Margaret Countess of Salisbury, for her burial place. Henry VIII.'s commissioners are answerable, on their own confession, for the destruction of the beautiful florid ornaments of this chapel; for, in the letter preserved in the British Museum, they say, " In the church we found a chaple and monument made of Cane (Caen) stone, perperyd by the late mother of Renold Pole for herr buriall, which we have caused to be defacyd, and all the armys and badgis clerely to be delete."

The eastern extremity of this church is formed by a spacious chapel, dedicated to the Virgin Mary, and supposed to have been built by the West family, ancestors to the Lords Delawar, about the end of the fourteenth century. There is some very fine carving in this chapel, and, immediately over it, there is a large room called St Michael's Loft, which has been used as a free grammar school since 1662.

The principal entrance to the church is under a large porch of the architecture of the fourteenth century, at the north-western extremity. The arches of the doorways were originally very beautiful. The square embattled tower, which rises at the west end of the church, was built in the fifteenth century by the Montacutes Earls of Salisbury. The great window, nearly thirty feet high, is embellished with tracery, and has over it the figure of our Saviour standing in a canopied niche, with his right hand raised, a cross in his left, and a crown of thorns on his head. The prospect, from the summit of the tower, includes a very extensive tract, teeming with rich meadows, enlivened by the windings of the Avon and the Stour. Within the church, there are some curious ancient monuments, especially one in alabaster, of a knight and his lady, supposed to have been erected to the memory of Sir John Chidiock, of Dorsetshire, who perished in one of the battles of York and Lancaster. The knight is in armour, with a collar of S. S. around his neck, and with his feet resting on a lion couchant; the lady is attired in the mitred head-dress and close garb of the fifteenth century. The monkish legend says, that the building of this church was expedited by a mysterious supernumerary workman, who always appeared at the hours of labour, though he never was present to receive either food or pay. To finish the building, a large beam was raised to a particular situation, but, after it had been so elevated, it was found to be too short. This occurred in the evening, and when the workmen returned to the church on the ensuing morning, they discovered that the beam had been placed in its right position, and that it now extended a foot longer than was necessary. They agreed that our Saviour alone could have thus assisted them, and to him, therefore, was the church dedicated. The miraculous beam is still shewn.

Christ Church is one of the smaller burghs which were permitted to return two members by the late reform act. It received its first precept from Edward I; but no returns were made, " through the poverty of the burgesses." It afterwards sent members in the reign of Elizabeth. The returns, recently made to Parliament by the burgh commissioners, make the number of houses in Christ Church five hundred and sixteen, of which one hundred and ninety-one are worth £10 per annum. The population is two thousand two hundred and sixty-two. The salmon and other fisheries, the breweries, the knitting of stockings, and the making of watch-springs, are the chief supports of the town. There is a handsome hotel, which commands a beautiful view of the sea, the Isle of Wight, and the Needle Rocks at the western extremity of it.

From Christ Church to Lymington, the country continues flat, cultivated, and enclosed. Scarce an object presents itself. A little to the right of the road you see a large house, built by Lord Bute, for the benefit of the sea air. It stands on a cliff directly opposite to Cherburgh, from which it is about sixty miles distant; and it overlooks the sea just in that point where Christ Church head and the western promontory of the Isle of Wight form an immense colonnade before it.

The road to the house runs directly to the front, narrow and contracted at the entrance, but opening by degrees. The house first appears, then the extent of the lawn, which is ample, with a pavilion at each extremity : These, from the sea, appear to connect it

with the house, and give it consequence. Beyond the
lawn, the grand colonnade just mentioned extends ; and,
beyond all, the expanse of the ocean.   There is something very amusing in thus contemplating an idea which
is continually dilating and opening itself from a narrow
tunnel into infinite space.   If it were the effect of chance
or necessity, we have only to admire the happiness
of it.

The cliff on which the house stands is about fifty or
sixty yards high.   It is not perpendicular, but the ground
being of a spongy, foundering nature, is continually
falling in huge masses, and affords an easy foundation
for winding stairs among the heaps of ruin which occupy
the slope.   At the bottom you are received by a clean
sandy beach, where, at the ebb of the tide, you may
continue your walk many miles.

The house is a sumptuous pile, and contains much
curiosity ; but as I am in quest only of scenery, my
subject forbids me to enter houses.   Lord Bute has
made an attempt to adorn the cliff around him with a
plantation.   But, if it should not thrive, I think the loss
not great.   Trees, in so exposed a situation, may perhaps
just get hold of the ground; but I should think it
impossible for them to produce either shelter or ornament.   Indeed, in views of this kind, I have my doubts
whether the rural idea should not purposely be excluded,
as interfering with the native grandeur of the scene.
Flowers, and flowering shrubs, at least, seem to be alien
beauties.

As we leave Lord Bute's, the country still continues
flat, cultivated, and enclosed.   Scarce a single opening
presents itself.   We observed, however, one species of
landscape, which, in so flat a surface, is singular, — those
hollows, or dells, mentioned in the general view of the
forest,* running across it to the sea.   They have not,
indeed, the consequence of mountain dells, yet some of
them afford pleasing scenery.   The most remarkable are
those of Chuton, Ashley, and Effort.   In each of these
there is a little rivulet, which the traveller, ignorant of

---

* See ante, page 125.

the country, will sometimes be surprised to see swollen to an extraordinary size, without any apparent cause. The case is, they communicate with the sea at a very little distance ; but, being totally skreened from it, and sheltered by wood on every side, they have the appearance of inland brooks, though, in fact, they are under the influence of a tide.

The cliff on which Lord Bute's house stands, runs two or three miles along the coast towards Lymington, and is known by the name of Hordwell Cliff. The summit of it is a fine carpet down, and is much frequented in the summer season by company from Lymington, for the sake of sea air and sea views. The sides of this cliff, as was observed, frequently fall in ; and, after one of these founders, as they are called, the masses of ruin form a bold rough bank against the sea, which secures the coast from another founder till that body of earth is washed away, and the land springs have loosened the earth above, when the cliff again falls in. Within these last twenty years, the sea has gained near a quarter of a mile in some places on this coast ; and the calculators of the country say, that Lord Bute's house cannot possibly stand above thirty years. He has taken, however, great pains to secure it, by diverting, at a great expense, the land springs ; so that he has little to fear but the action of the sea, which, though a rough enemy, is a much less dangerous one ; and against this he has endeavoured to guard, by facing the precipice in different parts with stone.

In this cliff, between Christ Church and Lymington, is found a great variety of fossil shells. About a hundred and twenty different sorts were collected by Mr Gustavus Brander of Christ Church, and presented to the British Museum. Mr Brander published also, in 1766, descriptions and very neat engravings of them, under the title of *Fossilia Hantoniensia.* These shells are found about fourteen or fifteen feet below the surface. The stratum above them is sand and gravel. The soil in which they are found is a bluish clay, and runs down from the gravelly stratum to a level with the sea, and probably much deeper. In every part of this cliff these shells are found, but chiefly about the village of Hord-well. It is difficult to get them : the collector must clamber up the sides of the precipice, and then extricate them from the clay, which is very stiff, by a tool. Their texture, too, is so brittle, that in cleansing them he runs a great risk of breaking them. What is remarkable, few of these shells belong to this coast, or indeed to any European coast; and many of them, as far as is known, are found no where else. It is remarkable, also, that this stratum of shells runs in a northerly direction quite through New Forest. Wherever the earth is opened to any depth, in digging marle, or on other occasions, shells are found; though I never saw them of any size except upon the coast.

A little below Hordwell the cliff fails, and the coast, becoming flat between this place and Lymington, is com-modiously formed into salterns, where great quantities of excellent salt have been made, though the trade has of late fallen off. The square bounded receptacles to receive the brine, are a glaring injury to the beauty of the shore.

Traces of the ancient *Salinæ*, or saltworks, may yet be discovered on the sea coast within the Manors of Milford and Hordle at very low ebbs of the tide.

About two or three miles farther along the coast, stands Hurst Castle, built at the point of an extraordinary natural causeway, which runs two miles into the sea, forming a narrow channel between the castle and the Isle of Wight. The causeway itself, also, is so narrow, that it scarce, at high water, exceeds two hundred yards in breadth. In high tides it is much narrower. The whole is covered with loose pebbles. The side towards the island is a bold shore, beaten into ledges, or terraces of pebbles, by the violence of the waves. The other side, which is sheltered, is undulating, marshy, and undetermined, forming the water, when the tide flows, into a smooth land-locked bay.

From this little peninsula, you are entertained with views on each hand. The island and the Needle Rocks are objects, dreary, vast, and grand, and not wholly unpicturesque. But to make them objects of the pencil, they must be well enlightened, and the foreground adorned with a little naval furniture, — an anchor, a net hanging to dry, a drifted boat, or some other object with which sea coasts abound. When I first saw this scene, it was in a sultry summer noon, and all the cliffs were overspread with that dingy indistinct hue, which sometimes accompanies a hot meridian sun. The sea, which was calm, was lighter than the land, though darker than the sky. But in the evening, the white cliff at the end of the island, together with the Needles, was tinged with the setting sun, and became very splendid; and the sea glowing with equal radiance, the whole view, and every part of it, was rich and harmonious.

On the other side of the peninsula, the Hampshire coast, extending far and wide, forms an immense bay, which appears flat, woody, and interspersed with a variety of distant objects. The parts are here and there picturesque; but the whole, though amusing, is too vast for the pencil.

Hurst Castle, lying level with the beech, fully commands the channel, which separates the coast of Hampshire from the Isle of Wight. It consists of a round tower, fortified by semicircular bastions, and was among the strongest of those castles which were built by Henry VIII. But since Portsmouth hath been a place of consequence, and always guarded by a fleet, this castle, as well as others of the same intention, are now neglected. In this castle the apartments are still shewn where Charles I was confined, when he was carried from the Isle of Wight; and very miserable they are.

" Here also," says the author of *Hampshire*, " was imprisoned, during a period of thirty years, a Roman Catholic priest named Atkinson, who was condemned to perpetual confinement for merely exercising the duties of his function. He died in October, 1729, at the age of seventy-four.

On the batteries we saw an instance of Hogarth's humour, when he was painter to the ordnance. The carriages have all crowns painted on them, with the king's initials. Below one of them, painted exactly in the vulgar style of the rest, Hogarth has formally put the initials of his name. The form of this castle at a little distance, set off by the rocks of the island as a background, is unpicturesque.

The Needles, which are of the same texture of rock with the neighbouring cliffs of the island, seem to have been washed from them by the sea. A gradual change has been observed, even in the memory of man. We may easily imagine with what violence a storm at sea pours in among these piles of formidable rocks, when the suction and eddies of tides and currents make them dangerous, almost in the serenest weather.

Besides the curious situation of Hurst Castle, there is another peculiarity on this coast, which deserves notice. It is an island called the Shingles, which sometimes rises fifteen or twenty feet above the water; and at other times totally disappears. It shifts its situation also, rearing itself at one time nearer the Isle of Wight, and at another, nearer the coast of Hampshire. The mystery of it is this. In that part of the channel lies a vast bank of pebbles, so near the surface, that it is beaten up into an island, by the raging of the sea, sometimes on one side, and sometimes on the other, as the tides and currents drive. From the same causes, too, all the prominent parts of it are as easily dispersed, and the island vanishes. When we saw it, it consisted of several acres : but it was then larger than had been remembered for many years. The sea, however, had found a passage through the middle of it, and it was lessening daily.

But as the country from Christ Church is flat, and the sea generally excluded from the sight, all these views of the Isle of Wight, the Needles, and Hurst Castle must be obtained by leaving the road, and getting a little nearer the coast. Other interesting views may be sought in the same way, both on the right and left of the road. At Milford, and in the neighbourhood of it, are several good views of these great objects. At Rookcliff, a little nearer the sea, the views are again varied, the island

and coast forming the appearance of an ample bay. On the other side of the road, about Pennington Common, from Mr Dixon's and other places, the distant views make a new appearance, just skirting the horizon, over a flat conntry, with a long sweep of the island, and intervening channel. But the most beautiful view on this side is from Mr Etty's drawing-room at Priestlands. The near grounds sink in the middle into a sort of wide valley, which is occupied in the distance by the island and the channel: and as they retire from the eye on the left, and wind rather towards it on the right, the whole has the appearance of a grand lake, bounded at this end, but running far into distance at the other. As the house stands in the centre of this view, it appears as if the house and view had been adapted to each other, which is one of the happiest circumstances that can attend a situation. A fine view is pleasing, but a fine view adapted to the situation of a house is more so. They who are unacquainted with the country should be apprised, that in all these views, and wherever the island is seen from the Hampshire coast, its insularity is no where discoverable. An extensive curtain of it only appears.

A little farther to the east stands Lymington, just at the point where the flat country we had been travelling from Christ Church descends to the river, which takes its name from the town. The brow and gentle descent of this falling ground the town occupies, forming one handsome street, which overlooks the high ground on the opposite side of the river. It is a neat, well built town, and pleasantly seated. The houses, especially on the side of the street next the coast, have views from the windows and gardens of the Isle of Wight and the sea.

Across the estuary, formed at the mouth of Lymington river, a dam with flood gates is thrown. The intention was to exclude the salt water from the meadows above; which, it was hoped, might have become good pasturage; but the purpose is not answered. A great beauty, however, arises from the influx of the tide, which forms a handsome piece of water above the dam, with many reaches and winding shores. We have already observed

6

the beauty of this estuary, when seen from the higher grounds, as it enters the sea.* The scenes are equally interesting which it affords when the eye pursues it up the stream, into its recesses in the forest. One of the best of them opens from the stable yard of the Angel Inn in Lymington, and the parts adjacent.

The channel between the isle of Wight and the shores of Hampshire is sufficiently deep, at all times, for ships of force and burden, which often pass through the Needles, as it is phrased; but if the weather be at all rough, it is thought an unsafe passage; and in general these narrow seas are frequented by smaller vessels. The port of Lymington particularly, which is entered by a long, narrow, shallow river, is chiefly frequented by light skiffs rigged, in the cutter form, with a jib and boom. These are, of all others, the most beautiful vessels which frequent a coast. To make a large ship a beautiful object, some peculiar incident is necessary. She must be fore shortened, for a ship in profile is formal. Her sails also must in part be furled, for the square sail without any contrast is disgusting. A degree of distance also is requisite, both to lessen the object and to soften the features of it. But the light skiff, with a single mast, a jib, and boom, is beautiful almost in any position. As she is often undecked, the lines of her sides are generally well contrasted, and the various turns and swellings of her sails almost always present some elegant form.

Of these vessels great numbers frequent the channel, between the isle of Wight and the coast of Hampshire. And what adds to the animation of the scene, the river forms two or three bold and beautiful curves, so that you see each little coasting vessel, as she tacks about in entering the harbour or leaving it, in every position in which she can possibly present herself. A small harbour therefore is much more productive of picturesque objects than one of larger size, frequented either by ships of war or of burden. A scene like this gave occasion to those very beautiful lines in Skakespeare:

* See ante, page 132.

She sat with me on Neptune's yellow sand,
Marking the embarked traders on the flood;
When we have laugh'd to see the sails conceive,
And grow big-bellied with the wanton wind,
Which she, with pretty and with swimming gait
Following, (her womb then rich with my young squire,)
Would imitate, and sail upon the land,
To fetch me trifles, and return again,
As from a voyage rich with merchandise.

As we leave the dam, and pursue our course along the shores of the river, we are entertained, if it be full, with some good lake scenes.

On the western side, just opposite to Vicar's Hill are the ruins of a Roman camp, which the country people know by the name of Buckland Ring, though in fact it is rectangular. It gives no value to the scene; but if your curiosity lead you to it, you will find it a very complete work of the kind. There are many larger in England, but few more perfect. It measures in length about two hundred paces; in breadth not quite so much, and hath been defended by two ramparts and two ditches. The whole of these works is entire, except the front towards the river, which is demolished, but in the demolition you may trace the double ditches. The ramparts seem to have been about twenty feet high. In the front the view is very extensive over the channel and all the environs of the river. On the opposite side the eye is carried far and wide into the forest.

Below the camp runs a creek from the river, where it is supposed the Romans used to land; and works have been thrown up there also, with a view, no doubt, to secure their landing. These works resemble those of the camp itself, only the area is less, and the rampart single.

This camp is supposed to have been formed by Vespasian, about the time that he conquered the Isle of Wight. " The inquisitive eye," says Mr Warner, " may still discern, in a morass which runs in a right angle from the western side of the river nearly to the foot of the intrenchment, the traces of a cut, or dock, evidently connected with the work, which, though in the lapse of ages it has been choked up and converted into a swamp, yet probably was sufficiently deep, in Vespasian's time, to receive the largest of the Roman galleys."

5

There has been also, on the other side of the river, exactly opposite to Lymington, another small fort. Nothing remains now except the artificial mount on which it had been erected, but it is generally supposed to have been a speculatory station to the grand camp of Buckland, as it commands a wide view of the channel.

SECTION VI.

REMARKS ON THE WESTERN PARTS OF NEW FOREST, IN A RIDE FROM VICAR'S HILL TO WILBERLY LODGE, BURLEY LODGE, BOLDREWOOD LODGE, RHINFIELD LODGE, SETLEY WOOD, BURNT HILL, &c.

HAVING thus taken a large circuit of near fifty miles round the western parts of the forest, I shall now conduct my reader through the same country again, *interiore gyro.* The internal parts of this extensive circle are supposed to contain some of the most beautiful scenery of its kind in the forest. But as we had here no turnpike road to guide us, and a great variety of paths to mislead us, we were obliged to put ourselves on horseback under the conduct of one of the under keepers.

Instead of holding the great road, as before, from Battramsley to Brokenhurst, we turned short to the left, into the open part of the forest, towards a noted landmark called Marl-pit-oak, well known to the deer stealer; who on this, or some neighbouring tree, often takes his stand in the dusk of a summer evening, to watch the herd as it leaves the woods to graze these open grounds.

This wild heath receives some beauty from its swelling in various parts. The swells are bold, but at the same time easy; the ground, seldom broken, generally falls gently into little valleys. These beauties, however, are obvious only to the picturesque eye, which, by a little imaginary finishing, can form these rough ground plots into pictures. As we attained the higher part of the heath, we had better landscape. We had been mounting gradually from the great road through two or three miles, when the country giving way on the right, a grand display of woody scenery was opened towards

Brokenhurst and Lyndhurst. On the left, the heath is but meagerly skirted with wood. To make amends, however, the cliffs of the Isle of Wight range beyond it in the distance.

Scattered about these wild grounds we meet with many tumuli. Between Shirley Holms and Setley Wood are four or five. Two of them are raised in contiguous circles, which is a circumstance rather uncommon. It seems to indicate that the persons to whose memory they were constructed had been nearly connected. On pacing the circumference of each, we find they have belonged to persons of unequal dignity, in the proportion of a hundred and eight to eighty-three. But a little to the east of Shirley Holms, near Peatmer Pond, arises a larger tumulus than either of these, called Shirley Barrow. Its circumference is one hundred and forty paces. There are many other tumuli on the great heaths of the forest, which I mention here, as I shall take no farther notice of them.

As we descended the gentle heights on which we were now raised, a beautiful valley, about a quarter of a mile in breadth, opened before us, arrayed in vivid green, and winding two or three miles round a wood. On the other side, the grounds, wild and unadorned, fall with an easy sweep into it. Beyond these a grand woody scene spreads far and wide into distance; and as it approaches the eye, unites gently with the other parts of the landscape. The valley was no other than that vast bog, already mentioned, known by the name of Long-slade Bottom.* Its deceitful surface, however, does no injury to its picturesque form, only, indeed, it deprives it of the appendages of grazing cattle. The nimble deer trip over it in summer without inconvenience, but no animals of heavier bulk dare trust themselves upon it. The name of the wood beyond this verdant valley is Hinchelsea.

As we leave Longslade Bottom on the right, the grounds which rise on the left are occupied by Sethorn Wood, a scene of considerable extent. Sethorn Wood was once the

* See an account of it, ante, p. 128.

noblest of all forest scenes.   The ground it stood on is
beautifully varied, and the grandeur and number of its
oaks were the admiration of all who saw them.   But its
glories are now over.   During the unremitted course of
thirty years, it continued to add strength to the fleets of
Britain, itself sufficient to raise a navy.   In this arduous
service, its vigour was at length exhausted, and it contains little more at present, than shrubs, and underwood,
and blasted trees.   In the midst of this wood rises a hill
called Oak Brow, from the stately oaks which once
adorned its summit and shaggy sides.   But its honours
fell a sacrifice, not like those of Sethorn, to its country's
good, but to the convenience of a potent neighbour.
Through the influence of Lord Delawar, whose views
it obstructed, its oaks were felled, long before any
inroads had been made among the woods which encircled
them.   And if the destruction of these oaks had been
partial, if a few here and there had been left as a
foreground, the injury, on the spot at least, might the
less be regretted; for the views which are thus opened
from its brow make great amends for the loss of its
woods.   They consist chiefly of two or three beautiful
lawns, skreened with forest scenery.   Yew-tree Bottom
denotes one of these scenes, and Even-water Bottom
another.   The former receives its name from the species
of trees which decorate it, the latter from a pool which
occupies its middle area.
     In forest language, valleys in general are called
bottoms, though, in fact, they are wide extended scenes.
Most of them have their little rivulets running through
them; but these forest streams are very unlike the streams
of a mountainous country, pouring among rocks, and
fretting among pebbles.   Theirs is a tamer nature : they
are seldom more than little oozing rills, which drain the
springy sides of rising grounds, and wander slowly,
unobserved and unobstructed, through the valleys of the
forest.   The landscape, however, seldom wants their
paltry assistance.   The only way in which these rivulets
are of any use in a forest scene, is when they spread
themselves into little pools in some part of the valley,
as they do here, in Even-water Bottom, and as they

frequently do in other scenes; and the merit of these little pieces of water chiefly consists in drawing all the cattle of the neighbourhood around their banks, which greatly animate and enrich the view.

In this part of the forest stands Wilverly Lodge, commanding beautiful views of these sweet wooded lawns and valleys, which, from the high situation of the lodge, are set off with the Isle of Wight as a background.

From Wilverly, we traversed the pales of a new timber enclosure, which is not less than four miles in circumference. If the wood which it is meant to defend should ever flourish, it would soon create a scene; but at present, this part of the forest is barren of beauty, and there is so very little appearance of the growth of timber, that people are apt to suppose it has been ignorantly planted or negligently attended. One reason, indeed, assigned for the ruin of the young wood, is the quantity of rabbits which breed in the dry sandy hills of these parts, and which it is difficult, amidst such shelter, to extirpate. A young oak just vegetating from the acorn, is esteemed by these pernicious inmates the most delicious food. Thus, it may be said, the glory of England may be nipped in the bud by a paltry rabbit.

After we leave these dreary pales, the country here and there breaks out towards Holmsley Lodge; but nothing is very interesting till we arrive at the brow of Burley Hill. Here the eye is greatly regaled: from this height it surveys a grand sweep of different removes of woody distance, spreading round a semicircular plain of several miles in extent, known by the name of Markway-bottom; the plain itself, consisting of a well proportioned intermixture of rich heath and green pasturage, is something between a forest lawn and a forest heath; too large for the one, and yet not large enough for the other. In two or three different parts, it is adorned with those attractive pools which enrich a landscape with the introduction of animal life.

The woods which encircle this grand savannah, as we survey them from the brow of the hill, are those of Bury on the left; adjoining to these, commence the woods of

Burley; and still more to the right, those of Rhinfield. All this rich scenery is in one continued, though varied and broken, sweep; and ranges at different distances from one mile to ten. The woods of Bury on the left, being the nearest and most elevated, entirely fill that part of the horizon under which they spread ; but beyond those of Burley rise, in fainter colouring, the two woody bosomed hills of Lyndhurst ; and beyond the woods of Rhinfield, a very remote forest view stretches into all the obscurity of distance. Every species of country, cultivated as well as uncultivated, when melted down into distance, has a fine effect, as we have often observed; but the forest distance is among the richest. Such is the grand view from Burley Hill, continually varying its appearance as we descend.

Our road led us over Markway Bottom to the Duke of Bolton's, at Burley, which is an excellent forest lodge, though an ordinary ducal seat. The late duke, having obtained a grant of it for thirty years, was at some expense in adorning it. He built handsome stables, fitted up the house, and laid out a lawn before it, which is bounded by a piece of embanked water. There is but little taste, however, shewn in the improvements; nor indeed does the situation deserve much attention. It is low; and, except that it stands in the midst of a beautiful forest, it is, on the whole, ill chosen.

The lawn of this lodge is adorned with some very grand oaks, which, from the dignity of their form and venerable appearance, as well as the number of the most respectable of them, have obtained the name of the Twelve Apostles.

In the woods around this lodge we saw a breed of small cattle, which the late Duke of Bolton procured from Scotland. While this herd was increasing, they were suffered to run wild in the forest; but, in a course of years, when he wished to reclaim a few of them, their habits were become so obstinate, and their nature so ferocious, that it was attempted without success, and they are now among the *feræ naturæ* of the forest. They are mischievous, however, only when attacked. We rode and walked among them without any molestation.

From Burley Lodge it is little more than two miles to Boldrewood Lodge, the seat of Lord Delawar. This house enjoys one of the finest situations of the forest. It stands high, with an extensive lawn before it, from which it commands a vast extent of forest scenery, spread around in great variety of distance, particularly towards Burley Lodge, where the woods stretch far and wide beyond a lengthened savannah, which sets them off to great advantage.* On the other side of the lawn, the distances are woody, but more broken, and not so remote.

Nor are the home views around this beautiful spot less pleasing than those at a distance. We wound near a mile round the lodge, through a succession of rich forest scenery, composed chiefly of beech. The trees themselves are among the most beautiful of their kind, having been secured from the axe by the protection of the house they adorn. But still the beech, even in perfection, is inferior to the oak, the elm, and the ash, in most of the characteristics of picturesque beauty. It has always too much of a spiry pointedness in the extremities of its branches, which gives a littleness to its parts. In its most beautiful form, it rarely shakes off this characteristic imperfection. If the trees, however, as individuals, were less pleasing, their combinations were highly beautiful, and exhibited much scenery from those natural openings and glades which are so often found in the internal parts of forests.

All the woods, not only around this lodge, but in its neighbourhood, abound in beech. The mast of this tree is the most fattening food for deer, and gives such repute to the winter venison of Boldrewood walk, that a stranger would have difficulty in getting a king's warrant for a doe executed in it.†

These woods also afford excellent feeding for hogs, which are led in the autumn season into many parts of the forest, but especially among the oaks and beeches of Boldrewood, to fatten on mast. It is among the rights of the forest borderers, to feed their hogs in the

* The same kind of situation, only varied, is described in page 133.
† Mr Samber's MS.

forest during the pawnage month, as it is called, which commences about the end of September, and lasts six weeks. For this privilege they pay a trifling acknowledgment at the Steward's Court at Lyndhurst. The word pawnage was the old term for the money thus collected.*

The method of treating hogs at this season of migration, and of reducing a large herd of these unmanageable brutes to perfect obedience and good government, is curious.

The first step the swineherd takes, is to investigate some close sheltered part of the forest, where there is a conveniency of water, and plenty of oak or beech mast, the former of which he prefers when he can have it in sufficient abundance.† He fixes next on some spreading tree, round the bole of which he wattles a slight circular fence of the dimensions he wants, and, covering it roughly with boughs and sods, he fills it plentifully with straw or fern.

Having made this preparation, he collects his colony among the farmers, with whom he commonly agrees for a shilling a-head, and will get together perhaps a herd of five or six hundred hogs. Having driven them to their destined habitation, he gives them a plentiful supper of acorns, or beech mast, which he had already provided, sounding his horn during the repast. He then turns them into the litter, where, after a long journey and a hearty meal, they sleep deliciously.

The next morning he lets them look a little around them—shews them the pool, or stream, where they may occasionally drink—leaves them to pick up the offals of the last night's meal—and, as evening draws on, gives them another plentiful repast under the neighbouring trees, which rain acorns upon them for an hour together at the sound of his horn. He then sends them again to sleep.

The following day he is perhaps at the pains of

---

* See Manwood *On Forest Law*, p. 201.
† Pliny seems to be of a different opinion. " Glans fagea suem hilarem facit, carnem coquibilem, ac levem, et utilem stomacho. Tradit Nigidius fungosam carnem fieri esculo, robore, subere." Lib. xvi. 6.

procuring them another meal, with music playing as usual. He then leaves them a little more to themselves, having an eye, however, on their evening hours. But as their bellies are full, they seldom wander far from home, retiring commonly very orderly and early to bed.

After this, he throws his sty open, and leaves them to cater for themselves; and from henceforward has little more trouble with them during the whole time of their migration. Now and then, in calm weather, when mast falls sparingly, he calls them perhaps together by the music of his horn to a gratuitous meal; but in general, they need little attention, returning regularly home at night, though they often wander in the day two or three miles from their sty. There are experienced leaders in all herds, which have spent this roving life before, and can instruct their juniors in the method of it. By this management, the herd is carried home to their respective owners in such condition, that a little dry meat will soon fatten them.

I would not, however, have it supposed, that all the swineherds in the forest manage their colonies with this exactness. Bad governments and bad governors will everywhere exist; but I mention this as an example of sound policy — not as a mere Platonic or Eutopian scheme; but such as hath been often realized, and hath as often been found productive of good order and public utility. The hog is commonly supposed to be an obstinate, headstrong, unmanageable brute; and he may perhaps have a degree of positiveness in his temper. In general, however, if he be properly managed, he is an orderly docile animal. The only difficulty is, to make your meanings, when they are fair and friendly, intelligible to him. Effect this, and you may lead him with a straw.

Nor is he without his social feelings, when he is at liberty to indulge them. In these forest migrations, it is commonly observed, that of whatever number the herd consists, they generally separate, in their daily excursions, into such little knots and societies as have formerly had habits of intimacy together; and in these friendly groups they range the forest, returning home at night in different parties, some earlier and some later, as they have been more or less fortunate in the pursuits of the day.

It sounds oddly to affirm the life of a hog to be enviable, and yet there is something uncommonly pleasing in the lives of these emigrants—something at least more desirable than is to be found in the life of a hog *Epicuri de grege.** They seem themselves also to enjoy their mode of life. You see them perfectly happy, going about at their ease, and conversing with•each other in short, pithy, interrupted sentences, which are no doubt expressive of their own enjoyments, and of their social feelings.

Besides the hogs thus led out in the mast season to fatten, there are others, the property of forest keepers, which spend the whole year in such societies. After the mast season is over, the indigenous forest hog depends chiefly for his livelihood on the roots of fern : and he would find this food very nourishing, if he could have it in abundance. But he is obliged to procure it by so laborious an operation, that his meals are rarely accompanied with satiety. He continues, however, by great industry, to obtain a tolerable subsistence through the winter, except in frosty weather, when the ground resists his delving snout; then he must perish if he do not in some degree experience his master's care. As spring advances, fresh grasses, and salads of different kinds, add a variety to his bill of fare ; and, as summer comes on, he finds juicy berries and grateful seeds, on which he lives plentifully till autumn returns, and brings with it the extreme of abundance.

Besides these stationary hogs, there are others, in some of the most desolate parts of the forest, which are bred wild, and left to themselves, without any settled habitation. As they cost nothing, either in food or care, their owners are content with the precarious profit of such as they are able to reclaim.

Charles I, I have heard, was at the expense of procuring the wild boar and his mate from the forests of Germany, which once certainly inhabited the forests of

* A hog from Epicurus's herd.

FOREST SWINE.

Todd Esc.

England. I have heard, too, that they propagated greatly in New Forest. Certain it is, there is found in it at this day a breed of hogs, commonly called forest pigs, which are very different from the usual Hampshire breed; and they have about them several of the characteristic marks of the wild boar. The forest hog has broad shoulders, a high crest, and thick bristly mane, which he erects on any alarm. His hinder parts are light and thin; his ears are short and erect; and his colour either black or darkly brindled. He is much fiercer than the common breed, and will turn against an ordinary dog. All these are marks of the wild boar, from whom I have little doubt that in part he derives his pedigree, though his blood may be contaminated with vulgar mixtures.* But though he is much more picturesque than the common hog, he is in much less repute among farmers. The lightness of his hind quarters, and the thinness of his flanks, appear to great disadvantage in the ham and the flitch.

We well remember an occasion when, in one of our New Forest rambles, we had thrown ourselves down at the root of a great beech tree, whence we looked abroad from underneath its wide canopy of foliage, on a small streak of sunshine, which, penetrating an opening in the wood and falling athwart the ground beyond, gave a broader and deeper effect to the shadows around. There was not a breath of air, and not a sound was to be heard, and we lay in all the listlessness of that dreamy musing which, to the idle mind, might seem as idleness, but which the philosopher and moralist may well know how better to appreciate. Suddenly a sound like that of warlike music, mellowed somewhat by distance, came upon our ears. We started up from our recumbent position so far as to lean upon one arm, and strained to listen, being almost persuaded, not without some degree of awe, that we were soon to have our eyes gratified by some pageant of the green garbed Elves. The sound increased, and grew harsher as it advanced; and as it drew yet nearer and nearer, the tramp of what might have passed for the fairy chivalry was mingled with it. Even yet we were ignorant of what spectacle awaited us, until at length the leading boar of a large herd of forest swine came

* See Vol. I. page 357.

grunting forward into the sunshine, followed by all the musical members of his harmonious detachment. Whether it was the cheering and cherishing effects of the sunshine, or that there was something savoury in the herbage of the spot, we know not, but the grunting swelled into a louder chorus, their snouts became more and more busy, their ears and tails were kept in continued and joyous motion, and their small eyes seemed to flash back the sun's rays with an unusual eagerness of expression. It was an interesting sight, and had swine not been the subject of it, we should tell the truth, and say, that it was a sight as beautiful as interesting. The creatures were in fine condition; their bristles shone like silver; their bodies were clean as if they had been daily washed and combed like a lady's lap-dog; and they seemed to be so free and so happy, that their very appearance filled our mind full of the romance of forest life and forest recollections. We sprang up in order to observe and to admire them more closely; but the noise we made alarmed them, and off they galloped in a terrible fright, helter skelter, *sauve qui peut*, with a speed which none of the porcine race, but such as are free swine of the forest, could have possibly exhibited; and long after the last of them had disappeared amid the more distant shades into which they penetrated, we still heard their retreating trumpets gradually dying away.

On leaving the beechen groves of Boldrewood, we were received by a large, open, swampy heath, called No Man's Walk, being under the peculiar jurisdiction of none of the keepers. The woods soon after commenced again, in which we passed a large forest vista, cut through them, from Lyndhurst to Burley Lodge; but it wanted the turnpike road which we found in the other vista.* I could not have supposed how much it lost from the want of this accompaniment. Without a road, there seemed to be no reason for a vista. In other respects, also, it wanted the variety of the Lyndhurst vista.

Along the confines of these woods, we skirted a forest lawn, called Warwicksted, which wheeled around us, in the form of a crescent, near two miles in circuit. It was a beautiful scene, hung with wood on every side.

* See ante, page 136.

Near this place stands Rhinfield Lodge, the situation of which is perhaps as pleasing, though not so grand, as that of Boldrewood. It stands on a spreading hill, encircled with groves of oak, among which, indeed, greater destruction hath been made, for the sake of the view, than seems to have been necessary. As the ground falls on every side from the hill on which the house stands, so on every side it soon begins to rise again, though very gently, expanding, by degrees, into a vast circle of forest scenery of every species,— extensive woods, skirted heaths, intermixtures of wood and lawn ; and all this landscape exhibited through the various removes of distance. When we were sated with these grand scenes, we had them afterwards presente more picturesquely, in parts, as we descended the hill on which the lodge stands. In this descent, we caught them every where to great advantage, through the boles and branches of the stately oaks which surrounded us. As the ground which immediately encircled this hill at the bottom is swampy, and watered with rivulets, the situation is sometimes in the winter rather uncomfortable. When the rains are abundant, the waters stagnate so much around the hill, that it is almost completely insulated.

The next scene we visited was a forest lawn, of grand dimensions. It seemed not less than nine or ten miles in circumference, bounded on every side, at least in appearance, with woods, some of which were on a level with it, and others on grounds elevated above it. Among these latter were the woods of Brokenhurst, adorned with the spire of the church shooting above them. The peculiarity of this lawn is, that its vast area is a perfect flat, a form which, though less beautiful than a playing surface, exceeds it in simplicity and grandeur. A small flat is trivial,—it is a mere bowling-green. It has neither beauty in its parts to set it off, nor greatness in the whole to make it interesting. A small piece of ground, therefore, should always be varied ; but an extensive flat, like this we are now examining, gives one grand uniform idea, which fills the imagination. The grandest idea of this kind is that of the ocean, the

greatness of which consists in its being a continued
flat. But the ocean presents grandeur without beauty.
In a view of this kind at land, the idea of beauty is,
more or less, impressed by the character of the scenery
around it. I remember being exceedingly struck with
the grandeur of an immense scene of this kind, on the
borders of Scotland, called Brough Marsh.* It is infinitely larger indeed than this, and is environed, not with
woods, which would lose their effect round so vast an
area, but with mountains. Romney Marsh, in Kent,
is a scene also of the same kind; but it is cut in pieces,
and deformed by parallel lines, hedges, and canals.
Nor are its boundaries good. Instead of woods or
mountains, it is bounded by the sea; and where the
sea appears in conjunction with a level surface, the
effect is bad; it joins one flat to another, and produces
confusion.

We agree as to the general principle laid down here; yet much
will depend on the accompaniments which are to be found in
each particular case, or, if we may so express ourselves, on
the frame with which such diminutive flats are surrounded.
A small portion of level lawn, short and velvety in its herbage
to a degree that inclines the spectator to fancy that it has
been worn down by the midnight revels of the fairy folk,
when surrounded by swelling banks, magnificent trees, or
wild rocks, affords one of the most delightful retreats that
ever poet imagined. There do we find, scattered about its
sunny margins, the early primrose, the glazed-cupped winter-
green, the nodding pyrola, the delicate adoxa moschatellina,
the enchanter's nightshade, the violet, and here and there
sparkling tufts of the sweet-scented woodruff, mingled with
many other pure and simple gifts of bounteous Flora, and
associated in our minds with our youthful years, and with all
that is lovely and all that is innocent. But let this small
portion of level surface be a little natural lake, or pond, even
aping in its dimensions the limited productions of art—let it
be crystalline, like that of the wild little lake of Belladron,
which sleeps at the foot of Craig Ellachie in Strathspey—let
it be garnished with its sloping turf and pensile birches, and
overhung with such steeps as tower, craggy and wooded, over

* See *Observations on the Lakes of Cumberland*, &c. vol. ii. page 109.

the tiny Highland pool we have mentioned,—and no poet could be trusted near to such a spot but with the risk of losing the small stock of wits which generally falls to the lot of such crazy pates.

The extensive forest lawn which gave occasion to these remarks is known by the name of Ober Green. It is chiefly pasturage, patched here and there with heath, and is esteemed one of the best feeding grounds, both for deer and cattle, in the forest.

Ober Green was the last of those beautiful lawns with which our ride through these parts of the forest was enlivened; and I imagine few counties in England could furnish so many pleasing woodland scenes in so small a compass. He who delights in such scenery will find it in much greater perfection in the wildness of a forest than among the most admired improvements of art. He will find it grander, more varied, and every where more replete with those wild, enchanting passages, which the hand of art cannot give. What are the lawns of Hagley,* or any other place celebrated for this species of artificial landscape, but paltry imitations of the genuine works of Nature?

Hinchelsea Wood, † which we left on the right in the morning, now again skirted our right, as we traversed Ober Green. Here it was as great an ornament as it was on the other side, at Long-slade Bottom. That vast bog which we had seen in the morning, winding so beautifully round Hinchelsea wood, now presented its deceitful surface directly in our way. An inexperienced traveller might have ventured to pass it without scruple: but our steps were better guided; we were carefully led through the skirts of the wood, to a place where a mole is thrown across this vast bog, with two or three wooden bridges to transmit the moisture.

Having passed this obstruction, we rose Blackamsley Hill, from whence, as in a table of contents, we had a view of all the country, the woods and the lawns we had passed, extending at least nine or ten miles in length.

* The late Lord Lyttleton's, in Worcestershire, now Lord Westcote's.
† See ante, page 161.

From Blackamsley Hill, we came to Setley Wood, near which we met again the great road we had left in the morning. But instead of continuing in it, we crossed it at a gate opposite to a gravel pit, as we leave Brokenhurst; and entered a wild heath called Brunt Hill, where some beautiful woody scenes immediately opened. On the left, along the declivities, hung . enclosures of cultivated meadow land, and likewise of rough grounds, both equally adorned with wood; and as these two species of landscape were here contiguous and exactly similar, excepting only the article of cultivation, they afforded a good opportunity of illustrating the doctrine of gradation, one of those great principles in landscape which contributes more than any other towards the production of effect. The force of gradation is most shewn in the management of light and colours; but it is shewn also in the union of objects. Abruptness, it is true, and strong oppositions, are often great sources of picturesque beauty, when properly and sparingly introduced. In profusion they are affected; but the great principle of gradation has universal influence, and enters more or less into every composition. The instance we saw of it here respected the union of objects.

On examining a piece of natural ground, we see, at a single glance, how gradually and beautifully Nature commonly unites one part with another, — the tree with the shrub — the shrub with the brake — that again with the weed — and lastly, these lowest decorations with the level ground, which is here and there still farther softened into them by patches of more luxuriant herbage.* But in the cultured field, however beautiful in its kind, you see no transition, no connection, or gradation among contiguous parts. Even if the hedges introduce no formality of lineal boundary, yet the smooth uniform surface, whether of grass or of corn, joins abruptly with the wood. This in a picturesque light is displeasing.

But you admire the artificial lawn, bounded only with wood? You then talk of contrast, rather than gradation, as a source of beauty?

* See Vol. I. p. 317.

3

We do; and scenes of this kind are often beautiful. But one of their great beauties arises still from grada- tion. When we talk of contrast, we do not mean simple opposition. Two contiguous stripes of black and white produce no effect. Strong oppositions we sometimes allow, but they must only appear in transient touches : gradation enters into the idea even of contrast. It is true, in the artificial lawn we commonly require neatness, so that the rude connections of Nature are excluded ; but still a lawn, bounded with regular wood, gives us little pleasure. It is the planter's care to obtain what gradation he can, by bringing some of his clumps forward, and thus connecting his lawn with his woods. Yet, with all his art, he can never do it in so nobly wild and picturesque a manner as Nature in her most beautiful works.

These remarks appear to us to be singularly applicable to the composition of music, as well as to that of landscape,— another proof, in our minds, of the verity of Mr Alison's theory of association.

The two different kinds of hanging grounds, bounded with woods, which occasioned these remarks, occupied our left. In front was an extended skirting of woody scenery, which, opening itself more and more as we proceeded, spread into a noble skreen. This scenery consisted of those vast woods which stretch from Heathy Dilton to Boldre Church.

These woods hang over the most pleasing meadows about Roydon, and along all the valley to Brokenhurst, that ever adorned a landscape. It is a landscape, indeed, of the cultured kind, and therefore little accommodated to the pencil ; but, of its kind, it is the most lovely. Through this valley, consisting of hanging meadows, variously bounded and adorned with wood, the river of Lymington, while it is yet rural, and only a forest stream, forms many a devious curve. But this pleasing scenery can only be traversed by the foot passenger, or the angler with his rod. Even on horseback you cannot pass the many wooden bridges, made of single planks, which are thrown athwart the several windings of the stream.

Leaving these scenes behind us, we entered the lanes of Roydon, broad, winding, and adorned in one part with an open grove, in others with an intermixture of beech and oak, which, stretching across, form a canopy above the head. These lanes open upon a heath called Sandy Down, which is supposed to enjoy the best air in its neighbourhood. Here the woods, which had before skreened our front, now winding round, appear with equal magnificence on the left. The summit is crowned with Boldre Church, which, discovering only its embattled tower among the trees, takes the form of a lofty castle.

Having crossed the river near the ruins of Haywood House, once a mansion of considerable note, we mounted the hill to the church, from whence we had beautiful views on the north to the forest, and on the south towards the white cliffs of the Isle of Wight, which are set off by intermediate woods. Indeed all the churches of the forest are loftily seated. For when the whole country was covered with woods, and before roads were cut through them, it was necessary to place the church in a lofty situation, that the inhabitants might the more easily find their way to it through the devious paths of the forest.

SECTION VII.

REMARKS ON THE MIDDLE PARTS OF NEW FOREST, BETWEEN THE RIVERS OF LYMINGTON AND BEAULIEU.

DIRECTING our course first towards Beaulieu, we passed the plantations of Sir Harry Burrard at Walhampton, which extend round his house, and are composed chiefly of fir. His gardens command extensive views of the Isle of Wight and the intervening channel; but they are views which may rather be called amusing than picturesque. They are too extensive for the use of the pencil: the distant coast exhibits too long a curtain, the hills are too smooth, and the water line is too parallel with the coast of Hampshire. The only way to obtain that species of beauty which we call picturesque, from so lengthened a view of distant coast, is to break it here and there with plantations, sometimes immediately on the foreground, and sometimes in the second distance. And indeed in many parts of the gardens, where such portions are intercepted by the woods, good pictures are obtained. After all, however, we must allow, that nine persons in ten would be better pleased with these extended views in their present amusing state, than if they had been more generally broken in a form to please the picturesque eye. Few people can distinguish between the ideas of beautiful and picturesque, but every eye is pleased with an amusing view.

We confess honestly that we cannot altogether approve of our author's use of the word amusing, as applied to scenery. We do not think that the term can be well applied to landscape at all. We may find scenes which are not picturesque, or, in other words, not easy to be painted, and that may yet be extremely delightful to look upon, and very gratifying to almost every eye that beholds them; but when the artist turns away from such scenes as these, he often does so, less from any want in the scenes themselves, than from his own feeling of incapacity to overcome the difficulty of doing them justice in the representation. Instead of sharing in the thousand various associations which endear such scenes to those around him, he has no other association with them, at least at the moment, than that of disappointment, if not of disgust, arising from the inefficiency of his own art.

To these sheltered recesses, which extend even to my garden gate, I am so much indebted, through the indulgence of their benevolent owner, for the quiet pleasures of many a studious hour, that I should gladly enter more minutely into a description of them, did not my subject, which holds me closely to the wild scenes of Nature, forbid. Yet there is one scene which I cannot forbear mentioning: it is so nearly allied to Nature, that it is closely allied also to my subject. The scene I mean, is a small lake, containing about a dozen acres, which has been formed out of a swamp: it is wooded on both sides, and the view of the whole together is very pleasing when you stand in the open part, towards Portmere Common, from whence the head which confines the water is concealed; and the woods on each side are united at the bottom with those of the garden. The walks on both sides are well managed, and contain many little pleasing recesses and openings to the water.

Walhampton was given by Richard de Redvers to the canons of Christ Church, who possessed it at the dissolution, when Henry VIII granted it to Sir Thomas Wriothesley, afterwards Earl of Southampton, from whose descendants it came into possession of the Earls of Arundel, and then to the family of Burrard.

Sir John D'Oyly and Mr Robbins, whose houses we pass in succession, have the same views towards the Isle of Wight and the Channel which are presented from the gardens at Walhampton; but they are seen under different circumstances.

Sir John D'Oyly's capital view is from a circular room at the top of his house, which commands a very great extent both of sea and land. On the land side the diversified woods of the forest appear stretching far and wide around his house, with all the intervening cultivation, houses, cottages, and farms. On the other side the sight extends along the channel of the Isle of Wight, in both directions; to the west as far as the open sea, and to the east as far as Spithead, where every motion of the fleet which is stationed there may be observed. His lawn has lately been new-modelled, and is now only in a state of improvement, so that its effect cannot yet be seen.

At Pilewell, Mr Robbins' views towards the sea are nearly the same as those from D'Oyly Park, only seen from a lower stand. Mr Robbins' lawn is a very extensive one. It is flat, indeed; but so much quiet space forms an excellent contrast with the busy scene of navigation which is spread beyond it. Still, however, these views are of the amusing kind. I should advise the picturesque eye, therefore, to seek the scenery of the island, as he will find it more broken in many parts of the walk which circles the lawn. The best view of the whole together, is from the dressing-room windows.

About a mile and a half from Baddesly we pass the edge of a piece of fresh water, above three miles in circumference, known by the name of Souley Pond. In an inland country it would have been thought a considerable lake; but its close neighbourhood to the sea diminishes the idea. It is not, indeed, skreened by such noble limits as dignify the lakes of Westmoreland and Cumberland,—rocks, mountains, and craggy promontories,—yet it is marked by an elegant irregular line. Its banks arise in gentle swells from the water; in some places the skirts of Beaulieu woods run down to its edge, and in others low points of level land shoot into it, which are always beautiful, especially when adorned with groups of figures or of cattle. On the whole, it is a pleasing scene. It produces great plenty of fish, and often affords a summer day's amusement to the gentlemen of the neighbourhood.

Souley was anciently denominated Fresh Water, as appears by the old charters, in which it is considered as bounding the possessions of Beaulieu Abbey. It is very deep in many parts. Its waters are now applied to turn the wheels of two large mills belonging to some iron works.

From Souley Pond the road leads towards the banks of Beaulieu river, which are rather high in this part, and much wooded; so that, of course, the water is skreened from the eye. The road, however, is very beautiful, passing through woody lanes and open groves; and the woods of Beaulieu are the more beautiful, as they are almost universally left untouched. You scarce see a maimed tree among them.

About two miles from Souley, a strange ruin attracts the eye on the left. It appears like the two ends of a barn, the roof of which has fallen in. But the curiosity of it is its amazing size. From one gavel end to the other, it extends eighty-one paces. The name it is known by is St Leonard's; and it is commonly supposed to have been a barn belonging to the monks of Beaulieu, who placed here a little establishment of their fraternity, to gather the fruits of the country in these parts. The vestiges of different buildings, and the walls of a small chapel, still remain. In a picturesque light, this ruin is of no consequence. We walked round it, and tried it, in every mode of perspective, if possible to make a drawing from it; but the two vast gavel ends would enter into no kind of composition.

Large barns were the common appendages of abbeys, and the vestiges of some of them still remain. There is a grand building of this kind at Battle Abbey in Sussex; though I should think it is more ornamented than was requisite for a barn. There is another very large one at Cerne in Dorsetshire. But the noblest edifice, I believe, in England, under the denomination of a barn, is to be seen at Choulsey in Berkshire, about two miles from Wallingford. This barn is still larger than that we are now surveying. It is somewhat above a hundred yards in length, and eighteen yards broad. It contains four threshing floors, and is supposed to have belonged to the rich abbey of Reading. Though carrying upon it the date of 1101, it is in good condition, and still performs the functions of a barn. Mighty castles and churches, in three or four centuries, have given way to time; but here is a barn, which has continued doing its offices to society, through the space of seven hundred years.

The Barn of St Leonard's is accounted for by its vicinity to Park Farm, anciently one of the granges belonging to the monks of Beaulieu. This farm lies pleasantly embosomed in fine woods, through which transient views of the Isle of Wight, and the neighbouring channel, are occasionally admitted. The granges appertaining to Beaulieu Abbey enjoyed the privilege of having divine service celebrated in them, a privilege which was granted them by a bull from Pope Alexander I. The chapel of Park Grange is yet standing, though much dilapidated. It is united at its south-eastern end with the farm house, which is a massive stone building of equal antiquity. The length of the chapel is forty-two feet, and its breadth about fourteen feet. The interior is divided by a stone skreen, which reaches to the roof. The floor of the altar part is elevated about six inches,

. and in the south wall there is a niche where the pix and crucifix were placed. In each division, the vaulting is supported by four plain ribs, uniting in a rose in the centre; and the interior is lighted by three painted windows. The anti-chapel has only two lancet lights at the south-western extremity. The remains of the chapel of St Leonard's, mentioned by Mr Gilpin, evince it to have been once extremely beautiful; but its original splendour is nearly obscured, from the ruin having been long applied to the base purposes of a goose house and hogs' stye. At the east end, on the side of the altar piece, is an elegant niche, adorned with lateral pinnacles, richly embossed, and a Saracenic arch, crowned with a cross.

From the ruins of St Leonard's the same woody road brought us soon to Buckler's Hard, a beautiful semicircular valley, or rather a dip of the bank, to the edge of the river, which forms before it one of its grandest sweeps. In this pleasing retreat the Duke of Montague, predecessor to the late Duke, proprietor of all this part of the country, proposed to build a town, which was to bear his name. He was at that time proprietor also of the Island of St Lucia in the West Indies; and as he enjoyed all the privileges, on the river, of the abbey of Beaulieu, which were great, and would have enabled him to invest his colony with many immunities, he expected to derive much advantage from a sugar trade, as sugars might thus be imported, and, from the plenty of fuel, refined at a much cheaper rate here than they could be anywhere else; and indeed the scheme had the approbation of many men of sounder judgment than the Duke. The limits of a town were accordingly planned, the streets were marked out, and the building grounds adjusted; but, at the peace of 1748, St Lucia was declared a neutral island, by which the Duke's property in it was lost; and, soon after, his only son dying, he dropped all farther intention with regard to his new town.

Buckler's Hard was, however, destined to receive a town, though of a different kind. The situation was commodious for ship building, as well as sugar boiling, and was taken for that purpose by Mr Adams, who made large contracts with government for building ships of war. Several very fine frigates have been built here, and some ships of more force.* The great number of workmen whom this business brought together, have given birth, by degrees, to a populous village.

From this busy scene we pursued our way to Beaulieu Abbey, which is about two miles beyond it. The road is still close and beautifully wooded. Within half a mile of it, you look down from the higher grounds into the circular valley, in which the ruins of the abbey stand.

The valley itself is extensive, and consists of great variety of ground; and the whole scene, but especially the hills which surround it, are woody. Through the middle of it runs the river, which, about two miles above Beaulieu, is a mere forest stream, and has no consequence but what it receives from the beautiful scenes through which it wanders. Under the walls of the abbey it meets the tide, which immediately gives it form and dignity. Here a bridge is thrown over it, on each side of which it spreads into a lake when the tide flows, shaping its ample sweeps around rich wooded shores. Both these grand basins might easily be kept constantly full, if a head were constructed, as I have heard it might be, across the river, at the second reach below the abbey. The tide, in all probability, would not obstruct a work of this kind, as it flows here with little force, scarce at the rate of four miles an hour.

The precincts of the abbey, which stands on the eastern side of the river, are, in circumference, about a mile and a half. The boundary wall is entire in several parts, and visible almost in all. The area within the boundary is nearly flat, and might easily be made a very

---

* The following is a list of the ships of war, and their number of guns, which have been built at Buckler's Hard:—

The Illustrious, of seventy-four guns—the Vigilant, Agamemnon, Indefatigable, and Europe, all of sixty-four—the Greenwich, and Hannibal, of fifty—the Woolwich, Romulus, Gladiator, and Sheerness, of forty-four—the Thames, Thetis, and Heroine, of thirty-two—the Coventry, Levant, Triton, Greyhound, Sibyl, and Brilliant, of twenty-eight—the Surprise, Fowey, and Mermaid, of twenty-four—the Kennington, of twenty—and the Scorpion sloop.

beautiful scene. Along the banks of the river the ground is a little varied, where a pleasant walk has been laid out, which is now picturesquely marked by the ruins of time. The bank is here somewhat higher than the river, and was formerly in this part the foundation of the boundary wall of the abbey, which, when the wall was entire, completely hid the river and all its beautiful appendages from the walk. Time has now restored them. Though the wall yet holds out in some places, it has in general failed. Large portions of it are gone; and, in other parts, there are chasms and fractures, through which the river and the surrounding woods appear often to great advantage from the walk. Old oaks, likewise, coevel with the abbey itself, are scattered profusely around the ruins of the wall—sometimes supporting it, and sometimes supported by it. They are everywhere beautiful appendages, and in many places unite with the ruins of the wall into the most pleasing foregrounds; while the river, spread here into a lake, and the woods beyond it, form a distance.

Among these ruins, I remember some years ago to have seen a very extraordinary instance of vegetation. The main stem of an oak arose in contact with a part of the wall, which was entire, and extended one of its principal limbs along the summit of it. This limb, at the distance of a few yards from the parent tree, finding a fissure in the wall, in which there might probably be some deposit of soil, shot a root through it into the earth. From hence, shooting up again through another part of the wall, it formed a new stem as large as the original tree, and from this again proceeded another horizontal branch like the former. In a great storm, which happened on the 27th of February, 1781, both the wall and the tree were blown down together.

Great part of the area between this beautiful walk and the abbey is occupied by an open grove, part of which is beautiful, and part deformed. The reason of the difference is, that one part is planted carelessly by the hand of Nature, the other regularly by that of Art.

Of the buildings of the abbey considerable parts remain—enough to shew that it has formerly been constructed in a rich Gothic style, though its dimensions were never large. The parts still in being of most consequence, are what is supposed to have been the refectory and the abbot's lodge. The refectory is now turned into a parish church, and forms a handsome aisle, which is worth looking into. The abbot's lodge is known by the name of the Palace, and was fitted up by the predecessor of the last Duke of Montague as a mansion, though he made little addition to it. The old hall still remains, and some of the other apartments. What he added is ill done, and what he did in the way of taste is whimsical and ill managed. He did nothing, indeed, that adorns this beautiful scene, many things which deform it, and some things so strangely absurd that no genius but his own could have conceived them. Instead of calling in some man of taste to assist him in making Beaulieu Abbey one of the most pleasing scenes in England, which it might have been, he employed an engineer, by whose help he drew a ditch around it—filled it with water—threw two or three drawbridges over it —secured all the avenues—and thus, by a wonderful stroke of art, converted an abbey into a castle. This achievement was performed about the time of a French war and a rebellion, when the duke had been raising a regiment, and his ideas had taken a military turn. It is said, too, that he made this strange metamorphosis under an apprehension lest some adventurous French privateer, taking the advantage of a full tide, might sail up the river, and endeavour to carry him off. Men of taste cannot enough lament, that a situation so well adapted to receive the beauties of art, should have fallen so unhappily into such wretched hands; and that more money had been spent in deforming it, than might have made it a scene of uncommon beauty.

Of the other parts of the abbey little remains. There is a court about sixty or seventy feet square, formerly perhaps a cloister, which is now converted into a garden.

In the inner walls remain several arches, now closed, two or three of which are of beautiful Gothic. Near this court, also, stands a small room, roughly arched. The arches are of stone, centering in a point at the top; but it does not easily appear for what purpose so small an apartment was intended. The kitchen is still very entire, as this edifice often is among the ruins of abbeys. It was a structure commonly of great strength.

But though the situation of Beaulieu Abbey is very pleasing, and perhaps more monkish than could easily have been found in the neighbourhood, yet, if a noble family mansion should be intended, a much grander situation might be chosen in many parts of this beautiful country, particularly on the high grounds a little to the north of Buckler's Hard, nearly about the point where the road from thence unites with that from Lymington. This situation commands a grand sweep over the river, together with its estuary,—the woods on both sides of it, which are rich and ample in a high degree,—and, in the distance, the Channel, and the high grounds of the Isle of Wight, from Cowes' Point to the Needles.

The privileges of the manor of Beaulieu, which were granted by King John, were very extensive, and are still preserved. No debtor can be arrested within its precincts, unless the lord's leave be obtained. The lords of Beaulieu also enjoy the liberties of the Cinqueports, and the same exemption from duties, which was the duke's principal reason, as was observed, * for building a town at Buckler's Hard. They hunt also, and destroy the king's deer if they stray within the purlieus of the abbey. On the day we were at Beaulieu, we found the hedges everywhere beset with armed men. There were not fewer than twenty or thirty. It appeared as if some invasion was expected. On inquiry we were informed a stag had been seen that morning in the manor, and all the village of Beaulieu was in arms to prevent his escape back into the forest. The fortunate man who shot him had a gratuity from the lord.

Beaulieu manor is an extensive scene, being not less than twenty-eight miles in circumference. It consists chiefly of woodlands; and, besides the deer which accidentally stray into it from the forest, contains a great number of deer in its own domains. Among

* See page 181.

these rough grounds are intermixed many valuable farms, and the whole yields annually about £4000.

Beaulieu Abbey, anciently *Bellus Locus*, or Fine Place, was founded in 1204, as we learn by reference to the article Hampshire, in the *Beauties of England*. The motives which impelled King John to such an act of piety, as it was then called, towards the brethren of the Cistertian order, a class to which he had been previously particularly adverse, have furnished the monks with an opportunity of resorting to the convenient system of miraculous interposition. In the outset of their legend, they observe, that the king, after various oppressive measures exercised against the Cistertians, summoned the abbots and principals of that order to Lincoln, whither they hastened, flattering themselves that he would there confer upon them some marks of his grace and favour. Instead of this, they tell us, that " the savage monarch ordered the abbots to be trodden to death by horses ; but none of his attendants being found sufficiently cruel to obey the sanguinary command, the ecclesiastics, dreadfully alarmed, retired hastily to their inn. During the course of the ensuing night, when the monarch slumbered in his bed, he dreamed that he was standing before a judge, accompanied by the Cistertian abbots, who were commanded to scourge him severely with rods and thongs ; and when he awoke in the morning, he declared that he still felt the smart of his beating. On relating this dream to a certain ecclesiastic of his court, he was advised to crave pardon of the abbots whom he had before so barbarously treated ; and assured that the Almighty had been infinitely merciful to him, in thus revealing the mysteries of his dispensations, and affording him paternal correction. The king, adopting this counsel, ordered the abbots to attend him, and, contrary to their expectations, received them with kindness ; and the remembrance of his dream still continuing to influence his conduct, he shortly after granted a charter for the foundation of the abbey." The endowments he bestowed on it were very great ; and in addition to various important privileges and immunities, he ordered a payment to be made of one hundred merks, towards the erection of the monastic buildings, which were raised on so very magnificent a scale, that, notwithstanding numerous pious donations made during the time of carrying on the works, as well as assistance derived from several other sources, the sum of four thousand merks remained undischarged at their completion. To enable the monks to pay this, they got a grant of the impropriation of the church and chapel of Cokewell, in Berkshire. Henry III confirmed all the benefactions of his predecessors, and invested the monks with the liberty of free-warren throughout their manor of Forenden, in Berkshire, which John had bestowed on them; together with the privilege of holding fairs and markets therein on stated days. Edward III confirmed all the preceding grants; and in the twentieth of his reign, ordered a tun of prisage wine to be delivered to the monks annually, for the celebration of mass. About this period the abbey was received under the special protection of Pope Innocent, who invested it with the privilege of sanctuary, exempted it from the payment of tithes, and conferred various rights upon its members. It is asserted by tradition that the abbot had the power of sitting in Parliament; but this report has not been corroborated by reference to any historical document. On the dissolution in the reign of Henry VIII, the possessions of the abbey, according to Dugdale, were estimated at the annual value of £326, 13s. 2d.; but according to Speed, at that of £428, 6s. 8d. In the following year, the manor of Beaulieu, with all its rights, privileges, and appurtenances, — the rectory and right of patronage excepted — was granted to Thomas Wriothesley, afterwards Earl of Southampton. This grant was confirmed to Henry Earl of Southampton, by James I. In the reign of William III, this estate became the property of Ralph Lord Montague, afterwards Duke of Montague, by his marriage with the heiress of the Wriothesleys. His son John, second Duke of Montague, transmitted it to his daughters, Isabella and Mary, from whom, by intermarriages, the manor has descended to the Lord Beaulieu and the Duke of Buccleuch.

Trusting that a more minute description of Beaulieu Abbey than our author has given us will not be unacceptable to the reader, we shall extract it from the article *Hampshire*, from which we have already had occasion to draw so largely: " The immediate precincts of the abbey were encircled by a stone wall, which, in several places, remains nearly entire, and is richly mantled with ivy; its circumference is about a mile and a quarter; the entrance is by an ancient stone gateway. Proceeding onward, the first object that attracts particular attention is an edifice, nearly of a square form, now called the Palace, but originally built for the abbot's lodging, and converted into a family seat after the dissolution.

Over the entrance is a canopied niche, in which stood the image of the Virgin Mary, to whom the abbey was dedicated. The hall is a well proportioned room, handsomely vaulted, the ribs springing from pilasters, and spreading over the roof in beautiful ramifications. Eastward from this edifice is a long building, supposed, from the extent and height of the apartments, to have been the dormitory; beneath it are several good cellars. The ancient kitchen is also standing, and near it is the refectory, a plain stone edifice, with strong buttresses : this is now the parish church of Beaulieu ; the abbey church, which stood to the north-east, having been entirely destroyed. The roof is curiously raftered with oak; the intersections of the ribs being embossed with rude sculptures of angels with shields, abbots' heads, and other figures. On the west side, elevated about twelve feet above the floor, is the ancient rostrum, or pulpit, from which lectures were read when the monks were assembled at their meals below. The ascent into it is by a flight of stone steps, curiously arched and ribbed over head, and enlightened by pointed apertures; its form is demioctagonal.

" The site of the abbey church may be traced by the unevenness of the ground ; but not a vestige of the building is remaining. Fragments of demolished tombs are occasionally dug up here, this having been the burial place of various illustrious personages ; and among them, of Queen Eleanor, mother of King John. Some traces of the cloisters are yet distinguishable, round an area of about a quarter of an acre ; now converted into a garden, in the west side of which is a gateway with rich mouldings, pillars, and capitals. Behind the gardens are ruins of some of the offices of the monastery, and particularly of the apartment in which the monks manufactured their wine. Some fields to the north of this building, spreading along a gentle declivity, with a southern aspect, still bear the name of the vineyards ; for there are numerous proofs of the vine having been cultivated in this southern part of England. Several of the fish ponds belonging to this monastery are yet entire, and abound in fish.

" During the period that Beaulieu Abbey was invested with the privilege of a sanctuary, its walls afforded a temporary protection to Margaret of Anjou, the courageous Queen of Henry VI, who, returning from the Continent in full expectation of being reinstated in her former dignity, was, on her arrival at Weymouth, informed of the imprisonment of her husband, the destruction of his army, the death of the Earl of

6

Warwick, and the elevation to the throne of her mortal enemy Edward IV. On this occasion her intrepid spirit bent beneath the pressure of accumulated woe, and, with her youthful son, she sought refuge within the friendly walls of Beaulieu, where, soon afterwards, the presence of the Earl of Devon, and some other faithful adherents, caused her to reassume her fortitude, and again prepare for active exertion. Another celebrated fugitive to whom the Abbey of Beaulieu afforded sanctuary, was Perkin Warbeck, whose real origin has been a theme of much argument, and is yet, perhaps, a subject for future historians completely to develope. Having landed in the west of England, and received a check before the gates of Exeter, he fled to this asylum, where he continued some time ; though every chance of escape was precluded by the conduct of Lord Daubeney, who invested the place with three hundred men. At length the promises of the King, Henry VII, allured him from his retreat ; and, after the publication of an actual, or pretended confession of imposture, he was committed prisoner to the Tower. Shortly afterwards, on a charge of treasonable practices, he was condemned to die, and was executed at Tyburn in the year 1499."

As we leave Beaulieu Abbey, along the Lyndhurst road, we skirt the upper lake, which is formed by the tide above the bridge. It is a beautiful sheet of water, about a mile in circumference, surrounded on every side with woods, which in many parts fall into it from the rising grounds. As the view opens, we look full up the lake. On the right the abbey appears among the woods to great advantage; on the left, a winding road runs along its margin, except where in some parts it is intercepted by clumps of trees. In front, the woods recede a little from the water, and leave a space of flat meadow, which has a good effect in contrast with the rising grounds and woods on each side. The whole scene is pleasing. Soon after we leave the lake, the river dwindles into a sluggish, little, bullrush stream. The meadows, however, through which it winds, are adorned with wood, and still continue beautiful.

At a place called the Fighting Cocks, well known to the lurking poacher, the manor of Beaulieu ends, and we entered the wild scenes of the forest. Deep woods received us: through these we rode near two miles, rising gently from the river, and then emerged into an open scene, called Culverly Heath, one of those beautiful woody skirted lawns, of which we had seen so many in the western parts of the forest; and yet the features of this were different from them all. We stood on a rough knoll, decorated with a few full grown oaks, descending in front into a lawn, which appeared to stretch about a mile in front, and a league on each side. It was skirted in every part with weeds, shooting out and retiring in skreens on each side, and folding over each other. The whole was a pleasing piece of forest perspective, and the lawn one of the most picturesque compositions we had met with in this mode of landscape.

Soon after we left Culverly Heath, we entered another scene of the same kind, larger, but less varied. In Culverly Heath the materials of landscape were brought together in so perfect a manner, as to produce a picturesque whole. Here, through an awkwardness in the composition, there was but an indifferent whole, though many of the parts in themselves were beautiful.

From this heath we entered a large wood called Denny. It has once been a noble scene, but it is now stripped of its principal honours, and consists chiefly of beech, with a few decrepid oaks straggling among them. Everywhere we saw noble stools, as they call the stumps of such trees as have been cut down; and could form an idea of their grandeur, by the respectful space they have formerly occupied. None of the trees in the neighbourhood seem to have approached within a considerable distance of them.

In this wood, which makes a part of Denny Walk, the lodge belonging to it is seated. Here we left the Lyndhurst road, which we had thus far pursued from Beaulieu; and turning to the left, directed our course to Whitley Ridge Lodge. In the neighbourhood of this place we found some beautiful scenes. One of them has peculiar merit. It is a small forest lawn, containing about seven or eight acres somewhat circular, and skirted with oaks, thickets, and open groves; but they are disposed in so happy a manner, and so much broken by clumps standing out from the other woods, that all the regularity of its form is removed. This lawn is the favourite haunt of deer in summer evenings; and their constant feeding upon it has given the finest texture to its turf. It is rough enough to shew its alliance to the forest; but, like some of Nature's fairest forms, it has so polished an appearance, that, with the smallest improvement, it might accompany the most cultivated scene.

From hence we continued our route through woods, like those of Denny, as far as Ladycross Lodge. These ravaged parts of the forest, though they still afford many pleasing scenes, yet, deprived of their noblest trees, are deprived also of their principal beauty. Though inferior wood, as we had frequent opportunity to observe, might produce distant scenery; yet when we enter the internal parts of a forest, we wish for objects of grandeur. In forest glades especially, where the scenes are small, large trees on the foreground are almost necessary.

From the woods of Ladycross, we entered the western side of that vast heath which occupies all the middle ground between the rivers of Lymington and Beaulieu. It is not a scene, like that of Culverly, and others, in which the woods and open country bear a proportion to each other, — it is diffuse, and unadorned. The circumambient woods are too inconsiderable; and yet it is everywhere surrounded with them. Those of Heathy Dilton occupied the right, and introduced, as we skirted this side of the heath, some little scenery; but all other parts were naked. In front, indeed, ranged a meagre skirting of wood, beyond which the high grounds of the Isle of Wight formed a distance.

As we proceeded farther on this heath, Norley Wood arose at some distance on the left. Towards this, across the heath, we bent our course, as we were told it afforded some of the most beautiful internal scenery of any part of the forest. Norley Wood stretches about two miles in length; and taking a semicircular turn, forms some heathy grounds, which hang to the south, into a bay. As a distant object, however, its woods possess only common beauties. To see its oaks in their glory we must enter its recesses. Their forms are remarkably picturesque, and their combinations are as pleasing as their forms. These combinations are greatly assisted by a profusion of holly, and other humble plants, which are interspersed among the trees. This delightful scenery also is happily opened. Several roads winding in different directions through the wood, form a variety of little recesses. Sometimes we were presented with a longer reach, sometimes with a sudden turn : and the beauty generally arose from seeing little removed clumps of wood, in Waterlo's style, variously rising behind one or two stately trees on the foreground, whose dark branches gave their enlightened foliage effect. Other varieties are introduced by the intersections of roads ; and others by the grass running among full grown trees, or clumps of underwood, —

> Where frequent tufts of holly, box, or thorn,
> Steal on the greensward ; but admit fair space
> For many a mossy maze to wind between.

In short, we found instances here, in great perfection, of every mode of scenery which I have already described in the internal parts of a forest.*

There is also a circumstance connected with this wood, which is rarely found in those woods which occupy the middle regions of the forest ; and that is a hamlet of those little trespassing cottages scattered about it, which have already been mentioned.† They commonly stand detached, and one or other of them meets the eye in various parts, and adds much to the scene. I have already explained how far such circumstances affect both natural and artificial landscape.‡

In a few years, however, all the beautiful scenery of Norley Wood will vanish. Its destruction has long been expected ; and was lately determined. In the beginning of the year 1781, a band of wood cutters entered it, with orders from the surveyor of the forest, to cut a hundred of the best trees, which he had previously marked for the use of the navy. These trees were set apart for building ships of the first and

---

. * See Vol. I. p. 312.   † *Ibid.* page 316.   ‡ *Ibid.* page 316.

second rates. The next year, another fall of the same kind of timber was ordered; and in three or four years, when all the noble trees are gone, the refuse will be destined to ships of inferior size,—frigates, sloops, and cutters. During seven years, it is supposed this wood will yield a considerable supply to the yards of Portsmouth. At present, however, a respite is given it; and the depredations which have been made have not yet greatly injured its beauty. In some parts they may have improved it,* by several openings which the woodcutters have made; though the scenes of Norley Wood admit improvements of this kind less than almost any other scenes in the forest, as they naturally abound in openings and recesses. If a few more attacks, however, be made upon it, its glory will be extinct; and Norley Wood, like other ravaged woods, will suggest only the remembrance of a scene.

And yet the various appendages of woodcutting,— piles of bark, and scattered boughs, and timber wains, —are not unpleasing objects.† The deep, hollow tone also of the woodman's axe, or of axes responsive to each other, in different parts of the wood, are notes in full harmony with the scene, though their music is a knell.

The fallen tree also, lying with its white peeled branches on the ground, is not only beautiful in itself, but if it be not scattered in too great profusion, (for white is an unaccommodating hue,) it forms an agreeable contrast with the living trees.

The white hue, if white can be called a hue, is but of momentary duration, if it ever exists at all. The peeled timber and branches are first of a mellow yellowish colour, which gradually changes into a rich reddish brown, by no means unpleasing to the eye, except from the association which it creates in the mind with the destruction of sylvan beauty, which its appearance necessarily tells us is going forward.

But when we see it deprived of its beautiful ramification, squared, and sawn in lengths, as it sometimes

* See Vol. I. p. 342.   † *Ibid.*

continues long to lie about the forest, it becomes an object of deformity; and we lament what it once was, without receiving any equivalent from its present state.

It may here also be remarked, that the king's timber is much more picturesque than such timber as is bought and cut by the merchant. He, with cautious and discerning eye, stands at the botttom of the tree while it is yet alive; and having examined every twisting limb, and destined every part to its proper service, lops them off, one by one, and then fells the tree, a deformed and mutilated trunk. The royal woodcutter is less nice: he fells the tree as it grows, and leaves the dockmen to ascertain the uses of its several parts. Two or three of the main limbs are generally reft and splintered in the fall; but that is not his concern: in the meantime, the ruin of the whole, with all its spreading parts about it, retains still a degree of picturesque beauty.

SECTION VIII.

A VOYAGE UP BEAULIEU RIVER.

THE river Avon is the boundary of the forest on the west, and the bay of Southampton on the east. Neither of these rivers, therefore, properly belongs to the forest. The only rivers which may justly be called forest rivers are those of Lymington and Beaulieu. The former of these we have already examined in various parts; the latter only about the abbey of Beaulieu. We determined, therefore, to investigate the whole by a voyage.

We took boat in Lymington river, which, at low water, winds beautifully before it enters the sea.* Its banks, indeed, are mud, but of the best species; for they are covered, like the other mud lands of this country, with sea grass, which gives them the air of meadows when the tide retires. The returning water overruns all the boundaries of the river, and makes it

* See ante, page 158.

necessary, for the use of vessels of any burden, to mark
its channel with stakes. The mouth of the river is
distinguished by a larger post, known among fishermen
by the name of Jack in the Basket. It stands about
three miles from Lymington harbour.

At this boundary we entered the channel, which
divides the coast of Hampshire from the Isle of Wight.
The former, which stretches along the left, appears as
a flat woody distance, just raised above the edge of the
water, and unmarked by any object of consequence.
They who are acquainted with the country can point
out, here and there, a house, just seen, among the trees.

On the right, the Isle of Wight makes a better
appearance, and yet not a picturesque one. It consists
of a double ridge of high lands, which, in almost
every part, are ill shaped, and in some parts, the upper
and lower grounds follow each other in a disagreeable
parallel. Indeed, we seldom see a continuation of high
grounds, through a space of near ten miles, forming so
unpleasant a delineation. At least, it seems such to
any eye assimilated to the grandeur of a mountainous
country.

The water line of the island appears to more advantage. Among many smaller indentations of the coast,
the bays of Totland and Newtown are considerable.
Totland Bay is formed by the western part of the island
called the Needle Cliffs, on one side, and on the other,
by that promontory which shoots out opposite to Hurst
Castle, usually called Sconce Point. It is a rude, wild
scene, though the cliffs themselves are rather of the
tame species, without any of those large parts and
projections which give a rocky coast its most picturesque
form. Newtown Bay affords an opening of a different
kind : it is a semicircular sweep into a country highly
cultivated, which, at a proper distance, when the several
objects of cultivation are massed together, has a good
effect.

As we approached the mouth of Beaulieu river, its
opening promised little. The eastern side forms a low,
lineal, disagreeable shore. The western side is still
more disagreeable. It consists of a flat tongue of land

called Needsore Point,* which runs out a considerable
way, and at lower water unites with the mud lands.
When the tide flows, it is in part covered with water.
We found it in this latter situation ; and our boat made
a short push over it, instead of going round by the
mouth of the river.

It is somewhat remarkable, that there is one of these
spits of land near the mouth of each of these forest
rivers, and also at the mouth of Southampton Bay.
Hurst Castle, formerly intended to guard the passage
through the Needles, occupies one near the mouth of
Lymington river ; and Calshot Castle another, at the
entrance of Southampton Bay. On Needsore Point,
which is the middle one, a fortress was thought unne-
cessary. But though these spits of land are remarkable,
they are easily accounted for. The united force of wind
and tide from the south-west and west, so much greater
and more continued than from any other quarter, is the
natural and obvious cause. The same thing happens
at the entrance of Portsmouth harbour. Spithead is the
barrier of its channel, which runs close along the eastern
shore under South Sea Castle and Portsmouth Wall,
much in the same manner as the channel of Beaulieu,
or rather Exbury Haven, runs close under the shore
from Leap. Wherever there is a low or gravelly coast
undefended, on the southern side of our island, it gives
way to the fury of the Atlantic winds and tides. The
rocks of Purbeck protect the gravelly coast about Pool
and Christ Church. To the east of these places, there
have certainly been depredations. Wight defends
Portsmouth, and the shores eastward as far as Arundel,
which would probably go to sea, if they were equally
unprotected from the west as from the east.

We had now entered Beaulieu river, which appears
to be about half a mile broad. For some time, Needsore
Point, on the left, continued a low winding shore,
closing us in behind, tedious and unvaried. But on

* Needsore, that is Needshore ; but the *sh* was not used in Saxon
orthography. Hence Needsore, Stansore, and other terminations of
that kind on this coast ; and Windsor, Hedsor, &c. on the Thames.

the other side the grounds began to form a beautiful bank.

As the reach opened, the skreens improved. The high grounds about Exbury formed themselves into a point covered with wood, through which Exbury chapel just appeared. The other side skreen was composed of ancient woods, where the axe seemed never to have entered. The river still continued as wide as at the entrance; stretching in front into an ample bay, confined by woods; but the extremity of the bay was softened by its length into a second distance.

By degrees we began to wind round Exbury Point, which still continued a principal feature in the view. But though it had greatly changed its appearance, the woods, and meadows, and rough grounds, were still very agreeably intermixed. On the other side, the woods had taken a sweep with the river, and were thrown into good perspective. They mantled down almost to the water, which was bordered only by a narrow edging of meadow. Here, the river affording easy access to the herds of the neighbouring pastures, they came down for refreshment during the sultry hours of a summer noon. While they cooled themselves in the river, the woods behind sheltered them from the sun, and formed a good background to their several picturesque groups. The front of this grand reach maintained long the same appearance, consisting chiefly of woody grounds softened by distance. Nor did the side skreens vary much. Continued woods still rose on the left; and on the right a portion of rough pasturage mingled with them.

We now came in sight of Buckler's Hard * on the left, where the large timber yards, houses, and ships on the stocks, made a violent chasm in the landscape. A quantity of timber scattered about a yard makes a very unpicturesque appearance. It affords a variety of parts without a whole. And yet, in a timber-yard, there are sheds and other circumstances, which are not wholly

* See an account of Buckler's Hard, page 181. The word *Hard* signifies only a firm causeway made upon the mud, for the sake of landing.

void of picturesque images.   In a ship on the stocks, through every stage as it advances, there is a degree of beauty, which consists chiefly in the variety of its sweeping lines.

At Buckler's Hard, the reach of the river is very interesting.   On the right are the woods of Beaulieu, winding round with great richness into a front skreen. On the left, where wood before abounded, the grounds now run more into pasturage, though far from being destitute of furniture.   One decoration they have, which is not unpleasing.   Where the meadows fall down to the water, they are secured from the tide by low, staked banks, which follow the winding banks of the river.   If they had run in a straight line, they would have been a great deformity; but as they wind, instead of being offensive objects, they give a sort of rough, irregular termination to the line of the river.   If we painted the scene, we should have no objection to introduce them, both for the reason given, and also for the sake of the reflections they form in the water.   They have sometimes also the beauty of contrast, when the other parts of the bank are without them.

From Buckler's Hard, the river takes a sweep to the right.   The woods likewise on that side follow its course, and spreading in great luxuriance to the water's edge, throw a gloom over half the river.   A noble bay, land-locked with wood, begins soon to open; as this scene removes, the woods take a different form, shaping themselves into removed skreens following each other. Another reach brought us within sight of Beaulieu, the bridge and the abbey forming the centre of the view; the river, in the meantime, losing very little of its grandeur from the first reach to the last.

Thus we finished our voyage up the river of Beaulieu, which, in a course of near three leagues from the sea, forms about five or six grand sweeps.   The simple idea it presents throughout, is that of a winding tide river flowing up a woody and uninhabited country, which is a singular character for an English river to assume. Here and there we see a house, and a few spots of cultivation, but so little, that they make no impression on the general character of the scene. The picturesque eye, used to landscape, easily overlooks these little obstacles, and carries on the general idea undisturbed. The busy scene of ship building at Buckler's Hard rather aided than injured the idea; for as no one would expect a scene of this kind in so retired a place, it seemed as if the adventurers, who had sailed up the river, had landed here either to refit their ships, or to build others for the purpose of pursuing their discoveries.

Miratur nemus insuetum fulgentia longè
Scuta virûm fluvio, pictásque innare carinas.

The idea of a wild country in a natural state, however picturesque, is to the generality of people but an unpleasing one. There are few who do not prefer the busy scenes of cultivation to the grandest of Nature's rough productions. In general, indeed, when we meet with a description of a pleasing country, we hear of hay cocks or waving corn fields, or labourers at their plough, or other circumstances and objects which the picturesque eye always wishes to exclude. The case is, the spectator sympathizes in the joys of a country, which arise from the prospect of plenty; and associating these ideas with the country itself, he calls it picturesque; by which he means only that it pleases him. Thus, too, in the grand and sublime scenes of Nature, if there be any mixture of horror in them, (which often adds greatly to the picturesque effect,) the associated ideas of unhappiness cloud the scene, and make it displeasing.

I mean not, when a person is among objects which in their remote consequences give delight, or in the midst of scenes which are connected with distress, that he should not feel the natural impressions they make,—all I mean is, to investigate the source of beauty, to limit the different modes of pleasure and pain, to separate causes and effects, and to evince that a scene, though it abound with circumstances of horror, may be very picturesque, while another may be entirely the reverse, though replete with incidents that produce joy and happiness.

I have an instance at hand to my purpose. One of

our voyagers * to the northern seas, in sailing up a river, thus describes the scene. " The country," says he, " on each side, was very romantic, but unvaried, the river running between mountains of the most craggy and barren aspect, where there was nothing to diversify the scene, but now and then the sight of a bear, or flights of wild-fowl. So uninteresting a passage leaves me nothing farther to add."

It is hardly possible, in so few words, to present more picturesque ideas of the horrid and savage kind. We have a river running up a country, broken on both sides with wild romantic rocks, which we know Nature never constructs in a uniform manner. We naturally therefore conclude, they ran out, in some parts, into vast diagonal strata ; on the ledges of which a bear or two appeared sitting on their hams, or howling at the boat. In other parts, the rocks would form lofty promontories hanging over the river, and inhabited by numerous flights of sea-fowl screaming around them. This is not an imaginary picture, but copied with exactness from Captain King's sketch. And yet he has no conception that a scene so savage could present any other ideas than such as were disgusting. He calls it an unvaried scene ; by which expression he meant nothing, I am persuaded, but that the rocks were neither intermixed with villages, nor with scenes of cultivation. Wood might probably be wanting, but in a scene of picturesque horror, wood is by no means a necessary appendage : it is rather indeed an improper one. Flourishing wood, at least, is out of place : the scene might perhaps admit here and there a scathed and ragged pine.

It is curious to observe how our author does himself unconsciously furnish illustrations of the theory of taste given by Mr Alison, whilst he is not only entirely ignorant of its principles, but is blindly groping after principles which are altogether untangible, because altogether without existence. He is thus continually in confusion, and perpetually compelled to yield up exceptions to the general rules he would lay down.

* Captain King, who succeeded Captain Cook, p. 207.

Beyond Beaulieu our boat could not pass. Thus far only the tide flows with any force. At Beaulieu, therefore, we waited till the tide turned, when we again embarked.

The views in ascending and descending a river, vary considerably through its several reaches. Yet the difference, though observable enough, cannot easily be described. Language wants colours to paint such nice distinctions. We shall therefore fall down the river with a quicker sail than we ascended. And yet we must not leave its retrospect views entirely unobserved.

The bay formed by the circling woods in the second reach as we descend is very beautiful. I know not whether its form is not more pleasing than we thought it in the morning.

The next reach loses in beauty. A long stretch of low land, sweeping across the river like a mole, which was less observable before, now greatly interrupts the beauty of the view.

The succeeding bay, where the woods of Exbury open in front, is very grand and extensive.

From Buckler's Hard, nothing can unite more happily than the rough uncultivated grounds of Exbury on the left, with the long succession of Beaulieu woods on the right.

After this the river soon becomes an estuary. When we entered it, as we looked up the stream, we had immediately the idea of a river winding into a woodland country: in the same manner, when we descended, we had as quickly an idea of a river entering the sea. For as the woods in the former case become at once the centre of the view, so does the sea and the Isle of Wight in the latter. The last reach, therefore, of the river continues long to exhibit a kind of mixed scenery. Exbury Point, and the woody grounds about it, still preserve the idea of the beautiful woodland scenes we had left; while Needsore Point, though it wind quite around, and shut us within a land-locked bay, is yet so low, that the sea and the island appear beyond it.

On opening the mouth of the river, our boatmen attempted to carry us across the mudlands as they had done in the morning, but they found it dangerous, and desisted; for if a boat should only touch the ground, the delay of a few minutes might endanger her sticking till the return of the tide, so rapidly do the waters retreat.

As the tide was thus leaving the mudlands, flights of sea-gulls hovered round, watching, on that event, to pick up the little wreck that remained. Sea fowl are the common appendages of all estuaries. Indeed few masters in landscape omit them.

> Æneas ingentem ex æquore* lucum
> Prospicit : Hunc inter fluvio Tyberinus amœno,
> Vorticibus rapidis, et multâ flavus arenâ,
> In mare prorumpit : Variæ circúmque, suprâque,
> Assuetæ ripis volucres et fluminis alveo
> Æthera mulcebant cantu, lucóque volabant.

Again,

> Ceu quondum nivei liquida inter nubila cygni,
> Cùm sese è pastu referunt, et longa canoros
> Dant per colla modos : sonat amnis———

And again,

> Piscoso amne Padusæ
> Dant sonitum rauci per stagna loquacia cygni.

On such classical authority we admire the flights of sea-gulls as a proper ornament in a scene like this. It was amusing to observe how quickly they discovered the relinquished shore, long before it was discoverable by us, and to see them running, in appearance, on the surface of the water. For though the tide had in those parts left the land, yet the mud, from its perfect flatness, long retained its glazed and watery appearance. The cormorant also sat watching the ebbing tide; but he seemed bent on matters of greater importance. He did not, like the idle gull, wheel round the air, nor pace about the ebbing shore, mixing business and amusement together. With eager attention he took his stand on some solitary post, set up to point the channel of the

---

* Æneas did not see the grove *ex æquore* from his ship, but he saw it rising *ex æquore* from the water's edge.

river, and from that eminence observed, from the dimpling of the waters, where some poor wandering fish had gotten himself entangled in the shallows, whom he marked for certain destruction.

But these are not the only birds which enliven a voyage up Beaulieu river. In the lines. I have just quoted from Virgil's description of Æneas' entrance into the Tyber, (the whole of which might serve, with very little alteration, for a description also of Beaulieu river,) two kinds of birds are introduced,—those which disport themselves *in fluminis alveo,* and those which *æthera mulcebant cantu, lucoque volabant.* With the actions of the former of these we have already been entertained ; but we have not yet listened to the music of the latter. I have been told it is extraordinary; and that all these woods on both sides of the river (so extensive are they, and unmolested) are filled with such innumerable flights of singing birds, that to sail up the river, in a morning or an evening in the spring, affords, in Virgil's language, an *avium concentus* hardly anywhere else to be found. The nightingale, the thrush, the blackbird, and the linnet, are the chief performers in the concert. Some of these you hear continually bursting out, either at hand or from a distance, while the various petty chirpers of the woods join the chorus; and though alone their little untuneable voices might be harsh, yet altogether (one softening the discordancy of another) they make a kind of melody, or at least an agreeable contrast to such of the band as are better skilled in their business.

I cannot leave this river scene without observing that, although it is picturesque in a high degree, yet it exhibits such a specimen of the picturesque (if I may speak in terms seemingly contradictory) as is not well calculated to make a picture. The whole is a succession of those softer nameless beauties which highly please, but cannot easily be described. Various beautiful accompaniments are exhibited ; but striking objects are wanting. If every reach had been adorned with a castle or a picturesque rock, such as Captain King's uninteresting river would have afforded, each successive scene would have been more picturesquely marked, though the character of the river, on the whole, might have been injured; but now the whole plays upon the eye in the same pleasing, though unvaried colours. A strong and peculiar character belongs to the river in general; but the parts, if I may so express myself, are lost in the whole. They are everywhere beautiful, but nowhere characteristic.

Here, again, Mr Gilpin is strongly at variance with himself; but entirely from his ignorance of those principles of association from which all our pleasure, arising from the contemplation of the works of Nature, is derived.

SECTION IX.

AN EXCURSION ALONG THE EASTERN SIDE OF BEAULIEU RIVER, THE COAST OPPOSITE TO THE ISLE OF WIGHT, THE WESTERN SIDE OF SOUTHAMPTON BAY, AND THENCE, BY DIBDEN, AGAIN TO BEAULIEU.

At Beaulieu we crossed the bridge, and, turning short to the right, had a better view of the first reach of the river from the land than we had before in our voyage from the water. The river itself had more the appearance of a lake, (for it was then high water,) and made a magnificent sweep round a point of wooded land; while the woods on the opposite side, following its course on an elevated bank, were as rich as a picturesque imagination could conceive them. The foreground, indeed, was not equal to a scene which was in every other respect so complete.

From hence we ascended a close lane, cut through a corner of Beaulieu manor, and enriched on both sides, but especially on the left, with forest scenery. At Hilltop Gate the lane opens into that extensive heath which occupies all the middle part of the peninsula between the river of Beaulieu and the bay of Southampton. As this peninsula shoots into length rather than breadth, the heathy grounds follow its form, and extend several miles in one direction, though seldom above two in the other. The banks of both rivers are woody; and these woods appeared, as we entered the heath, to skirt its extremities. Through these extremities, containing the most beautiful parts of the country, we meant to travel. At Hilltop, therefore, instead of crossing the heath, we turned short into a road on the right, which led us along the skirts of the woods, under the shade of which we travelled about a mile. Sometimes these woods shot like promontories into the heath, and we were obliged to ride round them ; but oftener our road, treading the clumps and single trees which stood forward, carried us among them. The richness and closeness of the forest scenery on one side, contrasted with the plainness and simplicity of the heath on the other, skirted with distant wood, and seen through the openings of the clumps, were pleasing.

From this heath we were received by lanes—but such lanes as a forest only can produce, in which oak and ash, full grown, and planted irregularly by the hand of Nature, stood out in various groups, and added a new foreground, every step we took—to a variety of little openings into woods, copses, and pleasing recesses.

While we were admiring these close landscapes, the woods on the right suddenly giving way, we were presented with a view of the river, Buckler's Hard beyond it, the men of war building in the dock there, and the woody grounds which rise in the offskip. This exhibition was, rather formally, introduced like a vista. The woods seemed to have been opened on purpose; but formality is a fault which we seldom find in Nature, and which, in the scene before us, she will probably correct, in a few years, by the growth of some intervening trees.

A mile farther brought us to the seat of Colonel Mitford, among the woods of Exbury. The house is no object; but the scenery consists of a more beautiful profusion of wood, water, and varied grounds, than is commonly to be met with. Here we proposed to spend the evening; but not finding Colonel Mitford at home, we took a ramble into his woods till supper, where we expected to meet him.

The richness of the scenes had led us imperceptibly from one to another. We had everywhere instances of the beauty of trees, as individuals, as uniting in clumps, and as spreading into woods,—for here all is pure Nature ; and as they were beginning now to put on their autumnal attire, we were entertained with the beauties of colouring as well as of form. Among these unknown woods, our way at length became perplexed, and the sun was now set. Having no time, therefore, to lose, we inquired at a lonely cottage which we found in a sheltered glade. Nothing could indicate peace and happiness more than this little sequestered spot, and we expected to find a neat, peaceful, contented family within. But we found that a happy scene will not always make happy inhabitants. At the door stood two or three squalid children, with eager famished countenances staring through matted hair. On entering the hovel, it was so dark that we could at first see nothing. By degrees a scene of misery opened. We saw other ragged children within, and were soon struck with a female figure, grovelling, at full length, by the side of a few embers upon the hearth. Her arms were naked to her shoulders, and her rags scarce covered her body. On our speaking to her, she uttered, in return, a mixture of obscenity and imprecations. We had never seen so deplorable a maniac.

We had not observed when we entered, what now struck us, a man sitting in the corner of the hovel, with his arms folded, and a look of dejection, as if lost in despair. We asked him who that wretched person was. " She is my wife," said he, with a composed melancholy ; " and the mother of these children." He seemed to be a man of great sensibility, and it struck us what distress he must feel every evening after his labour, when, instead of finding a little domestic comfort, he met the misery and horror of such a house—the total neglect of his little affairs—his family without any overseer, brought up in idleness and dirt—and his wife, for whom he had no means of providing either assistance or cure, lying so wretched an object always before him. We left him, strongly impressed with his calamity, which appeared to be a more severe visitation than the hand of Heaven commonly inflicts.

We found afterwards that we had been wholly mistaken, and that we had before us a strong instance of that strange fatality by which mankind are so often themselves the ministers of those distresses which they are so ready to ascribe to Heaven. On relating our adventure at supper, we were informed, that the man whose appearance of sensibility had affected us so much, was one of the most hardened, abandoned, mischievous fellows in the country—that he had been detected in sheep-stealing—and that he had killed a neighbour's horse in an act of revenge—and that it was supposed he had given his wife, who was infamous likewise, a blow in a quarrel, which had occasioned her malady.

The next morning we took a particular view of the beautiful scenery around us, of which the evening before we had only obtained a general idea.

The woods of Exbury, which are extensive, are chiefly oak, the spontaneous growth of the country; but Mr Mitford found many of the bare and barren spots about his house planted by his father and grandfather with fir groves of various kinds, though generally, according to the fashion of the times, in formal rows.

On a deliberate view of his grounds, he formed a general plan, resulting from the various scenes they exhibited. The boundary of his estate presents a series of views of three very different characters. Towards the west, he has a variety of grand river views, formed by the Ex, or, as it is commonly at this day called, Beaulieu river, as we had seen it in our voyage through the woods of Beaulieu and Exbury in its approach to the sea. The southern part of his boundary overlooks what was anciently called the Solent Sea, but now commonly the Channel of the Isle of Wight, which, at its two extremities, discovers the open sea through the eastern passage by Spithead, and, through the western, by the Needles. On the east and north his boundary views take a new form. We leave the shore, and wind into a woodland country, which, within a hundred yards, assumes so new a character, that we might easily conceive it to be as many miles from the sea. In these

woody scenes, intermixed with open grounds, we continue about four miles, till, winding round, we return
to those rising grounds on the west, from whence we
first had the views of the river.

This boundary circuit carries us through the space of
about eight miles.   Mr Mitford has done little besides
marking it out, by cutting through the woods as he
should wish to lead it.   To complete his plan would be
very expensive; though an expense equal to the natural
advantages of the scene, in good hands, would make
this one of the most varied and picturesque woodland
rides perhaps in England.

Within this boundary circuit Mr Mitford has marked
out an interior one, circling about a mile round his
house.   As the object of the larger circuit is to shew,
as much as possible, the extent of his views, the object
of this interior one is to break those distant views into
parts, to form those parts into the most beautiful scenes,
and to exhibit them with woody foregrounds to the best
advantage.   From many parts of this interior scenery,
the Isle of Wight makes its most picturesque appearance.
In various views of it from the Hampshire coast, we
have seen it spread in too lengthened a curtain, and its
hills too smooth and tame.   Both these inconveniences
are here, in a degree, obviated.   Seldom more than a
small part of the island is seen at once, and this part is
about the centre, which is the loftiest and the roughest.
Here rise two considerable hills, Gatescliff and Wrax-
hill, and one of them affords a circumstance of great
beauty.   Carisbroke Castle, seated on an eminence
about four miles within the island, is seen very advantageously against Gatescliff, when the sun shines either
on the castle or on the mountain, while the other is in
shadow.

In laying out this inner circle, Mr Mitford had his
greatest difficulties to contend with; for here he had all
his grandfather's formal groves to encounter; and it was
no easy matter to break their formalities, to make
judicious inroads through them, and unite them in one
plan.   He often lamented—what other improvers have
lamented before him—the injudicious sufferance of the

growth of trees. Next to the cutting down of trees improperly, the greatest mischief is to let them grow together too long : they soon ruin each other. He had suffered his woodward only to use his discretion in the distant woods. In the groves about his house he allowed no marking hammer but his own. The consequence was, he was so little on the spot that many of his best trees were injured. The fir especially, if its natural branches are once lost, as they always are by straitened quarters, never recovers them. These two circuits round his house Mr Mitford has joined by three cross walks.

In taking these circuits, we could not help remarking the comparative virtue of taste and expense. The former, with very little of the latter, will always produce something pleasing ; while the utmost efforts of the latter, unaided by the former, are ineffectual. The larger the proportion of misguided expense, the wider will the deformity spread ; whereas every touch in the hand of taste has so far its effect.

It is the same precisely in working the scenes of Nature as in forming an artificial scene. Set two artists at work, give one of them a bit of black lead and a scrap of paper ; every touch he makes, perhaps, deserves to be treasured in a cabinet. Give the other the costliest materials, all is a waste of time, of labour, and expense ; add colours, they only make his deformities more glaring.

True taste, in the first place, whether in Nature or on canvass, makes not a single stroke till the general design is laid out, with which, in some part or other, every effort coincides. The artist may work at his picture in this part or the other, but if his design and composition are fixed, every effort is gradually growing into a whole ; whereas he who works without taste, seldom has any idea of a whole. He tacks one part to another, as his misguided fancy suggests ; or if he has any plan, it is something as unnatural as the parts which compose it are absurd. The deeper his pocket, therefore, and the wider his scale, his errors are more apparent.

To an injudicious person, or one who delights in

temples and Chinese bridges, very little would appear
executed in the scenes I have described at Exbury.
There is scarce a gravel walk made, no pavilion raised,
nor even a white seat fixed; and yet, in fact, more is
done, than if all these decorations, and a hundred others,
had been added, unaccompanied with what has been done.
The greatest difficulty of all is surmounted, — that of
laying out a judicious plan.   The rest, though the most
ostensible, because the most expensive, is only a little
mechanical finishing.

From these pleasing scenes we pursued our journey
through part of the beautiful ride we have just described
to Leap, along lanes close on the left, but opening to
the right in various places to the river, which assumes
a magnificent form.   Needsore Point makes here an
appearance very different from what it made when we
navigated the mouth of Beaulieu river.*   It appears now
from the higher grounds, when the tide is low, to run
at least a league into the sea; flat, unadorned, and
skirted with drifted sand, making a singular feature in all
these views; and the more so, as every part of the
ground in its neighbourhood is woody, bold, and prominent.   This peninsula, of which Needsore Point is
the termination, belongs to the manor of Beaulieu.   It
contains some good land, consisting chiefly of pasturage;
and the whole of it is let out in a single farm.

In this remote part, it is supposed, somewhere near
Exbury, the Dauphin, after his fruitless expedition to
England, embarked privately, on the death of King John,
for France, burning the country behind him as he fled.
His embarkation from so obscure a place shews, in a
strong light, how much his hopes were humbled.

At Leap we met the sea, where the coast of the Isle
of Wight, as far as to Spithead on the left, makes
nearly the same unpicturesque appearance, which it
does from the other shores of the forest.   It extends
into length, and exhibits neither grandeur nor variety.
When it is seen, as we saw it from Mr Mitford's,
broken into parts, as it should always be when seen to

* See ante, page 196.

picturesque advantage,* it afforded several beautiful
distances. But here, when the whole coast was displayed
at once, it lost its picturesque form. Near Leap, however, we had one very beautiful coast view. A rising
copse on the left, adorned with a road winding through it,
makes a good foreground; from thence a promontory,
in the second distance, with an easy sweeping shore,
shoots into the sea, and is opposed on the opposite side
by a point of the island, leaving a proper proportion of
water to occupy the middle space.

Leap is one of the port towns of the forest; and as it
lies opposite to Cowes, it is the common place of embarkation in these parts to the island. It consists of about
half a dozen houses, and shelters perhaps as many
fishing boats. All the coast, indeed, from St Helen's to
the Needles, and around the island, is, in peaceable
times, a scene of fishing. In the whiting season
especially, fleets of twenty or thirty boats are often seen
lying at anchor on the banks, or a little out at sea.

Fowling, too, is practised on this coast, as much as
fishing. Numerous flocks of wild fowl frequent it in the
winter,—widgeons, geese, and ducks; and, in the beginning of the season especially, as they bear a price in the
country, they of course attract the notice of the fowler.
As the coast between Hampshire and the Isle of Wight
is a peculiar species of coast, consisting, when the tide
ebbs, of vast muddy flats, covered with green sea weed,
it gives the fowler an opportunity of practising arts
perhaps practised nowhere else.

Fowling and fishing, indeed, on this coast, are commonly the employments of the same person. He who
in summer, with his line or his net, plies the shores
when they are overflowed by the tide; in winter, with
his gun, as evening draws on, runs up in his boat
among the little creeks and crannies, which the tide
leaves in the mudlands, and there lies in patient expectation of his prey.

Sea fowl commonly feed by night, when in all their
multitudes they come down to graze on the savannahs of

* See ante, page 177.

the shore. As the sonorous cloud advances, (for their noise in the air resembles a pack of hounds in full cry,) the attentive fowler listens which way they bend their course. Perhaps he has the mortification to hear them alight at too great a distance for his gun (though of the longest barrel) to reach them; and if he cannot edge his boat a little round some winding creek, which it is not always in his power to do, he despairs of success that night. Perhaps, however, he is more fortunate, and has the satisfaction to hear the airy noise approach nearer, till at length the host settles on some plain, on the edge of which his little boat lies moored. He now, as silently as possible, primes both his pieces anew,—for he is generally double armed—and listens with all his attention. It is so dark that he can take no aim; for if he could see the birds, they also could see him; and, being shy and timorous in a great degree, would seek some other pasture. Though they march with music, they feed in silence. Some indistinct noises, however, if the night be still, issue from so large a host. He directs his piece therefore, as well as he can, towards the sound, gives his fire at a venture, and instantly catching up his other gun, gives a second discharge where he supposes the flock to rise on the wing. His gains for the night are now decided, and he has only to gather his harvest. He immediately puts on his mud pattens,* ignorant yet of his success, and goes groping about in the dark, happy if he have a little star light, in quest of his booty, picking up perhaps a dozen, and erhaps not one: so hardly does the poor fowler earn a few shillings, exposed in an open boat, during a solitary winter night, to the weather as it comes, rain, hail, or snow, on a bleak coast, a league perhaps from the beach, and often in danger, without great care, of being fixed in the mud, where he would become an inevitable prey to the returning tide. I have heard one of these poor fellows say, he never takes a dog with him on these expeditions, because no dog could bear the cold which he is obliged to suffer. After all, perhaps others enjoy more from his

---

* Mud pattens are flat pieces of board, which the fowler ties to his feet, that he may not sink in the mud.

labours than he himself does; for it often happens, that the tide next day throws on different parts of the shore, many of the birds which he had killed, but could not find in the night.

I have heard of an unhappy fowler, whom this hazardous occupation led into a case of still greater distress: in the day time, too, it happened, which shews the double danger of such expeditions in the night. Mounted on his mud pattens, he was traversing one of these mudland plains in quest of ducks; and being intent only on his game, he suddenly found the waters, which had been brought forward with uncommon rapidity by some peculiar circumstance of tide and current, had made an alarming progress around him. Encumbered as his feet were, he could not exert much expedition; but to whatever part he ran, he found himself completely invested by the tide. In this uncomfortable situation, a thought struck him, as the only hope of safety. He retired to that part of the plain which seemed the highest, from its being yet uncovered by water; and striking the barrel of his gun (which for the purpose of shooting wild fowl was very long) deep into the mud, he resolved to hold fast by it, as a support, as well as a security against the waves, and to wait the ebbing of the tide. A common tide, he had reason to believe, would not, in that place, have reached above his middle; but as this was a spring-tide, and brought in with so strong a current, he durst hardly expect so favourable a conclusion. In the meantime, the water, making a rapid advance, had now reached him: it covered the ground on which he stood, it rippled over his feet, it gained his knees, his waist, button after button was swallowed up, till at length it advanced over his very shoulders. With a palpitating heart he gave himself up for lost. Still, however, he held fast by his anchor: his eye was eagerly in search of some boat, which might accidentally take its course that way; but none appeared. A solitary head, floating on the water, and that sometimes covered by a wave, was no object to be descried from the shore, at the distance of half a league; nor could he exert any sounds of distress that could be heard so far. While he was thus making up his mind, as the exigence would allow, to the terrors of sudden destruction, his attention was called to a new object. He thought he saw the uppermost button of his coat begin to appear. No mariner floating on a wreck could behold a cape at sea with greater transport than he did the uppermost button of his coat. But the fluctuation of the water was such, and the turn of the tide so slow, that it was yet some time before he durst venture to assure himself that the button was fairly above the level of the flood. At length, however, a second button appearing at intervals, his sensations may rather be conceived than described, and his joy gave him spirits and resolution to support his uneasy situation four or five hours longer, till the waters had fully retired.

A little beyond Leap we were interrupted by a creek, which, when the tide flows high, runs considerably into the land, and forms a large piece of water. At all times it is an extensive marsh; its borders are edged with rushes and sedges, which grow profusely also on various little rough islands on its surface. Here the wild duck and the widgeon find many a delightful cover, amidst which they breed and rear their young in great abundance.

Near this part of the coast stands Lutterel's Tower, built as the station of a view; but as it is intended for a habitable house likewise, the offices, which it could not contain, are constructed of canvass around it. It is finished in the highest style of expense; and, if it were not for the oddness and singularity of the conception and contrivance, it is not entirely destitute of some kind of taste. But the building is so whimsical, and the end so inadequate to the expense, that we considered it, on the whole, as a glaring contrast to those pleasing scenes we had just examined at Exbury, in which true taste had furnished us with a delightful entertainment, at a trifling expense.*

The view which this tower commands over the circumjacent country is very extensive; but its sea view is

* See ante, page 209.

most admired, stretching from the bay of Southampton
to Portsmouth, from thence to St Helen's, and, on the
other side, all along the range of the Isle of Wight, and
beyond the Needles to the ocean.   The whole together
forms the appearance of a magnificent bay, of which
Spithead and St Helen's (where there is commonly a
fleet at anchor) make the central part.

But this view, like the other extensive views we have
seen, is by no means picturesque.   It might have been
supposed, that the Isle of Wight (on surveying its
appearance in a map) would have made such an angle
at Cowes Point, which is nearly opposite to this tower,
as would have thrown the eastern part of the island into
better perspective than the western assumes from any
part of the Hampshire coast.   And so indeed in some
degree it does.   But the eye is at too great a distance
to get much advantage from this circumstance.   If the
spectator were carried nearer Cowes, the coast towards
St Helen's might then fall away in good perspective.
But at this distance all is sea, the coast is a mere thread,
and the whole view together is without proportion.

And yet it is not merely the disproportion between
land and water which disqualifies a view of this kind in
a picturesque light: a picturesque view may consist
entirely of water.   Nor is it distance which disqualifies
it: the most remote distances are happily introduced on
canvass.   But what chiefly disqualifies it, is the want of
foreground to balance this vast expanse of distance.
Unless distances and foregrounds are in some degree
balanced, no composition can be good.   Foregrounds
are essential to landscape—distances are not.

A picturesque view, as was observed, may consist
chiefly, indeed entirely, of water; but then it is supposed,
that as there cannot be a natural foreground, an artificial
one must be obtained,—a group of ships, a few boats
with figures, a lighthouse, or something that will make
a balance between near and distant objects.   Such were
the sea pieces of Vandervelt, in which vessels of some
kind were always introduced to make an artificial foreground.   We sometimes, indeed, meet with amusing
views, such as that celebrated one at Hackfall, in

Yorkshire,* where there is a gradual proportion among the different parts of the retiring landscape; we can scarce distinguish where the foregrounds end, and where the distance begins; yet still there are objects nearer the eye, which in a degree set off the retiring parts, though they may not be fully proportioned to them. But the most advanced parts of water cannot form a foreground, if I may so speak. It wants, on its nearest parts, that variety of objects which, receiving strong impressions of light and shade, are necessary to give it consequence and strength. It turns all into distance. Such is the view before us over the Channel, and along the shores of the Isle of Wight. To the imagination, it is the simple idea of grandeur; to the eye, a mere exhibition of distance.

Besides, there is not only a want of natural proportion and balance between the foreground and the offskip, but a foreground here could not even artificially be obtained, because of the loftiness of the point. Take the same view from a lower stand—from the level of the sea for instance, or a little higher, where you may station a group of ships, the masts and sails of which rise above the horizon—and by thus giving the view a proper and proportioned foreground, you may turn it into one of Vandervelt's compositions, and give it picturesque beauty.

We have seen an exquisite picture, painted by the powerful pencil of the Reverend John Thomson of Duddingstone, which we conceive to be a triumph of art in its way. The whole subject is a portion of sea, with a fragment of sandy shore. It has a raw hazy atmosphere over it, almost blending with the water, and not an object, either animate or inanimate, is to be seen in it, except one solitary sea-gull on the wing. But there is so much truth and Nature in the work, that no one who looks upon it will say that the introduction of ships, boats, lighthouse, or any thing else, would improve it. We thus see that all these imaginary obstacles to picturesque effect may, in many instances, be overcome by the

* See *Observations on the Lakes and Mountains of Cumberland*, vol. ii. p. 191.

genius of the artist alone, without any alteration of the mate-
-rials which are to be worked upon, and if this can be effected
by genius in one instance, so would it be effected in all,
if the powers of human genius could only be sufficiently
extended; and thus would the character of the picturesque
become an universal property in Nature.

But though the view from Lutterel's Tower is not
picturesque, it is certainly, as we observed of those other
views over the island,* in a great degree amusing.
The whole area, constantly overspread with vessels of
various kinds, is a perpetual moving scene; while the
naked eye discovers in the distance a thousand objects,
and, through a telescope, a thousand more. Though
the telescopic pleasures of the eye are very little allied
to the pleasures of the painter, they still assist the
amusement. The cliff on which this tower stands, is
about forty or fifty feet high, and is formed into a terrace,
which runs a considerable way along the beach.

About a mile from this whimsical building stands
Calshot Castle, situated, like the Castle of Hurst,† on a
tongue of land shooting into the sea. Calshot is another
of those ancient coast castles which Henry VIII built
out of the spoils of the abbeys. It was originally
intended as a safeguard to the Bay of Southampton.
The views here are of the same nature as those at
Lutterel's Tower. They have a less extensive range to
the west, but this is compensated by a full view of
Southampton Bay. And they are the more picturesque,
as the point of view is lower.

Near the village of Fawley, which is among the
largest villages of the coast, stands Cadland, the seat
of Mr Drummond, an edifice of a very different kind
from that we had just been surveying. Though quite
plain, it is one of the most elegant, and seems to be
one of the most comfortable houses in the country.

It stands on a gentle eminence on the banks of
Southampton Bay, with a great variety of ground
playing beautifully around it, which is everywhere
adorned, and in some places profusely covered with

* See ante, page 177.　　　　† See ante, page 154.

6

ancient wood. The whole country, indeed, was so well wooded, that no addition of wood was any where necessary; in many parts it was redundant. This abundance of old timber gives the house, though lately built, so much the air and dignity of an ancient mansion, that Mr Brown, the ingenious improver of it, used to say, " It was the oldest new place he knew in England." The clumps, particularly, he has managed with great judgment. We observed some combinations of ash and other trees, which were equal to any clumps we had ever seen. They adorned the natural scene, and were just such as the picturesque eye would wish to introduce in artificial landscape. We regretted that the great storm in February, 1781, had blown down nineteen of these ornamental trees. There seemed, however, no deficiency; though, I doubt not, if we had known the situation of those which had fallen, we should have found they filled their station with great propriety. The park includes a circuit of about five miles.

Besides the beauty of the grounds themselves around the house, they command all the pleasing distances in their neighbourhood,—Southampton Bay, Netley Abbey, Calshot Castle, Spithead, the Channel, the Isle of Wight, St Helen's, Cowes, and all the other conspicuous parts of the island; and as many of these views are seen with the advantage of grand woody foregrounds, they have often an admirable effect.

The only thing that appeared affected about this elegant mansion is the parade which accompanies some of the appendant buildings. At the small distance of half a quarter of a mile from the house, stands a most splendid farm. The stables, the cow sheds, the pigeon-house, the granaries, the barns, are all superb. In another direction, the same honour, though in an inferior degree, is paid to poultry. This is too much, and tends only to lessen the dignity of the principal mansion.

As the horse is so nearly connected with his master, and contributes so much to his state and convenience, we allow so noble an associate to lodge under a roof proportioned to his master's magnificence. As he is expected also to be ready at a call, and may properly be the object of attention to persons of any rank, we allow his magnificent lodging to stand near the mansion to which it appertains. At the same time, if the stables be expensive, they should contribute to the magnificence of the whole, by making one of the wings, or some other proper appendage, of the pile.

But for the cow sheds and pig styes, they have no title to such notice. Let them be convenient and neat, but let them be simple and unadorned; let them stand in some sequestered place, where they may not presume to vie with the mansion they depend on, but keep a respectful distance. Herds of cattle are beautiful, in a high degree, in their proper place, among lawns and woods; but pent up, as they are obliged to be, in yards, amidst filth and litter, they are no objects of beauty. Neither should their habitations be considered as such : ornaments here serve only to call the attention to a nuisance.

From Cadland we proceeded to Hethe, through a variety of such beautiful country that we almost thought the house we had just seen might have been better stationed elsewhere. In a variety of pleasing situations, it is difficult to select the best. Something or other may excel in each ; and the eye, divided in its choice, is unwilling to lose any thing. As we cannot, however, possess every beauty and every convenience at once, we must forego that idea, and endeavour to make such a selection as will include the most ; though, perhaps, some striking beauty which we observe in other situations is lost. This probably is the case of the elegant mansion we have been surveying. No situation perhaps, on the whole, could have excelled it.

The pleasing landscape we met with between Cadland and Hethe, was of a similar kind to what we had already admired,—great profusion of full grown oak adorning great variety of playing ground. But what particularly recommended these scenes, were several dips, running down to Southampton Bay, wooded on each side, with a rich country beyond the water. They were of the same kind with those we admired between

Christ Church and Lymington,* but much richer and more beautiful. Two of the most striking of these scenes were from Stobland Common, and near Butt's Ash Farm.

At Hethe the whole bay of Southampton opened in one view before us ; but the scene it offers is far from being picturesque. The opposite shore is long and tedious, and the lines of the bay run parallel ; for though, in fact, there are two or three bold openings in it, formed by the mouths of rivers, yet, in the distance, which is about a league, they are totally lost.

Hethe is the ferry port to Southampton, which lies higher up in a diagonal across the bay, and upon a neck of land which shoots into it. The flowing tide, there-fore, carries the boat quickly to Southampton, and the ebbing tide returns it as expeditiously to Hethe.

From Hethe to Dibden the country, if possible, improves in beauty. The many inequalities of the ground — the profusion of stately trees — the sheltered enclosures appearing everywhere like beautiful little wooded lawns — the catches, here and there, of the bay — and, above all, the broad, green, winding lanes, adorned with clumps standing out in various parts, — exhibit a wonderful variety of pleasing landscape. I touch general features only ; for as these woodland scenes are nowhere strongly marked, it is impossible to give any particular detail of them by verbal description. One may say of them, as we sometimes say of a well written history, which runs into a variety of incidents, interesting indeed, but not replete with any important events, that no just idea of the contents of it can be given without referring to the book itself.

Dibden is an ancient village, called Depe-dene in the Doomsday Book, and from this authority, we know, that at the time of making the survey, it had a fishery and a saltern. The church is very old, but incommodious and mean ; several of the Lisle family of Moyle's Court, and Crux Easton, lie buried in this fabric. In the churchyard is an immense yew

* See ante, page 152.

tree, the bole of which is thirty feet round near the root. The trunk is hollow, but still sufficiently strong to support three stems of very considerable size. Above one hundred and forty acres of marsh and mudlands on the shore near Dibden have been securely embanked and cultivated at the expense of Lord Malmsbury. The manor of Bury Farm, three or four miles to the north of Dibden, is held by an ancient grant from the crown, by the tenure of the possessor presenting the sovereign with a pair of white greyhounds whenever he enters the New Forest. This custom, as we afterwards see, was observed in 1789. The breed is purposely preserved by the family. The house is a modern building, erected on the side of an ancient mansion, in removing which, and in digging the foundations of the present one, a considerable number of Roman coins were discovered. Eling, called Edlinges in the Doomsday Book, appears, from that record, to have been a place of some consequence, it having a church, two mills, a fishery, and a saltern, at the period of making the survey. In the reign of Edward the Confessor, the manor was held by the singular tenure of providing half a day's entertainment for the king whenever he should pass that way. The church has been enlarged at different periods, as appears from the variety in its architecture. In sinking a well in this parish, a few years ago, a quantity of fossil shells was discovered at the depth of thirty-six feet.

From Dibden we continued our route northward, till we entered a beautiful forest lawn. We had found many of these scenes in different parts, each of which had something peculiar to itself.* This, too, had its peculiar character.. It was about two miles in diameter. To the eye its limits appeared circular; and its form, descending gently to a wide centre, had some resemblance to that of a dish. Yet it was far from a regular scene. Its great beauty consisted chiefly in its noble skreens of forest wood, which, growing everywhere around it with great irregularity, broke out into the skirts of the area, not in clumps, which, in so large a scene, would have had little effect, but in corners of woods, adding variety to its limits; yet, without

* See ante, page 190.

encroaching on the simplicity and grandeur of the general idea. The name of this beautiful and extensive forest scene is Hound's Down, so named, probably, from the fair advantage it gives the hound in pursuit. If he can drive his chase from the thickets into this open plain, it is probable he will there secure him.

Through the middle of this wide down the Lyndhurst road passes to Southampton. The entrance into it, on the Lyndhurst side, is beautiful, particularly between the ninth and tenth stones, where the ground is finely diversified with those woody promontories just mentioned. As we approach the top of the hill towards Southampton, the beauty of the scene is gone; the extremity is a naked, barren boundary. One advantage, however, we obtain from it, which is a distance, — in forest scenery the more valuable, as the more uncommon. Distances are, at all times, an agreeable part of landscape, and unite with every mode of composition. Here it is introduced at first in its simplest mode: a plain foreground, without any ornament, is joined to a removed distance, without the intervention of any middle ground. In a composition of this simple kind, it is necessary to break the lines of the foreground, which may easily be done by a tree, or a group of cattle. As we rise to the verge of the eminence, the view enlarges itself. The grounds immediately below the eye are overspread with wood, and become a second distance, beyond which extends a remote one. Under a proper light, this landscape is calculated to produce a good effect. The parts are large; and if one vast shadow overspread the woods on the nearer grounds, an enlightened distance would form a fine contrast.

Hound's Down is one of the best pasture grounds in the forest, at least in patches, and is of course frequented with cattle, which are a great addition to its beauty. We rarely pass it in a summer evening without seeing herds of deer grazing in different parts, or forest mares with their colts.

One thing, indeed, disfigures it, and that is the straight course of the road which bisects it. The vista, which leads through the forest from Brokenhurst to Lyndhurst, we observed,* was both great in itself, and accompanied with infinite variety; and therefore it became both a grand and a beautiful object: but a simple, straight road like this, over a plain, has a different effect. Though, in fact, it is grander than a winding road, as being more simple and consisting of fewer parts, yet, as it is at best only a paltry object, and has not grandeur sufficient to arouse the imagination,† it is, on the whole, much less pleasing than a road playing before us in two or three large sweeps, which would at least have had variety to recommend it, and might easily have been contrived without lengthening the journey across it, on a trotting horse, above two minutes. But in matters of this kind, in which surveyors of high roads are concerned, we expect beauty only by chance, and when we obtain it, it is so much gain.

In our way to Hound's Down, we rode past a celebrated spot, called the Deer Leap. Here a stag was once shot, which, in the agony of death, collecting his force, gave a bound which astonished those that saw it. It was immediately commemorated by two posts, which were fixed at the two extremities of the leap, where they still remain. The space between them is somewhat more than eighteen yards.

About half a mile on the right, as we leave Hound's Down, stands Iron's Hill Lodge. It occupies a knoll in the middle of a kind of natural, irregular vista. In front the ground continues rising gently about two miles to Lyndhurst. The back front overlooks a wild, woody scene, into which the vista imperceptibly blends.

From Hound's Down we returned to Beaulieu, along the western side of that extensive heath, which, as I observed,‡ occupies the middle district between the river of Beaulieu and the bay of Southampton. In this part it consists of great variety of ground, and is adorned with little patches of wood scattered about it; and as it is in general the highest ground in its neighbourhood, it is not, like most of the heaths we have seen, termi-

* See ante, page 135.
† See this idea illustrated, page 172.
‡ See ante, page 204.

nated by a woody skreen, but by distances, which being commonly forest scenes, are picturesque, though not extensive. Among these were some woody bottoms on the right, which were pleasing.

SECTION X.

A TOUR THROUGH THE NORTHERN PARTS OF NEW FOREST.

HAVING now examined those parts of the forest which lie on the south side of the invisible line drawn from Ringwood to Dibden,* we proposed next to examine those parts which lie on the north side of it.† We directed our course first to Lyndhurst. This village stands high; and the church, standing still higher, is a landmark round the country.

Though Lyndhurst is but a small place, it may be called the capital of the forest. Here the forest courts are held; and here stands the principal lodge, which is known by the name of the King's House, and is the residence of the lord warden, though it is but an ordinary building. An assignment of timber was lately made to put it and some other lodges into better repair.

Behind the house lies a pleasant sloping field, containing about six or seven acres, which is planted round with shrubs, circled by a gravel walk, and secured from cattle by a railed fence. I mention this mode of enclosure only because I have often thought it a very good one, especially if a field like this consist of sloping ground; for the rails, which are in many parts hid, appear winding in others, and the eye is seldom offended, sometimes pleased, with pursuing them, and taking them up again, after they have for a while disappeared. There is something, also, not unpleasing in the perspective of winding rails. I do not, however, mention a fence of this kind as suitable to a regal mansion, or so proper, in many cases, as a sunk one, but only as a simple unaffected manner of enclosing a field near a

* See ante, page 124.　　　　† See ante, page 127.

plain common house, and perhaps less offensive than chains, wires, nets, or any of those slight unnatural fences, which cannot be hid, and yet appear so disproportioned. I should wish my rails, however, to be without ornament; and either to be left with their natural colour, or to be painted of some dingy olive-green hue: if they are of a bright green, of a white, or of any other glaring colour, they disgust. They are at best only disagreeable conveniences: ornament makes them objects. But above all ornaments, we are disgusted with the Chinese. That zigzag work, commonly called Chinese railing, is very offensive. Plain, simple posts, with one, two, or three rails, according to the sort of cattle we wish to exclude, make the least disgusting fence.

Opposite to the royal lodge stands a large square building, with a turret at each corner, where the king's horses, carriages, and staghounds, are kept.

Lyndhurst is beautifully situated. It has been considered as the capital of the New Forest ever since the era of its formation; and here the chief justice in Eyre for this forest exercised his jurisdiction, so long as he continued to exercise it, for there is no trace of it subsequent to the reign of Charles II. All the forest courts under the jurisdiction of the verdurers are still held here, as well as those of attachment, &c. as the swanimote; the former are held on such days as the presiding judges appoint, three times in a year; the latter on the 14th of September annually. An ancient stirrup is preserved here, said to have been that used by William Rufus at the time he was shot by Sir Walter Tyrrel. The king's stables are very large, and were probably considered as magnificent when first erected, that is, about the time of Charles II.

I do not find that the royal lodge of Lyndhurst has ever been visited by the sovereign from the time of Charles II till the year 1789, when George III passed through the forest in his road to Weymouth. So long a time had elapsed, that all the etiquette of receiving a royal visitor was almost forgotten. When the day, however, of his arrival was notified, all the keepers, dressed in new green uniforms, met him on horseback, at his entrance into the forest. He travelled without

guards, and was conducted by these foresters to Lyndhurst. When he alighted from his coach, Sir Charles
Mills presented him with two white greyhounds, by
which ceremony he holds certain forest privileges. His
majesty and the royal family (for the queen and three
of the princesses were with him) at first dined in public
by throwing the windows open, and admitting the crowd
within the railed lawn; but as the populace became
rather riotous in their joy, there was a necessity to
exclude them. The royal family, however, walked
abroad in the forest every evening. The king spent
his mornings in riding; and as he rides fast, he saw
greatest part of the forest, and seemed so much pleased
with it that he continued at Lyndhurst (poorly as he
was there accommodated) from Thursday the 25th of
June till the Tuesday following.

On the 22d of July, 1818, his Royal Highness the late
Duke of York, who had taken a journey into Hampshire to
settle various matters respecting the forest rights, honoured
the gentlemen of the New Forest Hunt with his company at
a grand entertainment given by them at the king's house,
Lyndhurst. As lord warden, his Royal Highness was pleased
to express the highest satisfaction at his reception on this
occasion. The Earl of Cavan and Viscount Palmerston
officiated as president and vice-president, and the company
consisted of a number of highly distinguished individuals. All
the villagers appeared dressed in their holiday clothes to
witness the Duke's arrival. Mr Nicoll had his fine pack of
hounds, with the whippers-in, displayed on the lawn before
the house; and the whole scene was extremely animated and
interesting.

Near Lyndhurst stands Cuffnells, the seat of Mr
Rose. It is not placed exactly as might be wished.
High ground rises immediately in front, which is always
a circumstance to be avoided. But Mr Rose has
happily managed an inconvenience which he found. He
has laid out a very handsome approach, which winds to
the house under the rising ground, and makes it of
much less consequence than when the road was carried
abruptly down the slope to the house. His improvements he has thrown to the back-front, where he is
leading a very beautiful walk through clumps of old

oak winding towards Lyndhurst. But his improvements are yet incomplete.

The author of the article Hampshire tells us that Cuffnells possesses many peculiar advantages of scenery, from its situation near the centre of the New Forest; and from its bold irregularity of surface being finely adorned with majestic oaks and noble beech trees, it affords some charming landscape compositions. These, whether contemplated in their foregrounds, middle distances, or remote backgrounds, cannot fail to gratify the eye of taste. When the late Mr Emes was called in to exercise his art of landscape gardening on this spot, he found that Nature had nearly superseded his intended operations, and he was obliged to confine himself to a few plantations and walks in the vicinity of the house.

Cuffnells stands on a rising ground embosomed in trees. It was the property of the late Sir Thomas Tancred, of whose heirs this spot was purchased by the late Sir George Rose, of the Treasury; and to those who have seen the little bare moorland spot in Scotland where stood the turf cot where that gentleman was born, and who have compared it with Cuffnells, it is gratifying, as well as stimulating to laudable ambition, to think how much may be achieved by prudence and steady exertion. Sir George made very considerable additions to the mansion. The south front is formed by a drawing-room thirty-six feet by twenty-four, a library forty-two feet by twenty-four, a handsome vestibule, and the conservatory. The collection of books, which was perhaps one of the most valuable in the possession of any private gentleman in the kingdom, came into Sir George's hands as executor of the Earl of Marchmont, who died in 1792. There were also a number of the Marchmont portraits here, and, amongst others, an original picture of William III, with whom Sir Patrick Hume, afterwards created Earl of Marchmont by this sovereign, returned to England. The earl's picture was also here. The events in the life of this zealous patriot and eminent statesman were various and extraordinary. From his first election into the Scottish parliament, in the year 1665, he distinguished himself by an active and able opposition to the encroachments made on the liberties of his country.

" It was not possible," says Mr Chambers in his *Scottish Biographical Dictionary*, " that a person who entertained so free a spirit in such an age, could long escape trouble. In 1675, having remonstrated against the measure for establishing garrisons to keep down the people, he was committed by the Privy Council to the Tolbooth of Edinburgh as a factious person, and one who had done that which might usher in confusion." He was afterwards confined for six months in Stirling Castle; and altogether he suffered imprisonment for about two years, having at last been liberated in April, 1679, through the earnest intercession of his friends. He then went to England, where he became acquainted with Monmouth, Shaftesbury, and the Lord Russel; and with them he held many conferences on the state of Scotland, and on the measures to be adopted to secure the kingdom against popery and arbitrary power, in the event of a popish successor. Notwithstanding they were perfectly innocent of any design against the lives of the king or the Duke of York, yet the government contrived to fasten on them a charge of that nature, and Lord Russel and Mr Baillie of Jarviswood were the victims of it. A party of guards was despatched to arrest Sir Patrick Hume; but the leader having halted them for refreshment at a house where the lady secretly favoured the cause of the Presbyterians, she had the ingenuity to discover the object of the expedition which her guests were engaged in, from their inquiries as to the way that led to Polwarth. With inconceivable adroitness she plucked a feather from a plume, and enclosing it in a blank cover, she despatched it to Sir Patrick Hume by a nimble-footed boy, who took the shortest cut over the hills, and, in the meanwhile, she detained the party as long as she could without exciting suspicion. No sooner had Sir Patrick received this enigmatical communication, than the consciousness of his then perilous situation enabled him fully to interpret it. He saw that his kind monitor meant that he should fly, and that not a moment was to be lost. But whither could he fly, where no secure retreat seemed now to remain for him on the face of the earth? At length, as he could think of no place of safety above ground, he bethought him of the family burial vault in Polwarth churchyard, about two miles distant from Redbraes Castle, where he usually resided; and he quickly resolved there to take refuge, among the mouldering remains of his ancestors. His place of concealment was known only to his own family, and to one trusty humble friend, a carpenter, named Jamie Winter, on whose fidelity they could depend. This man contrived to convey a bed and bedclothes to his dismal place of retreat; and there Sir Patrick remained, without fire, during the strict search that was made for him in every direction. His daughter, Grizel Hume, afterwards Lady Grizel Baillie, who was then about eighteen years of age, was intrusted with the task of conveying food to him, but, to avoid all risk of suspicion, it could only be carried to the vault at midnight. She had been bred up, as our great Scottish Shakespeare tells us, " in the usual superstitions of the times," that is, with her full share of dread for ghosts and apparitions of every description ; but her strong affection for her father, and her conviction of the high and sacred duty she was engaged in performing, raised her mind far above any such childish fears ; and when her mother asked her, after her return from her first adventure, whether she had not been frightened in passing through the churchyard, she replied, that her only fears had been occasioned by the minister's dogs, which had barked at her from the manse, that stood close to the churchyard. Apprehensive that the barking of these animals might lead to a discovery, her mother sent for the clergyman next morning, and, by pretending an alarm for mad dogs, she prevailed on him to destroy them, or to shut them up.

But this was not all the difficulty they had to encounter ; for as they dared not to trust the servants, so they could neither prepare nor take provisions openly, without the certainty of exciting suspicion. The only mode, therefore, which was left for them, was stealthily to abstract from their own table as many fragments as might satisfy the wants of their beloved prisoner. In this even there was great danger and risk ; and what at any other time would have been considered as rather a ludicrous circumstance, was very nearly turning out a very fatal event for them. Sir Patrick Hume was extremely fond of that old Scottish dish, a sheep's head boiled in broth, and his daughter, the Lady Grizzel being aware of this, she one day took advantage of all eyes being turned from her, and contrived, unseen, to slip the larger part of a sheep's head into her napkin. But whilst she was secretly congratulating herself on her own cleverness, she was considerably alarmed by the innocent question put by her brother, a boy too young to have been trusted with a matter of importance so vital, who suddenly observing that the sheep's head had disappeared, exclaimed, in great surprise, " Mother, mother! while we have been supping the broth, Grizzy has eaten up all the sheep's head!" A single ray of light found its way into Sir Patrick's gloomy abode, through a narrow slit at one end ; and, availing himself of this, he was wont to amuse himself by reading and reciting Buchanan's Latin version of the Psalms; and when we think of the beauty of the imagery of these holy aspirations, and how much many of the subjects of them were applicable to his lamentable situation, we do not wonder at his selection, especially seeing that the confidence in the protection of the Almighty which breathes throughout them all, was admirably calculated to keep up within him that rational hope of succour from on high, which is ever our best support during all the afflictions of this life. In this way he spent several weeks, until, the hottest period of the search for him being over, they at length ventured to conceal him in the house, and finally he succeeded in escaping to France. There he assumed the disguise of a travelling physician, in which character he journeyed to Brussels, where he embarked for Holland, and on his arrival there, he was cordially received by the Prince of Orange. In 1685, Sir Patrick returned to his native country with the unfortunate Earl of Argyle's expedition; and he and his companion in arms, Sir John Cochrane, having made a desperate resistance with their small party against a large body of cavalry, at a place called Muirdykes, they escaped in the dark. Sir Patrick ultimately embarked in a vessel from the west coast, by Dublin to Bourdeaux, and finally reached Holland, whence he returned in triumph with the Prince of Orange in 1688, to be rewarded, by rapid preferment, for all the perils he had encountered in his country's cause. He was created a peer, made Chancellor of Scotland, a Commissioner of the Treasury, &c. His grandson, the last Earl of Marchmont, died in 1798. He was remarkable as a statesman, and was the friend of Pope. The representative of this family, through a female line, is the present Sir Hugh Purves Campbell Hume, of Marchmont, Baronet.

Cuffnells now belongs to Sir Edward Poore, Baronet; and so far as our knowledge of him extends, we are disposed to think that this beautiful place will lose none of its fascination from its having come into his hands.

Mr Ballard also has a house near Lyndhurst, which stands high, and commands an extensive view. The king walked up to it, and with his glass continued some time examining the distant objects. He was so pleased with it, that on leaving it, he gave it the name of Mount Royal.

We still entertain a most grateful recollection of the kind reception we met with, some twenty-six years ago, from the favoured inhabitant of Mount Royal. We remember having been conducted into the house by such a way, that all idea of a distant prospect was banished from our thoughts. We were ushered into a splendid apartment, and thence directly out upon a balcony, whence we looked over Lyndhurst and Cuffnells, and the whole New Forest, stretching towards the sea, with all its variety of surface and magnificence of timber, the distance being closed in by the Isle of Wight. We have seldom since looked upon a more gorgeous scene, or a scene which had in it a more close association with the national glory of Britain.

From Lyndhurst along the Rumsey road, the forest opens beautifully on the right, upon a lawn swelling in different parts, and supported with wood at various distances. This lawn is used as a race-ground, where the little horses of the forest, of which there is a mart at Lyndhurst, are commonly brought to try their strength and agility.

That noble vista which we described after we left Brokenhurst,* is interrupted by Lyndhurst, but commences again on the other side of the town. Here, however, it is of little value. It is but ill adorned with wood. The trees, which are rare, scathed, and meagre, are in general not only ugly, but ill combined. Some formalities also give it a bad effect. Before, it was irregularly great and simple; here, the road rises to the eye in three regular stages. The summit, too, is formally abrupt. The road cut through the wood forms here a gaping chasm, opening like a wide portal, discovering the naked horizon, and making, as it were, a full pause in the landscape: we discover it plainly to be artificial, and this hurts the eye. The effect is beautiful on the other side of Lyndhurst, where the chasm of the vista, as you approach, is filled with the tops of retiring trees, which excites the idea of something beyond it, and gives it a more natural air.

This gaping chasm appears long the striking feature

* See ante, page 136.

of the view as we rise the hill. In our approach to it, however, the eye is here and there agreeably drawn aside; particularly by a forest lawn, which presents itself about a mile and a half from Lyndhurst, opening both on the right and left. It is decorated irregularly with wood—rises before the eye—blends itself leisurely with a few scattered trees and clumps, which come forward from the distant woods to meet it, and then loses itself imperceptibly in the depths of the forest.

Somewhere in this part, between Lyndhurst and Rumsey, a charitable scheme was projected in favour of a body of Palatines, who took refuge in England in the reign of Queen Anne, and engaged the humane part of the nation in endeavouring to provide means for their support. Many benevolent projects were formed, and, among others, this of settling them in New Forest; and the matter was thought so practicable, that it was digested into a regular plan, and laid before the Lord Treasurer Godolphin.

The arrangement was this :—A square plot of ground, containing four thousand acres, was to be marked out, and equally divided into four parts by two roads running through it, and crossing at right angles in the centre. Each of these four parts was to be subdivided into five, so that the whole plot might be proportioned into twenty farms, each of two hundred acres. This provision of farms being made, twenty of the best and most respectable Palatine families were to be looked out and put in possession of them; the rest were to be day labourers. Each farmer was to be intrusted with a capital of two hundred pounds, to be exempted from taxes for twenty years, and to have an assignment of forest timber for building and repairs.

This scheme, which seems to have been well digested, is said to have been first hinted by the famous Daniel de Foe : but got no farther than the Treasurer's Board— whether the soil was thought incapable of being improved, or whether it miscarried from being the production of so wild a genius, which made it suspected as chimerical.

We had now arrived at the summit of the vista, which

in prospect had appeared so formal. On a close approach, its formality wore off, and we found ourselves surrounded by beautiful scenery. The summit itself is a fine wooded knoll, rising on the left, and falling on the right into open groves. As we descended the hill on the other side, the close wooded scenery still continued beautiful, and we found the grand vista better supported with wood.

In wooded scenes like these, the plano-convex mirror, which was Mr Gray's companion in all his tours,* has a pleasing effect. Distances, indeed, reduced to so small a surface, are lost; it is chiefly calculated for objects at hand,† which it shews to more advantage.

When we examine Nature at large, we study composition and effect. We examine also the forms of particular objects. But from the size of the objects of Nature, the eye cannot perform both these operations at once. If it be engaged in general effects, it postpones particular objects; and if it be fixed on particular objects, whose forms and tints it gathers up with a passing glance from one to another, it is not at leisure to observe general effects. But in the minute exhibitions of the convex mirror, composition, forms, and colours, are brought closer together; and the eye examines the general effect, the forms of the objects, and the beauty of the tints, in one complex view. As the colours, too, are the very colours of Nature, and equally well harmonized, they are the more brilliant, as they are the more condensed.

In a chaise particularly the exhibitions of the convex mirror are amusing. We are rapidly carried from one object to another. A succession of high-coloured pictures is continually gliding before the eye. They are like the visions of the imagination, or the brilliant landscapes of a dream. Forms and colours in brightest array fleet before us; and if the transient glance of a good compo-

---

* See Gray's *Memoirs*, page 352.

† Mr Gray, on viewing the ruins of an abbey, says, " They were the truest objects of his glass he had met with anywhere." He does not, indeed, assign the reason; but, if he had considered it, he might have seen it was because they presented a happy display of present objects. See his *Memoirs*, page 380.

sition happen to unite with them, we should give any price to fix and appropriate the scene.*

After all, perhaps the chief virtue of this deception may consist in exhibiting the beauties of Nature in a new light. Thus, when we close one eye, and look through the lid of the other half shut, we see only the general effect of objects ; and the appearance is new and pleasing ; or when we stoop to the ground, and see the landscape around us with an inverted eye, the effect is pleasing for the same reason. We are pleased also when we look at objects through stained glass. It is not that any of these modes of vision is superior, or even equal, to the eye in its natural state : it is the novelty alone of the exhibition that pleases. If the mirror have any peculiar advantage, it consists in its not requiring the eye to alter its focus, which it must do when it surveys the views of Nature — the distance requiring one focus, and the foreground another. This change of the focus, in theory at least, (I doubt whether in practice,) occasions some confusion. In the mirror we survey the whole under one focus.

Those who are much accustomed to sketch from Nature are well aware of the advantage they receive from occasionally surveying the subject they are drawing with half-closed eyes. When the landscape is thus looked on carefully, for a few moments, the minuter parts of Nature disappear, and only the grander and more characteristic features are retained ; and as these are all that strike the eye of him who merely looks at Nature in the ordinary way, so they are all that it becomes necessary for the artist to represent. In poring over any subject of which we are anxiously desirous to make an accurate portrait, we may be said to regard it almost microscopically : every leaf of the tree, every blade of the grass of the bank, and every small crack in the rock before us, is discovered and impressed upon the retina by our long looking at them. But, in what may be termed our ordinary observation of the scene, all these would be overlooked by us : to represent them, therefore, minutely, is to draw or paint things that certainly do exist in Nature,

* " I got to the parsonage a little before sunset, and saw in my glass a picture that, if I could transmit to you, and fix in all the softness of its living colours, would fairly sell for a thousand pounds."— Gray's *Memoirs*, p. 360.

but which never appear, in our eyes, as ingredients in landscape, and which therefore give offence to all who are of
true and sound taste, when too liberally brought forward by
the artist. The secret of frequently looking with half-shut
eyes at the subject we are sketching, is most valuable.

On the other hand, the mirror has at least one disadvantage. Objects are not presented with that depth,
that gradation, that rotundity of distance, if I may so
speak, which Nature exhibits, but are evidently affected
by the two surfaces of the mirror, which give them a
flatness something like the scenes of a playhouse,
retiring behind each other. The convex mirror also
diminishes distances beyond Nature, for which the
painter should always make proper allowance. Or, to
speak perhaps more properly, it enlarges foregrounds
beyond their proportion. Thus, if you look at your face
in a speculum of this kind, you will see your nose
magnified. The retiring parts of your face will appear,
of course, diminished.

About a mile beyond the woody summit we had
passed, we entered another forest lawn, which, though
very confined, has its beauty; as all these openings must
have, however confined, if surrounded with ancient
wood. But about half a mile farther, where the Romsey
and Salisbury roads divide, another forest lawn, of much
larger dimensions, presents itself. This is very spacious,
well hung with wood, and (what in all these scenes adds
greatly to their beauty) adorned in various parts with
woody promontories shooting into it, and clumps and
single trees scattered about it. On an eminence near
this lawn, stands a new house, belonging to Mr Gilbert:
it seems to enjoy a good situation, but we did not ride
up to it. In this part of the forest are a few scattered
houses, known by the name of Cadenham, remarkable for
standing near that celebrated oak, of which I have given
an account in the early part of this work.*

Not far from hence lies Paulton's, the seat of Mr
Welbore Ellis. Paulton's was one of the first works
of Mr Brown, and therefore deserves the attention of
the curious, though in itself, indeed, it is a pleasing
scene. The situation of the house is that of an abbey,—

* See Vol. I. p. 247.

low, sheltered, and sequestered. It is contained within
a paled boundary of about five miles in circumference;
but the whole is so woody, that the boundary is nowhere
visible. When Mr Brown first undertook this place, it
was full of ancient timber, and nothing was wanting
but to open the area judiciously into ample lawns,
skreened with wood.

A polished scene like this, in the midst of a forest,
addresses us with the air of novelty; and when natural,
as this is, cannot fail to please. It will not, however,
bear a comparison with the wild scenes of the forest.
We enter them again with pleasure, and speak of them
as we do of the works of a great literary genius, which
contain greater beauties, though perhaps blended with
greater defects, than the laboured works of a less exalted,
though more correct writer. Every thing in these cultured scenes may be perfectly correct—nothing may
offend—yet we seek in vain for those strokes of genius
which rouse the imagination, and are so frequently found
among the wild scenes of the forest. Some things, however, at Paulton's, did offend, particularly an attempt to
improve a little forest stream (by forming a head) into
a river. Attempts of this kind seldom answer; and the
misfortune here is the more glaring, as a great white
Chinese bridge stands everywhere in sight to remind us
of it. We wish for simple ornaments on all occasions—
ornaments which the eye is not obliged to notice. Here
the ornament was particularly out of place, as it was not
only a fault itself, but led the eye to the detection of
other faults.

We cordially agree with Mr Gilpin in these remarks upon
Paulton's, and this we do boldly, not from any recollection
of it, but merely on the slight sketch which he gives us of
the nature of the improvements (so called) which Mr Brown
effected there. That style of landscape gardening which
may be called the shaving and dressing style, is everywhere
bad when carried beyond the mere precincts of the mansion;
but it is most of all intolerable when thus introduced, like a
piece of wretched patchwork, in the midst of such a world
of wild Nature as the New Forest affords! Chinese bridges
over a serpentine ditch of unvarying width, and green banks

so regular and smooth, that they might be taken for painted boards ! Well may we exclaim with Mr Knight, —

> Hence, hence ! thou haggard fiend, however call'd,
> Thin, meagre genius of the bare and bald ;
> Thy spade and mattock here at length lay down,
> And follow to the tomb thy favourite Brown —
> Thy favourite Brown, whose innovating hand
> First dealt thy curses o'er this fertile land ;
> First taught the walk in formal spires to move,
> And from their haunts the secret Dryads drove ;
> With clumps bespotted o'er the mountain's side,
> And bade the stream 'twixt banks close shaven glide ;
> Banish'd the thickets of high-towering wood,
> Which hung reflected in the glassy flood ;
> Where, screen'd and sheltered from the heats of day,
> Oft on the moss-grown stone reposed I lay,
> And tranquil view'd the limpid streams below,
> Brown with o'erhanging shade, in circling eddies flow.
> Dear, peaceful scenes, that now prevail no more,
> Your loss shall every weeping muse deplore.

We remember an anecdote told us by the late Duke of Gordon, which seems to be somewhat in place here. His Grace, being desirous to improve the scenery of Gordon Castle, invited a certain landscape gardener from England,— one whom we shall forbear to name, though he is long since dead ; but we shall say of him, that he was one of that class who

> With charts, pedometers, and rules in hand,
> Advance triumphant, and alike lay waste
> The forms of Nature, and the works of taste.
> To improve, adorn, and polish they profess ;
> But *shave* the goddess whom they came to *dress*.

The gentleman was delicate and indolent — the weather was gloomy and unfavourable for some eight days or so, and he preferred the comforts of a book and an easy chair in the drawingroom to exposing himself to the raw damps which prevailed abroad. But, as he thus lacked exercise of limb out of doors, he made up for the want of it by exercise of jaws within ; and the Duke's venison, and hock, and claret, suffered seriously from his daily attacks. But ten days' enjoyment of this Castle of Indolence had not gone over his head, when certain alarming twinges in his toe taught him, one evening, that an old monitor was about to revisit him, to remind him of the infinite nothingness and vanity of all human happiness, and next day he was laid up in bed with a swingeing fit of the gout. Some weeks of great suffering and of gradual convalescence brought him again to his easy chair, and by degrees he became so far well as to be able to return to his venison and claret, and, finally, one clear sunshiny day, he ventured forth on crutches into the lawn before the castle. There, levelling his opera-glass silently around him for some time, he at last begged to know in what direction lay the course of the river Spey; and, on this being explained to him, — " Ha!" said he gravely, " I thought so ;" and then pointing to a grove of magnificent old forest trees which stood at some distance in the park, — " we must open a view in that direction. Your Grace will please to order those trees to be cut before next season, when I shall have the honour of revisiting Gordon Castle, to judge of the effect of their removal before going farther." Next morning this tastemonger took his departure. The noble trees which he had condemned bowed their mighty heads before the axe, as many noble heads have bowed before it, under the sentence of judges no less unworthy and merciless. The seasons revolved, and so did the wheels of the tastemonger's carriage, which brought him back to Gordon Castle, where the same scene of sloth, easy chair, eating, venison, hock, claret, gout-admonitory and gout-mordant, recovery, and revisitation of the ground, took place. Now, it happens that the Spey opposite to Gordon Castle cuts against lofty friable banks, of a bright red coloured mortar, which are perpetually crumbling down ; and although these were, even at the time we speak of, for the most part hidden by the younger and more distant woods towards the boundary of the park, yet it so happened, that whereas no part of the water of the Spey was visible, the tastemonger had no occasion even to use his opera-glass to discover a broad sketch of blood-red bank, which, being higher than the rest, was seen towering most offensively over the delicate greens of the offscape, like a troop of heavy dragoons looking over a hedge. " We must throw a clump up in that direction," said the tastemonger, waving his hand towards the place with a very important air ; " we must have a clump on that gentle swell, to shut out yonder hideous brickfield." " A clump !" exclaimed the Duke, with horror in his eyes. " Why, my good Sir, on that very gentle swell grew those goodly trees which you ordered to be cut last year, and, if you choose to satisfy yourself of the fact, you may go yonder to look at the roots which are yet remaining !" The gentleman was silent ; the Duke left him to his own meditations ; and the result was, that he had shame enough left to desire.

his carriage to be got ready, and to order it to transport him whence he came, an order which his Grace took no measures to thwart or to retard.

But, now that we have indulged the reader and ourselves in this story, so admirably exemplifying the manner in which Nature was tortured and murdered some fifty years ago, (not to be too particular as to time,) yet we have pleasure in saying, that such matters are much better understood now. We have had occasion to appreciate the sound judgment and good taste of Mr Gilpin, a near relation of our author, whose advices regarding the operations of landscape gardening, given to various individuals of our acquaintance, have always appeared to us to be so rational and judicious, as to do him the greatest possible credit.

From Paulton's we entered an extensive tract of rising ground, which bounds the forest on the north, along the borders of Wiltshire, and stretches on the left towards Fordingbridge, the river Avon, and the county of Dorset. This side of the forest, however, is by much the narrowest: its limits hardly extend, from east to west, above four miles; whereas the boundary of the forest, in the same direction near the sea, extends at least fourteen.

This lofty plain, consisting chiefly of furze and heath, as far as we surveyed it, appeared in itself little adorned with any forest furniture. The little wood in any part of its area bore no proportion to its extent; but it overlooked very grand views. In a picturesque light, therefore, we considered it as a vast theatre, from whence we might view almost all the regions of the forest which we had passed. Towards the north, indeed, in some parts, it commands views into Wiltshire; but the country is cultivated, and not removed enough to lose its formalities. This part, therefore, may be considered only as a foil. The grand opening is towards the south. Here we found a station which commanded a very noble view. The heath, making a gentle dip, presents a vast bay, which spreads the whole forest in a manner before the eye as far as the sea, in one vast expanse of scenery. Bramble Hill, one of the lodges, standing on a knoll on the left, about half a

4

mile below the eye, occupies one side of the opening into this immense woody distance, and another prominence, on which stands the ruins of Castle Malwood, occupies the other. The station may easily be found by this direction. Between these two promontories the eye is conducted from wood to wood, over lawns and heaths, through every shade of perspective, till all distinction at length is lost, and the eye doubts whether it is still roving over the tufted woods of the forest, or is landed upon the distant shores of the Isle of Wight, or is wandering among the hazy streaks of the horizon. At least it had that dubious appearance when we saw it. But it is one of the choice recommendations of these extensive scenes that they are subject to a thousand varieties from the different modifications of the atmosphere.

A vast scene, however, like this is unmanageable, as we have often observed, though it may be highly picturesque. But our observations on this subject may be carried farther than we have yet carried them.

It is a common assertion among landscape painters, that if the picture be justly painted, an extensive distance in miniature will have the same effect on the mind of the spectator, as if it were painted on the largest scale. Stand near a window, they tell you, and the whole may be brought within the circumference of a pane of glass. If then the same landscape were exactly painted on the pane of glass, it would have the same effect in a picture which it has in Nature.

This reasoning, I fear, is false. It depends entirely on the supposition, that we collect all our notices of external objects from the eye, agreeably to that construction of it which the anatomist gives us. Whereas, in fact, the eye is a mere window. It is a pane of glass through which the imagination is impressed by the notices it receives of outward objects; which notices, though sometimes true, are often false, particularly with regard to the size of objects, and will mislead it, unless corrected by experience. The mathematician talks of the angle of vision, and demonstrates that the size of the object in the eye must be in exact proportion

5

to that part of the cone of rays which it intercepts; and it is on this supposition the painter asserts, that an extensive distance exactly painted, though in miniature, will affect the spectator like the natural scene. But many things are mathematically true, though experimentally false. Such is the famous puzzle of Achilles and the tortoise. The mathematician demonstrates, that the tortoise must win the race, though not one jockey at Newmarket would bet on his side. Just so the imagination revolts from the mathematical account of vision. If I examine, for instance, the height of that tree by the side of a notched stick, it is scarce an inch. But no mathematical proof can persuade me, that I see it under those dimensions. I am well assured, that the tree not only is, but appears to me, much larger.

If, indeed, my imagination could be so far deceived as to believe the landscape which is painted on a pane of glass were really the landscape transmitted through it, I might then suppose it of the dimensions of Nature. On no other supposition I can give it credit. But if a deceit of this kind could not easily be practised on a pane of glass, much less could it be practised in a picture. We could never so far impose upon ourselves as to conceive a little object, of the dimensions of a foot by six inches, hung against a wall, can be a just representation of a country twenty or thirty miles in extent.

I mean not to debate the structure of the eye with the philosopher. All I mean to assert is, that the picturesque eye has nothing to do with tunics, irises, et retinas. It judges of nothing by a focus or a cone of visual rays. The imagination, guided by experience, presides solely over vision, as far at least as the bulk of objects is concerned; and it pictures them, not as painted on a mathematical point, but on an extended plain, and of their natural size. How Nature manages this matter is beyond the painter's power to explain. The fact is certain—let the philosopher, if he can, account for it.

To bring the argument to the point before us: there must be real space to interest the imagination, and excite ideas of grandeur. In a picture, the imagination cannot be imposed upon. Two or three inches may give us the form of the landscape, the proportion between the foreground and the offskip, the hue of distance and its general appearance; and we may be pleased with these things even in miniature. But it is impossible, within such scanty limits, to raise any of those feelings which landscape, in its full dimensions, will excite. Try the matter experimentally—examine such a landscape as this vast extended forest view before us alternately, first with the naked eye, and then with a diminishing glass, (which at least gives as just a representation of the perspective and keeping of Nature as any artificial landscape can do,) and you will be convinced how much the idea loses under the latter experiment. At the same time, if such a distance as this, extensive as it is, were painted on a larger scale than common, and properly accompanied and balanced with foreground, we might be tempted to forget its under size; and, seeing so large a picture, might acknowledge something like an equality with Nature: we might be inclined to forget the deception, and might, in some degree, feel those sublime ideas which Nature itself excites.

Besides this grand and extensive distance which we surveyed between Bramble Hill and the ruins of Castle Malwood, we found many views of the same kind as we traversed the high and heathy grounds towards Fritham and Fording Bridge. But the hills about Boldre Wood and Lyndhurst occupy the middle space between the northern and southern parts of the forest; and as they rise considerably, and intercept our views, the more we proceed in a western direction, I know not whether, on the whole, the view we have just taken is not one of the most extensive and most amusing which the whole forest exhibits. I cannot, therefore, conclude a description of New Forest more properly than with this grand exhibition, which, in a manner, comprehends the whole.

As I have more than once, however, observed, that scenes of all kinds, and distances the most of all, are so diversified by the circumstances under which they are examined, that no single view can give an adequate idea of them, I wish, before I shut up these forest scenes, to add a fuller illustration of this great picturesque truth, which should always be in the recollection of every picturesque observer of Nature. The example I shall select for this purpose shall be the scenery around the parsonage house at Vicar's Hill; not so much because it is a pleasing scene in itself, as because lying constantly before my eye, it is the best instance I can have; for no one can make remarks of this kind on a scene which he has not frequently examined. I must first describe the scenery before I remark the several circumstances under which it is often varied.

Vicar's Hill is a knoll, falling gently on the east to a grand woody bank, part of the wild grounds of Sir Harry Burrard; on the south, towards the Channel and the Isle of Wight; and, on the west, towards Lymington river, all which it overlooks. As it stands on the edge of the forest, the situation of it is nearly conformable to the wish of the poet:

> —— Be my retreat
> Between the groaning forest and the shore,
> A rural, shelter'd, solitary scene.*

The two last of these epithets, indeed, belong not to it. It stands rather lofty, though not high, and is so far from being solitary, that it enjoys a good neighbourhood.

From this knoll the views are engrossed by two houses, Mr Cleavland's and the vicarage, the united plantations of which exclude the prospect from all other parts of the hill. From both these houses the views are beautiful; but they are of different kinds. Mr Cleavland's standing on the west side of the knoll, has a view of Lymington river, which forms one of its best sweeps below his lawn. From hence the eye is carried along the river to its opening into the Channel, of which, together with the shores around, the island beyond, and the town of Lymington, the distant landscape is formed. These distances are varied as you view them from the upper and lower parts of the lawn; and, in general, as they are circumscribed by the high lands which bound the estuary, they are much more picturesque, and, in the eye of a painter, more beautiful than those vast extensive views.

* Thomson's *Winter*.

of the island and Channel which we have so often seen from various parts of the coast. We have had other occasions to remark . the picturesque beauty of this estuary.*

As Mr Cleavland's has a better view of the water, the vicarage has a better view of the woods. A house built where it could command both scenes, would enjoy a grand situation. The view, however, is so good, that it will bear a division, and yet each part form a whole. The vicarage stands in the garden, closed on every side but the south, which is the aspect of the best rooms. Before it is spread a small lawn proportioned to its size. At the end of the lawn, which is also the boundary of the forest, is a sunk fence, connecting it with the meadows beyond. These meadows declining to the south and east, form the brow of Vicar's Hill in those directions, and are skreened by the grand woody bank above mentioned, wheeling gently round, which shapes the lower part of them into a sort of semicircular valley. To the hanging woods of this picturesque bank, a close descending walk from the house, following the direction of the forest boundary, unites the garden.

The woody bank, which is the grand circumstance of the view, having thus circled the meadows, falls away towards the estuary of the river, and becomes one of its high enclosures. On the other side, it is intersected by a rising ground, on which stands the town of Lymington, at the distance of a mile.† Over the dip, formed by this intersection, rises, as if fitted for the place, a lofty part of the Isle of Wight; from which a ridge of high land continues, passing over the town as a background. Below the island appears a small catch of the Channel; but the intervening woods of the eastern skreen have now almost intercepted it, interposing one beautiful circumstance in the room of another.

Some of the chief modes of incidental beauty which vary these few parts of landscape are these :

In a morning the effect is often beautiful, when the sun, rising over the trees of the eastern bank, pours his sloping rays upon their tufted heads, while all the bottom

* See ante, page 132 and page 158.
† See the situation of Lymington described, page 157.

of the valley, not yet having caught the splendour, is dusky and obscure.*

The effect still continues beautiful as the sun rises higher. Some prominent part of the woody skreen always catches the light, while the recesses among the trees still hold the depth of the morning shadow.

The disposition of the landscape is as well adapted to receive the effects of an evening as of a morning sun. As all the eastern skreen is richly and picturesquely wooded, the illumination of the trees from the west is generally pleasing, especially as the meadows, descending to the east and south, and of course declining from the summer sun, present large masses of shade.

But the effect of light is best seen in an evening storm, when it rises from the east, behind the woody bank; while the sun, sinking in the west, throws a splendour upon the trees, which, seen to such advantage against the darkness of the hemisphere, shews the full effect of light and shade.

In winter, the island is generally of an indistinct gray hue; but in summer, when the evening sun gets more to the north, its declining ray strikes the distant cliffs and broken grounds of the island shores, and gives them a great resplendency. As these broken grounds run behind the town, the effect of the chimneys and houses, when seen in shadow against the warm tints of the island shores, is often very picturesque; much more so than when the sun throws its light upon them. And here we see exemplified a truth in landscape, that the light breaks a town into parts, shews its poverty, and dissipates its effect; whereas all the parts of a town, seen in shadow are blended together, and it becomes one grand object. I speak, however, chiefly of towns in the situation of this, placed along the ridge of an eminence, and about a mile from the eye. In remote distance, a ray of light thrown upon a town has often a good effect. These splendid lights of an evening sun upon the cliffs and broken shores of the island, appear first about the beginning of April; but they grow

* See an effect of this kind described more at length, Vol. I. p. 328.

stronger as the power of the sun increases. Various
other tints also, of a bluish, purplish, and yellowish hue,
the effects of evening suns in summer, occasionally
invest the island.

But haziness and mists are here, as in other places,
the great sources of variety. In general, they have a
good effect, but sometimes a bad one. As the remote
part of the landscape, which consists of the Isle of
Wight, does not immediately connect with the woods
on one side, and the town of Lymington on the other,
but is separated from them by the channel, which is
about two or three leagues across, it of course happens,
that when a partial fog removes the island alone from
the sight, a violent chasm is left in the landscape : there
is no gradation ; the rising ground on which Lymington
stands appears staring against a foggy sky without any
support of distance. Nothing can shew more strongly
the use of distances in completing the harmony of a
view. When the several parts of a country melt into
each other, as in the grand distance we have just been
surveying from Castle Malwood, a fog, or mist, can
never introduce any great mischief. It comes gradually
on, and therefore only gradually obscures. It is the
chasm which occasions the blank. At the same time,
notwithstanding the island is not gradually connected
with the other parts of the country, the landscape loses
in no other modification of the atmosphere. If the mist
be more general, so as to obscure not only the island,
but the town also, and, in proportion, the nearer parts
of the view, the effect is often beautiful. The woods of
the eastern bank being obscured, the firs of the lawn
standing much nearer, rise strongly in opposition : the
eye is pleased with the contrast, while the imagination
is pleased also with diving into the obscurity, and
forming its own objects.

The line, also, which the high grounds of the island
form upon the sky, is sometimes strong, and sometimes
faint; sometimes also a part of it is broken, or intercepted by clouds, which gives a contrast to the other
part.

Again, the mist is sometimes so light, that it removes

the island several leagues farther from the eye; yet still the landscape, partaking of the general effect, preserves its harmony.

Sometimes, also, after a heavy shower, when the air, as the rain goes off, becomes perfectly diaphanous, like an Italian sky, and all the vapours are precipitated, the island will advance many leagues nearer the eye; every part of it will be perfectly conspicuous; even the little divisions of property will appear faintly sketched upon it; yet still the clearness of the other parts of the landscape according with it, all will be in place, and a general harmony preserved.

These are chiefly summer effects. I have often, however, seen beautiful effects in winter of a similar kind, especially in a morning somewhat inclining to frost, when the rays of the sun have appeared, as it were, struggling between the haziness of the island, the smoke of the town, and the splendour of the rising sun. In one part distinctness has prevailed, in another obscurity. I have seen also something of the same effect in a winter noon, only rendered, perhaps, still more beautiful by streaks of ruddy sunset passing along the horizon, and joining in the conflict.

In the year 1783, when such uncommon fogs prevailed over Europe, the appearances of the island were often very strange. Earth, clouds, and water, confounded together in vast combinations, seemed often to have exchanged places; the water would appear above the island, and the clouds below both. But these appearances were so uncommon, that they scarce deserve mention, nor indeed were they often in themselves picturesque.

I omit mentioning here the variety which the seasons produce on this landscape; though as it is a woody scene, the effect is often singularly beautiful, especially in autumn.

If, then, so great a variety of incidents arise from the few circumstances of landscape which are found at this place, with what variety may we suppose landscapes of a larger size, and composed of more complicated parts, may be attended — particularly extensive distances, which are of all others attended with the greatest variety

of incidental beauty! Every landscape, indeed, hath
something peculiar to itself, which disposes it more or
less to receive the incidents of light and weather in some
peculiar manner. An open sea coast one should think
of so simple a construction, as to be little liable to
receive any change; and yet I have stood upon a sea
coast, on a sunshiny cloudy day, when the wind has
been rather brisk, and have, in less than an hour, seen the
whole picture under a dozen different forms, from the
varying of the lights in the sky, on the horizon, on the
surface of the water, or on some part of the coast.

The conclusions from all these remarks are, that every
landscape is in itself a scene of great variety—that there
are few landscapes which have not, at some time or
other, their happy moments—that a landscape of extent
and beauty will take the full period of a year to shew
itself in all the forms it is capable of receiving—and
that he who does not attend to the variations of the
atmosphere, loses half the beauty of his views.

The atmospherical phenomena, which Mr Gilpin notices
above as having occurred in the year 1783, though certainly
not picturesque, are extremely curious. They have been
frequently noticed by others, and especially by Mr William
Scoresby, junior, who observed some very wonderful appearances of distant objects, whilst navigating the icy sea in
the ship Baffin, in the immediate neighbourhood of West
Greenland, during the summer of 1820; of which he gave
an account to the Royal Society of Edinburgh, in December
of the same year. " The first of these," says he, " consisting chiefly of images of ships in the air, occurred on
the 28th of June, in latitude seventy-three degrees thirty
minutes, and longitude eleven degrees fifty minutes west.
For two or three days previous, the weather had been
intensely foggy, with the wind from the south-east, east,
and north-east, blowing fresh. The day alluded to was
beautifully clear; not a cloud, excepting the most delicate
cirri, having appeared in the sky for twenty-four hours.
The thermometer varied between thirty-seven and forty-two
degrees, and even at this moderate temperature the sun was
so powerful, that its intense light produced a very painful
sensation in the eyes, whilst its heat softened the tar in the
rigging of the ship, and melted the snow on the surrounding
ice with such rapidity, that pools of fresh water were formed

Appearance of the Holderness coast as seen by the naked eye, from the altitude of 60 feet above the level of the Sea. June 24th 11 A.M. 1826.

The same coast seen at the same time, from the height of 40 feet.

The same coast seen at the same time, from the height of 20 feet.

on almost every piece, and thousands of rills carried the excess into the sea. There was scarcely a breath of wind —the sea was as smooth as a mirror—the ice around was crowded together, and exhibited every variety, from the smallest lumps to the most magnificent sheets. Bears traversed the fields and floes in unusual numbers, and many whales sported in the recesses and openings among the drift ice. About six in the evening, a light breeze at north-west having sprung up, a thin stratus, or "fog-bank," at first considerably illuminated by the sun, appeared in the same quarter, and gradually arose to the altitude of about a quarter of a degree. On this most of the ships, navigating at the distance of ten or fifteen miles, amounting to eighteen or nineteen sail, began to change their form and magnitude; and, when examined by a telescope from the mast-head of the Baffin, exhibited some extraordinary appearances, differing in effect at almost every point of the compass. One ship, bearing north-west by west, had a perfect image, as dark and distinct as the original, united to its mast-head in a reverse position; two others, at north-west, presented two distinct inverted images in the air, one of them a perfect figure of the original, the other wanting the hull. Two or three more, bearing about north, were strangely distorted, their masts appearing of at least twice their proper height, the top-gallant-masts forming one-half of the total elevation; and, at the same time, some vessels, bearing north-north-east and east, exhibited an appearance totally different from all the preceding. These, five in number, were at the distance of twelve or fifteen miles, and, consequently, considerably beyond the natural horizon; but, owing to the influence of some peculiar vapour in the air, they now seemed to advance so near that they became distinctly visible, and the ice, for some minutes, appeared beyond them. Their masts seemed to be scarcely one-half of their proper altitude, in consequence of which, one would have supposed that they were greatly heeled to one side, or in the position called careening. Along with all the images of the ships, a reflection of the ice, in some places in two strata, also appeared in the air. The upper stratum of ice, in which the images of the ships terminated, was fifteen minutes of altitude from the apparent horizon. These reflections suggested the idea of cliffs, composed of vertical columns of alabastar. The stratus which occupied the space intermediate between the reflection of the ice and the horizon, was, in some positions of the sun, highly illuminated, and shone like a sheet of .stant water in a calm; but, in other cases, it was a little darker in colour than the higher region of the atmosphere. To this fog, or stratus, then, it is probable all the reflections were owing; the double images being produced by two or more strata of fog; while a highly tremulous transparent vapour, resembling the steam of water before condensation, which could occasionally be discerned floating across the ice with the breeze from the north-west and north, occasioned, it is likely, the singular distortions observed in the form of every distant object seen through it. Hence, not only ships, but also the ice, was sometimes deformed by the refractive property of this vapour. The verge of the ice, in one place, became a considerable precipice; in another, it appeared like distant land clad with snow; and a large hummock on the horizon was reared into the air in the form of an obelisk. The appearances now described occurred between six and twelve P.M. The reflected images of the ice continued visible above two hours; of some of the ships, about half an hour; and of others, presenting double reflections, about five minutes. The whole of the phenomena were seen about the same time. There were some vessels in the south-east quarter, which were not in the least changed from their natural form or dimensions.

" The atmosphere was again in a similar state to that just mentioned, on the 15th, 16th, and 17th of July. Our latitude was then seventy-one degrees thirty minutes, longitude seventeen degrees west. Ice fields and floes, with many smaller pieces, were in abundance around us. The wind was extremely light, the sky cloudless, and the temperature in the shade between forty and forty-eight degrees; the sun, at the same time, was bright, and its rays powerful. On each of these three days, curious reflections from fog banks, or refractions from tremulous vapour, were observed. The ice in the horizon was reflected in one, two, or three parallel strata, at the altitude, as seen from the deck of the Baffin, of ten to thirty minutes above the verge of the sea; and where water occurred on the horizon, a blackish gray undulating streak appeared in the atmosphere above it, exactly resembling the slight waves produced by a gentle breeze of wind, of which it was doubtless a reflection. In some places the reflected ice was in narrow faint streaks; in others, in bold bright patches, resembling cliffs of white marble of the basaltic structure. Sometimes the phenomenon extended continuously through half the circumference of the horizon, at others it appeared in detached spots, in various quarters. From the deck of the ship, with a telescope, the inverted images of distant vessels were often seen in the air, while the ships themselves were far beyond the reach of vision. Some ships at the distance of six or eight miles, like those seen on the 28th of June, were elevated to twice their proper height, and others compressed almost to a line. Hummocks of ice here and there were surprisingly enlarged; and every prominent object, in a proper position, was either magnified or distorted. These appearances, though often visible to the naked eye, were not generally very striking; but when examined through a telescope, they presented a never-varying scene of the most interesting imagery. Most of the phenomena now mentioned were seen on the 16th of July, at five o'clock in the afternoon. A stratus was then observed in the east, extending north about as far as the north-west. In the latter quarter, including the azimuth of the sun, the sky was whitish and resplendent, so that the fog was concealed in the general glare.

" Another instance of curious refraction will only be mentioned. This occurred on the 18th of July, under similar circumstances of weather, &c. as those already described. The sky was clear. The tremulous vapour was particularly sensible and profuse, though perfectly transparent. The temperature of the air at 9 A.M., the time when the phenomenon was first noticed, was forty-two degrees; but in the evening preceding, it must have been greatly lower, as the sea was in many places covered with a considerable pellicle of new ice. Such a circumstance, in the very warmest part of the year, must be considered as very extraordinary, especially when it is known, that ten degrees farther to the north, no freezing of the sea, at this season, that I am aware of, has ever been observed. The latitude of the ship was at this time seventy-one degrees twenty minutes north, the longitude seventeen degrees thirty minutes west. Having approached, on this occasion, so near the unexplored shore of Greenland, that the land appeared distinct and bold, I was wishful to obtain a drawing of it; but on making the attempt, I found I could not succeed with any degree of accuracy, since the outline changed as fast as I proceeded. The odd form of many of the hills induced me to examine the land with a telescope from the mast head, on which, finding it much disfigured by refraction, I contented myself with sketching a few of the most remarkable objects. The land at this time in sight, extended from west to north-north-west, per compass; the nearest part at west-north-west being about thirty-five miles distant. It seemed to be a barren and lofty country, abounding in mountainous ridges and peaks. There was much less snow on it than we usually find on Spitzbergen at this season; but in other respects it very much resembles that inhospitable country.

The general telescopic appearance of the coast was that of an extensive ancient city, abounding with the ruins of castles, obelisks, churches, and monuments, with other large and conspicuous buildings. Some of the hills seemed to be surmounted by turrets, battlements, spires, and pinnacles; while others subjected to one or two reflections, exhibited large masses of rock, apparently suspended in the air, at a considerable elevation above the actual termination of the mountains to which they referred. The whole exhibition was a grand and interesting phantasmagoria. Scarcely was any particular portion sketched, before it changed its appearance, and assumed the form of an object totally different. It was perhaps alternately a castle, a cathedral, or an obelisk; then expanding horizontally, and coalescing with the adjoining hills, united the intermediate valleys, though some miles in width, by a bridge of a single arch of the most magnificent appearance and extent. Notwithstanding these repeated changes, the various figures had all the distinctness of reality; and not only the different strata, but also the veins of the rocks, with the wreaths of snow occupying ravines and fissures, formed sharp and distinct lines, and exhibited every appearance of the most perfect solidity."

The same gentleman read another paper, on the same subject, to the Royal Society of Edinburgh, in January, 1827. It was no less interesting. " In the session of 1820-21," says he, " I had the honour of communicating to the Royal Society a description of some remarkable atmospherical refractions observed in the Greenland Sea. Since that period, additional opportunities for observation, under circumstances peculiarly favourable, afforded a great number of other examples of a similar kind, along with some still more singular. Among these, the most extraordinary was the inverted image of a ship, which appeared in the lower part of the atmosphere, so distinctly and beautifully defined, that I could venture to pronounce it to be the representation of my father's ship, as indeed it proved to be, though we were then distant from each other about twenty-eight miles, and some leagues beyond the limit of direct vision.

" The phenomena I have now to describe occurred during

the last summer, about Bridlington Bay, and were seen from my residence at Bridlington Quay. I shall first describe the appearance of the shipping in the bay.

" In the afternoon of the 12th of June, about five o'clock, after a clear hot day, the phenomena were first observed. All the shipping, at a sufficient distance, began to loom, and were variously distorted, and many vessels, when examined by the telescope, exhibited inverted images immediately above them. A portion of the extreme verge of the sea seemed to separate, as by a transparent fog bank, and between the real horizon and this refracted horizon, all the distortions and inverted images occurred. Some of the ships were of their natural proportions, with an inverted fac-simile above. Others, at distances, or in situations such that the top of the masts reached more than one half the height of the refracting interval, were abridged of their upper sails. One brig, nearer than the rest, only exhibited its hull and courses, with an inverted resemblance of the same over the top; and what gave it a still more curious appearance, was a narrow clear space between the vessel and the image, as if there were in that place (in the line of the top-sails of the brig) a perfect void. In one or two cases, besides the inverted image, there was also an imperfect erect image, placed upon the upper line of the horizon. Most of the vessels, though they appeared situated upon the true horizon, were, in reality, greatly more distant, and many of them altogether beyond the limit of ordinary vision. Hence, whilst the eye was fixed upon them, owing to the perpetual changes of the atmosphere, one or other of them would frequently disappear, and remain for some time invisible, and then suddenly start into sight as before. Objects within the horizon, (about six miles distant,) were scarcely, if at all, affected by the refraction. The upper or refracted horizon was often irregular in its outline, and sometimes broken. It was generally dark, and well defined ; but the interval between it and the real horizon was frequently more faint in its shade, as if by attenuation. Sometimes there was a treble horizon exhibiting parallel streaks. The low coast of Holderness (forming the southern part of Bridlington Bay) was slightly influenced by the same refraction. The air on this occasion was clear and calm, — occasionally there was a gentle sea breeze.

" Twelve days after this, (June 24th,) the phenomena were repeated with several new peculiarities, especially in regard to the land, as hereafter noticed. The interval between the true and refracted horizons, (measuring between one and two minutes of a degree,) was, as before, of a bluish gray colour, and resembled a thin mist. But, besides the usual appearances of the ships, there were many erect images perched, as it were, upon the upper line of the horizon, and belonging to vessels that were evidently far out of sight! This occurred at noon, when the temperature was eighty degrees in the shade. In the afternoon, the temperature becoming more equable, most of the phenomena disappeared; but in the evening, with the change of temperature, they were renewed in their principal varieties. On this day the sky was again cloudless, with a slight breeze from the eastward, though occasionally it was quite calm. The following day there were very beautiful repetitions of the phenomena. The upper horizon was occasionally double and broken. A second erect image of some of the ships appeared between the two upper lines. Again, there was a renewal of these interesting appearances on the 26th of June; the day was, as before, clear and hot, but with a smart sea breeze. The horizon began to separate about ten A. M., and between eleven and twelve every object at sea beyond the distance of six miles became influenced by the unequal refraction. There were, on this occasion, several instances of a single inverted image of a ship, clearly defined, though the ship to which it referred was altogether out of sight! The images were, in most respects, very similar to what I have formerly observed in the Arctic Regions, though scarcely so distinct and well defined. In high latitudes, indeed, I have seen them as sharp and definite as if cut with a graver.

" On June the 24th, already referred to, the Holderness coast was most singularly affected by the state of the atmosphere. In the forenoon of this day, the sun having intense power, the low and uninteresting part of the promontory, terminating at the Spurn, assumed a new appearance to the naked eye. Slight hummocks and knolls, on the ridge of the land, were raised into parallel vertical pillars, resembling immense detached columns of basalt; and the whole range, for a considerable extent, seemed to be surmounted by a horizontal and almost continuous platform. This platform, or causeway, which it resembled, seemed, in many places, entirely unsupported, the clear view of the sky being obtained beneath it. But this apparent platform was, in reality, the refracted image of the stratum of land beneath, forming continuous columns where the land was highest, and the image joined the protuberances, but leaving vacant interstices where the land was low, and the resemblances more remote. Having made a sketch of the appearance of the coast from my window, which is at the height of about forty feet above the level of the sea at low water, (the state of the tide at the time,) it occurred to me that there might possibly be a difference of appearance at another level; and on ascending to the attic story, (about sixty feet above the sea,) I was surprised to find the phenomena altogether changed, and the natural form of the land almost restored. I returned to the sitting-room, and found the refracted state, before observed from thence, remaining unchanged. I next descended to the cellar flat, (about twenty feet above the sea,) where, on a level platform, by the side of the house, there was a clear view of the same coast. Here, again, I experienced another surprise, in finding the appearance almost perfectly what it ought to be at that level, scarcely any remains of the refractive influence being observable; yet at the middle position, in the sitting-room, the phenomena continued unaltered!

"On a subsequent day, objects within four miles of the observer were slightly influenced by the refraction, though the greatest effects occurred in respect to objects six to ten miles distant. The phenomena continued to preserve their character, as seen from the three different levels, for above an hour, and then the appearance, as seen from the sitting-room, began to descend; so that eventually, as the heat of the day increased, or rather became more general and uniform, the view from the sitting-room became nearly that which was before seen from the attic, whilst that which had been seen from the sitting-room was now seen from a level ten or fifteen feet lower. Shortly after mid-day, it appeared so striking from the level of the street, (ten feet below the sitting-room,) that it began to attract the notice of all the inhabitants in the neighbourhood. From two until five P.M. the phenomena were more indistinct, and less interesting; but as the heat began to abate, (towards six P.M.) the appearances observed in the morning were in a great measure repeated. On several other occasions, the coast of Holderness was seen through unequally refractive media; but there was no appearance so interesting as the one above described.

"No other cause requires to be sought for in explanation of

the phenomena, than that of different parallel strata of air of
unequal density, so ably demonstrated and illustrated by Dr
Wollaston, and so strikingly exemplified by Dr Brewster, in
his experiments, resembling the very effect in Nature, with
hot and cold strata of water or glass.   Nor is the striking
peculiarity observed on the Holderness coast, of the phenomena being confined to a particular level in the position of the
observer, of difficult explanation.   In this case, it is perhaps
only necessary to suppose (I speak doubtfully, however) that
the distant coast, observed from the upper altitude, was seen
altogether through an upper stratum of air, of pretty uniform
density ; and also observed from the lower station, that it was
either seen chiefly through a lower stratum, or through
different strata, amid which the rays of light passed from the
distant coast converging, but not having arrived at a focus ;
but that from the middle altitude, the rays from the land
passed so obliquely out of one medium into the other, that a
part was refracted back again into the former medium, so as
to double the object, by presenting an inverted image.

" The occasion of the frequency of these phenomena during
the last summer, and of their extraordinary character, may
perhaps be accounted for from a remarkable and sudden change
in the temperature of the air.   The cool weather of the preceding spring had continued down till the beginning of June.
The sea, even near the coast, was in consequence at its winter
temperature, whilst the air became quickly heated by the
fervent glare of an unclouded sun.   When, therefore, the air
near the surface of the earth became greatly warmed, the
stratum immediately in contact with the sea was chilled by
its coldness, whereby media of unequal density and refracting
power were produced.   And through these unequal media
the rays of light, both from the shipping and the Holderness
coast, had to pass to the eye of the observer, an uninterrupted
surface of water in all cases lying between the objects and
myself.   The passing of the rays of light, at an extremely
small angle, through these different strata of different refracting powers, would sufficiently account, on the principles
already referred to, for most of the phenomena observed."

The *Fata morgana*, a remarkable phenomenon sometimes
seen in the Straits of Messina, between the Island of Sicily
and the Italian coast, is somewhat allied to these singular
optical illusions we have been describing.*   When the rays

---

* These have been particularly described by Minasi.

6

of the rising sun fall at a particular angle on the sea of Reggio, and the bright surface of the water in the bay is unruffled, an individual standing on an eminence of the city, with his back to the sun, and his face to the bay, sees on the water, as in a catroptic theatre, numberless pilasters, arches, well delineated castles, regular columns, lofty towers, superb palaces with balconies and windows, extended valleys of trees, delightful plains with herds and flocks, armies of men on foot and on horseback, and many other strange figures, in their natural colours and proper actions, passing rapidly in succession along the surface of the sea. But, if the atmosphere be highly impregnated with vapour and dense exhalations at the time, it then happens that in this vapour, as in a curtain extended along the channel to the height of about twenty-four or twenty-five feet, and nearly down to the sea, the observer will behold the scene of the same objects, not only reflected from the surface of the sea, but likewise in the air, though not so distinct or well defined. Lastly, if the air be slightly hazy and opaque, and at the same time dewy, and adapted to form the iris, then the above mentioned objects will appear only at the surface of the sea, as in the first case, but all vividly coloured or fringed with red, green, blue, and other prismatic colours. Minasi considers all these as images of the objects on the two coasts. He holds the sea to be an inclined speculum, on account of the rapid current which runs through the straits; and he supposes that the opposing eddies divide it into different planes. He ascribes the aërial *morgana* to the refractive and reflective power of effluvia suspended in the air. Dr Wollaston tells us, that this class of phenomena may be imitated, either by viewing a distant object along a red-hot poker, or through a saline, or saccharine solution with water and spirit of wine floating upon it.

A very extraordinary phenomenon, precisely of the same nature as those noticed by Mr Scoresby, has been recorded by Mr Vince. The castle of Dover, which, with the exception of the turrets, is concealed from the view at Ramsgate by the intervening hill, appeared, on the 6th August, 1806, as if it had been brought over and placed on the side of the hill next to Ramsgate. This phenomenon must have arisen from some variation of density in the intermediate air. Between the observer and the land from which the hill rises, there was about six miles of sea, and from thence to the top of the hill about six miles more.

The mysterious appearances on the Souter Fell, in Cumberland, are more attributable to reflection than refraction. The first of these was observed in 1743, by Daniel Stricket, then servant to John Wren, of Wilton Hall, who, together with his master, saw the figure of a man, with a dog, pursuing some horses along Souter Fell side—a place so steep, that a horse can scarcely travel on it at all; yet they appeared to run at an amazing pace, till they got out of sight at the lower end of the Fell. Stricket and his master ascended the Fell next morning, in full expectation of finding the man and animals all lying dead, but no vestige of either was to be discovered. The following year, 1744, on the 23d of June, as the same Daniel Stricket was walking, about half-past seven o'clock in the evening, a little above the house of Mr Lancaster, of Blakehills, with whom he then lived, he saw a troop of horsemen riding on Souter Fell side, in pretty close ranks, and at a brisk pace. Remembering that he had been laughed at for mentioning what he had seen the previous year, he continued to observe them in silence for some time; but, being at last convinced that the appearance was real, he went into the house, and begged Mr Lancaster to come out, as he had something very curious to shew him. They went out together; but, before he spoke, his master's son had already discovered the aërial troopers. The whole members of the family were then informed, and the strange spectacle was seen by all. These visionary horsemen seemed to come from the lowest part of Souter Fell, and they became visible at a place called Knott. They moved in regular troops along the side of the Fell, till opposite to Blakehills, when they went over the mountain, in this way describing a curvilinear path; and both their first and last appearance was bounded by the top of the mountain. They went at a regular swift walk, and they continued to appear and disappear for more than two hours, till night put a stop to any farther exhibition of them. Many troops were seen in succession; and frequently the last, or last but one, in a troop, would quit his position, and gallop to the front, where he marched on at the same rate as the others. These wonderful appearances were seen by every human individual within the distance of a mile, and they were the same to all. The spectators were above twenty-six in number.

The natural explanation of this phenomenon is, that a troop of those who were preparing to rise in the subsequent Rebellion, were exercising in some hollow and concealed

part of the mountain, and that their figures being received
upon a dense cloud floating in the air, were reflected downwards on the mountain's side. It was a similar optical accident
that rendered a whole army most distinctly visible to a farmer
and his son near Inverary—a circumstance which, though
extremely interesting and well vouched for in all its particulars, is too long to be given within our present limits. We
shall therefore conclude this subject with saying, that we have
no doubt that many of those strange mysterious visions, such
as those of processions and of funerals, so often seen in the
Highlands of Scotland, and other mountainous countries, are
quite explicable on the same principles.

SECTION XI.

OF THE ANIMALS WHICH FREQUENT THE FOREST.

HAVING thus taken a view of the most beautiful scenes
of the forest, it is, lastly, proper to people them. No
landscape is complete without its figures. I shall make
a few observations therefore on such animals as frequent
the forest, which the imagination of the reader may
scatter about as he pleases in the several scenes which
have been presented to him. The human inhabitants of
the forest have already been mentioned.*

A diminutive breed of horses run wild in New Forest.
In general, however, the horse is private property,
though sometimes with difficulty ascertained. Numbers
of people who have lands in the neighbourhood of the
forest have a right of commoning in it; and most of the
cottagers who border on it assume that right. Many of
them have two or three mares, and some, who make it
their business to breed colts, have droves.

The horse is gregarious. Herds of twenty or thirty
are often seen feeding together, in summer especially,
when they have plenty of pasturage, and can live as
they please. In winter they are obliged to separate,
and seek their food as they can find it. In general,
indeed, they are left in all seasons to take their chance

* See ante, page 116.

in the forest. Where there is no expense there can be no great loss; and what is saved, is so much gained. In marshy parts, a severe winter often goes hardly with them; but in dry grounds, where heath and furze abound, they pick up a tolerable winter subsistence, especially if they have learned the little arts of living which necessity teaches. Of these arts, one of the most useful is to bruise and pound with their fore feet the prickly tops of furze. This operation, which I have often seen performed, prepares the rigid diet of a furze bush in some degree for mastication, and renders it rather less offensive to the palate.

When such colts as have long run wild are to be caught for sale, their ideas of liberty are so unconfined, from pasturing in so wide a range, that it is matter of no little difficulty to take them. Sometimes they are caught by sleight of hand, with a rope and a noose : but if this method fail, they are commonly hunted down by horsemen, who relieve each other. Colt hunting is a common practice in the forest. The colts which feed on Ober Green are sometimes taken by the following stratagem. In this part runs a long bog, described under the name of Longslade Bottom, which is crossed by a mole thrown over it.* With this passage the colt is well acquainted; and, on being pursued, is easily driven towards it. When he is about the middle of the mole, two or three men start up in front, and oblige him to leap into the bog, where he is entangled and seized.

These expedients naturally put one in mind of those used by the Spanish Americans, to catch the horses of the Pampas. " When we came to the post," says Captain Head in his *Travels*, " I found about twenty gauchos assembled to commence breaking in the young horses — an operation which was to be continued for many days. As the carriage was many hours behind me, I resolved to see this, and, getting a fresh horse, I rode immediately to the corral, and soon made friends with the gauchos, who are always polite, and on horseback possess many estimable qualities, which, at the door of their hut, they appear to be devoid of. The corral was quite full of horses, most of which were young ones, about three and

* See ante, page 173.

four years old. The capataz, mounted on a strong steady horse, rode into the corral, and threw his lasso over the neck of a young horse, and dragged him to the gate. For some time he was very unwilling to leave his comrades; but the moment he was forced out of the corral, his first idea was to gallop away; however, the jerk of the lasso checked him in a most effectual manner. The peons now ran after him on foot, and threw the lasso over his four legs, just above the fetlocks, and, twitching it, they pulled his legs from under him so suddenly, that I really thought the fall he got had killed him. In an instant a gaucho was seated upon his head, and with his long knife, in a few seconds, he cut off the whole of the horse's mane, while another cut the hair from the end of his tail. This, they told me, is a mark that the horse has been once mounted. They then put a piece of hide into his mouth to serve as a bit, and a strong hide halter on his head. The gaucho, who was to mount, arranged his spurs, which were unusually long and sharp, and while two men held the animal by his ears, he put on the saddle, which he girthed extremely tight; he then caught hold of the horse's ear, and, in an instant, vaulted into the saddle; upon which the man who was holding the horse by the halter, threw the end of it to the rider, and from that moment no one seemed to take any farther notice of him. The horse instantly began to jump, in a manner which made it very difficult for the rider to keep his seat, and quite different from the kick or plunge of an English horse; however, the gaucho's spurs soon set him going, and off he galloped, doing every thing in his power to throw his rider. Another horse was immediately brought from the corral, and so quick was the operation, that twelve gauchos were mounted in a space which, I think, hardly exceeded an hour.

" It was wonderful to see the different manner in which the different horses behaved. Some would actually scream while the gauchos were girthing the saddle upon their backs; some would instantly lie down and roll upon it, while some would stand without being held, their legs stiff, and in unnatural directions, their necks half bent towards their tails, and looking vicious and obstinate; and I could not help thinking, that I would not have mounted one of these for any reward that could be offered me; for they were invariably the most difficult to subdue.

" It was now curious to look round and see the gauchos on the horizon, in different directions, trying to bring their

horses back to the corral, which is the most difficult part of
their work, for the poor creatures had been so scared there,
that they were unwilling to return to the place. It was
amusing to see the antics of the horses: they were jumping
and dancing in different ways, while the right arms of the
gauchos were seen flogging them. At last they brought the
horses back, apparently completely subdued and broken in.
The saddles and bridles were taken off, and the young horses
immediately trotted towards the corral to join their companions, neighing one to the other. Another set were now
brought out, and as the horses were kept out a very short
time, I saw about forty of them mounted. As they returned
to the corral, it was interesting to see the great contrast which
the loss of the mane and the end of the tail, made between
the horses which had commenced their career of servitude,
and those which were still free."

Again, Captain Head tells us, that on leaving San Luis,
they drove a set of loose horses before them, and about
twelve o'clock stopped to change. " The horses were driven
to the edge of a precipice which was quite perpendicular, and
which overhung a torrent, and we formed a semicircle about
them, while the peons began to catch them with the lasso,
which they were much afraid of. The horses were so
crowded and scared, that I expected they would all have
been over the precipice; at last the hind legs of one horse
went down the cliff, and he hung in a most extraordinary
manner by the fore legs, with his nose resting on the ground
as far from him as possible, to preserve his balance. As soon
as we saw him in this situation, we allowed the other horses to
escape, and in a moment the peon threw his lasso, with the most
surprising precision, and it went below the animal's tail like
the breeching of harness. We then all hauled upon it, and
at last lifted the horse, and succeeded in dragging him up:
during the whole time he remained quiet, and to all appearance perfectly conscious that the slightest struggle would
have been fatal to him. We then mounted our fresh horses,
and although the path over the mountains was so steep and
rugged, that we were occasionally obliged to jump a foot or
two from one level to another, we scrambled along, with the
loose horses before us, at the rate of nine or ten miles an
hour."

At all the neighbouring fairs, the New Forest horses
are a principal commodity, and are bought up for every

purpose to which a horse can be applied. Diminutive as they are, you may often see half a dozen of them straining in a waggon; and as it is fashionable to drive them in light carriages, their price has been enhanced. It is a little fortune to a poor cottager if he happen to possess three or four colts that are tolerably handsome, and match well. He may probably sell them for ten or twelve pounds a-piece.

In point of value, the New Forest horse would rise higher if the same care were taken in breeding him which was formerly taken,* and which is still, in some degree, taken in the neighbouring forest of Bere, where, I have heard, the keepers are ordered to destroy all horses which, at three years of age, are under thirteen hands, and all mares under twelve.

There is another evil, likewise, which tends to injure the forest colt, and that is, putting him to business at too early an age. Though a small horse attains maturity earlier than a large one, yet these horses, bred chiefly by indigent people, and generally of little value, are introduced much sooner to labour than abler and better horses commonly are.

The fame and exploits are still remembered of a little beautiful gray horse, which had been suffered to run wild in the forest till he was eight years of age, when he had attained his full strength. His first sensations on the loss of his liberty were like those of a wild beast. He flew at his keeper with his open mouth, or, rearing on his hind legs, darted his fore feet at him, with the most malicious fury. He fell, however, into hands that tamed him. He became, by degrees, patient of the bit, and at length suffered a rider. From this time his life was a scene of glory. He was well known on every road in the county, was the favourite of every groom, and the constant theme of every hostler. But in the chase his prowess was most shewn. There he carried his master with so much swiftness, ease, and firmness, that he always attracted the eyes of the company more than the game they pursued.

---

* See Manwood *On Forest Law*, page 29.

The New Forest horse is often supposed to be of Spanish extraction, from ancestors imagined to have been shipwrecked on the coast of Hampshire, in the time of the Armada ; but I look on this as a species of the ancient vaunt, *genus a Jove summo,* and to deserve as little attention. Some of them have a form which would not disgrace so noble a lineage. The horse represented in the annexed plate, is among the most beautiful ; but in general the croup of the forest horse is low, and his head ill set on, having what the jockeys call a stiff jaw. Of this defect a resemblance is given in the horse on the left, whose head is set on as those of the forest horses commonly are. Their claim, there-fore, to high lineage must in general rest more on their good qualities than on their beauty, on the hardiness of their nature, on their uncommon strength, on their agility and sureness of foot, which they probably acquire by constantly lifting their legs among furze.

We are disposed to think, that there may be some truth in the tradition, that these New Forest horses have Spanish blood in their veins. If so, they can boast of a common ancestry with the horses of the American Pampas, which have just been noticed. Captain Head says, that the horses of the Pampas are like the common description of Spanish horse, but rather stronger ; from which we should be disposed to believe that their strength had through ages increased, in consequence of superior pasture. " They are of all colours, and a great number are piebald. When caught, they will always kick at any person who goes behind them ; and it is often with great difficulty that they can be bridled and saddled ; however, they are not vicious, and when properly broken in, will allow the children to mount by climbing up their tails. Although I rode many thousand miles in South America, I was quite unable to learn how to select either a good horse or an easy going one, for by their appearance I found it impossible to form a judgment ; indeed, I generally selected for myself the worst looking horses, as I sometimes fancied that they went the best." This of the unpromising form of the horse of the Pampas wonderfully corresponds with Mr Gilpin's description of the New Forest horse.

It is astonishing how much the horse has spread himself

NEW FOREST HORSES

over the American continent, since his first introduction there by the Spaniards. Herds of ten thousand individuals are often found together. These consist of many families united, as it were, into one nation, for each male has his own wives and progeny around him, of whom he takes the guidance, and to whom he gives his particular protection. Their great enemies are the wolves, and against these they defend themselves by forming the whole body into a solid mass, the younger animals being placed towards the centre, and the older males on the outside, with their heads turned inwards, so that they are prepared to repel with their heels any attack that may be made upon them at any point. The most prevalent colours in these nations, are dark brown, black, and bay, the last being the most common. In Siberia, large herds of wild horses are found, as well as in the great Mongolian deserts, and among the Kalkas, to the north-west of China. They are also found in the deserts along the Don, where they are supposed to have descended from the Russian horses employed in the siege of Asoph, in 1697, which were turned loose for want of provender. There are numerous wild horses at the Cape of Good Hope, but they are small, vicious, and untractable. They are also found wild in other parts of Africa. But the Arabian race of horses is the finest. These occur wild in the deserts of that country, and the natives employ many stratagems to take them, when they select the most promising for breeding. Many suppose that Arabia is the original country of the horse.

But though the form of the New Forest horse is seldom beautiful, yet as the ornament of the forest scene, he is very picturesque. The horse, in his natural state, rough, with all his mane about him, and his tail waving in the wind as he feeds, is always beautiful; but particularly in so wild a scene as this, which he graces exceedingly.

On this subject I cannot forbear digressing a little (and I hope the critical reader will not be too fastidious) on the great indignity the horse suffers from the mutilation of his tail and ears. Within this century, I believe, the barbarous custom of docking horses came in use, and hath passed through various modifications, like all other customs, which are not founded in Nature and truth. A few years ago, the short dock was the only tail (if it may be called such) in fashion, both in the army and in carriages. The absurdity, however, of this total amputation began to appear. The gentlemen of the army led the way. They acknowledged the beauty and use of the tail as Nature made it. The short dock everywhere disappeared, and all dragoon horses paraded with long tails.

The nag tail, however, still continued in use. Of this there are several species, all more or less mutilated. The most deformed one is the nicked tail; so named from a cruel operation used in forming it. The under sinews of the dock being divided, the tail starts upwards, directly contrary to the position which Nature intended. The nag tail is still seen in all genteel carriages. Nor will any person of fashion ride a horse without one. Even the gentlemen of the army, who have shewn the most sense in the affair of horse tails, have been so misled as to introduce the nag tail into the light horse; though it would be as difficult to give a reason now for the nag tail as formerly for the short dock.

Two things are urged in defence of this cruel muti- . lation,—the utility and the beauty of it. Let us, briefly as possible, examine both.

To make an animal useful is, no doubt, the first consideration; and to make a horse so, we must neces- sarily make him suffer some things which are unnatural, because we take him out of a state of Nature. He must be fed with hay and corn in the winter, which he cannot get in his open pastures; for if he have exercise beyond Nature, he must have such food as will enable him to bear it. As it is necessary, likewise, to make our roads hard and durable, it is necessary also to give the horse an iron hoof, that he may travel over them without injuring his feet. But all this has nothing to do with his tail, from which no encumbrance arises.

" Yes," says the advocate for docking, " as it is necessary for the horse to travel, to hunt, and to race, it is useful to lighten him of every encumbrance. And as it is necessary for him to travel through dirty roads, it is useful to rid him of an instrument which is con- tinually collecting dirt, and lashing it over himself and his rider."

To ease your horse of every encumbrance in travelling is certainly right. You should see that his bridle and saddle (which are his great encumbrances) are as easy as possible, and that the weight he carries or draws be proportioned to his strength. But, depend upon it, he receives no encumbrance from Nature. It is a maxim among all true philosophers, that Nature has given nothing in vain; and there can be no reasonable doubt, but that Nature has given the horse his tail to balance and assist his motions. That this is the case seems plain from the use he makes of it. When the animal is at rest, his tail is pendent; but when he is in violent action, he raises and spreads it, as a bird does in the same situation. Would the swallow or the dove be assisted in their flight by the loss of their tails? or the greyhound in his speed by docking him? For myself, I have no doubt but if the experiment were tried at Newmarket, which I suppose it never was, the horse with his long tail, however the literati there might laugh at him, would not be in the least injured in his speed, and would certainly answer better, in all his sudden turns, to the intention of his rider. He would extend and spread his helm; it would steer his way, and we should seldom hear of his running out of his course, or on the wrong side of the post.

Besides, his tail probably assists him even in his common exertions, and balances his body when he trots, and prevents his stumbling. I have heard a gentleman who had travelled much in the East remark, that the Turkish and Arabian horses rarely stumble, which he attributed, and with much appearance of truth, to their long tails.

But whatever use the tail may be to the horse in action, it is acknowledged on all hands to be of infinite use to him at rest. Whoever sees the horse grazing in summer, and observes the constant use he makes of his long tail in lashing the flies from his sides, must be persuaded that it is a most useful instrument, and must be hurt to see him fidget a short dock backward and forward, with ineffectual attempts to rid himself of some plague which he cannot reach.

As to the objection against the tail as an instrument which is continually gathering dirt and lashing it around, if there be any truth in what I have already observed, this little objection dissolves itself; especially as the inconvenience may with great ease be remedied when the road is dirty, either by knotting up the tail, or by tying it with a leathern strap.

But whatever becomes of utility, the horse is certainly more beautiful, we are told, without his dangling tail. " What a handsome figure he makes when he carries both his ends well!" This is the constant language of horse dealers, stable keepers, and grooms ; and such language, though originating in tasteless ignorance and mere prejudice, has drawn over men of sense and understanding. It is inconceivable how delusively the eye sees, as well as the understanding, when it is fascinated and led aside by fashion and custom. Associated ideas of various kinds, give truth a different air. When we see a game cock, with all his sprightly actions and gorgeous plumes about him, we acknowledge one of the most beautiful birds in Nature ; but when we see him armed with steel and prepared for battle, we cry, " What a scarecrow!" But a cockfighter, with all the ideas of the pit about him, will conceive, that in this latter state he is in his greatest beauty; and, if his picture be drawn, it must be drawn in this ridiculous manner. I have often seen it.

Let jockeys, and stable boys, and cockfighters, keep their own absurd ideas; but let not men, who pretend to see and think for themselves, adopt such ridiculous conceits. In arts, we judge by the rules of art. In Nature, we have no criterion but the forms of Nature. We criticize a building by the rules of architecture; but in judging of a tree, or a mountain, we judge by the most beautiful forms of each which Nature hath given us. It is thus in other things. From Nature alone we have the form of a horse. Should we, then, seek for beauty in that object in our own wild conceptions, or recur to the great original from whence we had it? We may be assured, that Nature's forms are always the most beautiful, and therefore we should endeavour to correct our ideas by hers. If, however, we cannot give up the point, let us at least be consistent. If we admire a horse without a tail, or a cock without feathers, let us not laugh at the Chinese for admiring the disproportioned foot of his mistress; nor at the Indian for doting on her black teeth and tattooed cheeks. For myself, I cannot conceive why it should make a horse more beautiful to take his tail from him, than it would make a man to clap a tail to him. * With regard, indeed, to the natural beauty of a horse's tail, we want little reasoning on the subject. In conjunction with his mane, it gives him dignity : it hides his stradling buttocks, which is a decency in Nature we should admire rather than destroy. It forms a contrast among the legs. The four equal legs of every animal are its greatest deformity, and their sameness, of course, gives the painter the most trouble in the management of them. In many of her forms, indeed, where Nature does not seem to aim at beauty, she neglects this economy; but as if she meant the horse for one of her most elegant productions, she has provided for him in this respect also, by giving him a graceful flow of hair, which, hiding sometimes one leg, and sometimes another, introduces a pleasing contrast among them all. The accidental motion, also, of the tail gives it peculiar beauty, both when the horse moves it himself, and when it waves in the wind. The beauty of it, indeed, to an unprejudiced eye, is conspicuous at once; and in all parade and state horses it is acknowledged, though even here there is an attempt made to improve Nature by art: the hair must be adorned with ribands, and the bottom of the tail clipped square, which adds heaviness, and is certainly so far a deformity.

The captain of an English man-of-war gave me an account, some time ago, of his landing in one of the piratical states of Barbary, while his ship anchored in the bay. He was received by the Dey (I think, of Tripoli) with great civility, and, among other things, saw his stables. They were lined with a very long

* See Lord Monboddo on that subject.

double row of the most beautiful Barb and Arabian horses. He was struck with their beauty, to which their grand flowing tails, combed and oiled in the nicest manner, were no little addition. As he continued his walk through the stud, he came to a couple of horses with nag tails. On inquiring into their history, he found they were English horses, which had been presented to the Dey. The horses themselves were fit to appear anywhere; but the contrast of their tails, he thought, in such company, made so very strange and disgraceful an appearance, that he was ashamed of his countrymen. The case was, his eye having been thus accustomed to the beautiful forms of Nature, had gotten rid of its prejudices; and being a rational man, saw the matter in its proper light.

I shall conclude my remarks on this cruel mutilation with an epigram by Voltaire. That celebrated wit was in England about the time when the barbarous custom of docking horses was in high fashion. He was so shocked at it, that he wrote the following verses, which, it is said, he gave to Lord Lyttelton :

> Vous, fiers Anglois, et barbares que vous êtes,
> Coupent les têtes a vos rois, et les queues a vos bêtes.
> Mais les François plus polis, et aimant les loix,
> Laissent les queues a leurs bêtes, et les têtes a leurs rois.*

There is more indignation than wit, I think, in these verses. Voltaire seems to consider docking a horse and killing a king as equal crimes, which, however, is carrying the matter somewhat farther than the picturesque eye wishes to carry it.

The same absurd notions which have led men to cut off the tails of horses, have led them also to cut off their ears. I speak not of low grooms and jockeys; we have lately seen the studs of men of the first fashion, misled probably by grooms and jockeys, producing only cropt horses.

---

* Hail to that public wisdom, which defends
  The docking kings and steeds at different ends.
  Alas! in France the folly still prevails,
  Of leaving kings their heads, and steeds their tails.

6

When a fine horse has wide, lopping ears, as he sometimes has, without spring or motion in them, a man may be tempted to remove the deformity. But to cut a pair of fine ears out of the head of a horse is, if possible, a still greater absurdity than to cut off his tail. Nothing can be alleged in its defence. The ear neither retards motion, nor flings dirt.

Much of the same ground may be gone over on this subject which we went over on the last. With regard to the utility of the ear, it is not improbable, that cropping it may injure the horse's hearing; there is certainly less concave surface to receive the vibrations of the air. I have heard it also asserted with great confidence, that this mutilation injures his health; for when a horse has lost that penthouse which Nature has given him over his ear, it is reasonable to believe the wind and rain may get in, and give him cold.

But if these injuries are not easily proved, the injury he receives in point of beauty may strenuously be insisted on. Few of the minuter parts of animal nature are more beautiful than the ear of a horse, when it is neatly formed, and well set on. The contrast of the lines is pleasing, the concavity and the convexity being generally seen together in the natural turn of the ear. Nor is the proportion of the ear less pleasing. It is contracted at the insertion, swells in the middle, and tapers to a point. The ear of no animal is so beautifully proportioned. That of some beasts, especially of the savage kinds, as the lion and pard, is naturally rounded, and has little form. The ears of other animals, as the fox and cat, are pointed, short, and thick. Those of the cow are round and heavy. The hare's and ass's ears are long, and nearly of the same thickness. The dog and swine have flapping ears. The sheep alone has ears that can compare with the horse. The ear of the horse receives great beauty also from its colour as well as form. The ears of bay and gray horses are generally tipped with black, which melts into the colour of the head. But the ear of the horse receives its greatest beauty from motion. The ear of no animal has that vibrating power. The ears of a spirited horse are continually in motion; quivering and darting their sharp points towards every object that presents; and the action is still more beautiful, when the ears are so well set on, that the points are drawn nearly together. Virgil, who was among the most accurate observers of Nature, takes notice of this quivering motion in the ears of a horse.

———— Si qua sonum procul arma dedere,
Stare loco nescit; micat auribus.*

The same word, which he uses here to express the motion of a horse's ears, he uses elsewhere to express the gleaming of arms, the glittering of a gem, and the vibrating motion of a serpent's tongue. But it is not only the quivering motion of the horse's ears that we admire—we admire them also as the interpreters of his passions, particularly of fear, which some denominate courage, and of anger or malice. The former he expresses by darting them forward, the latter by laying them back.

This digression hath carried me much farther than I intended; but the mutilation of the tail and ears of this noble animal is so offensive to reason and common sense, that I have been imperceptibly led on by my indignation. Though nothing I can say on the subject, I am well persuaded, can weigh against the authority of grooms and jockeys, so as to make a general reform; yet, if here and there a small party could be raised in opposition to this strange custom, it might in time perhaps obtain fashion on its side. We commonly suppose, that when mankind in general agree in a point, there is truth. I believe no nation upon earth, except the English, have the custom among them of docking, nicking, and cropping their horses. The wisdom, too, of all antiquity decides fully against the practice. Instances, perhaps, might be found in the bas-reliefs of the Antonine column, and other remains of Roman antiquity, both of the cropt ear and of the hogged mane, (which, I take for granted, were never practised, except in cases of defect;) but I am persuaded no one instance can be found, in all the

* ———————— Or if the sound
Of war approach, he points his quivering ears,
And paws the ground.

Anger or intended Mischief

Under no impression of passion.

Cropt Horse

Short, dock.

Nicked tail

Square tail

Switch tail

remains of Grecian or Roman antiquity, of a short dock or a nag tail.

We really hope, for the sake of humanity, good taste, and we think we may add, common sense, that these brutal infringements upon Nature are becoming less and less frequent every day.

Besides the horse, the forest is much frequented by another animal of his genus, inferior indeed in dignity, but superior in picturesque beauty,—I mean the ass. Among all the tribes of animals, scarce one is more ornamental in landscape. In what this picturesque beauty consists, whether in his peculiar character, in his strong lines, in his colouring, in the roughness of his coat, or in the mixture of all, would be difficult perhaps to ascertain. The observation, however, is undoubtedly true; and every picturesque eye will acknowledge it. Berghem bears full testimony to its truth. In his pictures the ass makes often the most distinguished figure; and a late excellent landscape painter,* I have heard, generally kept this animal by him, that he might have it always at hand, to introduce in various attitudes into his pictures. I have heard also that a plaster cast of an ass, modelled by him, is sold in the shops in London; but I never saw it.

It is a remarkable fact, that the ass was actually extinct in Britain in the time of Elizabeth. Hollinshed informs us, that in his time, " our lande did yeelde no asses." We know that they existed before that period, and to our great comfort we have now no reason to complain of any lack of them. It does not appear, however, from what cause the animal became extinct, or how the race was restored. The ass was originally a native of Arabia and Syria, where it is even now found in the wild state, though rarely. Its chief natural habitat is Tartary, where it is the wild native of the dry and mountainous deserts. It is also met with, though less frequently, in Africa. The wild ass stands higher on its limbs than those which are domesticated, and its legs are more slender in proportion. Its hair is very fine, light coloured, soft, and silky, and on some parts marked by a few obscure waves or

* Mr Gainsborough.

undulations. The only exception exists in the native ass of
India, which is feeble, small, bow-legged, and apt to be short
winded. Wild asses are gregarious like horses, but they live
in smaller herds, each of which is regularly conducted by a
leader, and they owe their safety to their timidity and
vigilance, aided by their great acuteness in hearing and
smelling. The ass was imported into America by the
Spaniards, as well as the horse, and it has now multiplied so
much as to be even troublesome from its numbers. In their
wild state they have all the fleetness of horses, and neither
declivities nor precipices interrupt the fury of their career, and
when they are attacked, they have the singular power of
defending themselves by means of their heels and mouth, with
so much address, that they often maim their pursuers without
so much as slackening their pace. But after capture, and
after having been compelled to bear their first load, their
swiftness seems to forsake them, and they contract all that
stupidity of look and dullness for which they are proverbial.

The animal seems in general to grow to greater perfection
in warm than in cold climates. They are rare in Sweden,
and not at all known in Norway. Even in Britain, they were
long rare even in the south of Scotland; and one of the most
striking changes which Edinburgh and its neighbourhood
presents to an individual who has been much absent from it
for a good many years back, is the great number of small ass
carts now in use, whereas such a thing was never to be seen
formerly except as a rarity, and that generally when driven
by some gipsy tinker. In the northern parts of Scotland the
animal is still rarely met with. In Spain, the breed of asses
has been greatly improved by care and attention, so that they
often rise to fifteen hands high, and are strong, elegant, and
even stately animals. In Egypt and Arabia also these animals
have been brought to so great perfection, that they often fetch
a higher price than horses, and they even manifest a degree
of noble gracefulness superior to those of Spain. They
combine quickness, alacrity, and ease in all their paces, with
extreme sureness of foot; and being more hardy than horses,
they are preferred to them for long journeys, or for pilgri-
mages across the desert.

When young, the ass is uncouthly proportioned, large
headed, and altogether of an unprepossessing appearance;
but he is gay and frolicsome, until age, harsh treatment,
and overworking, break his spirit, and render him slow, dull,
and headstrong. When laden beyond his strength, he

expresses his uneasiness by lowering his head, and bending down his ears. If greatly abused, he will open his mouth and draw back his lips in a disagreeable manner. But with all this, there is no animal more alive to kindness than an ass; and if ass proprietors are disposed to doubt this fact, we should humbly entreat them—tinkers, costermongers, and all, not forgetting those smugglers who work them in their vocation all night, and who let them out all day for carrying the sea bathing nymphs of the watering places—to try the truth of what we assert, by putting it to the test of experiment. But little opportunity is allowed the poor ass to shew his sense of kind treatment, for where, says he, is kind treatment to be met with? But we know that he is belied in being accused of sulkiness, as well as in being supposed to want intelligence. For as he is remarkable for treasuring up an accurate recollection of localities, so he often displays a strong attachment to his master, whom he recognizes even in the greatest crowd; and if he is capable of all this under the detestable usage he experiences from the demons in human form, who seem to take sport and pleasure in his miseries, what effect would not kindness work upon him? We remember an anecdote of an Irishman at Ramsgate, who being asked to name the hardest wrought creature in existence, replied, " Och! a Ramsgate donkey to be sure; for, faith, afthur carrying angels all day, be the powers he is forced to carry speerits all night." To which we think that he might have added that his drivers were devils. But could we only persuade people to try the effect of kindness on the poor ass, he might be so much improved both physically and morally, as to be a much more useful animal than he even now is. To the poor he is in many circumstances invaluable, from his frugal mode of faring; thistles and plantain leaves, and such road-way-side plants being all he asks; for, even in his wild state, his favourite food is the wild plants of the desert, and especially those herbs which are bitterly lactescent; and it is likewise worth notice, that he actually prefers brackish water when thus left to his own choice.

One reason, indeed, for replenishing the forest so much with asses, is the pro agation of mules, of which great numbers are bred ip many parts of it; at least the breed was much encouraged before the troubles of America, whither several were every year exported.

The mule is by no means so picturesque an animal as the ass, and is rarely introduced in landscape, chiefly,

I suppose, because he has not so determined a character. He is neither a horse nor an ass, and yet has a resemblance to both. To make an object truly picturesque, it should be marked strongly with some peculiar character. Besides, the mule varies in form as much from himself as he does either from the horse or the ass. He follows his sire. A mule bred from an Arabian differs as much from the offspring of a forester as the two sires themselves. This also injures his picturesque character. The mule from which the annexed drawing was taken was a mule of blood. The ass also varies from itself, but not so much as the mule. It is here represented under one of its most elegant forms, that it may the more justly be compared with a mule of the same description.

It is a strange anomaly in Nature, that, whereas it is a well known fact, that horses and asses have a certain degree of constitutional antipathy to each other, so that it is difficult to induce young horses even to pass an ass on the road, they should yet be made to breed together, so as to give rise to the hybrid offspring called mules and hinnies. The former is the produce of a jack-ass and mare, and is much preferred to the latter, which is the produce of the horse and the she ass. The mule is much the larger of the two, and partakes much more liberally of the qualities of the nobler parent. Its fore parts are better shaped; the chest is broader, and more elegant; the rump fuller, the haunches are smoother, and the sides rounder; and on the head and other extremities, it bears some resemblance to the sire. The hinny, on the contrary, obviously partakes of the dimensions and appearance of the mother ass. Its chest, however, is thinner, its back is more rigid, its rump sharper, and its head longer, and not so thick in proportion; whereas the head of the mule is both thicker and shorter than that of the mare. The ears of the mule are longer than those of the horse, and those of the hinny are shorter than those of the ass. The mule is by much the most robust and hardy, and more fitted for the purposes of riding, draft, and burden. It is a very remarkable fact, that the mule is longer lived than either the horse or the ass, less liable to disease, and more capable of vigorous exertion. In Spain, fifty or sixty guineas is a common price for a good mule; and they are used in carriages of people of the first rank. We have had ourselves occasion to

THE MULE

NEW FOREST ASS

see a pair of beautiful mules driven as leaders in the Defiance Edinburgh and Aberdeen coach. These regularly perform one of the stages to the northward of Perth, which they do twice a day; and the coach, which is one of the fastest in the kingdom—its time, we believe, being about nine miles and a half, or ten miles an hour, stoppages included—loses no ground during the stage in which these animals are employed.

The *Literary Gazette* relates a curious anecdote, on the testimony of an eye-witness: " It is customary in Spain to guide the mules without reins, and merely by calling to them. The animal, when called by its name, punctually follows the orders of his driver. But it is a very peculiar circumstance, that they must always be yoked at the very same place which they have been accustomed to, otherwise they will not draw. After the battle of Cordura, several waggons were required to carry away the effects of King Joseph Napoleon from Madrid. While the waggons were loading, most of the drivers unyoked their mules, under pretence of feeding them, and then put them to again at an unaccustomed place. The animals refused to draw. The drivers at first seemed to give themselves all possible trouble to make them go on. The French, who escorted the train, attempted to assist, and dealt out their blows liberally on all sides. The Spanish drivers, however, contrived to get out of the way, and the mules kept their place in spite of all their beating. This occasioned a long delay, for the French sought in vain the cause of the obstinacy of the mules. At last, a part of the escort of cavalry were obliged to dismount, and their horses were harnessed to the waggons. But during this time, a part of the Spanish cavalry, whose approach appears to have been known to the drivers, had made a detour about Madrid, and so they captured all the baggage of poor Joseph, who is said to have narrowly escaped being made prisoner."

The obstinacy for which the mule is proverbial is much to be attributed to the ill treatment to which, like the ass, the creature is subjected. Our own experience in Alpine travelling has taught us how inestimable the services of this creature are, in traversing those wild regions, on those narrow rock-worn tracks by which alone they are accessible. If the traveller will only give his mule rein enough, and allow him to take his own way, and to pick his own steps, we conceive that he is safer in the saddle than scrambling on his own feet. In the Andes they are no less valuable. Captain

Head, in his lively manner, gives us some interesting anecdotes of mules, one of which is as follows:—

" As I was looking up at the region of snow, and as my
mule was scrambling along the steep side of the rock, the
capataz overtook me, and asked me if I chose to come on, as
he was going to look at the ' Ladera de las Vaccas,' to see if
it was passable, before the mules came to it; for when the
Cordillera is first opened by the melting of the snow, the
Ladera is for some time impassable, till it broadens towards
the end of summer. He accordingly trotted on, and in half
an hour we arrived at the spot. It is the worst pass in the
Cordillera. The mountain above appears almost perpendicular,
and in one continued slope down to the rapid torrent which
is raging underneath. The surface is covered with loose earth
and stones, which have been brought down by the water. The
path goes across this slope, and is very bad for about seventy
yards, being only a few inches broad; but the point of danger
is a spot where the water which comes down from the top of
the mountain either washes the path away, or covers it over
with loose stones. We rode over it, and it certainly was
very narrow and bad. In some places the rock almost touches
one's shoulder, while the precipice is immediately under the
opposite foot, and high above the head are a number of large
loose stones, which appear as if the slightest touch would
send them rolling into the torrent beneath, which is foaming
and rushing with great violence. However, the danger to the
rider is only imaginary, for the mules are so careful, and seem
so well aware of their situation, that there is no chance of
their making a false step. As soon as we had crossed the
pass, which is only seventy yards long, the capataz told me
that it was a very bad place for baggage mules, that four
hundred had been lost there, and that we should also very
probably lose one. He said that he would get down to the
water at a place about a hundred yards off, and wait there
with his lasso to catch any mule that might fall into the
torrent, and he requested me to lead on his mule. However,
I was resolved to see the tumble, if there was to be one; so
the capataz took away my mule and his own, and then
scrambled down on foot, till he at last got to the level of the
water, while I stood on a projecting rock, with the two English
captains of the mines, the three Cornish miners, the assayer,
and the surveyor, who were all anxious to witness the passage
of the baggage.

" The drove of mules now came in sight, one following another; a few were carrying no burdens, but the rest were either mounted or heavily laden; and as they wound along the crooked path, the difference of colour in the animals, the different colours and shapes of the baggage they were carrying, with the picturesque dress of the peons, who were vociferating the wild song by which they drive on the mules, and the sight of the dangerous path they had to cross, formed altogether a very interesting scene.

" As soon as the leading mule came to the commencement of the pass, he stopped, evidently unwilling to proceed, and of course all the rest stopped also. He was the finest mule we had, and, on that account, had twice as much to carry as any of the others; his load had never been relieved, and it consisted of four portmanteaus, two of which belonged to me, and which contained not only a very heavy bag of dollars, but also papers which were of such consequence that I could hardly have continued my journey without them. The peons now redoubled their cries, and leaning over the sides of their mules and picking up stones, they threw them at the leading mule, who now commenced his journey over the path. With his nose to the ground, literally smelling his way, he walked gently on, often changing the position of his feet, if he found the ground would not bear, until he came to the bad part of the pass, where he again stopped, and I then certainly began to look with great anxiety at my portmanteaus; but the peons again threw stones at him, and he continued his path, and reached me in safety; several others followed. At last a young mule carrying a portmanteau, with two large sacks of provisions, and many other things, in passing the bad point, struck his load against the rock, which knocked his two hind legs over the precipice, and the loose stones immediately began to roll away from under him: however, his fore legs were still upon the narrow path. He had no room to put his head there; but he placed his nose upon the path on his left, which gave him the appearance of holding on by his mouth. His perilous fate was soon decided by a loose mule who came, and in walking along the Ladera, knocked his comrade's nose off the path, destroyed his balance, and, head over heels, the poor creature instantly commenced a fall which was really quite terrific. With all his baggage firmly lashed to him, he rolled down the steep slope, until he came to the part which was perpendicular, and then he seemed to bound off, and, turning round in the air, fell into the deep torrent on his back, and upon his baggage, and instantly disappeared. .. I thought of course that he was killed, but up he rose, looking wild and scared, and immediately endeavoured to stem the torrent which was foaming about him. It was a noble effort; and for a moment he seemed to succeed, but the eddy suddenly caught the great load which was upon his back, and turned him completely over ; down went his head with all the baggage, and as he was carried down the stream, all I saw were his hind quarters, and his long, thin, wet tail lashing the water. As suddenly, however, up his head came again, but he was now weak, and went down the stream, turned round and round by the eddy, until, passing the corner of the rock, I lost sight of him. I saw, however, the peons, with their lassos in their hands, run down the side of the torrent for some little distance ; but they soon stopped, and, after looking towards the poor mule for some seconds, their earnest attitude gradually relaxed, and when they walked towards me, I concluded that all was over. I walked up to the peons, and was just going to speak to them, when I saw, at a distance, a solitary mule walking towards us !

" We instantly perceived that he was the Phaeton whose fall we had just witnessed, and, in a few moments, he came up to us to join his comrades. He was, of course, dripping wet; his eye looked dull, and his whole countenance was dejected; however, none of his bones were broken, he was very little cut, and the bulletin of his health was altogether incredible. With that surprising anxiety which the mules all have to join the troop, or rather the leading mule which carries the bell, he continued his course, and actually walked over the pass without compulsion, although certainly with great caution."

With horned cattle, of course, the forest, like all other wastes, abounds ; and this is a source of great picturesque beauty. The enclosure presents only a small number at once, the property of some single person; but in the forest, the cattle of all the neighbouring hamlets and cottages pasture together. We see them often in large herds ; and in summer, the season of landscape, they are drawn in numbers to favourite spots, particularly about pools and rivulets, where the various combinations and attitudes they form are beautiful and picturesque in the highest degree. Besides, they appear in a forest to much more advantage than they can possibly do within the formality of hedges.

But how much more picturesque must have been the appearance of the native cattle of Britain when they were the wild inhabitants of its forests! We cannot positively fix the time when these creatures ceased to exist in this island in a state of freedom; but we can at least say that they did so exist within these three hundred years; and the specimens of them which yet remain in some of our parks are sufficient to enable us to understand how important they must have been as picturesque objects, and as productive of picturesque circumstances among the sylvan scenery of the olden time. Bewick tells us that they are still to be found in the parks of Chillingham Castle in Northumberland, at Wollaton in Nottinghamshire, at Gisburne in Craven Yorkshire, at Lime Hall in Cheshire, and at Chartley in Staffordshire. These wild cattle are distinguished chiefly by their colour, which is invariably white; their black muzzles; the whole insides, and about one-third of the outside, of their ears, from the tip downwards, red; horns white, with black tips, very fine, and bent upwards; and some of the bulls have a thin upright mane, about an inch and a half or two inches long. About twenty years since there were a few at Chillingham, with black ears, but they were destroyed by the park keeper. The ears and noses of all those at Wollaton are black. At Gisburne there are some perfectly white, except the inside of their ears, which are brown. They are without horns, very strong boned, but not high, and are said to have been originally brought from Whalley Abbey in Lancashire, upon its dissolution in the thirty-third of Henry VIII. Tradition says they were drawn to Gisburne by the power of music.

At the first appearance of any person, the wild cattle set off in full gallop, and, at the distance of two or three hundred yards, make a wheel round, and come boldly up again, tossing their heads in a menacing manner; on a sudden they make a full stop, at the distance of forty or fifty yards, looking wildly at the object of their surprise; but, upon the least motion being made, they all again turn round, and fly off with equal speed, but not to the same distance; forming a shorter circle, and again returning with a bolder and more threatening aspect than before, they approach probably within thirty yards, when they make another stand, and again fly off; this they do several times, shortening their distance, and advancing nearer, till, they come within ten yards, when most people think it prudent to leave them, not choosing to provoke them farther; for there is little doubt that in two or three turns more they would make an attack.

The mode of killing them was perhaps the only modern remains of the grandeur of ancient hunting. On notice being given that a wild bull was to be killed on a certain day, the inhabitants of the neighbourhood came mounted, and armed with guns, &c. sometimes to the number of a hundred horse, and four or five hundred foot, who stood upon walls, or got into trees, while the horsemen rode off the bull from the rest of the herd, until he stood at bay, when a marksman dismounted and shot. At some of these huntings twenty or thirty shots have been fired before the creature was subdued. On such occasions the bleeding victim grew desperately furious, from the smarting of his wounds, and the shouts of savage joy that were echoing from every side: but, from the number of accidents that happened, this dangerous mode has been little practised of late years, the park keeper alone generally shooting them with a rifle at one shot.

When the cows calve, they hide their young for a week or ten days in some sequestered situation, and go and suckle them two or three times a-day. If any one comes near the calves, they clap their heads close to the ground, and lie like a hare in form to hide themselves: this is a proof of their native wildness, and is corroborated by the circumstance, that a calf of two days old was found so hidden, in a very lean and weak state. On stroking its head, it got up, pawed two or three times like an old bull, bellowed very loud, stepped back a few paces, and bolted with all its force at the legs of the person who discovered it; it then began to paw again, bellowed, stepped back, and bolted as before; but the gentleman having stood aside, it missed him, fell, and was so very weak, that it could not rise, though it made several efforts to do so. But it had done enough: the whole herd were alarmed, and coming to its rescue, they obliged him to retire; for the dams will not allow any one to touch their calves, without furiously attacking them.

When any individual happens to be wounded, or is grown weak and feeble through age or sickness, the rest of the herd set upon it, and gore it to death.

The weight of the bulls is from forty to fifty stones the four quarters; the cows about thirty stones. The beef is finely marbled, and of excellent flavour.

3

Those at Burton Constable, in the county of York, were all destroyed by a distemper. They varied slightly from those at Chillingham, having black ears and muzzles, and the tips of their tails of the same colour : they were also much larger, many of them weighing sixty stones ; probably owing to the richness of the pasture in Holderness, but generally attributed to the difference of kind between those with black and with red ears, the former of which they studiously endeavoured to preserve. The breed which was at Drumlanrig, in Scotland, had also black ears.

Cows are frequently turned out among the wild cattle at Chillingham, and it is somewhat extraordinary that the calves produced by this means are invariably of the same colour with the wild breed, (white with red ears,) and retain a good deal of the fierceness of their sire.

But of all animals with which the forest abounds, the stag is, in a peculiar manner, adapted to its scenes. The wildness of his nature harmonizes with them, and the beauty of his form adorns them. We admire his erect front, his spreading horns, on which he sometimes wears above twenty antlers, his limbs finished with so much elegance, and his stately measured pace.

But here, perhaps, the advocate for docking horses will glory in the short tail of the stag. He has no reason. There is no doubt Nature has provided for the exigencies of the stag in his speed, as well as for those of the horse. It is true, the shortness of the tail in so beautiful an animal rather seems a defect. But as, in the language of religion, the well ordered mind acknowledges every thing right in the works of God ; so, in the language of painting, the picturesque eye acknowledges every thing beautiful in the works of Nature. Some objects, indeed, may please less than others, and be less accommodated to the rules of painting ; but all objects are best as Nature made them. Art cannot mend them. Where art interferes, beauty vanishes. We dress the polished lawn ; but we only remove what may there be a deformity, though elsewhere a beauty. When we endeavour to improve the object—when we clip the holly, and trim the box,—we introduce deformity.

We sometimes, indeed, artfully remove a branch, but it is to open the landscape, not to improve the tree.

This is the most satisfactory admission which Mr Gilpin has yet made, and the explanation here given of the term picturesque is sufficiently clear, and perfectly correct.

The stag, during his first year, is called a calf, and does not assume the name of a stag till his fifth; being known in the intermediate years by certain technical names, which none but foresters can remember. In his sixth year he takes the respectable title of a hart. Some authors hath given it to his fifth; but I follow the authority of Manwood.* Besides this title, he may still attain two higher degrees of honour,—those of a hart-royal, and of a hart-royal proclaimed.

If he be hunted by the king, and escape, or have his life given him for the sport he has afforded, he becomes from thenceforward a hart-royal. If he be hunted out of the forest, and there escape, the king hath sometimes honoured him with a royal proclamation, the purport of which is, to forbid any one to molest him, that he may have free liberty of returning to his forest. From that time he becomes a hart-royal proclaimed. Manwood mentions a fact of this kind, which he found on record in the castle of Nottingham. It is dated in the time of Richard the First, who, having roused a hart in Sherwood Forest, pursued him as far as Barnsdale, in Yorkshire, where the hart foiled, and escaped his hounds. The king, in gratitude for the diversion he had received, ordered him immediately to be proclaimed at Tickill, and at all the neighbouring towns.

An affair of this kind, it is not unlikely, was the original of white-hart silver, as it is called, in the forest of Blackmore, in Dorsetshire. Some gentlemen, in the time of Henry III, having destroyed a white hart, which had given the king much diversion, (and which, it is probable, had been proclaimed,) the king laid a heavy fine on their lands, an acknowledgment of which was paid into the exchequer so late as in the reign of

* See Manwood, page 99.

Elizabeth.* Hutchings, in his *History of Dorsetshire*, says it is paid to this day.†

Instances of favourite stags, and of the warmth with which mankind have espoused their cause, when injured, occur so frequently, that Virgil thought a circumstance of this kind a proper incident for the whole plot of his Æneid to turn on:

> ———— quæ prima malorum
> Causa fuit, bellóque animos accendit agrestes.
> Cervus, erat formâ præstanti. ‡

In general, the stag is a harmless, inoffensive animal. At one season only, when he is engaged in his seraglio, he is fierce. You hear him roaring and bellowing at that time, about the forest, meditating revenge on his rival, whom he meets, head to head, and foot to foot. While he is able with his antlers to parry the attack, he stands his ground; and if he happen to be of equal prowess with his rival, the conflict is obstinate. But a weak adversary soon feels the strength of his opponent. He cannot resist his push. His flanks give way; and he is presently driven off the field.

At these seasons of riot, the stag is said to be dangerous. If, therefore, in passing through the forest, you see him at a distance in your path, you had better avoid him, by turning a little to the right or left. If you do not approach, he will not pursue. I have heard old foresters, however, say, they did not remember an instance of his ever doing voluntary mischief at any time, and assert, that he will always avoid the passenger if he can.

We believe that a red deer stag, having the whole forest before him, would, even in the rutting season, rather fly from a man than stay to assault him. But the matter is different when he is confined within the boundary of a park, however extensive it may be, for then an old stag becomes ferocious, even when not occupied in his amours. We remember a

---

* See Camden's *Brit.* p. 59. † Vol. ii. p. 492.

‡ ———— a favourite stag
 Was of this dire distress the leading cause.
 It raised suspicions first, then roused the sons
 Of violence to war.

circumstance which happened to a friend of ours in the park of Cullen House. The gentleman had seated himself under a large tree at the extremity of the park, in order to sketch a distant view of the house. He was intently occupied in his subject, when he was suddenly alarmed by a sound of pawing and stamping, and on looking up he beheld a huge stag, with a royal head, stooping his horns, and retreating slowly back in order to give greater effect to the charge he was about to make against our unfortunate friend. In one instant the gentleman had thrown down his sketch book and drawing utensils, and in the next he sprang at a horizontal bough over his head, and coiled himself up into the tree, with an agility that very much surprised himself. The stag, though thus disappointed, was not so easily put off; for he walked to and fro under the tree like a sentinel, turning his eye upward every now and then ; and this he continued during two or three hours, till at last, becoming tired of his watch, he sulkily retreated, and left our friend to gather up his sketching materials, and to retreat over the park wall, without waiting to finish his drawing.

But it is on all hands agreed that he is highly dangerous when hard pressed by the hounds and driven to extremity. When the chase is well nigh over—when that elastic vigour with which at first he bounded along the plain is changed into a heavy gallop—when his mouth becomes black and dry, his tongue hanging from it—and his eye marked with horror and dismay, (cruel, surely, to turn such agony into sport!) his reverence for man is gone: he is driven to despair, and all his powers are collected into terror and undistinguishing fury.

Some years ago a stag in New Forest, pressed by the hunters, and just entering a thicket, was opposed by a peasant, who foolishly, with his arms extended, attempted to turn him. The stag held his course, and darting one of his antlers into the man, carried him off some paces sticking upon his horn. The man was immediately conveyed to Lymington, where he lay dangerously ill for some time, but at length recovered. I have heard, also, that when the Duke of Bedford was lord warden of the forest, his huntsman had a horse killed under him by a stag which he crossed in the same imprudent manner.

We have a beautiful description in Shakespeare, which I cannot forbear introducing, both for the sake of the picture, and for the knowledge it conveys. The sorrows of the dying stag—his sighs, his tears, and the unfriendly return his distresses find from all his former companions, are circumstances in his history well known to the naturalist, the forester, and the huntsman. The melancholy Jacques is introduced by the poet reposing on the ground:

> ———— As he lay along
> Under an oak, whose antique root peeps out
> Upon the brook that brawls along this wood,
> To the same place a poor sequester'd stag,
> That from the hunter's aim had ta'en a hurt,
> Did come to languish ————
> The wretched animal heaved forth such groans,
> That their discharge did stretch his leathern coat
> Almost to bursting; and the big round tears
> Coursed one another down his innocent nose
> In piteous chase.
> ———— Anon a careless herd,
> Full of rich pasture, bounding comes along,
> And never stays to greet him. "Ay," quoth Jacques,
> "Sweep on, ye fat and greasy citizens;
> 'Tis just the fashion: wherefore look ye not
> Upon that poor and broken bankrupt there?"

The hind, also, in defence of her calf, is equally for-- midable, as far as her strength allows, and her powers of exerting it. She has been known to strike a dog so violently with the spring of her fore feet, as to strip his skin from his flesh, and lay his side bare.

As it is now many years since New Forest has been a scene of royal diversion, the breed of stags is generally diminished. It is a rare thing now to meet them in the southern parts of it; though within the memory of man, they were so numerous that I have heard an old forester, pointing to the side of a hill on Beaulieu Heath, say, he had seen them lying there in herds, like cows and horses. There are still, however, many in the northern parts of. the forest, particularly about Boldrewood and Burley Lodges; but, in general, the fallow deer are more. encouraged.

The stag might easily be trained, like the rein deer of Lapland, to draw a carriage, if we had not animals more proper for the purpose. The present Earl of Orford, I have been informed, bred two by way of experiment, which by domestication became manageable, were bitted, and drew a light cutricle with great gentleness and expedition. The stag is a native of our island, as indeed he is found in most parts of the world, differing only in a few accidental varieties.

The red deer is now chiefly to be found in the Scottish Highlands, as in the Rae Forest in Sutherland, in those of Athol and Braemar, and in some others. As it is only at particular seasons that red deer frequent the woods, the greater part of their life being spent in the mountain glens and on the open mountain sides, it is not natural to suppose, that they can become numerous within the confinement of an English forest. But from the extent of ground devoted to them by many individuals in Scotland, and the great care which is exerted for their preservation, we have every reason to think, that although their number for a long time declined, they are now rather increasing in North Britain. The stag is larger in some countries than he is in Britain; yet we have known the animal attain the weight of above three hundred pounds, exclusive of head, skin, and offals. In Bavaria, where they are very numerous, they are larger; but it is in America that they grow to the largest size, and there indeed they are magnificent animals. The stag also varies somewhat in colour in different countries. In Britain, he is brown above and whitish beneath, with some black about the face, and a list of the same down the hind part of the neck. In summer, the brown hue grows gradually redder, whence the animal acquires its name.

The annual loss and reproduction of the horns of a stag, is one of the most wonderful phenomena of animal physiology. The power of the nutritive process of the bloodvessels is strikingly exhibited by it, since a stag's horn, weighing perhaps twenty-five pounds, is completely formed in ten weeks. It exhibits a singular instance of a limited duration in life of a part of the system entirely independent of the life of the whole. What is very remarkable, the branches of the external carotid arteries which supply the horn with nourishment, are remarkably dilated and extended in ramification during its growth, and are again curtailed and diminished in calibre when the process has ceased. The stag begins to shed his horns in the latter end of February, or the beginning of

March. Very soon after the old horn falls off, a soft tumour begins to appear, which is covered with a velvet looking down, and from that time forward, it continues to grow, and to shoot forth into antlers. The skin covers the horns for some time, and the bloodvessels with which it is furnished serve to supply the growing horns with nourishment. These vessels are placed within those furrows which appear on the horn, after the skin has been removed ; for when the horns have reached their full growth, they acquire strength and solidity, and the velvet skin, with its bloodvessels, dries up and begins to fall off, and hastens this process by the itchy feeling which is then produced, inducing him to rub them against trees ; in this manner, the whole head gradually acquires its complete hardness, expansion, elasticity, and beauty.

The elasticity of the horn of the red deer is remarkable. The late Duke of Gordon shewed us two heads, which were linked together by the horns in a very singular manner. The wife of one of his Grace's keepers was one day alarmed by a very unusual noise near her cottage. On going to the door, she was surprised and somewhat terrified to behold an immense stag, with his head down, and pushing at another which lay dead on the ground. Her husband being absent, the woman did not dare to approach them, but ran into the house, in a state of alarm. The cottage stood on the edge of a sloping bank ; and the live stag, having the advantage of the declivity, gradually pushed the dead body of the other downwards, till he reached the level ground below, where he could push it no farther, and where he remained, chained by the head. The woman, who had ventured to take occasional stolen glimpses at what was going forward, informed her husband, the moment he returned home, and the keeper, on hurrying to the spot, was surprised to find that, in the desperate rush which the two infuriated animals had made at each other, he that survived had driven his horns fairly through between those of his opponent, and that, after they had so passed between them, their instantaneous expansion to their natural stretch had irrecoverably fixed them, one within the other, whilst at the same time one of the dog antlers, by taking a diagonal direction under the throat, had divided the jugular vein, and thus produced the death of the vanquished. The gamekeeper soon revenged his fate; for, after cutting the throat of the conqueror, he separated the two animals, by decapitating both, and carried the united heads to Gordon Castle, where they found a place in the Duke's museum.

There is a curious sympathy between the growth of the horns and the generative functions, for the destruction of these organs impedes the increase, alters the form, or altogether prevents the renewal of the horns. Anomalous instances of the females possessing horns have occurred, which have been noticed by Stahl, Leopold, Roy, and others. It is a remarkable thing that the old horns are seldom or never found, from which it is believed that the animals have a practice of burying them; and in this way some people have been led to account for horns being so frequently found in mosses, without any skeleton attached to them. We did once pick up a roebuck's horn; but it was whilst the dogs were running the animal it belonged to through a dense young wood, and the horn being about to drop naturally, was easily knocked off by a cross branch whilst he was going at full speed. After the stag has shed his horns, as if conscious of his weakness, he seeks the most retired parts of the woods, and only comes forth to feed during the night; but after his horns have become solid and polished—that is, about July or August—he quits the thickets for the more open forest, and begins to sound his loud and tremulous note of love, and he flies from place to place in search of the females. They become extremely furious in their ardour, their necks swell, they strike with their horns against trees and other obstacles. The rutting season usually lasts about three weeks, during which time the stag frequents the sides of the rivers and pools of water, into which he often rushes to quench his thirst, and to cool his heat. He swims with great ease and strength; and it is said that he sometimes ventures out to sea, allured by the hinds, and that he will even swim from one island to another, though at a considerable distance. The hinds go with young eight months and a few days, and seldom produce more than one fawn. They bring forth in May, or in the beginning of June, and conceal their young with great care in the most obscure retreats they can find. They will even expose themselves to the fury of the hounds, and suffer all the terrors of the chase, in order to draw off the dogs from the place where they have concealed their treasure. The hind also boldly defends her offspring against all sorts of enemies, and even in those countries where the wolf is found, he is compelled to retreat from her upon such occasions. But the stag is one of her most dangerous foes, for he would often destroy the fawñ, were it not that the hind so carefully conceals her offspring. The fawn never quits the dam during the whole summer; and in winter the stags and hinds of all ages keep together in herds, which are more or less numerous according to the mildness or rigour of the season. From fifty to sixty is no uncommon number in one herd, but several hundreds are sometimes to be seen at once in the Highland mountains. They separate in the spring; the hinds retiring to bring forth, while none but the young ones remain together.

The age of a stag may be pretty well guessed at by the number of its antlers. The first year exhibits only a short protuberance; the second year the horns are straight and single; the third year produces two antlers; the fourth three; the fifth four; and when arrived at the sixth year, the antlers amount to six or seven on each side. We have seen the head of a hart, shot near Innes House, in Morayshire, which had eight tines, or antlers, on each side, sixteen in all. " Lykewyse," says the *Book of Saint Albans*, " as in the boke of hawkynge aforsayde, are wryten and noted the termys of playsure belongynge to gentylmen; havynge delyte therin. In the same manere this boke folowynge shewyth to suche gentyle persones the manere of huntynge for all manere of bestys, whether they ben bestys of venery, or of chase, or rascall; and also it shewith al termys convenyent, as well to the houndes as to the beestys aforsayd. And in certen there ben many dyvers of theym, as is declaryd in the boke folowynge:

BESTYS OF VENERY.

Where so ever ye fare, by fryth or by fell,
My dere chylde, take hede how Trystam doo you tell,
How many manere bestys of venery there were:
Listen to your dame, and she shall you lere.
Foure manere bestis of venere there are:
The fyrste of theym is the harte, the seconde is the hare,
The boare is one of tho; the wulfe, and not one mo.

BESTYS OF THE CHASE.

And where that ye come in playne or in place,
I shall you tell whych ben bestys of enchase:
One of theym is the Bucke, another is the doo:
The Foxe, and the Marteron, and the wylde Roo.
And ye shall, my dere chylde, other bestys all,
Where so ye theym fynde, Rascall ye shall them call.
I fryth, or in fell, or in the forest, I you tell.

NOTE HERE THE AEGE OF AN HARTE.

And for to speke of the harte, yf ye woll it lere :
Ye shall hym a Calfe call at the fyrste yere ;
The seconde yere a Broket, so shall ye him call ;
The thyrde yere a Spayad lernyth thus all ;
The fourth yere a Stagge call hym by ony waye ;
The fyfth yere a grete Stagge your dame bydde you saye ;
The syxte yere call hym an Harte :
Dooth soo, my chylde, whyles ye ben in quarte.

TO KNOWE THE HEED OF AN HARTE, AND THAT IS DYVERS.

And of the hornys that he thenne beryth abowte,
The fyrste heed shall be jugyd wythout.
Therein fynden we suche dyversyte,
Netheless the syxt yere evermore at the leest,
Thou shalt well juge the perche of the same beest.
Whan he hath auntelere wythout ony lette :
Ryall and Suryall also there isette.
And that in the toppe so whan ye maye him ken :
Thenne ye shall calle hym forchyd an harte of ten.
And whan he hath in the toppe thre of the selve,
Then ye shall call hym trochyd an harte of twelve.
And afterwarde in the toppe whan there foure beene,
Thenne shall ye call hym sommyd an harte of syxtene.
And from foure forwarde what so befall,
Be he never of so many, ye shall him sommyd call,
Ryght of the nombre evyn that he is :
Callyth hym from foure sommyd I wys
Also have ye seele : an harte heeded weele.

THE DYSCRYVYNGE OF A BUCKE.

And ye speke of ye bucke : the fyrste yere he is
A Fawn soukynge on his dame, say as I you wys :
The seconde yere a Prycket, the thyrde yere a Sowrell,
A Sowre at the fourth yere, the trouth I you tell ;
The fyfth yere calle him a Bucke of the fyrste hede ;
The syxte yere calle hym a Bucke, and doo as I you rede.

OF THE HORNYS OF A BUCKE.

The hornes of a grete Bucke, or he soo be,
Must be sumonyd as I saye herkenyth to me.
Two braunches fyrste pawmyd he must have :
And foure avauncers the soth yf ye woll save.
And xxiiii espelers, and then ye maye hym call ;
Where so ye be a grete Bucke I tell you all.

AN HERDE.

My chylde callyth herdys of harte and of hynde,
And of bucke and of doo where ye theym fynde.

A LYTELL HERDE, A MYDDYLL HERDE, A GRETE HERDE.

Twenty is a lytyll herde, though it be of hyndys;
And thre score is a myddyll herde to call hem by kyndis;
And foure score is a grete herde, call ye them soo:
Be it harte, be it hynde, bucke, or elles doo.

HOW YE SHALL SAYE A GRETE HARTE, AND NOT A FAYR AND OTHER.

A grete harte whan ye hym se so shall ye hym call:
But never a fayre harte for noo thynge that maye be fall.
A grete hynde, a grete bucke, and a fayr doo;
My sones, where ye walke call ye theym soo.
So ye sholde name suche dere: and doo as I you lere.

The eye of the stag is peculiarly beautiful, soft, and sparkling, and in him the senses of hearing, smelling, and seeing, exist in a degree of acuteness perfectly wonderful. When listening, he raises his head, erects his ears, and catches up every noise however distant. When he approaches a thicket, he stops to look around him on all sides, and attentively surveys every object near him: if the cunning animal perceives nothing to alarm him, he moves slowly forward; but on the least appearance of danger, he flies off with the rapidity of the wind. He listens with great tranquillity and delight to the sound of the shepherd's pipe, which is sometimes made use of to allure him to his destruction. If he be called to with a loud voice, or a loud whistle, as he is going carelessly through the forest, he will stop and look round for a little time. This we can answer for on our own experience, and, we believe, is often a means employed to ensure to the marksman a more steady shot.

The stag is nice in the choice of his pasture, eats slowly, and when his stomach is full, he lies down to chew the cud at leisure. The great length of his neck renders this a tedious operation, and one which is not effected without great straining. Indeed, the grass is returned from the first stomach, through the narrow passage of his long neck, with a kind of hiccup, which continues during the whole time he is engaged in ruminating. The older the stag grows, the stronger his voice becomes, and the more it quivers: in the rutting season it is even terrible. We ourselves remember to have heard the stags of Braemar roaring to one another, whilst we were groping our way down from Ben Mach Dhuie, in a dark night, and although this was in autumn, we thought the sound more allied to the roaring of wild beasts of prey, than to the voice of any of our herbivorous animals. The note of the hind is not so loud ; indeed it is seldom heard, but when excited by apprehension for herself or her young. The stag was supposed to be extremely long lived, but more recent observations have settled the extreme duration of his existence as being from thirty-five to forty years.

The stag is capable of making a very bold defence. William, Duke of Cumberland, caused a tiger and a stag to be enclosed in the same area ; and the stag made so bold a defence, that the tiger was obliged to give up the contest. But this is not wonderful, as we have heard of a jackass beating off a tiger with his heels.

It is a strange mistake that Bewick and some other English zoologists fall into, in saying that the flesh of the stag is " poor and ill flavoured." These gentlemen, by saying so, only prove that they have never had the good fortune to eat a bit of red deer venison in good season, such as used to be shot by the late Duke of Athol. Certainly no carrion can be worse than red deer venison when it is out of season, but when the animal is killed in proper season, and in good plight, his flesh is as far superior to that of park venison as can possibly be conceived. The fat is then several inches thick, and the flavour of both that and of the lean, is quite enough to endanger the life of any alderman who may be seated before it.

The stag used to afford royal sport in the olden time, by being driven "with hound and horn." Nothing can be more true to Nature, or more enlivening, than the description of the stag hunt, with which the poem of the *Lady of the Lake* opens. It is exquisitely beautiful, and better describes the ancient mode of hunting than any thing we have met with in prose ; but it is much too long to quote in this place. Another poem of smaller dimensions, but of merit little inferior, has fallen into our hands accidentally. As the gentleman to whom it really belongs has not chosen to give it to the world himself, perhaps we shall be accused as being guilty of a piece of presumption in now producing it here. But as our present editorial capacity gives us large licence to poach upon the manors of others, we shall perhaps be forgiven by the highly gifted poet and historian, Mr P. Tytler, who, we believe, is its author ; and we are so sure of the thanks of the reading world for having rescued so beautiful a morçeau from oblivion, that they must greatly overpay us for any censure we may incur for our boldness.

I.

Hark! through the greenwood ringing,
Peels the merry horn;
On gallant steed,
O'er dewy mead,
Sir Asquetin is borne.
Many a brave and noble knight
Pranceth proud on left and right.
With beagle good
They draw the wood,
And loud and shrilly raise
The music of the chase.

II.

Deep, deep within the forest,
Fast by fountain clear,
With dew-drop dank
Upon his flank,
Stands the noble deer.
See, he starts! for, heard afar,
Come the notes of the woodland war;
And up he springs,
And on the wings
That mock the mountain wind,
Leaves hound and horn behind.

III.

Sweet, sweet upon the mountain
Sinks the setting sun;
The coursers fleet
Scarce drag their feet,
The weary chase is done.
But where's the antler'd king, who late
Ranged his realms in fearless state?
Alas! alas!
Upon the grass
That his best heart's blood dyes,
The captured monarch lies.

William Barclay, in his treatise *Contra Monarchomachos*, gives us the following picture of a royal hunting, with which the Earl of Athol treated Queen Mary. " In the year 1563," says he, "the Earl of Athol, a prince of the blood royal, had, with much trouble and vast expense, a hunting match for the entertainment of our most illustrious and most gracious Queen; our people call this a royal hunting. I was then a young man, and was present on that occasion. Two thousand Highlanders, or wild Scotch, as you call them here, were employed to drive to the hunting ground all the deer from the woods and hills of Athol, Badenoch, Marr, Moray, and the counties about. As these Highlanders use a light

dress, and are very swift of foot, they went up and down so
nimbly, that in less than two months," (we cannot conceive
how it could have taken so long a time, for more could now
be collected in less than as many weeks, with the same force,)
" they brought together two thousand red deer, besides roes
and fallow deer ; the Queen, the great men, and a number of
others, were in a glen, when all these deer were brought
before them.   Believe me, the whole body moved forward in
something like battle order.   This sight still strikes me, and
ever will strike me, for they had a leader whom they followed
close wherever he moved.   This leader was a very fine stag,
with a very high head.   This sight delighted the Queen very
much, but she soon had cause for fear ; upon the Earl's (who
had been from his early days accustomed to such sights)
addressing her thus : ' Do you observe that stag who is foremost of the herd? there is danger from that stag; for if
either fear or rage should force him from the ridge of that
hill, let every one look to himself, for none of us will be out
of the way of harm ; for the rest will follow this one, and
having thrown us under foot, they will open a passage to this
hill behind us.'   What happened a moment after confirmed
this opinion; for the Queen ordered one of the best dogs to
be let loose on one of the deer ; this the dog pursues ; the
leading stag was frighted, he flies by the same way he had
come there ; the rest rush after him, and break out where the
thickest body of the Highlanders was ; they had nothing for
it but to throw themselves flat on the heath, and allow the
deer to pass over them.   It was told the Queen that several
of the Highlanders had been wounded, and that two or three
had been killed outright ; and the whole body had got off,
had not the Highlanders, by their skill in hunting, fallen upon
a stratagem to cut off the rear from the main body.   It was
of those that had been separated, that the Queen's dogs and
those of the nobility made slaughter.   There were killed that
day three hundred and sixty deer, with five wolves, and some
roes."   Of this species of hunting, called the tenchel, Sir
Walter Scott has given us an admirable description in
Waverley.

But the mode of hunting the red deer, which is now most
in use, is that called deer stalking.   A party of deer stalkers
should be as small as possible, in order to secure success ;
because there will be the less chance of their being detected
by the animals they wish to approach ; and youth, activity,
patience, and a thorough carelessness of encountering cold,

wet, and hunger, are qualifications absolutely necessary to the individuals. Much will depend upon the accurate knowledge of locality possessed by the keeper who attends the party, as upon his information the motions of the whole must in a great measure be regulated. It is his business to direct his telescope to the sides of the hills, and carefully to examine them, so as to ascertain what deer may be grazing in the corries or hollows of its surface. A herd is discovered, a council of war is held, the various lines of approach are well considered, and finally, the plan of operations is determined on. Much caution is necessary; for, independent of the wonderful powers of seeing, hearing, and smelling, with which the red deer are gifted, they always take the precaution to establish a sentinel, generally a hind, in such a position as she may be enabled to give an early alarm; and the moment she gives the signal, the whole herd disappears with the rapidity of lightning. It is absolutely necessary to approach them up the wind, otherwise they would nose their coming enemy a great way off. Unbroken silence, also, must be preserved, for the smallest noise would alarm them; and it is equally essential that the party should be entirely concealed. The whole members of it, therefore, must take such a route as may afford most inequalities of surface, under cover of which they may advance unseen; and where no such inequalities exist, they must creep on their bellies through the long heather, like serpents. It very often happens that the deer stalker must make a circuit of some miles ere he can hope to approach the herd; and not unfrequently, when almost within shot of them, he meets with some piece of plain ground, over which he cannot hope to pass unnoticed, in which case he must wait sometimes for hours, till the deer happen to change their position, so as to permit him to advance with some hope of success. Again, it occurs, that as his heart is beating with eagerness, as if it would burst his breast, and when a few yards of nearer approach will place him within the reach of " the grete harte," suddenly, alarmed by some unknown cause, every horned head is thrown into the air, and in a moment every winged heel is bounding over the mountain's brow. Such are the blanks in the lottery of deer stalking; but it has its prizes also. Suppose the sportsmen, after hours of labour, and strange vicissitudes of hopes and fears, at last arrived within a reasonable distance. The rifles — for each has generally more than one — are carefully examined; and while each conceals himself as perfectly as he can, each takes

his independent aim, and all fire as much at once as possible.
Some of the deer fall dead ; others, perhaps, are wounded ;
but whilst these, as well as the other uninjured individuals
of the herd, start with amazement, and stand for a moment
doubtful in which way to fly, a second volley is given, and,
to secure the wounded, some large deer dogs are let loose
from the leash, who run upon the track of the blood, and
never leave it until the animal drops, or until they pull him
down, or until they bring him to bay in some stream, where
they keep him occupied till the sportsman arrives to despatch
him.   And now, very great care must be taken not to
approach him too rashly ; for if he should break his bay, and
run! at the hunter, it is more than probable that the life's
blood of both might be poured out together.   An instance is
mentioned of eleven deer out of a herd of fifteen having been
killed by one person, owing to the accidental circumstance
of an echo producing the sound of the shot on one side,
whilst the flash appeared on the other, so that the deer were
unable to determine which way to fly, till the four which
were left were driven to desperation, and in that way broke
recklessly away from the fancied circle in which they supposed
themselves to be enclosed. We have done our best to give some
idea of this most interesting sport ; but if the reader would
have it more perfectly, let him peruse Mr Fraser's novel, called
The Highland Smugglers, and he will there find a picture of it
which is as true to the life as it is fascinating in its details.

The fallow deer is much more limited by Nature in the
place of his abode, and in this island, particularly, has
been received only by importation.   He is supposed to
have but two varieties, — the spotted and the dark brown.
The former is of Indian extraction ;* the latter was
brought from Denmark by James I.   They are now,
indeed, much intermixed ; but in general the spotted
race are more the inhabitants of the park.   The brown,
which is the hardier species, occupy the forest.   The
latter is the more picturesque animal.   The uniform spot
of the variegated deer is not so pleasing as one simple
brown tint, melting away by degrees into a softer hue,
which produces a sort of natural light and shade, as
indeed all colours do which blend gently into each
other.

* See Pennant's *Zoology.*

Forest deer, though pasturing at large, seldom stray far from the walk where they are bred; and the keeper, who is studious that his deer may not travel into the limits of their neighbours, encourages their fondness for home, by feeding them, in winter, with holly, and other plants, which they love, and browsing them in summer with the spray of ash. When he distributes his dole, he commonly makes a hollowing noise to call his dispersed family together. In calm summer evenings, if you frequent any part of the forest near a lodge, you will hear this hollowing noise resounding through the woods; and if you are not apprized of it, you will be apt to wonder each evening at its periodical exactness.

Deer feed generally in the night, or at early dawn, and retire in the day to the shelter of the woods. Their morning retreat is thus picturesquely described:

———— The day pours in apace,
And opens all the lawny prospect wide;
The hazy woods, the mountain's misty top,
Swell on the sight; while o'er the forest glade
The wild deer trip, and, often turning, gaze
At early passengers. ————

Mr Pennant tells us,* that in Germany the peasants frequently watch their corn the whole night, to preserve it from the depredations of deer. He needed not, on this head, to have carried so far from home, — the borderers of New Forest are equally subject to the depredations of these animals; and are often obliged, when the neighbouring deer have gotten a haunt of their corn lands, to burn fires all night to deter them. I heard a farmer say, that it cost him five pounds one summer to guard eight acres of wheat. It is a remark among foresters, that all the deer kind are particularly offended by disagreeable smells. The farmer commonly, therefore, smears the ropes with tar which he sets up as fences, and throws fetid substances into his nightly fires, to disseminate the odour in the smoke.

We need not wonder if such depredations provoke

* See *British Zoology.*

acts of violence. Though protected by law, these atrocious marauders very often, and deservedly, suffer death for their offences.

A farmer, however, not long ago paid dear for taking the administration of justice into his own hands on an occasion of this kind. He had frequently lamented the depredations on his corn; and being at all events determined to retaliate, he narrowly observed his fields; and having found the track along which the nightly plunderer advanced, he took his station near it, as evening drew on, with a rifled barrel well loaded. After much listening, and many little alarms, he at last heard the bushes crackling and giving way in earnest. He now made himself sure of his prey; and, lying close, he levelled his piece, so as just to take the stag as he emerged from the thicket. The night was dark, but, however, allowed him sufficient light to take aim at so large a body. He fired with effect, and had the pleasure to see his enemy fall; but, on running to him, he was struck with finding he had killed one of the best horses of his own team.

We knew a case similar to this, but unfortunately much more tragical, which happened in the north of Scotland. There the peasantry are in many districts compelled to watch their crops night after night; and more lamentable mistakes than that of shooting a valuable horse have been sometimes committed. Whilst the people mount guard, to defend their crops from the deer, they do so, perhaps, not without a secret hope that the depredators may not fail to come. About two or three years ago, two different parties went out near Fochabers, unknown to each other, each armed with guns, to keep watch in this way. An individual of one party mistook a man of the other party for a deer, fired at him, and the result was, unfortunately, fatal.

Before quitting the subject of deer, we cannot help regretting that the scenery of New Forest should not be enlivened by that most beautiful of all our species of deer, — the roe buck. The *Book of Saint Albans* bids us call any number of roes assembled together, a Bevy,

———————— a Beeve of Rooes what place they ben.

And it farther tells us —

WHAT IS A BEVY OF ROOES, GRETE OR SMALLE.

And syxe is a Bevy of Rooes on a rowe ;
And ten is a myddyl bevy full well I it knowe.
A Grete Bevy is twelve whan they togyder be,
And so call them, sones, where that ye them se.
The more nombre than ywys, the gretter the bevy is.

OF THE ROO HUNTYNGE, BREKYNGE, AND DRESSYNGE.

Whan ye hunte at the Roo, then ye shall saye thore,
He crossyeth and tresonyth your hondes byfore ;
A grete Roo Bucke ye call hym not soo,
But a fayr Roo Buck and a fayr Doo.
Wyth the bowellys and wyth the blood,
Rewarde ye your houndes, my sones, soo good.

OF THE ROOBUCKE.

And yf ye of the Roobucke woll knowe the same ;
The fyrste yere he is a Kydde soukynge on his dame ;
The second yere he is a Gerle, and so ben suche all ;
The thyrde yere an Hemule loke ye hym call ;
Roobucke of the fyrste heed he is at the fourth yere ;
The fyfth yere a Roobucke hym call I you lere.
At Saynt Andrewe's daye his hornes he will caste ;
In moore or in mosse he hydyth them faste,
So that noo man maye theym soone fynde ;
Elles in certayn he dooth not his kynde.
At Saynt Jamy's daye where soo he goo :
Thenne shall the Roobucke gendre wyth the Roo ;
And soo boldly there as ye sojourne,
Then he is called a Roobucke gooynge in his tourne.

OF THE CRYENGE OF THYSE BESTYS.

An Harte belowyth, and a Bucke groynyth, I fynde ;
And eche Roobucke certain bellyth by kynde.
The noyse of thyse bestys thus ye shall call,
For pryde of theyr make they use it all ;
Saye, chylde, where ye goo, your dame taught you so.

The roebuck was once common in England and Wales ;
but it had for ages ceased to exist in these countries till the
year 1800, when the Earl of Dorchester turned four or five
brace of these animals into his woods near Milton Abbey, in
the county of Dorset. Some of these were procured at a
great expense from Brooke's menagerie in London, and some
were presented to him by the Earl of Egremont. These
roebucks had the full range of the woods of Mr Pleydell of
Whatcombe, as well as of those belonging to Lord Dorchester ;
and Mr Pleydell readily lent his aid to his Lordship in taking
every means to preserve them from injury.

A writer in the *Sporting Magazine* of 1817, tells us that the roebucks increased very rapidly, producing generally two, and sometimes three fawns at a birth, so that they not only stocked the woods into which they were originally turned, but they also migrated into many of those belonging to the neighbouring gentlemen, till they finally became pretty common in that part of the country.

The country around Milton is wild, with a large proportion of woodland; and, consequently, it is well adapted for deer of all descriptions. The valleys are rich and fertile, but the hills which surround them are high, very steep, and for the most part covered with copsewood or plantations.

From the great increase of those roe deer, Mr Pleydell thought that he might venture to hunt them now and then, without interfering with the preserves of Lady Caroline Damer, who was by this time the possessor of Milton Abbey; and accordingly, with her Ladyship's concurrence, and that of his other neighbours, he commenced the chase of them with his pack of harriers. The woods in the neighbourhood being in general large and full of hares, Mr Pleydell at first encountered some difficulty, particularly as his hounds had never been accustomed to hunt deer; but after having been out a few times, and having at last succeeded in killing a roebuck, the hounds became so well settled to the scent, that he experienced little or no inconvenience afterwards.

When trying for roebucks, the covers are drawn in the same manner as for a fox. When first roused, they run short, and keep but a small distance before the hounds; the cry of the pack is, consequently, extremely animated and cheerful, every hound enjoying the scent, which seems to be peculiarly grateful, and eargerly exerting itself in the pursuit. From this circumstance, a roe deer, in a little time after it has been roused, has often appeared to be so much exhausted, that a sportsman unused to this species of hunting, would naturally imagine that it was on the eve of being caught; but after having suffered itself to be more than once overtaken by the hounds, and even after having been seen in the very midst of them, it has been known to leave the wood, and the chase has been continued for more than two hours, before it has been ultimately taken. There is no risk of the roebuck being chopped, or mobbed, by hounds, as hares and foxes often are, for the strength and agility of roe deer always enable them to evade their pursuers; they are therefore never taken by surprise or accident, but always after they are completely tired. The oldest bucks are never seen to stand at bay; but they finally suffer themselves to be overpowered, without making any attempt to oppose or to resist their foes, a circumstance which arises from their heads being undefended by brow antlers, as those of the other kinds of deer are. This species of chase is very severe for the hounds, for the roebuck runs as much in the cover as he possibly can; and as the agreeable nature of the scent keeps the hounds going nearly the whole time at their full speed, they are generally very much fatigued when they return to kennel.

In Mr Somerville's beautiful poem of *The Chase*, we have the following short description of this species of hunting : —

> ———— Heaven-taught, the roebuck swift
> Loiters at ease before the driving pack,
> And mocks their vain pursuit; nor far he flies,
> But checks his ardour, till the steaming scent,
> That freshens on the blade, provokes their rage.
> Urged to their speed, the weak deluded foes
> Soon flag fatigued; strain'd to excess, each nerve,
> Each slacken'd sinew fails; they pant, they foam;
> Then o'er the lawn he bounds, o'er the high hills
> Stretches secure, and leaves the scatter'd crowd
> To puzzle in the distant vale below.

But however correct the first part of this description may be, and however beautiful the whole of it may appear, certain it is, that although the roebuck is stronger than the fallow deer, and capable of enduring a much longer chase, yet Mr Pleydell's hounds gave the lie to the latter part of Mr Somerville's statement; for the article in the *Sporting Magazine* to which we have alluded, informs us, that, at the time it was written, Mr Pleydell had been forty-four times out in pursuit of roebucks, that the hounds found a deer every day excepting two, and that they had killed twenty-six in all. When they failed, it was chiefly owing to changing, and rarely from any deficiency in the scent. In general, the roe deer do not go to any great distance from the woods which they inhabit; but some of Mr Pleydell's chases were to the extent of seven or eight miles in length, and many of them were more than three hours in duration. The roebuck possesses his full strength in winter, as well as in summer. They are not inclined so much to take soil as other deer; for although the course of the Stour, the principal river in Dorsetshire, is not far distant from the woods in which they are found, two deer only have made their way to that river, and they were both killed soon after they had reached it.

The roe deer are extremely nimble and active, and at times take immense leaps. We remember one on the banks of the Findhorn, which cleared a broad road and a paling at one bound. But when running before the hounds, and even when in view, they do not seem to exert themselves, nor do they then appear to possess any great degree of swiftness; certainly not sufficient to enable them to escape from greyhounds in an open country.

The roebuck was once much more common in Scotland than it is at present; but it is still very plentiful in some places; and we can say from our own knowledge, that it has very much increased of late years, and that the increase of plantations in the south of Scotland has been the means of spreading it much farther in that direction than we formerly remember it to have been found. Roe deer are now to be met with in Fifeshire, immediately opposite to Edinburgh. And on a late occasion, we saw a roebuck running across the fields near Bathgate, in Linlithgowshire. They would soon increase were it not that their numbers are kept down from the idea that they devour young trees. This they no doubt do in a small degree, but by no means to any great extent; indeed, the great mischief they occasion is at the time the skin and vascular system of the horns are drying up and dropping off, when they rub them against the trees, in order to aid the progress of Nature; and in this way indeed they destroy the bark. The tree they always prefer at this time if they can find one, is a young elm; and their selection is probably owing to the mucilaginous juice of that tree cooling and soothing that itching which then gives them so much uneasiness. We have seen many young trees disfigured by these operations of the roebuck, but we have very rarely seen them altogether destroyed. The roebuck is much more common in America than in Europe, and its size is also much greater in the New World than in the Old. In Louisiana the inhabitants live very much upon its venison.

" The form of the roebuck," says Bewick, " is elegant, and its motions light and easy. It bounds seemingly without effort, and runs with great swiftness. When hunted, it endeavours to elude its pursuers by the most subtle artifices; it repeatedly returns upon its former steps, till, by various windings, it has entirely confounded the scent. The cunning animal then, by a sudden spring, bounds to one side; and, lying close down upon its belly, permits the hounds to pass by without offering to stir." We cannot speak as to the truth of this last manœuvre of the roebuck, but we can corroborate all that is said about its doubling when chased. And we can also say, that, when wounded, they have sometimes escaped our most active search, even where the covert was so small as to lead us to believe that it was impossible they could have been passed over by the dogs.

They do not herd in great numbers, like other deer; but they live in separate families, which, as the Book of Saint Alban's has already told us, are properly called bevies. We have seen as many as thirteen individuals in one bevy; but this is extremely rare, though five, or even seven, are not uncommon. For a great part of the year they are to be found in pairs, the buck and doe together. The sexes unite about the beginning of August; but their true rutting season continues fifteen days, from the latter end of October to the beginning of November, during all which time the fawns are driven away from them. This last union only is productive. The doe goes with young five months and an half, and brings forth about the end of April or beginning of May. She produces two fawns at a time, and sometimes, though very rarely, three. At this time she separates from the buck, and conceals herself and progeny in some thicket in a retired part of the forest. In ten or twelve days the fawns are able to follow the doe; but even then, whenever danger occurs, she hides her young in some thicket, and leads away strangers or dogs, by offering herself to their attention. We have frequently found these beautiful little creatures, when almost new dropped; though we have never been successful in rearing any of them. But it is by no means impracticable to bring them up; and as to their being incapable of attachment or familiarity with their keeper, as asserted by Bewick and others, we can vouch for the contrary being most particularly the fact, for we have frequently known them as pets. One we remember to have seen so tame, that it followed the young ladies to whom it belonged in all their walks, came into the drawing-room with them, and, notwithstanding the appearance there of a crowded company of strangers, it went about from one person to another, tamer than any dog, and eat sugar or cake out of the hands of any one who chose to present it with such delicacies. It was extremely playful, and seemed to have a curiosity to taste every thing that came in its way,—a circumstance which at last unfortunately occasioned its death, which occurred in consequence of its having eaten a lady's glove ; and the same young ladies had one, on a former occasion, equally tame, which died from having eaten a piece of cork. But as pets in general are liable to accidents, so of all others such a pet as this is doubly so. We remember a beautiful young roe belonging to another lady, which was equally tame, and which died in consequence of having been pursued by greyhounds.

The horns of the roebuck begin to sprout when they are about eight or nine months old. They shed their horns in the latter end of autumn, and renew them in the winter ; whereas the horns of the stag fall off in the spring, and are renewed in summer. A roebuck lives about twelve or fifteen years.

The roebuck is usually hunted by slough hounds, which are turned into that part of the wood where the game is supposed to lie; and they are accompanied by the keepers, who advance through the covert in line, so as to drive the roebuck towards some narrow pass at the farthest extremity of it, where the sportsmen are planted in ambush with their guns. We have had much experience in this sport ; and we always found that if by any accident we were baffled in getting a shot, our hounds, when high mettled, generally pressed so hard upon the roebuck, and so close to the scent, that they forced him to quit his country ; and, as they continued to follow him for miles, our sport was at an end for the day. It is remarkable that the scent of the roebuck is so very fascinating, that we have heard an old huntsman say he could break his hounds off running any thing but that of roe deer, and that the devil himself could not stop hounds if they got upon the slot of a roebuck. We must confess, however, that the note of the dogs echoing through the forest, mingled with the shouts of the keepers, and the occasional *mot* of a bugle-horn, with a dropping shot now and then, exciting one's liveliest curiosity, were all circumstances extremely fascinating. But then it was often cold work standing at the passes, during the depth of winter, when the roe deer are most in season ; and accordingly we fell upon a mode of hunting the animals, which we very much preferred. This was, by having three or four brace of particularly large, well bred, true nosed cocking spaniels, which we taught to range around us as we walked through the forest, keeping a circuit, the circumference of which was never less than two hundred yards from us. In this way, when a roebuck was roused, the chances were rather more than equal that he was driven in our direction; and if this did not happen, the result was, that although the whole of our little pack went off yelping, hot upon the scent, yet they came back to us again, after running him for perhaps a quarter of an hour or twenty minutes, during which time, by the way, it very frequently occurred that he was again brought round in our direction; but, at all events, we thus had our dogs ready, in a very short time, to renew the sport somewhere else. We found these little animals very pertinacious in the pursuit, where the deer was wounded. This was by far the liveliest, as well as most successful mode of roebuck hunting; and instead of standing for a long time freezing behind a tree or bush, we had always the advantage of being continually in exercise. Roe deer venison is said, by those who are ignorant of it, to be very indifferent food. All admit that it makes very delicious high flavoured soup, and that the pasty is not to be despised; but we who have killed roebucks in season—that is, when they have fat upon the kidneys—will aver that, when the haunch in such a state is properly kept, properly treated, and properly cooked, nothing can be more delicate.

The sheep does not frequent the forest in any abundance. Here and there you find a little flock on a dry gravelly hill; but, in general, the forest abounds with swamps and marshy bottoms, highly pernicious to the sheep,—the only animal perhaps, except one, which pursues with the greatest avidity what is most destructive to it. It is the less, however, to be lamented that the lawns of the forest are not decorated with these animals, as they are certainly less adapted to a forest scene than deer, though in themselves, perhaps, more picturesque. The forest is wild, and they are domestic.

With hares and rabbits the forest abounds. The latter are the under keeper's perquisite, and of course well looked after. There are many dry, sandy knolls where colonies of these inmates are settled, which are not among the least amusing of the minute inhabitants of the forest.

In the same class we rank the squirrel. He is not of consequence to be numbered among the picturesque ornaments of a scene; but his form and manners, his activity and feats of dexterity, are very amusing. On extraordinary occasions, when he is agitated by love or

anger, his muscles acquire tenfold elasticity. He descends
a tree in a rapid spiral as quick as thought—darts up
another in an opposite direction—flings himself from
tree to tree with amazing exactness—and pursues his
mate or his rival among the mazy branches of an oak
with a velocity that eludes the sight.

Pheasants, also, greatly abound in many parts of the
forest. In the manors of Beaulieu, Fawley, and other
places, where they are protected, they multiply beyond
belief. They are seen often in flocks feeding like
poultry in the fields, and adorning the woods and copses
with their elegant shape and glossy plumage.

The partridge is not so fond of the wild scenes of the
forest as the pheasant. She is more the bird of cultivation. Where the plough flourishes she thrives, and
seldom chooses to inhabit a country in a state of Nature.
The pheasant has no objection to a field of corn; but he
can procure his living without it. He can make a hearty
meal of the wild berries of the woods, or content himself
with a bellyfull of acorns. To him, therefore, corn is a
luxury—to the partridge it is a necessary. She is generally found gleaning the stubble, or basking under a
hedge, and gets into many a difficulty which she might
have avoided by feeding more at large. Sometimes,
indeed, she is found in the forest, but it is chiefly when
she is hunted by men and dogs from her favourite
haunts.

The blackcock, on the other hand, is more a forester
than even the pheasant. He has no connection with
man. He scorns the enclosure, and all the dainties of
the stubble. The wild forest is his only delight, and
there his pleasures lie more in its open than in its woody
scenes. This bird was formerly found in great abundance in New Forest; but he is now much scarcer,
though he has the honour, which no other bird can boast,
of being protected as royal game. To this day, when
the chief justice in eyre grants his warrants to kill game
in the forest, he always excepts the blackcock, together
with red and fallow deer.

The plaintive ring dove, also, is a great admirer of
the woody scenes of the forest. Many suppose her a

solitary bird; at least that she flies only with her mate, confounding her habits, perhaps, with those of the turtle dove, which, I believe, is solitary. But the ring dove is certainly gregarious. I have often seen in the forest large flocks of this species together in the winter months; so well the poet knew their nature, by contrasting them with the woodcock,—

> While doves in flocks the leafless trees o'ershade,
> The lonely woodcock haunts the watery glade.

It is quite true that the ring dove (*Columba palumbus*) is gregarious, towards autumn and during winter; but in spring these birds separate into pairs, for the purpose of breeding; and as they are supposed to breed at least twice a year, they continue in pairs, until stormy weather begins to drive them again into large societies.

The woodcock, indeed, is sometimes seen in the forest; but the rough lawns and heaths he finds there do not entirely suit his appetite. He is curious in the choice of his haunts. He must have some sweet woody glen, watered by little oozing mossy rills, into which he may easily thrust his beak; and these he cannot everywhere meet with in the forest.

It is a remarkable fact, that when woodcocks first arrive from their long flight, they are more commonly to be found among the heather in the moors than anywhere else.

The snipe, less delicate in her haunts, is the frequent inhabitant of the wildest scenes. Any swamp or marshy spot will please her; and of these she finds abundance in various parts of the forest.

Plover of different kinds are common, also, in its heathy parts. I have sometimes seen large flocks of the gray species, and have stood admiring them as they encircled the air. In their regular mode of flight they in some degree resemble water fowl; but they are not so determined in their course, wheeling about and forming various evolutions, which are very amusing. Sometimes they appear all scattered, and seem in confusion, till, closing together as if by the word of command, they get again into form.

With regard to all the songsters of the grove, the woody scenes of the forest are vocal with them. The thrush, the blackbird, the linnet, and the nightingale, abound on every spray. The nightingale, above all, delights in the wild scenes of the forest. The blackbird and the thrush are often seen tripping over the embellished lawn, or flirting from the neat trimmed holly hedge. But the nightingale rarely frequents these cultured spots. To her they afford little pleasure. Her commonest haunts are those of Nature,— the brake, the copse, the rough hedge, or the forest, where she sings her melodious strains to woods and solitude, and often

——— wastes her sweetness on the desert air ;

only that her voice, so varied, clear, and full, is heard far and wide when the evening is still—almost at hand, though in the distant wood.

Among the birds of harmony there are two, which I shall find it difficult, perhaps, to establish in that class, — the jay and the woodpecker. Their screams, however discordant in themselves, or when out of place, accord admirably with the forest, and produce that kind of local harmony which one of our old poets* ascribes to the sound of a drum : it may be dissonant in one place, though musical in another :

> What sound is that, whose concord makes a jar ?
> 'Tis noise in peace, though harmony in war.
> The drum, whose doubtful music doth delight
> The willing ear, and the unwilling fright.

" We take music, however, here (according to a very good definition of it) in the large and proper sense of the word, as the art of variously affecting the mind by the power of sounds."†

But besides the harmony arising from the agreement of these wild notes with the scenes of the forest, there is another source of it in the sympathetic feelings of the mind. These wild notes excite ideas of those pleasing forest scenes where we have commonly heard them. But I shall give my meaning in better words than my own.

* D'Avenant.   † Gregory's *Comparative View.*

There is in souls a sympathy with sounds;
And, as the mind is pitch'd, the ear is pleased
With melting airs or martial, brisk or grave.
Some chord, in unison with what we hear,
Is touch'd within us, and the heart replies.
　How soft the music of those village bells,
Falling at intervals upon the ear
In cadence sweet! now dying all away,
Now pealing loud again, and louder still,
Clear and sonorous as the gale comes on!
With easy force it opens all the cells
Where memory slept.　Wherever I have heard
A kindred melody, the scene recurs,
And with it all its pleasures. *

We entreat the reader's attention to the unconscious admission which Mr Gilpin here makes of the grand principle of Mr Alison's theory, which equally applies to sounds as to the objects of vision; and the illustration which he has selected in the quotation, is no less striking.

But however discordant the notes of these birds may be to the fastidious ear, their rich, yet harmonious plumage, must at least recommend them as highly ornamental to every scene which they frequent.　The woodpecker, particularly, is arrayed in the richest plumage of any bird we have, except the kingfisher; yet all his splendid tints are perfectly harmonious.　The jay, also, is beautifully tinted on his back and breast with a light purplish hue, intermixed with gray; and his wing is perhaps the most admirable piece of workmanship in the whole feathered creation.

On the same ground with the jay and the woodpecker, I should not scruple also to rank the kite, if his manners did not disturb the harmony of the woods as much as his voice supports it.　Independent of his manners, he is one of the most harmonious appendages of the forest, where Mr Pennant makes him indigenous.†　He is too small for picturesque use, but highly ornamental to the natural scene.　His motions are easy and beautiful in a great degree.　He does not flap his pinions like the rook or the magpie, and labour through the air : he sails along with steady wing, as if he were lord of the element on which he rode.　But what harmonize chiefly with the

* Cowper.　　　　† *British Zoology.*
3

forest are his wild screams, which strike notes in peculiar unison with those scenes over which he sails :

————— Kites, that swim sublime
In still repeated circles, screaming loud,
Have charms for me. —————
Sounds, inharmonious in themselves and harsh,
Yet, heard in scenes where peace for ever reigns,
Please highly for their sake. —————

It is remarkable that we seldom see more than two of this species together,— the male and the female.   They seem to divide the forest into provinces ; each bird hath his own, and, with more than princely caution, avoids his neighbours.   It is his great employment to circle through the air, as the poet describes him above, in various evolutions over his own woody dominions, where, with keen eye and keener talons, he still preserves the spirit of the old forest law.

The kite (*Falco milous* of Linnæus,) is a remarkably cunning bird.   A kite which happened to be caught by some accident, was brought to us alive in a basket.   It soon began to manifest symptoms of dying, and as we looked at it in the open basket in the house, its form gradually stiffened, it turned over upon its back, thrust out its legs, and closed its eyelids, as if in the last agony of death.   Compassion for the creature induced us to take it out of doors, and we set down the basket on the airy brink of a bank that sloped suddenly downwards.   To our great astonishment our bird came suddenly alive again, and in one instant its wings were spread, and it soared away down over the grassy lawn, and by degrees sweeping round and round in successive circles, it towered into the upper regions of the sky.   The whole of its sickness was manifestly nothing more than a feint.

We conceive that the *Falco butea*, the common buzzard, also must be a bird of the New Forest, though we do not know that it is.   He is often confounded with the kite, or glead ; but the kite is a longer and slenderer bird, and the most perfectly distinguishing mark is his forked tail, which the buzzard has not.   The buzzard is a very beautiful bird.   We had one in so tame a state, that although he lived in the trees in the neighbourhood of the house, he depended altogether upon us for food.   The moment we called to him he appeared, and when we held up a piece of meat, he would swoop down from the top of the tallest tree, and carry it off; and one day that we held it on the point of a fork extended horizontally, he carried off fork and all in his talons. There was a little girl with red hair, who used to come bareheaded every morning, to carry breakfast to her father, who was one of the labourers about the place. Whether it was that the girl's red hair had some resemblance to the meat he was in the habit of being fed with, we know not, but certain it is, that the buzzard swooped down two or three times at her head, to the great terror of the poor little girl, who made the best of her way, like a dove to the covert; and she took care never to come abroad afterwards without the protection of her bonnet.

Very often the eagle himself is found in the forest. Mountainous and rocky countries are his delight. On the ledge of some steep prominent rock he builds his eyry, and rears his royal progeny. But when food becomes scarce in those desolate regions, as it sometimes does, he finds it convenient to make an excursion into the forest. Here he hunts the leveret and the fawn, and screens his atrocious deeds in the closest woods. Wherever he is seen, the watchful forester endeavours to keep him in sight till he bring him to the ground. And yet I have heard of a pair of eagles, which took possession of a part of the forest called King's Wood, where they eluded all the arts of the keeper, and continued their annual depredations for several years. Some time ago an eagle was killed, after three discharges, near Ashy Lodge, and was extended, like the imperial arms, in the court-room of the King's House at Lyndhurst.

The eagle is by no means fond of entangling himself amid the mazes of the forest. His weight, and his length of wings, render it rather a difficult matter for him to rise from the level ground, and still more so when he is becalmed by surrounding trees. The bird seems to be aware of all this, for it must be very acute hunger, and something very tempting indeed in the way of repast, that will induce him to trust himself amidst foliage. Several deer were found by the keepers of the New Forest, dead, and with their eyes torn out. After a careful watch, a deer was discovered in great agony, struggling with an eagle, which had seized him by the head and shoulders. The keeper fired, and killed the bird, which was beautifully preserved, and it afterwards formed one of the objects in Bullock's London Museum.

Of all the feathered inhabitants of the forest, I should have thought its scenes, in all respects, the best adapted to the rook. Here he might build his habitation, and rear his young, far from the prying eyes of men. Here, also, he might indulge his social temper without limits, and enlarge his aërial town from wood to wood. But he has no such ideas. I cannot learn that he ever thought of forming a settlement in the forest, which is the more extraordinary, as he is, in fact, a lover of its scenes, and rejoices in 'them at all times but in the breeding season, when one should imagine he stood most in need of their shelter. At that time he seems sedulously to court the faithless habitations of men; through what propensity or instinct of Nature, the naturalist is wholly at a loss to determine. After his family is reared, and he has carried off in safety such of his progeny as have escaped the arts of men and boys, he · retires every evening, at a late hour during the autumn and winter months, to the closest covers of the forest, having spent the day in the open fields and enclosures in quest of food. His late retreat to the forest is characteristic of the near approach of night: .

> —— Night thickens, and the crow
> Makes wing to the rooky wood. ——

And again,

> Retiring from the downs, where all day long
> They pick their scanty fare, a blackening train
> Of loitering rooks, thick urge their weary flight,
> And seek the shelter of the grove. ——

But in his economy there is something singular. Though the forest is his winter habitation, (if I may call that his habitation, which, like other vagrants, he uses only as a place to sleep in,) he generally every day visits his nursery, keeping up the idea of a family, which he begins to make provision for in earnest very early in the spring.

Among all the sounds of animal nature, few are more pleasing than the cawing of rooks. The rook has but two or three notes; and when he attempts a solo, we cannot praise his song. But when he performs in concert, which is his chief delight, these two or three notes, though rough in themselves, being mixed and inter-mixed with the notes of a multitude, have all their sharp edges worn off, and become very harmonious, especially when softened in the air, where the band chiefly exhibits. You have this music in perfection when the whole colony is roused by the discharge of a gun. The cawing of rooks, however, is a sound not so congenial to the forest as it is to the grove.

Early association has made the rook very dear to us. We delight in his choral music. In no part of his vast creation is the wisdom of Almighty God more clearly manifested, than in the instinctive economy and management exhibited by rooks. We have watched them in the morning, when leaving the wood where they have had their dormitory. We have seen them rise into the air before the sun, like a vast cloud, where the whole army would wheel round and round with the most wonderful evolutions. Then would they break off into four grand *corps d'armée*, four grand divisions, which would each take its course to an opposite point of the compass. After flying a mile or two, each in its own direction, the four bodies might severally be observed to take post for a while in some large grass field, whence again rising after a time, and forming evolutions like those which were at first performed by the main body, they would subdivide themselves into brigades, which would each take its own separate way over the country. On watching any one of these brigades, it could be traced to some spot where it would again subdivide itself into regiments, if we may so call them, and so would these birds go on breaking themselves into smaller divisions, until they were scattered all over the face of a country, in parties of not more than two or three together. Were the whole nation of rooks to set forth in one body, and to alight on any one field of grain, they would devour the whole of it in a few hours. But scattered as they thus providentially are, the damage they do to each individual is so small, that it is hardly worth notice. Towards evening, we have seen these small parties collecting, and every rendezvous recognized in the morning, is regularly revisited at night, and the com-panies, the regiments, the brigades, the *corps d'armées*, and finally, the great national army itself, are all made up in

succession, in the same places, and in the same manner exactly
as they were subdivided in the morning; and after a variety of
beautiful aërial evolutions, and one harmonious chorus of
thanks to that beneficent Being who has liberally provided for
their wants, they all at once settle down on the tall trees of
the wood, with the shades of night, there to enjoy their repose
till morning.

We are surprised that Mr Gilpin has not mentioned the
raven (*Cervus corax*) among the inhabitants of the forest, for
although we have no personal knowledge of its existence
there, yet it is impossible to suppose that the bird does not
build about the cliffs of the Isle of Wight, and if so, it is
certain to be a prowler in the forest. From our own experience, we are not disposed to admit that it is ever found to
build in trees, we mean in trees rising from the level ground
of a forest, let their altitude be what it may. Rocks, which
are almost, if not altogether inaccessible, and withered, old,
picturesque trees, which shoot out their bare and gnarled
limbs from the face of some precipice, are the only positions
which we have ever observed the raven choose for the purpose
of nidification. But he has no objection to haunt the forest
for prey, and he is so strong on the wing that he will come
a long way to take his prey, or to feed on the carrion which
accident may have provided, which he scents at an immense
distance. The raven is an amazingly sagacious bird. His
thefts are very curious. We remember a tame raven, which
belonged to a stand of chairmen at the head of North Hanover
Street, in Edinburgh, some thirty years ago : he was a most
amusing bird, and his adroitness in catching anything was
so great, that we found it quite impossible to throw a piece
of sugarcandy at him, even though we used all our force in
doing so, without his catching it in his beak before it came
to the ground. But he began to indulge in long flights, and
like many rustics corrupted by a city life, he became very
impudent and full of tricks. Often have we seen him flying
along George Street, and peeping into all the open windows ;
and one day, to the great surprise of the passengers in the
street, he was observed soaring away with a pair of handsome
black silk breeches streaming from his beak, whilst a gentleman, half dressed, was seen stretching himself from a garret
window, and looking most anxiously after his stolen property.
The history of this transaction was, that the gentleman was
dressing to go out to dinner, and whilst his head was in the
basin during the operation of washing his face, the raven,

who had been eyeing him from the roof, very knowingly took his opportunity of flying through the open window, and carrying off the silk breeches from the back of the chair over which they were hanging. A hue and cry was raised after the thief—the populace shouted—the bird became alarmed, and dropped his silken prize, which came slowly to the ground with many a strange gyration; and the garment was recovered in time for the mortified beau to be encased in it, and to hurry to the feast to which he had been bidden.

Among the winged inhabitants of the forest we should not forget the honey bee, which everywhere covers the surface of it. These wide demesnes are in many parts spread with heath, which is one of the favourite vegetables of this industrious insect. Where this abounds, the cottager commonly carries out his hives in winter, hiding them as he can from observation, and fencing them from the annoyance of cattle. There he leaves them till swarming time, when they necessarily become the objects of his care; and if he is fortunate, his profits are considerable. I knew a cottager who made above fifteen guineas in one year of his forest honey, though he sold it only at threepence a pound. Sometimes the hive is discovered and stolen, though in general it is a garrison which can defend itself pretty well; however, as the prudent peasant never places all his wealth in one place, he generally, at worst, secures enough to repay his trouble. Hampshire honey is in good esteem, but it is rather the honey produced in the northern parts of the county than what is commonly called forest honey.

We are informed that a man at Logan House, in the middle of the Pentland Hills, near Edinburgh, has sometimes made five or six pounds sterling, not of his honey, but by merely taking in bee-hives to board for the season of the heather bloom, at the rate of one shilling per hive.

Another species of fly should not be passed over, which is one of the greatest nuisances of the forest. In form it is not unlike the common black fly, and about its size, but its colour is different. It is a bright-coated, brown insect, well cased, strong, and very retentive of life.*

* Vivit, cursitat, immo coit, dempto licet capite.

Linnæus de *Hippobosca.*

It has a sidelong, crawling motion like a crab. The horse is its favourite quarry, though it attacks the cow and other animals. You may sometimes see hundreds of these insects nestling under the tail and belly of such horses as are patient of them, as the New Forest horse commonly is by long sufferance. But to such horses as are unaccustomed to these teasing insects, they are a grievous torment, though it is doubtful whether they are blood suckers, or subsist only on such juices as exude through the skin. In this latter case they offend the horse only by tickling him, for which operation their legs are well adapted, appearing, in a microscope, armed with sharp talons like pothooks.

This is the (*Hippobosca equina*) of Linnæus. It is one of the most tormenting of insects, though the torment it inflicts is entirely occasioned by the insufferable titillation it creates by the insertion of its proboscis into the pores for the purpose of suction, and to the wriggling gait which it has over the skin with its many-clawed feet. It chiefly inhabits the bodies of birds — such as swallows and partridges. We have found it on the grouse, and we have sometimes been subjected to the annoyance produced by its traversing the surface of the skin, by its having found means to make its way from the dead grouse in our game bag, and to insinuate itself within the defences of our clothes; and no one who has not had experience of the misery it creates when crawling with its wriggling and sideling motion over the back, can form any idea of it. And then it claps so close with its flat body and bowed legs, that one may undress and dress again a dozen times before it can be detected; and when detected, it is very difficult to kill it, for it lies quite flat, and appears to have no substance, and when any attempt is made to crush it, the moment the pressure is removed, away it runs wriggling as if nothing had happened to it. It is commonly known by the name of the New Forest Fly, and although it is to be found elsewhere, and especially in the Highland moors, it is nowhere, that we know of, so common as in the New Forest. The New Forest horse, or any horse which has been for some years naturalized to the New Forest, appears to be little annoyed by it; but it is a very dangerous thing to go there with riding or machine horses which have never experienced this plague, for we have seen such animals driven actually frantic, and rendered quite unmanageable by the assaults of myriads of these vexatious creatures. They are, as Mr Gilpin says, not unlike the common house fly; but this likeness is only at a first and careless view, for the differences which they exhibit, even on a brief inspection, are sufficiently evident; and these are, the very particular bright glaze which appears over the whole of the insect, the greater spread of the wings, the singular bowed legs, the very flat scale looking form, and the very strange wriggling motion, like that of some house-fly grievously wounded. It can move in all directions, but with most rapidity sideways, for it does not seem to run easily straight forward. It is thus most wonderfully adapted by Nature for making its way among the feathers of birds, which grow in transverse rings around the animal. These characters will enable any one at once to detect the New Forest fly.

It is not impossible that this creature may serve a beneficial purpose in the great scale of God's creation, by continually removing from the pores that perspiration which would otherwise be lodged about the feathers; and it may perhaps act, at the same time, as a kind of stimulant to the skin. Although there are seldom more than two or three on a small bird, yet, from their size, they must remove a great deal of the matter excreted by the skin, as they appear seldom to leave the bird they live upon, and they even remain on it after it is dead.

Such are the inmates of the internal parts of the forest. Along its shores, bordering on the Isle of Wight, it is furnished with a new set of inhabitants,—those various tribes of sea fowl which frequent the brackish waters of an estuary.

Among the most common, as well as the most beautiful, is the gull. Water-fowl, in a particular manner, discover in their flight some determined aim. They eagerly coast the river, or return to the sea, bent on some purpose of which they never lose sight. But the evolutions of the gull appear capricious and undirected, both when she flies alone, and, as she often does, in large companies. The more, however, her character suffers as a loiterer, the more it is raised in picturesque value by her continuing longer before the eye, and displaying, in her elegant sweeps along the air, her sharp-pointed wings and bright silvery hue. She is beautiful, also,

not only on the wing, but when she floats in numerous
assemblies on the water, or when she rests on the shore,
dotting either one or the other with white spots, which,
minute as they are, are very picturesque, and may
properly be introduced in landscape, giving life and
spirit to a view.   Sea painters particularly make great
use of this bird, and often with good effect.   The
younger Vandervelt was fond of introducing it; he
knew the value of a single bright touch in heightening
his storms.

As the wheeling motion of the gull is beautiful, so
also is the figured flight of the goose, the duck, and the
widgeon, all of which are highly ornamental to coast
views, bays, and estuaries.   We often see innumerable
bodies of these and other sea-fowl congregated in close
array, and filling the air with their resounding cries.*
They are not hyperbolically described as

> ——————— Living clouds,
> Infinite wings, till all the plume-dark air,
> And rude resounding shore, are one wild cry.

In a picturesque light, these living clouds are of little
value ; unless, indeed, some wild, forlorn, and rocky
coast is presented, where these sea-fowls commonly
breed, and where in great bodies they are characteristic.

Among the solitary birds which frequent the estuaries
of rivers, the heron and the cormorant are of too much
consequence to be omitted.

The form in which the heron contracts his long neck
in flying, his outstretched legs, the solemn flapping of
his wings, his easy deliberation in taking the ground,
the bluish tint of his plumes, softening into white, and
his patient and attentive posture as he stands fishing on
the shore, are all circumstances, as far as they go,
picturesque.   His hoarse note, too, at pausing intervals
as he passes through the air, though harsh and discordant
when unaided by its proper accompaniments, like other
notes of the same kind when the scenes of Nature act
in concert with it, hath its full energy and effect.   I call

---

* See ante, page 212.

the heron a solitary bird, because his common habits and manner of seeking his food are solitary; we seldom see more than two in company, though, like the rook, he breeds in large societies.

Nothing can be more picturesque or interesting than a heronry. We know one on the banks of the river Findhorn, which has called forth the admiration of all who have had the good fortune to see it, especially when in full occupation, during the breeding season. The rocks on the river at the place where the herons have established themselves, are of the flœtz formation. On the left bank the under strata rise abruptly over the bed of the stream, whilst the upper strata recede from it, so as to form a broad piece of plain. On the rock immediately over the river some very venerable old oaks, of great height, rise from among the smaller wood, which everywhere clusters along the brink. On the elevated heads of these trees the greater number of the herons have established their nests, whilst the rocks, which rise in perpendicular cliffs to an immense height on the opposite side of the river, including the whole of the existing strata, have, here and there, a nest adhering to some prominent shelf. So far as we can learn, there is reason to believe that this heronry has existed upon these trees, and upon their predecessors, and upon the rocks in their neighbourhood, for ages. The neighbouring proprietors are zealous for its preservation, and no one is allowed to injure or to alarm the birds whilst occupied in rearing their young. The only enemies they have are the mischievous jack-daws, who build in the crevices of the cliffs. We have often been amused, for hours together, in watching their predatory warfare from the brow of the cliff, whence the spectator can see down into the nests on the top of the trees, on the opposite side of the river. These nimble little birds no sooner perceive that a heron has quitted her nest than they dart into it, and carry off an egg; and nothing can be more ludicrous than the attempts made by the unwieldy herons to pursue their enemies, and to recover the eggs, or to punish the depredators. The heron was formerly royal game; and it is possible that those birds have frequented this place since the time that Thomas Randolph, Earl of Moray, Regent of Scotland, held his court within the ancient hall of Tarnawa.

Heysham gives us a curious anecdote of herons, the circumstances of which he says occurred at Dallam Tower, in Westmoreland, the seat of Daniel Wilson, Esq.

" There were two groves adjoining to the park, one of which, for many years, had been resorted to by a number of herons, which there built and bred ; the other was one of the largest rookeries in the country. The two tribes lived together for a long time without any disputes. At length the trees occupied by the herons, consisting of some very old oaks, were cut down, in the spring of 1775, and the young brood perished by the fall of the timber. The parent birds immediately set about preparing new habitations, in order to breed again ; but as the trees in the neighbourhood of their old nests were only of a late growth, and not sufficiently high to secure them from the depredations of boys, they determined to effect a settlement in the rookery. The rooks made an obstinate resistance ; but, after a very violent contest, in the course of which many of the rooks and some of their antagonists lost their lives, the herons at last succeeded in their attempt, built their nests, and brought out their young. The next season the same contests took place, which terminated, like the former, by the victory of the herons. Since that time peace seems to have been agreed upon between them. The rooks have relinquished possession of that part of the grove which the herons occupy ; the herons confine themselves to those trees they first seized upon ; and the two families live together in as much harmony as they did before the quarrel."

Nor is the cormorant without his beauty. His eager, steady, determined flight—his plunging into the waters—his wild look, as if conscious of guilt—his bustle on being alarmed—shaking the moisture from his feathers, and dashing about till he get fairly disengaged,—are all amusing circumstances in his history. But he is a merciless villain, supposed by naturalists to be furnished with a greater variety of predatory arts than any bird that inhabits the waters. When the tide retires, he wings his ardent flight, with strong pinions and outstretched neck, along the shores of the deserted river, with all the channels and currents of which he is better acquainted than the mariner with his chart. Here he commits infinite spoil. Or, if he find his prey less plentiful in the shallows, he is at no loss in deeper water. He dives to the bottom, and visits the eel in her retirement, of all others his favourite morsel.* In vain the

* See other parts of his history, ante, p. 212.

fowler eyes him from the bank, and takes his stand behind the bush. The cormorant, quicker sighted, knows his danger, and parries it with a glance of his eye. If he choose not to trust his pinions, in a moment he is under water—rises again in some distant part—instantly sinks a second time, and eludes the possibility of taking aim. Even if a random shot should touch him, unless it carry a weight of metal, his sides are so well cased, and his muscular frame so robust, that he escapes mischief. If the weather suit, he fishes also dexterously at sea. Or perhaps he only varies his food between sea fish and river fish, as his palate prompts. When he has filled his maw, he retires to the ledge of some projecting rock, where he listens to the surges below in dozing contemplation, till hunger again awaken his powers of rapine.

Bewick tells us that the *Pelicanus carbo*, or Great Black Cormorant, is gregarious during the breeding season. These birds assemble in flocks on the summits and inaccessible parts of the rocks which overhang, or are surrounded by, the sea, upon which the female makes her nest of the withered sea-tang, weeds, sticks, and grasses, which are cast ashore by the waves. She lays four or more greenish-white eggs, of the size of those of a goose, but of a longer shape. But they are too fetid to be eaten even by the Greenlanders. They are said to remain throughout the year in Greenland. The lower bill of this creature is covered, towards its lower extremity, with a naked yellowish skin, extended under the chin and throat, where it hangs loose, and forms a kind of pouch, which, together with the springing blades on each side, forming its rim, is capable of distension to a great width, and enables the bird to swallow prey apparently too large to be admitted into its throat. The natives of Greenland make use of this pouch as a bladder to float their fishing darts after they are thrown. Their skins, which are tough, are used for garments, and their flesh is eaten; and, strange as it may seem, we have been informed by some gentlemen, of good taste too, that cormorant soup very much resembles hare soup.

These birds are very destructive both in lakes and in the sea. They dive from an immense height, never fail in catching the prey they have aimed at, or in returning to the surface with it held across their beak. They then, with wonderful adroitness, throw it up into the air, and opening their enormous maw,

they invariably swallow it head foremost. Their common
station on shore is on some projecting rock, where they preserve an erect posture by propping themselves up on the stiff
feathers of the tail. And after a full meal, they remain dozing
in a semi-stupified state, so that they may be even sometimes
taken by throwing nets over them. When accident brings
them into places to which they are unaccustomed, they will
bear to have repeated shots fired at them without stirring.
Dr Heysham mentions that, about the year 1759, one of those
birds " perched upon the Castle of Carlisle, and soon afterwards removed to the cathedral, where it was shot at upwards
of twenty times without effect; at last a person got upon the
cathedral, fired at it, and killed it. In another instance, a
flock of fifteen or twenty perched, at the dusk of evening, in
a tree on the banks of the river Esk, near Netherby, the seat
of Sir James Graham. A person who saw them settle, fired
at random at them in the dark six or seven times, without
either killing any or frightening them away. Surprised at
this, he came again at daylight and killed one, whereupon the
rest took flight." Notwithstanding their natural wildness,
there seems to be no doubt that certain species of the cormorant have been so far subjected to the wishes of man as to be
rendered subservient to the purpose of fishing, as the different
kinds of hawks were for fowling. Whitlock tells us that he had a
cast of them manned like hawks, which would come to hand.
He took much pleasure in them; and he relates that the best
he had was one presented to him by Mr Wood, Master of the
Cormorants to Charles I. Willoughby says that they were
hoodwinked in the manner of falcons till they were let off to
fish. " When they come to the rivers they take off their
hoods, and having tied a leather thong round the lower part
of their necks, that they may not swallow down the fish they
catch, they throw them into the river. They presently dive
under water, and there for a time, with wonderful swiftness, they
pursue the fish; and when they have caught them, they arise
presently to the top of the water, and pressing the fish tightly
with their bills, they swallow them, till each bird hath in this
manner swallowed five or six fishes; then their keepers call
them to the fist, to which they readily fly, and little by little,
one after another, vomit up all their fish, a little bruised with
the nip they gave them with their bills. When they have
done fishing, setting the birds on some high place, they loose
the string from their necks, leaving the passage to the stomach
free and open, and for their reward they throw them part of
the fish they have caught, to each, perchance, one or two

fishes, which they, by the way, as they are falling in the air, will catch most dexterously in their mouths." This practice is said to be in use in China to this day.

" This tribe," says Bewick, " seems possessed of energies not of an ordinary kind ; they are of a stern, sullen character, with a remarkably keen penetrating eye, and a vigorous body, and their whole deportment carries along with it the appearance of the wary, circumspect plunderer, the unrelenting tyrant, and the greedy insatiate glutton, rendered lazy only when the appetite is palled, and then sitting puffing forth the fetid fumes of a gorged stomach, vented occasionally in the disagreeable croakings of their hoarse hollow voice. Such is their portrait ; such is the character generally given of them by ornithologists ; and Milton seems to have put the finishing hand to it, by making Satan personate the cormorant, whilst he surveys, undelighted, the beauties of Paradise :

> Thence up he flew, and on the Tree of Life,
> The middle tree, and highest there that grew,
> Sat like a cormorant.

It ought, however, to be observed, that this bird, like other animals, led only by the cravings of appetite, and directed by instinct, fills the place and pursues the course assigned to it by Nature." And we may add to this last most judicious remark, that the human cormorant, who, in defiance of that reason with which his bountiful Creator has gifted him, devours his blessings till he renders them curses, is yet more disgusting than the creature here described ; and that when talking of that cormorant, who metaphorically devours the widow and the orphan, we speak of an animal much more cruel and detestable than any of God's creatures of prey which blindly obey those instincts which their Creator has, for wise purposes, implanted in them.

SECTION XII.

CONCLUSION OF THE WHOLE.

THUS I have carried my reader through all the varieties I know of woodland scenes. I considered first the single tree as the origin and foundation of all. I considered next the various combinations of trees, under the several beautiful forms of scenery which they compose ; and as the forest is of all others the grandest and most interesting combination of trees, I dwelt the longest on this part of my subject, selecting New Forest, in Hampshire, as an example to illustrate the several observations I had made. Through this picturesque country I have led my reader geographically; and have presented him with a great variety of beautiful scenes, —woods, lawns, heaths, forest distances, and sea-coast views. I have adorned these scenes also with their proper appendages,—wild horses, deer, and other picturesque inhabitants. I might greatly have multiplied both my general and particular remarks; but I fear I ought rather to apologize for my redundances than my omissions.

I now close my observations with a sigh over the transitory state of the several scenes I have described. I mean not, with unphilosophic weakness, to bemoan the perishable condition of sublunary things, but to lament only, that, of all sublunary things, the woodland scene, which is among the most beautiful, should be among the most perishable.

Some species of landscape are of permanent nature, — such, particularly, as depend on rocks, mountains, lakes, and rivers. The ornamental appendages, indeed, of these scenes — the oaks and elms that adorn them — are of a more transient kind. But the grand constituent parts of them may be supposed coeval with Nature itself. Nothing less than some general convulsion can injure them.

Such landscape, again, as depends for beauty on old castles, abbeys, and other ruins, generally escapes for ages the depredations of time. If the woody appendages of these scenes, like those of lakes and mountains, are open to injury, yet a quick vegetation restores them speedily to Nature, unless, indeed, the persevering hand of improvement intervene.

But the landscape which depends chiefly on woodland scenery is always open to injury. Every graceless hand can fell a tree. The value of timber is its misfortune. It is rarely suffered to stand, when it is fit for use; and in a cultivated country, woods are considered only as large corn fields, cut as soon as ripe: and when they are cut for the uses to which they are properly designed, though we may lament, we should not repine. But when they are cut, as they often are, yet immature, to make up a matrimonial purse, or to carry the profits of them to race-grounds and gaming-houses, we cannot help wishing the profligate possessors had been placed, like lunatics and idiots, under the care of guardians, who might have prevented such ruinous and unwarrantable waste.

The depredations which we have seen made in every part of New Forest, and the vast quantities of timber which are felled every year for the navy, and regularly assigned for various other purposes, cannot but make a considerable change in its scenery. The description, therefore, which I have given of it, is not the description of what it was in the last century, nor of what it will be in the next. Many alterations in particular scenes have taken place, even since this work was begun. In a foreground, the cutting down of two or three stately trees makes an essential alteration; and much change of this kind hath been made in many places. In these instances, therefore, the remarks here offered must be considered as history, rather than as description. They attempt to chronicle scenes which once existed, and are now gone. That grand vista which hath been described between Brokenhurst and Lyndhurst hath, since these remarks were made, undergone much change. Many of the nobler trees which adorned it have been felled; and many of the old decaying trees, and others which had been stunted under the shade of those that had been felled, are now grown still more decayed and ragged. They are ill clad and thin; and their withered branches everywhere stare out, unadorned and naked, through their meagre foliage. From these causes, and the deformed gaps which the felling of good trees hath occasioned, this avenue hath lost much of its beauty. The reader will still remember, that, when in the early part of the work,* I considered the maladies of trees as a source of picturesque beauty, I meant it only with regard to individuals placed in particular circumstances. Here, where we are contemplating the beauties of what should be a rich forest scene, they are out of place. It

* See Vol. I. page 49.

must, however, be added, that although these changes are continually happening among the ancient oaks of the forest; yet, as young trees are growing old, Nature is also continually working up new foregrounds to her landscapes, though it is a much easier business to deform than to restore.

We remember a whimsical circumstance that occurred to us, which is now brought to our recollection by the above remark as to the change frequently produced by cutting down foreground trees. On one occasion we were engaged with a friend in sketching some ruined cottages at the skirt of a wood in the county of Haddington. Some magnificent oaks rose in the foreground, and with the ruined moss covered walls and chimneys of the deserted cottages in the middle ground, backed by wood, they made out a very beautiful, and simple, local subject. It was on a Saturday, and we were intently occupied, when we were suddenly addressed by a rustic who came up to us. " Ye had better no put thae trees in your plan," said he, pointing to the foreground oaks, "for gif ye do, your plan winna be right."—"How ?" demanded we. " Ou, because thae muckle trees are to be fell'd on Monday; sae gif ye want yere plan to be right, ye 'll no put them intilt." The reader will easily imagine that this information only sharpened our exertions ; and although the trees themselves have doubtless been long ere this worn out in the different works to which their timber may have been applied, we have the good fortune still to retain their picturesque forms in our portfolio.

In the distant scenery of the forest, indeed, where effect depends on vast combinations of trees, and may be produced even from the inferior kinds, the inroads of the axe are less observed. Though the choicest oaks, therefore, may be removed, yet, if a sufficiency of meaner trees is left, no considerable change will happen for many years in the distant landscapes of the forest. The lawns and heaths, in which its greatest beauty consists, will preserve their ornaments; and, unless where their dimensions are small, (in which case stately trees are required as foregrounds,) they may long remain the objects of admiration.

6

INDEX.

THE END.

EDINBURGH:
Printed by ANDREW SHORTREDE, Thistle Lane.

14 DAY USE
RETURN TO DESK FROM WHICH BORROWED
BIOLOGY LIBRARY

This book is due on the last date stamped below, or
on the date to which renewed.
Renewed books are subject to immediate recall.

LD 21–40m-10,'65
(F7763s10)476

General Library
University of California
Berkeley

ND - #0243 - 020523 - C0 - 229/152/20 - PB - 9780282157722 - Gloss Lamination